So Easy to Use . . . the Internet

So Easy to Use . . . the Internet

by David Peal

Dulles, VA

So Easy to Use . . . the Internet

Published by

AOL Press

An imprint of Hungry Minds, Inc.

909 Third Avenue

New York, NY 10022

www.hungryminds.com

www.aol.com (America Online Web site)

Library of Congress Control Number: 2001096745

ISBN: 0-7645-3666-4

Printed in the United States of America

10 9 8 7 6 5 4

1B/SX/QS/QS/IN

Distributed in the United States by Hungry Minds, Inc. and America Online, Inc.

For general information on Hungry Minds' books in the U.S., please call our Consumer Customer Service department at 800-762-2974. For reseller information, including discounts and premium sales, please call our Reseller Customer Service department at 800-434-3422.

Welcome to AOL Press™

AOL Press books provide timely guides to getting the most out of your online life. AOL Press was formed as part of the AOL family to create a complete series of official references for using America Online as well as the entire Internet — all designed to help you enjoy a fun, easy, and rewarding online experience.

AOL Press is an exciting partnership between two companies at the forefront of the knowledge and communications revolution — AOL and Hungry Minds, Inc. AOL is committed to quality, ease of use, and value, and Hungry Minds excels at helping people understand technology.

To meet these high standards, all our books are authored by experts with the full participation of and exhaustive review by AOL's own development, technical, managerial, and marketing staff. Together, AOL and Hungry Minds have implemented an ambitious publishing program to develop new publications that serve every aspect of your online life.

We hope you enjoy reading this AOL Press title and find it useful. We welcome your feedback at AOL Keyword: **Contact Shop Direct** so we can keep providing information the way you want it.

About the Author

David Peal has been associated with America Online since 1995, when he was the editorial manager of the Internet Connection. (Back then, there was an AOL channel devoted exclusively to the Internet.) At AOL, he developed forums about the Internet and helped create AOL's first comprehensive online source of Internet help. In 1996 he developed and wrote the first edition of this book and has been closely involved with it since then. Before coming to AOL, David was product manager at Sybex, an independent computer book publisher, where he initiated several of the first books about the Internet, including *Access the Internet*, which he wrote in 1994. David has written four other books for AOL: *Your Official America Online Guide to Pictures Online* (Hungry Minds), *Your Official America Online Guide to Digital Imaging Activities* (Hungry Minds), *Picture This!* (AOL Press), and *The Student's Guide to the Internet* (AOL Press). Currently he is adjunct associate professor in the Educational Technology Leadership M.A. program at George Washington University.

Credits

America Online

Technical Editors

Chris Deegan
Caroline Curtin
Holly Hawkins
Bruce Stimpson
Pam Irvine
Jim Bradey
Joel DiGiacomo
Jim Hoscheit
Fate Freeman
Tom Love
Roy Ben-Yoseph
Laurie Zamora
Jennifer Canestraro
Chris Johnson
Dan Pacheco
Kristine Krantz
Elizabeth Ward
Janine Wilkin

Cover Design
Daniela Richardson

Hungry Minds

Senior Project Editor:
Nicole Haims

Acquisitions Editor:
Richard Graves

Copy Editor:
Rebecca Huehls

Technical Editor:
Lee Musick

Permissions Editors:
Carmen Krikorian
Laura Moss

Publishing Director:
Andy Cummings

Editorial Manager:
Leah Cameron

Media Development Manager:
Laura Carpenter VanWinkle

Editorial Assistant:
Jean Rogers

Associate Project Coordinator:
Ryan Steffen

Layout and Graphics:
LeAndra Johnson
Brian Torwelle
Erin Zeltner

Proofreader:
Betty Kish

Indexer:
Sherry Massey

Author's Acknowledgments

It is a pleasure to thank everyone at AOL who has supported this book since the first edition, which covered AOL 3.0. For this new edition, devoted to AOL 7.0, my gratitude goes in particular to Kathy Harper and Dan Shilling for fielding questions and providing access to AOL's technical gurus.

The book's publisher, Hungry Minds, has seen this book through several editions, and for the second time, I have been lucky enough to work with Senior Project Editor Nicole Haims, who coordinated every detail from outline through production. Copy Editor Becky Huehls did a close and careful read for which I am grateful, because she made me clarify many points along the way. Jean Rogers did a tremendous job making sure all my Ts were crossed (many weren't, as it happens). Along with Nicole and Becky, Technical Editor Lee Musick made many pointed recommendations for improvement. A book written in a short period, even by the standards of Internet time, relies on vigilant proofreaders.

Finally, Rich Graves, Andy Cummings, and Walter Bruce made sure that the book was published on time and to everyone's satisfaction, and it is hard to thank them enough for doing so.

On the home front, thanks to my family, who inspired, informed, and supported this book in more ways than I can say.

Contents at a Glance

Table of Contents

Introduction

This book offers much more than a guide to the latest version of the AOL software. You can think of this book as a cross between a map and a manual. It's a map to help you understand what you will find, and where, in the online world. It's a manual showing you how to use AOL to explore that online world's diverse destinations and communities.

If you're interested in a more thorough tour of AOL 7.0, check out *So Easy to Use America Online 7.0,* by David Marx and Jennifer Watson, and published by Hungry Minds.

How This Book Is Organized

The book is primarily organized by what you can do on AOL and the Internet. You might, for example, want to communicate with others by e-mail or search for information. I'm assuming your interest in going online is to stay in touch with the people you care about, learn a new field, do research on a medical condition, go shopping, or do something else related to your daily interests. If you're unclear about what you can do online, don't worry. I'll cover that, too.

The next few pages show you in more detail what you'll find in this book, chapter by chapter.

From AOL to the Internet

In the first four chapters, I try to answer some basic questions about AOL, the Internet, and AOL's Internet tools and services.

- Chapter 1 addresses some of your initial questions: What is the Internet? What drives it? How are the Internet and AOL are related? What's in it for you?
- Chapter 2 introduces you to AOL features that allow you to use the Internet.
- Chapter 3 shows how the AOL software can be adjusted to work for you, putting you in control of as much of your online experience as possible.

- Chapter 4 introduces AOL's helpful tools for making the Internet safe and fun for everyone in your family. It also introduces some of the Web-based resources that make the Internet indispensable for families and to learners of all ages.

Discovering the World Wide Web

The World Wide Web has been all the rage for years now, and for good reason. Chapters 5-9 explore browsers and searching in detail:

- Chapter 5 identifies a variety of useful destinations for people planning a job change, investing for retirement, buying a new car, shopping for a house, buying things, planning a trip, and more.
- Chapter 6 shows how to use AOL's browser to effortlessly enjoy the entire Web and take advantage of the many new multimedia features that bring you sounds, pictures, animation, and video.
- Chapter 7 introduces the Netscape Navigator 6 browser. More than a great browser, Netscape has built-in tools for sending messages and searching the Web.
- Chapters 8 and 9 cover the large subject of searching AOL and the Internet at large for specific information. Chapter 8 focuses on AOL Search, AOL's comprehensive search tool. Chapter 9 discusses the special-purpose Internet resources that can be used to locate authoritative legal and medical information, as well as information in special formats.

Communicating on AOL and the Internet

The most popular Internet tools seem to be those that make it easy to stay in touch with friends, family, and the people you care about. Chapters 10-14 look at four important groups of communication tools: e-mail, instant messaging, mailing lists, and newsgroups.

- Chapters 10 and 11 provide a thorough guide to e-mail. In Chapter 10, you can read about reading and managing your mail, whether it's on AOL or an AOL Anywhere device such as a handheld computer or wireless phone. Chapter 11 is about writing and styling your mail.
- Chapter 12 provides a guide to instant messaging. Messaging with online buddies can be compared to a conversation in which you are typing instead of talking. Software called AOL Instant Messenger℠ now makes it possible for AOL members and other Internet users to chat online.
- Chapter 13 provides what you need to find, join, create, and participate in *mailing lists*. Based on e-mail, these communities provide a framework for acquiring and sharing information with people who share a strong professional or personal interest.
- Chapter 14 covers newsgroups, which, like mailing lists, deliver the human knowledge that makes the Internet a thriving learning community.

Extending Your Internet Connection

Although you can do a lot through AOL's Internet tools, you can also extend your connection through other tools, faster connections, and new ways of taking part in daily activities, from sharing pictures to making phone calls.

- Chapter 15 shows how to extend your Internet connection by downloading and installing software and multimedia files from the Internet.
- Chapter 16 profiles specific downloadable programs that can extend the range of things you can do online and offline, from playing music, to managing files, to creating Web pages.
- Chapter 17 introduces high-speed Internet connections delivered over phone lines and cable wires, and through the air. A high-speed connection can enhance the quality of your online experience by speeding up just about everything you do online.
- Chapter 18 profiles some of the important online activities supported by AOL and the Internet, including reading books, listening to music, and sharing pictures.

Using AOL 7.0 on Different Operating Systems

AOL 7.0 works with Windows 95, Windows 98, Windows Millennium Edition, Windows 2000 Professional, and Windows XP. If you have Windows 3.*x*, you need to use AOL 4.0, which is available at AOL Keyword: **Upgrade**. AOL 7.0 for the Macintosh operating system is also available, but can only be accessed from a Macintosh.

This book is based on AOL 7.0 running under Windows 98. AOL 7.0 looks and works the same regardless of which version of Windows you use. However, from time to time you will come face-to-face with the Windows operating system. In the following cases, you may notice differences in the following procedures because of minor differences in the underlying operating system:

- Saving, opening, and printing files.
- Accessing and launching programs (software).
- Setting an association, which identifies the program that opens when you double-click a file.
- Setting browser preferences.
- Using the browser to download files from the Internet.
- Finding program icons. (For example, in Windows 98, they can be placed on the desktop, Start Menu, taskbar, Program Folder, and system tray.)

- Using music and video players. Use the AOL 7.0 Preferences box (available from the Settings menu) to adjust multimedia preferences.

Please consult the documentation for your version of Windows as needed.

Using This Book

The beauty of books is that they don't require instructions. Still, you may be interested in some book features that can help you get more out of your time wandering through these pages. Each chapter begins with a list of topics covered in the chapter. This is not a table of contents, but a list of the chapter's major themes. Each chapter ends with a brief summary and a bulleted list indicating where to go next — within the book and online. The Table of Contents provides page numbers for every section in the book, to help you get the precise information you need at a given moment.

AOL Toolbar and Menu Bar Selections

Tasks relating to AOL as a software application are grouped in a horizontal *menu bar.* The menu bar has six menus lined up horizontally at the top of the AOL window: File, Edit, Print, Window, Sign On, and Help. You'd use the File menu, for example, to select a music file to play in the AOL Media Player and the Print menu to print any document displayed in AOL.

Below the menu bar is the AOL toolbar, where you access tasks relating to the online experience itself—reading e-mail, browsing the Web, using the white pages, finding movie times, and many others. The brightly colored toolbar has its own menus, indicated by small downward-pointing triangles. Click any menu name to see the options available in the menu. You can read more about menus and toolbars in Chapter 2.

Throughout the book, I show menu bar and toolbar selections by using the ⇨ symbol. For example, you may see the following instructions:

- Choose Edit⇨Dictionary from the menu bar.

  This means to click the Edit menu, move the mouse down the menu, and release the mouse button when the Dictionary command is highlighted.

- Choose Settings⇨Preferences from the AOL toolbar.

  This tells you to click Settings on the AOL toolbar and move the mouse down the menu until the Preferences command is highlighted. This particular command tells the AOL software to open the Preferences window.

AOL Keywords

Keywords are AOL's shortcut to nearly everything on the AOL service. They are indicated in this book as follows: AOL Keyword: **AOL Search**. The boldface indicates what you are to type. Keywords are not case sensitive, so you can type **aol search**. Where do you type keywords? Use AOL's Keyword window (click the Keyword button on the toolbar) or the address box (in the center of the toolbar). Chapter 2 has more to say about using keywords.

Boldface

In addition to AOL keywords, you may see other text that you need to type in boldface. The boldface helps you distinguish what you're supposed to type from the rest of the text.

Tips, Notes, Cautions, and More

In the margins you will find icons next to certain points in the text. These comments can have different purposes:

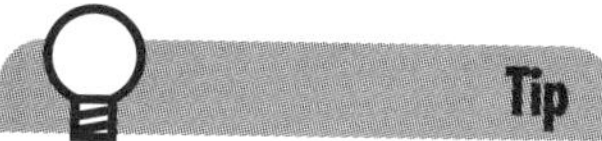

Find a shortcut or piece of useful advice using this icon.

Notes point out a piece of information worthy of further mention.

This icon explains a new or unfamiliar term used in the text.

Use this icon to find online resources related to the text.

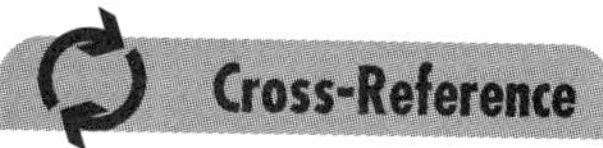

Find related information with this icon.

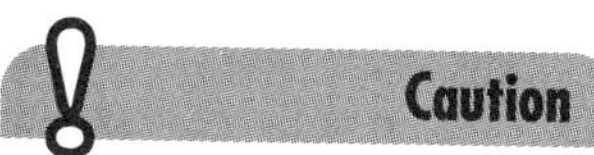

This icon gently warns of potential problems or dangers; you won't find many of them.

Chapter 1

AOL, the Internet, and You

This chapter introduces you to AOL, explains what AOL and the Internet have to do with each other, and helps you get started exploring them both.

The Online World: There When You Need It

While working on this book, I went online for many reasons. Usually I needed to find out something, but whatever the reason, I never thought twice about the fastest way to find what I needed. Thanks to AOL, the Internet is always there when I need it.

The *Net* is standard shorthand for the *Internet,* a global network of information services and human communities. The *Web,* World Wide Web, is only a part of the Net, though the easiest-to-use and most visual part. Chapters 5 through 9 are devoted to the World Wide Web.

Online refers to any content available on a network. Commonly, online refers to AOL and the Internet.

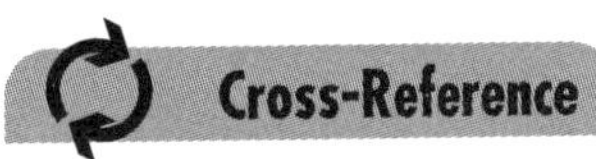

For more about AOL Media Player, see Chapter 18.

First of all, I had to get up-to-date about the many topics in this book, from high-speed access to online music. Finding the information I was looking for rarely took much time and never cost a thing.

I also used the Internet to plan a week at the beach, my family's favorite end-of-summer destination. I found out about beaches in a state we'd never visited. On the World Wide Web, I learned about tourist attractions, found a house to rent, rented it, printed some local maps, and got driving directions that included the estimated mileage and driving time. I did all this without waiting on hold, spending a nickel (except for the rental), or even standing up. Chapter 5 introduces trip-planning resources available from AOL and from the Internet.

AOL also helped me plan a quick family trip to the Big Apple. I checked Amtrak's online train schedules (`www.amtrak.com`). On the day of our departure, I checked the local weather at AOL Keyword: **Weather**, so that we could dress appropriately. Online, my family chose and bought tickets for a play, kid-appropriate of course.

While making these various travel arrangements, I listened to radio stations that you can normally listen to only in other cities and abroad, as well as a few stations that exist only on the Internet. I tuned in to all these radio stations by using the AOL Media Player.

During coffee breaks, I played Tetris, a 1980s-vintage computer game that has been spiffed up for the World Wide Web (`www.shockwave.com`). Listening to music and playing multimedia games used to require special software, and the experience was often pokey and unsatisfactory. Today, the software, hardware, and connections are much quicker. The music approaches CD quality, and the games are actually engaging to play.

Closer to home, I did some research on possible pets for my son, including frogs, turtles, hamsters, mice, and even ferrets. He did the searching, which has become second nature for him, too. We learned a thing or two together along the way, before settling on a hamster. In the past month or so, he has gone online by himself to view airplane photos, get instructions for paper airplanes, and find current-event stories from newspapers for school. With Parental Controls, covered in Chapter 4, I know that he'll stay out of trouble.

Using AOL Keywords and Web Addresses

Some online content is available only on AOL. To access this content, you must be an AOL member. Some content is available on the Internet; anyone can use it. Being an AOL member gives you access to both.

- To visit an online area available only on AOL, you often use an AOL keyword. To go to a keyword, first sign onto AOL. In the address box, type your keyword and then click Go. How do you learn the keyword for an area of possible interest? Press Ctrl+K to open the Keyword window (shown in the following figure) and then click Keyword List to see all available AOL keywords. Chapter 2 has more about keywords.

- To visit a Web site, you use the address box. Type in any Web address and click Go. Chapter 6 has more about Web addresses and Web navigation.

On both AOL and the Web, after you've accessed information, you can almost always find *links* that you click with your mouse to go to related information.

Finally, I used the Web to buy a digital camera as a gift. On CNET, I compared prices (AOL Keyword: **CNET**). At the Digital Photography Review site (`www.dpreview.com`), I read users' opinions of specific models and experts' in-depth technical discussions, and then compared online pictures of the same subject taken with different cameras. Using the Digital Photography newsgroup (`rec.photo.digital`), I read more opinions and got some hard information about the model I was considering. I also bought a book or two about digital photography at an online bookstore.

Lastly, I check my e-mail several times a day. It has become my favorite way of staying in touch with friends, family, colleagues, editors, and others.

What's the Difference between AOL and the Internet?

America Online has been called a world unto itself, a beautifully organized world of content and community available only to AOL members. While AOL is a private network, the Internet emerged in the 1970s as a public solution to the strategic problem of connecting diverse computers located anywhere, so that people could reliably share information. While no one controls the Internet, AOL does have community guidelines, which you can read about at AOL Keyword: **TOS**. Finally, *because* no one owns the Internet or controls what's available there, it has become a lush garden filled with information and entertainment resources of every type.

For a decade, AOL has also been the place from which AOL members can enter the wonderfully overgrown world of the Internet. AOL provides, in fact, several layers of value to your Internet experience:

In this book, I use the terms *e-mail* and *mail* interchangeably.

- AOL offers a well-integrated set of Internet tools for browsing the Web, reading e-mail, downloading files, and taking part in online discussion groups. AOL also offers security features that protect you and your family from junk e-mail and offensive content. These and other tools are thoroughly covered in this book.

- You get guidance in using AOL's tools and services to maximum benefit.
- AOL editors work continuously to find, link, and describe Net resources, so you get both navigational tools and places to go.
- As an AOL member, you are part of a very large community whose sheer size can translate into shopping services (like Shop@AOL) and community features (like Groups@AOL) that you cannot find elsewhere. As well as being unique, these services come to you in an integrated format (with shared features such as the Screen Name Service, described in Chapter 3) and are increasingly consistent in the way they look and work.
- You can use AOL's tools to run any Internet software, including other browsers, other file-download programs, special music players, and Web filters to keep kids safe on the Net.

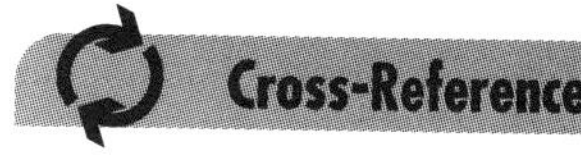

You can find out more about free software in Chapter 16.

AOL and the Net: A Blurring Boundary

Despite the early differences between AOL and the Internet, the boundary between them is beginning to blur.

Easy-to-use software and a friendly environment, combined with community tools such as chat and e-mail, have made AOL the world's largest online community. Now, AOL is developing easy-to-use services for the larger world of the Internet.

That's just one area where the boundary between AOL and the Net is blurring. For example:

- You can now exchange instant messages with AOL members and Internet users, thanks to the AOL Instant Messenger software, as you'll see in Chapter 12.
- You can insert clickable links to Web sites or to favorite places in e-mail messages, message-board postings, and instant messages. Sending links is the easiest way to share your favorite Web sites with someone else on AOL or the Net. Read all about Favorite Places in Chapter 3, AOL Mail in Chapter 11, and messaging in Chapter 12.

Definition

A *link* is a short bit of text that's often underlined or a small picture. You can click text or a picture by passing your mouse arrow over it and clicking when the arrow turns into a picture of a pointing finger.

- Groups@AOL (AOL Keyword: **Groups**) gives AOL members the ability to create communities consisting of AOL and Internet users. These communities have their own Web sites, outfitted with communication tools such as a Group mailing list, a private message board, and the AOL Instant Messenger chat software. Chapter 12 introduces Groups.
- You can use AOL Search to search AOL and the Web simultaneously. Searching for facts and opinions of every stripe has never been easier. Read about AOL Search in Chapter 8.

The boundary between AOL and the Web becomes even blurrier when you consider the large-scale Web sites and services that AOL has recently updated. With sites like the following, AOL has created some of the most visited Web sites on the planet:

You can reach all these sites from the AOL.COM home page (`www.aol.com`).

- **My AOL:** You can customize the content on your My AOL Web page. This content is updated many times a day and can be accessed anywhere by using a handheld computer, wireless telephone, or other AOL Anywhere device, as you'll see in Chapter 10.
- **AOL Mail on the Web:** When you're away from home, you can read your e-mail via the Web. You don't have to be logged onto AOL, but you do need to provide your AOL screen name and password. See Chapter 10.
- **AOL People & Chat:** Use the AOL Instant Messenger software to take part in one-to-one electronic conversations. Or you can chat with several others on AOL or the Internet. See Chapter 12.
- **AOL Search:** Use this tool to find specific information on the Web as well as in encyclopedias, news archives, message boards, and other services. See Chapter 8.
- **Shop@AOL:** With this huge collection of well-known stores, you can comparison shop and order online in a secure online environment. Just go to AOL Keyword: **Shopping**. See Chapter 5.
- **AOL Web Channels:** Channels offer carefully selected directories of Internet (and some AOL) content on big topics like Real Estate, Health, and Women.

AOL's home base on the Web is the new Internet Connection, shown in Figure 1-1. From here you can reach all of AOL's content through the channel links in the lower left. At the same time, you can go to the Web. If you know a Web address, you can type it into the Go to Web box to visit the Web site. If you want to do a Web search for anything, type in **hamsters**, **paper airplanes**, or whatever interests you into the Search box. You can reach the Internet Connection by clicking the Internet button on the AOL toolbar or by going to AOL Keyword: **Web**. (See the sidebar, "Using AOL Keywords and Web Addresses.")

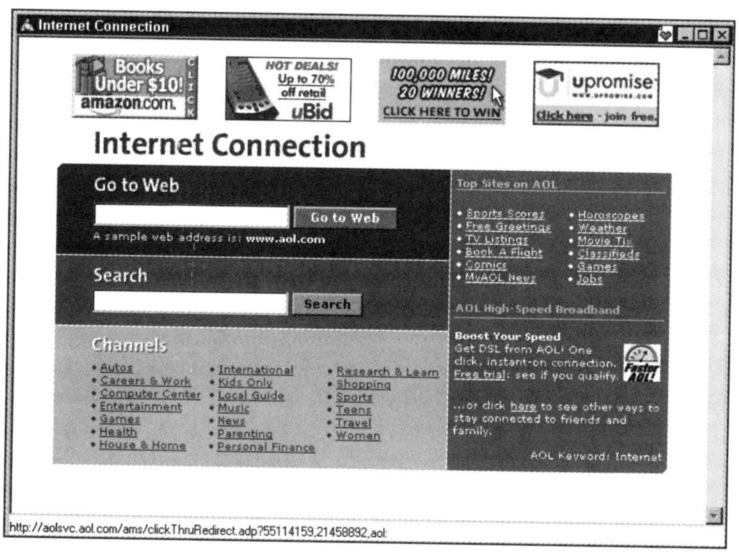

Figure 1-1. The Internet Connection sits on the boundary between AOL and the Net, providing access to AOL and Web content.

Taking AOL with You: AOL Anywhere

At the same time that AOL has expanded its content to the Web, AOL is providing easier access to that content through hardware other than the personal computer (PC) and software other than the AOL software.

AOL Anywhere is a cluster of related services, each of which offers a new method for accessing AOL's content. Here are some of the new ways of accessing AOL:

- Wireless phones
- Handheld computers, such as Palms and PocketPCs

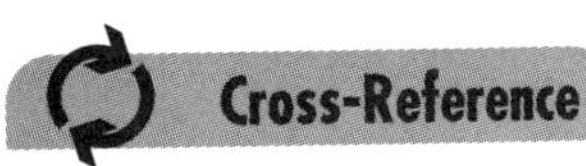

Cross-Reference

For more information, start at AOL Keyword: **Anywhere**. Chapter 10 introduces you to the major AOL Anywhere services, and pagers. Chapter 18 covers AOLTV.

- Television (AOLTV)
- Mobile Communicator, a miniature two-way messaging device

Even if you don't own a wireless phone or handheld computer, you can use AOL Anywhere to access many of your favorite AOL services. With a simple telephone, you can get your mail and other AOL features (AOLbyPhone). With a Web browser, you can read your mail and log onto AOL Web sites such as "You've Got Pictures" from computers that don't have AOL installed (AOL at Work). See Chapter 10 for more.

What's New in AOL 7.0

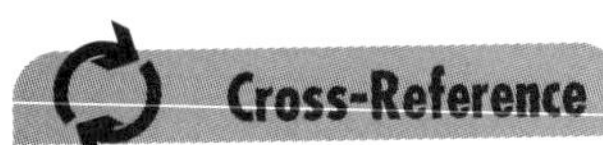

Cross-Reference

If younger people in your family will be using e-mail and other AOL features, you can learn about Parental Controls in Chapter 4. Find out more about using e-mail in Chapter 10.

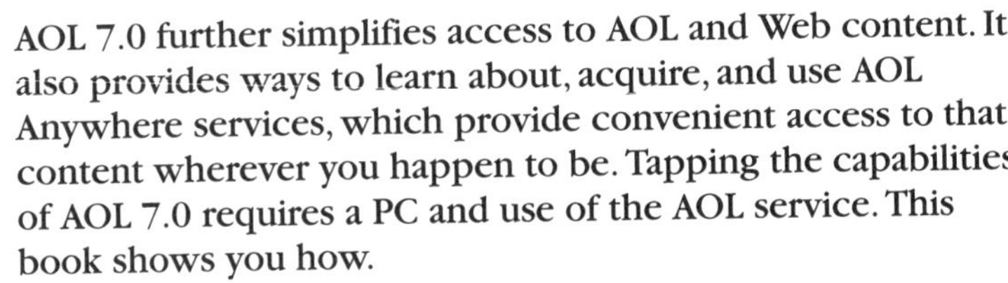

AOL 7.0 further simplifies access to AOL and Web content. It also provides ways to learn about, acquire, and use AOL Anywhere services, which provide convenient access to that content wherever you happen to be. Tapping the capabilities of AOL 7.0 requires a PC and use of the AOL service. This book shows you how.

Many of the changes in AOL 7.0 are under-the-hood refinements affecting the quality, speed, and smoothness of the online experience. Here is a summary of the changes you are more likely to notice:

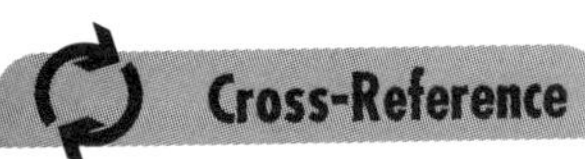

Cross-Reference

Your *Address Book* (Chapter 11) can keep track of information about all your friends and acquaintances (phone numbers, e-mail addresses, birthdays, etc.). Your *Buddy List* (Chapter 12) shows you which of your online friends and acquaintances is online when you are.

- **Parental Controls:** This essential AOL feature, which is designed to keep young children as safe as possible online, has a new set of Mail Controls. The Mail Controls make it easier to customize a child's e-mail access.
- **E-mail and Address Book:** To help you use e-mail and your Address book, AOL has added several new features.
  - When you type the e-mail address of a person to whom you want to send an e-mail message, AOL tries to match the letters you have typed with names in your Address Book. This feature speeds up address entry and reduces spelling mistakes.
  - In the Address Book, which is available online and offline, you can now denote a person's default (primary) e-mail address whenever the person has more than one address. Your Address Book is

available regardless of how you get online — from your PC, your handheld, a wireless phone, and other AOL Anywhere services.

- From the Buddy List, you can now select a buddy's name and click the Information button to send the person mail or an instant message; add the buddy's screen name to your Address book; view the person's Web page or Member Profile, if there is one; and locate the person if he or she happens to be in a chat room at the time. Like the Address Book, your Buddy List is always available, regardless of how you access AOL.
- When you attach files to an AOL e-mail message, the file size is no longer limited.
- You can now display larger e-mail messages — up to 63K. If you receive a message that is over 63K, the message is converted into an attachment. This refinement allows you to receive longer messages.

▶ **Instant Messaging:** New IM features simplify the service even more.

- Just as in e-mail, when you type the address of the person to whom you want to send an instant message, you see a list of suggestions based on the entries in your Address Book.
- Enhancements to the Away Message allow you to see a buddy's Away Message so that you don't have to send an instant message first.
- Also new is the Idle Indicator in your Buddy List window, which shows buddies who have stepped away from their computers without turning on their Away Message.

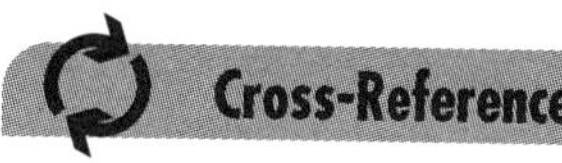

See Chapter 13 for more about mailing lists and Chapter 12 for the details on Instant Messenger.

▶ **Enhancements:** The AOL toolbar has a brighter, rounded look. The toolbar buttons include a new button that takes you to a new AOL service: AOL Radio (see Figure 1-2). AOL Radio has been revamped, while the AOL Media Player has new features and increased ease of use.

The Welcome and Goodbye screens now have a new look and more links to local content, as well as features for members with high-speed access.

Also changed is the AOL Calendar, whose key features have also been made easier to use.

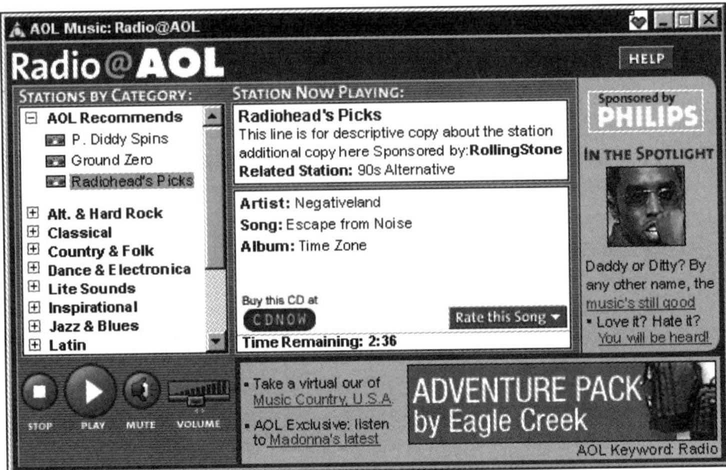

Figure 1-2. AOL Radio lets you listen to more than 75 channels of music.

Ways to Think of the Internet

The Net encompasses a vast set of places to visit and things to do. In addition to information, it provides a home for communities of every size. For some people, a community means a group of people with similar interests, such as a shared profession, hobby, or parenting concern. For others, community means nothing more than the pleasures of socializing. AOL provides a set of tools for taking advantage of these informational and community resources. Enabling these tools is a vast network of networks — millions of computers that are wired together and that you fortunately never have to think about. Here are four ways to think of the Net, which together begin to capture the unique qualities of the world's biggest work in progress.

The Net as a Million Places to Visit

AOL Search (AOL Keyword: **Search**) takes most of the work out of finding what you want. See Chapter 8 for more details.

What draws tens of millions of new people to the Internet every year? Primarily, it's the sights, sounds, and pure information that all these online destinations offer. The World Wide Web (the visual and easy-to-use part of the Internet) combines ease of use and ease of participation; anyone can contribute "pages" to the Web, making the Web a more interesting place to visit.

The Internet has become the most popular way to learn about ancient civilizations, inkjet technology, and just about everything else. It's also the place for timely facts, such as the weather, driving directions, and a great deal more. For example, Figure 1-3 shows a multimedia clip that explains the latest breakthrough in the study of dyslexia.

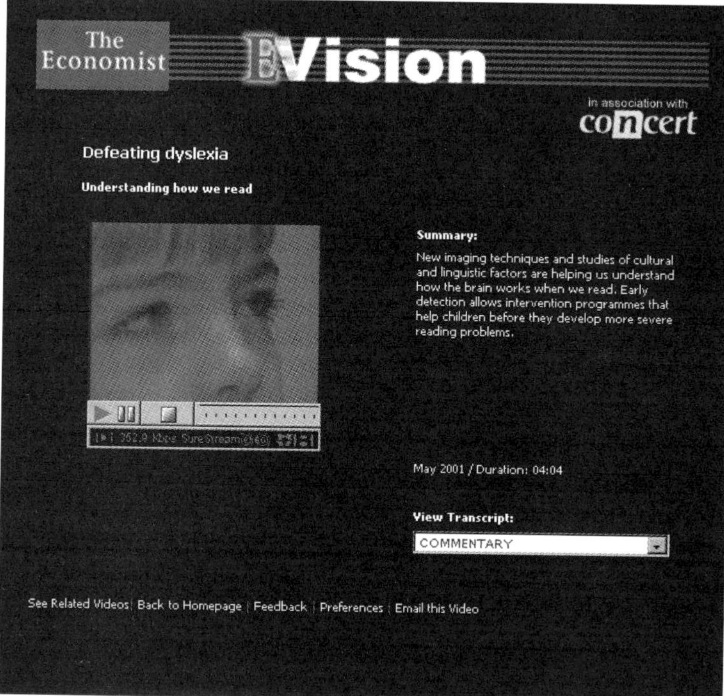

Figure 1-3. England's *The Economist* magazine produces eVision, with audio and video broadcasts that summarize underlying trends — from the magazine's viewpoint, of course (`www.economist.tv`).

Note

With about 80,000,000 visitors a month when this book was written, the combined Web sites of AOL Time Warner were the most visited Internet destinations on the World Wide Web, as reported in CyberAtlas (`www.cyberatlas.com`).

The Net as Many Communities

Many people think of the Net not as a library, but as a pub or coffee bar — a place where chatting is encouraged. Using AOL, you can create your own communities, such as interactive Web pages and Groups. These communities differ from real-world ones in their strongly voluntary character and the high degree of motivation among their participants.

Any AOL member can start a new community, or Group, using AOL's Groups@AOL service. Both AOL members and Net buddies can join. Each Group has a Web site, message board, chat, and more. See Chapter 12 for more information. AOL members can also start their own community by creating a mailing list,

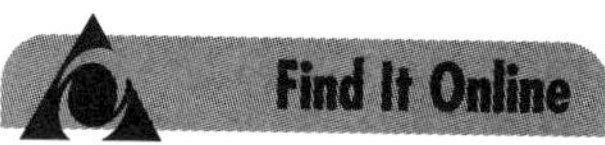

Find It Online

AOL's People Connection recently launched Communities (AOL Keyword: **Communities**). Each Community is devoted to a theme and has its own chat rooms, message boards, and members' Web pages.

using either the Address Book or a hosting site like Topica (Chapter 13).

Online communities can create brand-new content when members simply talk to each other and answer each other's questions about community themes. But even if a site's purpose isn't creating community, its content can generate active communities of interest. For example, photo.net (`www.photo.net`) is the place to go to learn about photography, but this site is so popular that it supports an online community as well.

The Net as a Set of Tools

In this book, *tool* refers to software that helps you carry out a specific task. Using the Internet requires the use of many tools.

How do you get to all these destinations and all this content? Internet tools allow you to reach across computers and networks to access specific information and to communicate with individuals and groups. Tools help you find files to download and then download them, while other tools help you upload messages and Web pages in order to share them. A tool such as AOL's Web browser lets you read the newspaper in any place in the world that has a newspaper and that has gone to the trouble of putting it online. AOL's e-mail tool puts you in touch with friends and colleagues.

This book provides guidance in using the major Internet tools available on AOL:

- The AOL browser as well as the Netscape browser (Chapters 6 and 7)
- All the related tools that are necessary for writing and managing e-mail (Chapters 10 and 11)
- Messaging tools, for "live" online communication (Chapter 12)
- Discussion groups on AOL, the Internet, and the Web (Chapter 14)
- The tools for uploading and downloading files (Chapter 15)

The Net as a Network of Networks

What makes all these online destinations and communities possible?

A *network* is a group of computers linked together in order to allow communication within the group and with the larger

The Net in Numbers

For current collections of statistics on Internet usage, CyberAtlas (`www.cyberatlas.com`) is a good place to start. Using this source in 2001, I found the following statistics:

- More than 130 million adults in the U.S. — 66 percent of the adult population — have Internet access at work or home. A higher percentage of Asians than whites, and of whites than African Americans, have Internet access.
- One quarter (25 percent) of retired people are on the Web. Internet usage among people 55 to 64 years old stands at about 43 percent, which is an increase of more than 10 percent in about a year. The most common activity for the 55-to-64 age group? E-mail.
- Four out of five college students in the class of 2001 turn on the computer instead of the radio or TV to get news and information. Nine out of ten use e-mail daily or frequently. Only 13 percent write letters by hand. (You be the judge of whether this is a good thing!)
- The world is catching up. The U.S. share of Internet usage fell from 40 to 36 percent in 2000-2001. So, while growth continues everywhere, America's hypergrowth is tapering off. Active Net users in Sweden and Canada, as a percentage of population, exceed the percentage in the U.S.
- The number of people around the world with Internet access approached 400 million in mid-2001, while the number of active users surpassed 200 million. This is a huge number in absolute terms, but around the globe, only one person out of thirty is wired in any active, meaningful sense.
- In the urban areas of China, India, Russia, and the rest of the developing world, just one person out of every three or four has even heard of the Internet.

world. The Internet is the network that connects millions of these networks (sometimes called *domains*) into a very big network. Each computer on any network can more or less openly communicate with any other computer on any other network.

Think of the Internet — with its vast stores of content, constant data flows, efficient ways of retrieving knowledge, and considerable ability to create new content — as a growing brain, always adding new neurons.

You can find a good general history of the early days in *Where Wizards Stay Up Late: The Origins of the Internet,* by Katie Hafner and Matthew Lyon (Simon & Schuster, 1997). The Internet Society's All About the Internet page includes timelines, interviews, and statistics (`www.isoc.org/internet-history`).

Where to Go from Here

For all the technical complexity, AOL has taken the lead in simplifying its tools and services. This book tries to make the experience of accessing and using the Internet manageable, useful, and fun. How you use this book depends on how you learn and what you want to do.

- Start with Chapter 2 for a thorough overview of the AOL software. Chapter 2 shows you where you can find AOL's Internet tools and services.
- Chapter 3 shows the many ways of customizing AOL's Internet tools and services to work the way you and your family want them to work.
- Chapters 5-9 explore the World Wide Web in depth.
- Chapters 10-14 introduce a broad range of personal communication tools, such as e-mail and instant messaging.
- Chapters 15-18 show how to use software and hardware to extend your Internet connection as far as you want to take it.

Chapter 2

Getting Familiar with AOL 7.0

IN THIS CHAPTER **PAGE**

Ready to go? This chapter takes you on a tour of AOL, starting with the familiar sights you see every time you use AOL: the Welcome Screen, toolbar, menus, Channel menu, and more. Read this chapter if you are new to AOL or if you want to learn about AOL's Internet tools, services, and help resources.

Learning Your Way around AOL

When you sign on to AOL, you see something like Figure 2-1. The toolbar and the Welcome Screen provide the dashboard for your life online. Note in particular the following major parts of the AOL display:

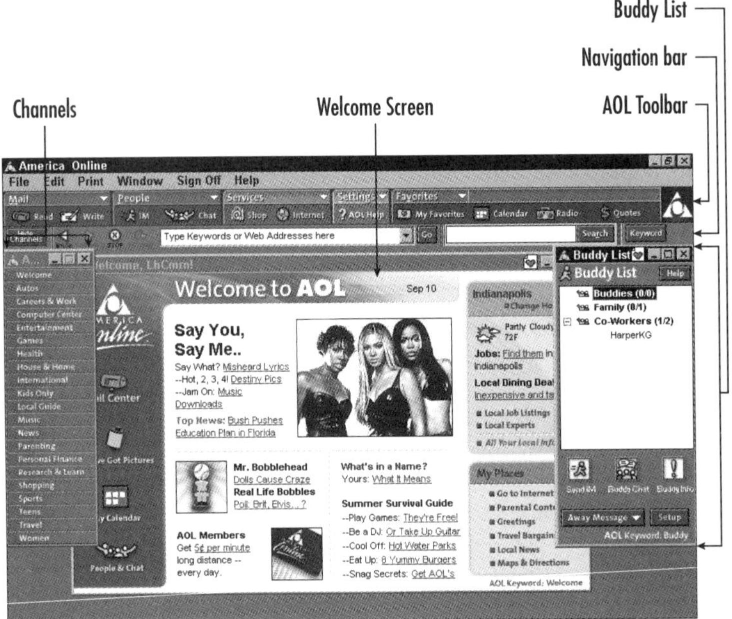

Figure 2-1. AOL 7.0 looks a lot like AOL 6.0: The toolbar and navigation bar give you access to all of AOL and the Internet.

- **The Welcome Screen:** This screen, in the center of the AOL display, provides direct access to many key features and AOL destinations, such as your electronic mailbox, your local weather, and online White Pages for the entire United States.
- **The AOL toolbar:** The toolbar, with its menus and buttons, includes major Internet tools and many important online destinations. The navigation bar is in the bottom half of the toolbar.
- **The menu bar:** The menu bar, which is at the very top of the AOL window, lists options for opening files, switching windows, playing music, and more.
- **The Buddy List:** This shows you which of your friends and acquaintances are online at the same time as you are.
- **The Channel menu:** Just click the name of a channel to go to one of AOL's 21 *channels* (including the Welcome Screen), which are online hubs of information and community devoted to health, entertainment, parenting, learning, sports, and other big subjects. Many individual channel screens have been redesigned for AOL 7.0.

The Welcome Screen: AOL's Red Carpet

The Welcome Screen, shown in Figure 2-2, gives you direct access to basic AOL features such as your e-mail, "You've Got Pictures," your local weather, your online/offline calendar, the Web, and Parental Controls (for keeping young people safe online).

The Welcome Screen is always available when you're signed on to AOL. Closing the Welcome Screen *minimizes* it without really making it go away. You can always view it again by choosing Window⇨Welcome from the menu bar.

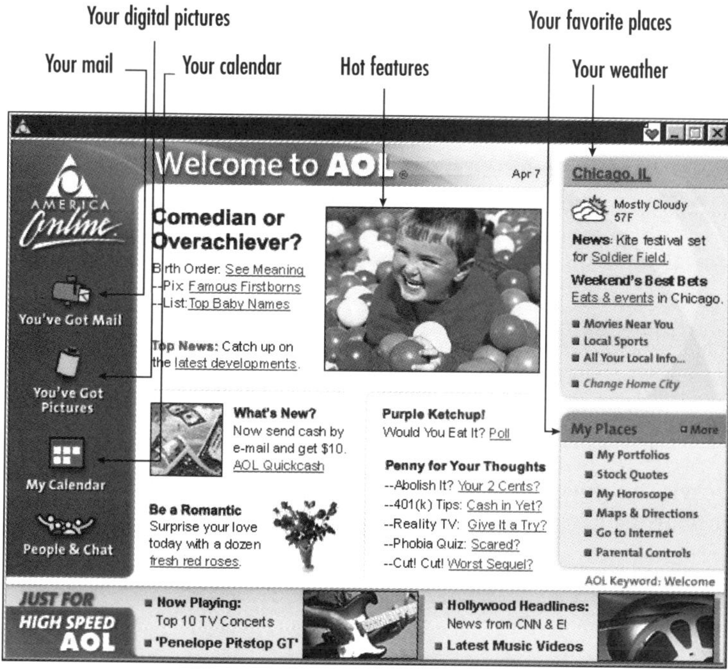

Figure 2-2. The AOL 7.0 Welcome Screen.

When you sign on to AOL, you can access the following features from the Welcome Screen:

- **"You've Got Pictures":** Underneath the famous You've Got Mail icon on the left side of the Welcome Screen, you can find an icon for AOL's "You've Got Pictures" service. "You've Got Pictures" provides online space for you to store digital images. Through this AOL service, you can also take rolls of film to a participating retailer and receive both digital *and* paper images. The digital images are posted directly to your AOL screen name. You can view them online, put them on your Web page, attach them to e-mail messages, or print them.
- **"My Calendar"[SM]:** You can use the My Calendar service to keep track of your appointments, meetings, deadlines,

Chapter 18 introduces "You've Got Pictures." For a complete guide, see my book, *Your America Online Guide to Pictures Online* (Hungry Minds, Inc.), available at AOL Keyword: **Shop Direct**.

dinners, and all the diverse goings-on that never quite fit into that wall calendar. On the left side of the Welcome Screen is a handy My Calendar icon that you can click to use the service. You'll also see a Calendar button on the toolbar. You can use the calendar offline or online, and can even use the service to buy tickets and coordinate outings with online friends. (For details, see Chapter 3.)

On AOL or on the Web, a *link* is a bit of text or a picture that you click to get related information. Text links usually appear underlined and in a different color.

- **My Places:** This customizable area allows you to add links to your favorite AOL areas. Chapter 3 has instructions on how to use My Places and also shows how to use AOL's Hot Keys, which serve a similar purpose — making *your* favorites directly accessible whenever you are online.

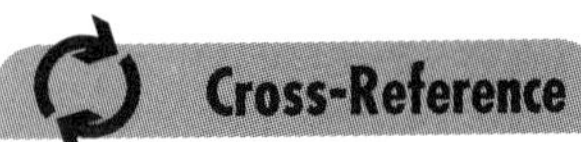

Chapter 3 looks at ways of customizing AOL, including tracking your schedule with My Calendar and customizing My Places.

- **Go to the Internet:** Below My Places is the handy Go to the Internet button. Like the Internet button on the toolbar, it takes you to the Internet Connection, an excellent place to starting exploring either AOL or the Internet.
- **Parental Controls:** The lower-right corner of the Welcome Screen also offers a handy link to AOL's Parental Controls.

Chapter 4 covers Parental Controls in depth.

Down the middle of the Welcome Screen are links to AOL's new areas, live events, and special promotions, as well as to breaking news stories. These links change throughout the day and night.

Where to Find Internet Tools

AOL comes with a full set of Internet tools. On AOL, you can use any additional (third-party) Internet tools you want — as long as they work on your Mac or Windows operating system, of course. You can also easily use different types of tools at the same time and use AOL's tools with third-party tools. Figure 2-3 shows you where AOL's tools are located.

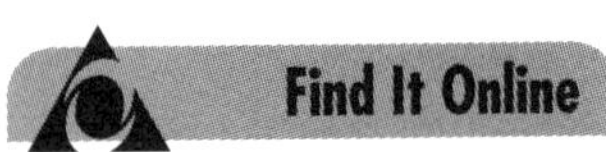

The easiest way to access the Internet is to click the Internet button on the AOL 7.0 toolbar. It takes you directly to AOL's Internet Connection page.

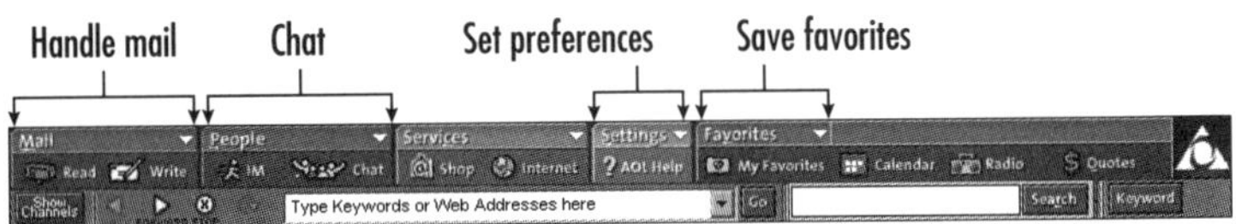

Figure 2-3. The Net's tools at your fingertips.

Following is a list of tools that help you use different parts of the Internet. All these tools are built right into your AOL software (on your computer) or are directly available from AOL:

- **E-mail:** You use e-mail to exchange messages or files with anyone on AOL or the Internet. On the toolbar, click the Read button to read your e-mail or the Write button to write a message. Or you can use the keyboard equivalents: Ctrl+R to read mail and Ctrl+M to write a message.
- **Web browser:** You need a browser to search and view any of the billion-plus documented pages on the World Wide Web. Select Services⇨Internet⇨Internet Start Page to go directly to the Web. A browser also opens whenever you click a Web link in a document, on your Windows desktop, in an e-mail message, or elsewhere.
- **Newsgroups:** You can start using newsgroups by choosing Services⇨Internet⇨Newsgroups from the toolbar or by going to AOL Keyword: **Newsgroups**. Newsgroups are discussion groups that work like public bulletin boards. Anyone with Internet access can post to a newsgroup and read messages on it.
- **The file-transfer service (FTP):** You can use FTP to download and upload files, and this service is indispensable if you want to create a Web site of your own. AOL provides this service at AOL Keyword: **FTP**. FTP is also available by choosing Services⇨Internet⇨FTP from the toolbar.

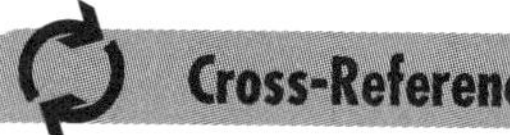

See Chapter 6 on AOL's browser and Chapter 7 on the Netscape browser.

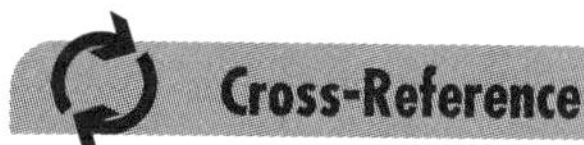

See Chapter 14 on newsgroups.

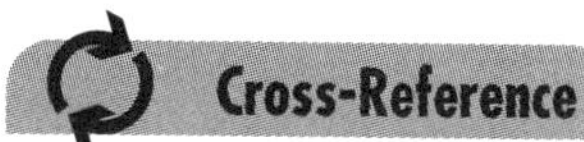

Chapter 15 covers the numerous ways to access and use FTP on AOL.

Using AOL's Toolbar

The AOL 7.0 toolbar retains the look and organization of the toolbar in earlier versions. The toolbar actually consists of *two* bars.

- The *toolbar proper* has menus (like Mail and File) and buttons (like Internet and Radio) that you can use to access online tools and visit major AOL destinations on the Web.
- The *navigation bar* helps you get around AOL and the Internet. It has an Address box, which can be used for AOL keywords and Web addresses. It includes navigation buttons (Back, Forward, Stop, and Reload) that enable you to move between online destinations and stop or reload online content. And it allows you to search AOL and the Internet by using the Search box on the right.

A *menu* is a list of choices. To see menu options, click the menu's name (*File*, for example) and move the pointer through the menu options. When your mouse highlights the option you want, click.

Using Toolbar Buttons and Menus

The toolbar consists of buttons and menus, as shown in Figure 2-3. The buttons give you direct access to common functions, such as writing e-mail, sending an instant message, shopping, going to the Internet, and using your calendar. These buttons have been selected from the many choices available on the toolbar menus. Here's how the buttons and menus work:

The buttons are handy shortcuts to the most popular AOL features. For example, say you want to send an e-mail message to an online buddy. You can either

- Click the Mail menu and run your mouse down the list of options that appears. Click Write Mail.

  or

- Simply click the Write button, which is located just below the Mail menu.

You can even use the keyboard shortcut, Ctrl+M, by pressing down the Control key and pressing M. However you get there, a fresh new Write Mail dialog box appears.

Whenever you move your mouse arrow over a toolbar button or toolbar menu, you see a short description of what the button or menu does. Click a button name to actually do something.

Displaying Only the AOL Toolbar Menus

You can customize AOL's toolbar to display only words instead of words and icons, freeing up some space and reducing visual distraction.

To adjust the toolbar so that it displays only words, follow these simple steps:

1. Choose Settings⇨Preferences and click Toolbar & Sound.
2. Click the Text Only radio button and then click Save at the bottom of the window. Your customized toolbar appears after you click Save.

The button and menu options on the toolbar are divided into the following five areas:

- **Mail:** These options give you access to your new and saved e-mail messages, your Filing Cabinet, mail preferences, your Address Book, Automatic AOL, and more.
- **People:** Use these options to send an instant message, take part in AOL chat, visit an online community, and use the online White Pages.
- **Services:** Here you can find the most popular AOL destinations in one convenient place. These include Moviefone, a fantastic recipe finder, AOL's guide to government services, and more.
- **Settings:** Use the options in this area to customize the way online tools and services work. Select Preferences for access to just about everything you can customize on AOL. You can also create passwords and screen names, and check billing information.
- **Favorites:** Use the buttons and menu choices to go to popular AOL features or your own Favorite Places. When you make a place into a Favorite Place, you store a link to it in your Favorite Places folder.

For more about customizing the AOL toolbar and creating Favorite Places, see Chapter 3.

Using the Navigation Bar

The navigation bar, shown in Figure 2-4, helps you get from one online destination to another.

If you have ever seen Netscape or Microsoft Internet Explorer, you will be familiar with the Back and Forward buttons. Unlike these browsers, AOL's navigation controls apply to AOL areas as well as Web sites. The Back, Forward, Stop, and Reload buttons are especially useful when you're exploring the Web.

Sometimes you may see a Web address referred to as a URL, or *Universal Resource Locator*. The URL identifies the exact location of a Web page. See Chapter 6.

Also, while other browsers have a single box for typing an address, AOL 7.0 has two boxes for typing text:

- **Address box:** You use the Address box for Web addresses or AOL keywords. After you type the address or keyword into the box, click Go or press Enter to go that destination.
- **Search box:** You can type search terms into this box and then click Search or press Enter. The Search box is to the right of the Address box and is set in a yellow frame.

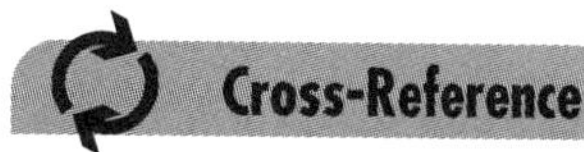

In Chapter 8, on AOL Search, you'll become more familiar with the Search box.

Notice the Search box to the right of the address box? You use it when you need to find specific online information. Type a search term such as **lightning bug** or **Bob Dylan** in the Search box and click Search. This way, you'll be using AOL Search to search AOL *and* the Internet.

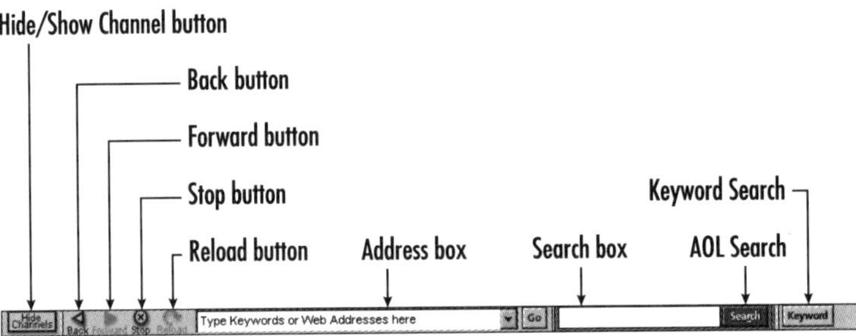

Figure 2-4. The AOL navigation bar.

Using AOL's Menu Bar

As Windows software, AOL has a menu bar at the very top of the display (refer to Figure 2-1). This menu bar contains some familiar (and some less-familiar) menus:

- **File:** Open, save, and organize your files.
- **Edit:** Edit text, look up words, and do copying-and-pasting.
- **Print:** Set your printing options and find printing services.
- **Window:** Keep track of open windows and prevent the clutter caused by too many open windows.
- **Sign Off:** Sign off or switch screen names without signing off.
- **Help:** Find help using AOL or one of AOL's many tools and services; help is available even when you are offline.

If you can access a menu option by using a keyboard shortcut, then the shortcut appears to the right of the menu option. Rather than choose Mail⇨Write Mail, for example, you can press Ctrl+M.

Tucked away in the AOL menu bar are some important features:

- On the File menu, you can access AOL's Picture Gallery for managing the digital pictures you download from "You've Got Pictures" or use in your Web pages. The Picture Gallery provides essential image-editing features, such as cropping and brightening, and is available even when you're offline.

To play music or a video on the AOL Media Player, choose File⇨Open and select the file from your computer.

- Also on the File menu, the handy New option lets you create a document with AOL's built-in word processor. Use this feature to create documents with styled text and pictures. Use the word processor to create to-do lists, drafts of important e-mail messages, rough outlines, and anything else you want. Save formatted text as .RTX, and it can be opened in Word.
- Whenever you are reading or writing, take advantage of the Edit menu's Dictionary, Thesaurus, and Spell Checker.
- The Find command (Edit⇨Find in Top Window) looks for a specific word in a list or other document. You can use this feature to go through new messages (in your electronic mailbox), old messages (in your Filing Cabinet), and postings (on a message board).
- *For people with scanners,* the Capture Pictures command (Edit⇨Capture Pictures) lets you start and control your scanner from AOL. This tool is available whether you're online or offline. You can use it to scan an image, capture a photo, or view what's in the AOL Picture Gallery.
- The Window menu lets you see which AOL screens and browser windows are currently open, so you can quickly switch between them. Also, the menu supports AOL's Favorite Places feature. By clicking the heart in the upper-right corner of any window, you can add an online destination to your Favorite Places folder and this menu. If a window fills the AOL screen (when it's *maximized*), you can't see the heart. In this case, choose Window⇨Add Top Window to Favorite Places (or just press Ctrl++).
- The Print menu gives you control of your printer, of course, when you want to print something that's displayed in AOL. The menu also takes you to a series of online sites collectively called Print Central. There, you can stock up on papers and inks; find dozens of home activities; and take advantage of the design, printing, binding, and delivery services provided by Kinko's.

Cross-Reference

The File menu also takes you to AOL features such as the Filing Cabinet (see Chapter 10) and Download Manager (see Chapter 15).

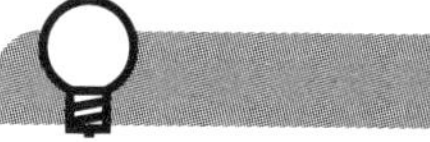

Tip

The Edit menu's Find command (Ctrl+F) is one of the most useful features on AOL because it works in so many different contexts: Use it in any list or text document to find an instance of a word.

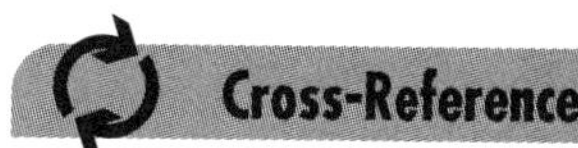

Cross-Reference

Favorite Places can be Web pages, AOL areas, and e-mail messages. Chapter 3 explains how to manage and use your Favorite Places.

About AOL Keywords

An AOL *keyword* is a word or phrase that takes you directly to a specific area of AOL (or sometimes a Web site) when you type the keyword into the toolbar's address box or into the Keyword window (Ctrl+K).

If you visit an AOL window that has a keyword, you will see it in the window's lower-right corner. Also, references to keywords appear throughout this book. On AOL and in this book, keywords follow the words *AOL Keyword.* So, to visit the Health Channel at AOL Keyword: **Health**, simply type **Health** into the Address box and click Go.

Using the Buddy List

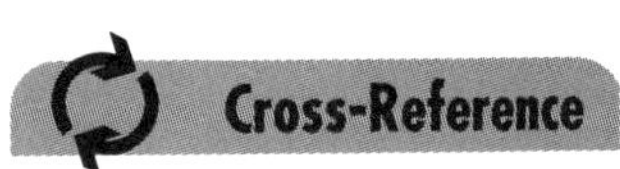

Chapter 12 shows how to create a Buddy List on AOL.

The Buddy List, shown in Figure 2-5, lets you know which of your friends and acquaintances is online when you are online. You can set up your Buddy List to include friends, family, and coworkers who have AOL or AOL Instant Messenger accounts. Through AOL, you communicate with other members by using instant messages. Just click the IM button on the toolbar.

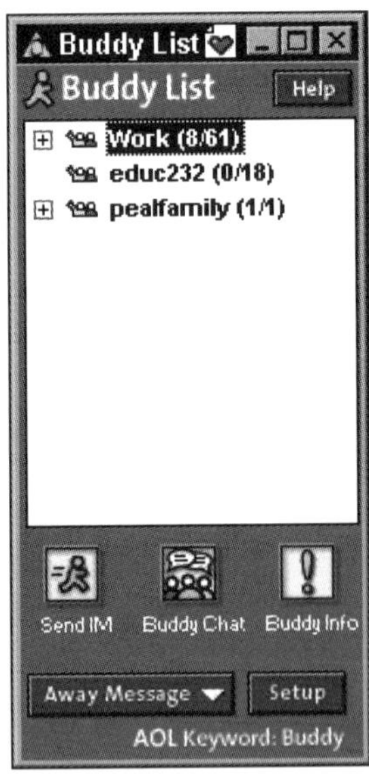

Figure 2-5. My Buddy List showing which of my friends and acquaintances are online. Click a group to see individual screen names.

If ever you are using a computer that doesn't have AOL installed on it, you can still use AOL Instant Messenger (AIM) or AIMExpress to send instant messages.

Channeling Your Energy

AOL arranges its online universe into 21 channels, including the Welcome Screen, which serves as a sort of guide to the other channels. AOL channels are listed in the Channels window (refer to Figure 2-1). Click the Hide Channels button on the toolbar to hide this menu from view. Click it again to bring it into view once again.

You can move the Channels menu (AOL Keyword: **Channels**) to any location on your screen. With the window open, just click the title bar (top of the menu) and drag the window.

Each channel brings together reference information, message boards, links to Web sites, shopping opportunities, and more, all arranged as large, familiar subjects. The Careers & Work Channel, shown in Figure 2-6, for example, combines networking opportunities, job-search tips, message boards for different professions, and an online employment service from Monster.com (`www.monster.com`).

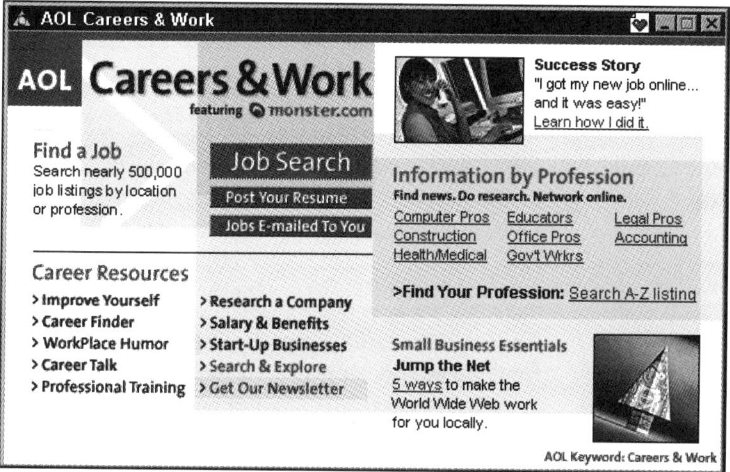

Figure 2-6. Use AOL's Channel window to go to the Careers & Work Channel.

Here's another way in which the boundary between AOL and the Internet is blurring: Every AOL channel takes you to dozens of handpicked Web sites directly related to the channel's theme. The Computing Channel, for instance, offers resources for using specific Internet tools, building Web pages, buying Internet software, and learning to program.

Getting Help with AOL and the Internet

Even if you already know your way around, Net technology changes so fast and new destinations emerge so frequently that you may need AOL's resources for getting help and staying up-to-date. The following overview helps you navigate AOL's abundant help resources.

Newcomers eager to get started might want to start at AOL Keyword: **QuickStart**, which has tips, a tour, and fast facts.

Help resources come in all sorts of levels and formats, so you can choose the one that matches your needs and the way you like to learn. Some resources help you learn to use certain AOL and Internet tools; others help you deepen your knowledge or do troubleshooting. Use these resources (and this book) whenever you need help. See Table 2-1 for help in finding the answers to your questions.

Table 2-1. Getting Help on AOL

Help Resource	*How to Find It*	*What's There*
AOL Online Help	Go to `www.aol.com/nethelp`, or from `www.aol.com`, click Help	Help with AOL Instant Messenger, newsgroups, mailing lists, FTP, the Web, and more. Look for the Mega Glossary!
AOL Help	Choose Help⇨AOL Help from the toolbar or go to AOL Keyword: **Member Services**	Task-oriented procedures for setting up AOL, signing on, using AOL, using the browser, and so on.
AOL Help Community	Go to AOL Keyword: **MHM**	Members help other members by using message boards about a range of Internet and AOL topics.
AOL Quick Help	Go to AOL Keyword: **Quick Help**	Help with AOL (connecting, billing information, passwords, Parental Controls, and so on). From here you can get live technical help.

Help Resource	*How to Find It*	*What's There*
AOL QuickStart	Go to AOL Keyword: **QuickStart**	For newcomers: AOL tips; a tour of essential services, such as Parental Controls; info about how to set passwords; and much more.
AOL & Computer Basics	Go to AOL Keyword: **Basics**	Classes on graphics editing, HTML, e-mail, and more. Many classes have online transcripts that you can read.
Internet Help	Go to AOL Keyword: **NetHelp**	The part of AOL Help focused on the use of AOL's Internet tools.
Computing Channel message boards	Go to AOL Keyword: **Computing Communities**	The place to ask other AOL members for their technical advice or product opinions.
Help Illustrated	Go to AOL Keyword: **Visual Help**	Beginners' message boards; AOL Slideshows; visual help in sending e-mail, downloading from the Web, using chat, and so on.
Get Help Now	Go to AOL Keyword: **Get Help Now**	Thorough advice for using Windows and AOL, in a how-to format.
Kids Only Help	Go to AOL Keyword: **KO Help**	Kid-friendly instructions for using various online features. Includes online safety articles.
Secrets of AOL	Go to AOL Keyword: **Secrets of AOL**	More advanced tips for using e-mail, instant messages, your Buddy List, and other essential tools.

Tip

Many of AOL's Internet tools have comprehensive sources of help. For e-mail, the Mail Center (Mail⇨Mail Center) helps you with everything mail-related. Other services, such as AOL Hometown and "You've Got Pictures," have a Help button.

Where to Start When You Need Help

At AOL Keyword: **Help Community**, you can find general help-related message boards and a list of frequently asked questions, with answers.

When you need help, check out AOL's help resources (AOL Keyword: **Help**), shown in Figure 2-7.

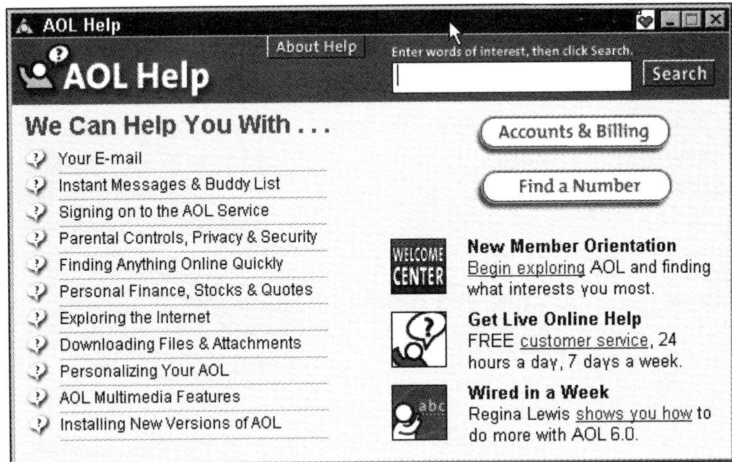

Figure 2-7. AOL's comprehensive help resources. Keep clicking until you find what you need. Click Exploring the Internet for help with Internet tools.

Finding NetHelp on the Web

Tip

NetHelp on the Web includes a large glossary of Internet terms.

Help with the Web is also available on the Web at the following address: `www.aol.com/nethelp`. Each topic leads to a list of subtopics with the specific information you're seeking.

Getting Help You Can See

Help Illustrated is for all of us "visual learners." At AOL Keyword: **Visual Help**, you can find more than 30 simple illustrated introductions to basic AOL tasks and a few Internet tasks, as shown in Figure 2-8. Bear in mind that a tutorial provides a single set of steps and can't capture every particular context or need.

When you type a Web address in to the address box, you don't have to type the `http://` part.

Taking an Online Class

Chats can be online free-for-alls. Several people in one place communicate by typing messages, and people come and go all the time. Chat-based classrooms have more structure, but they retain chat's openness. AOL Keyword: **Basics** provides a growing list of chat-based classes, led by knowledgeable AOL members. These classes may be AOL-focused or Net-focused, or they may cover both worlds. For each topic, information is available in several forms, so you can learn the way you like.

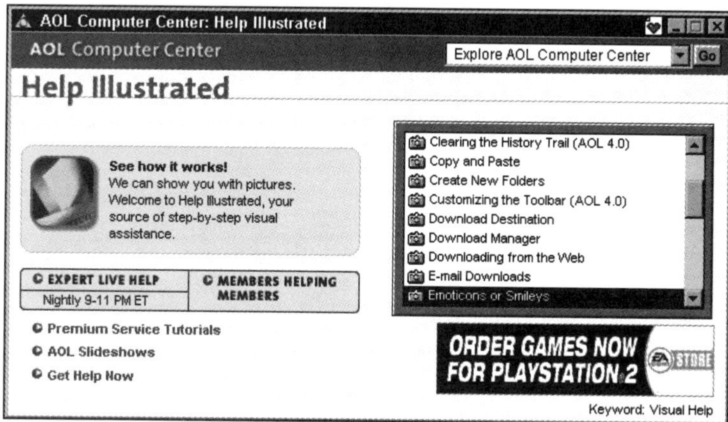

Figure 2-8. At AOL Keyword: **Visual Help**, you get illustrated overviews of basic Internet tasks. Shown here is part of the list of topics with Emotions or Smileys highlighted.

Getting Help from Other AOL Members

Message boards are public bulletin boards in which you can find out about specific topics. Whereas chat and AIM-based online conversations come and go, the questions and answers posted on a message board can be available for weeks. Some message boards give AOL members the chance to ask each other for advice when buying a printer or coping with a malfunctioning scanner. Other members can strut their stuff, share experiences, and provide links to AOL and Internet resources.

The Computer Center Channel has the most numerous and perhaps the best Internet-related message boards on AOL. Go to AOL Keyword: **Computing Communities**, which has recently been revamped and reshaped into the format of AOL's new communities. Every AOL community (AOL Keyword: **Communities**) brings together focused message boards, dedicated chats, home pages, and resources dedicated to a particular subject. The Computer Community includes classes, tutorials, transcripts, how-to documents, frequently asked questions and answers, and more. Figure 2-9 shows the hot message boards in the Computing Community.

The Computing Channel focuses on PCs and Windows. At the channel's Help Desk (AOL Keyword: **Get Help Now**) you can acquire basic Windows skills, such as copying files, creating folders, and formatting disks.

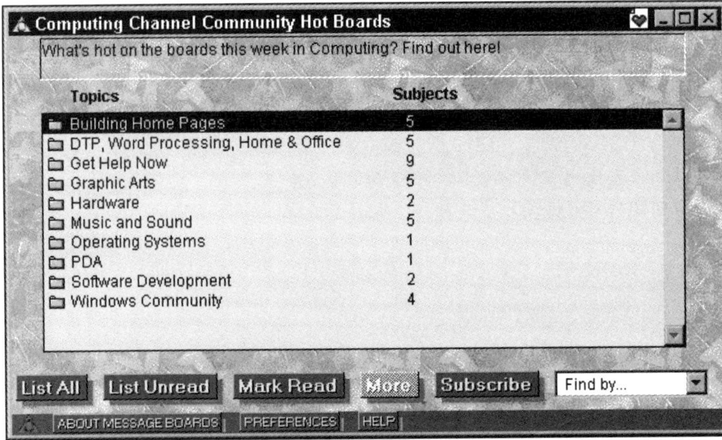

Figure 2-9. A message board at AOL Keyword: **Computing Communities**, where you can get answers to pressing questions.

Staying Informed with Electronic Newsletters

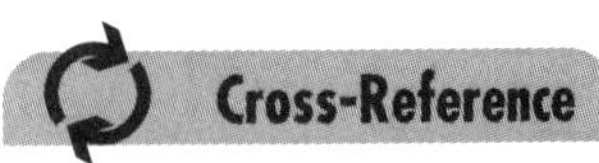

Chapter 13 goes into mailing lists in depth and introduces newsletters available by channel.

Many channels and areas on AOL have their own newsletters, most of them delivered weekly. Newsletters arrive in your online mailbox and contain news, product information, online events, and other tidbits of likely interest to people who frequent a particular area or channel. AOL Keyword: **Newsletters** lists AOL newsletters by channel, allows you to subscribe by simply pushing a button, and archives back issues.

Getting Information When You Are Not Online

If you want to use AOL's offline features such as the Picture Finder or Calendar, help is available at Help⇨AOL Help from the menu bar. The task specific, to-the-point information is formatted in standard Windows fashion, with short procedures, definitions of technical terms, and links to related information. Like all Windows-style help, the absence of context and examples makes the material a bit dry, but useful enough for people who know exactly what they are looking for and who have some experience with Windows applications, such as AOL.

Where to Go from Here

The new AOL 7.0 software incorporates Internet features just about everywhere. This chapter introduced the software and showed where the tools are. Changes in the software and on AOL's computers provide a richer and simpler experience of the Internet. Whenever you have a question or problem, AOL offers help in text and pictures, offline and online.

- Chapter 3 shows how to define your preferences and customize how AOL and its Internet tools work.
- Chapter 4 explores the family perspective on AOL, including the many ways AOL provides a safer online experience.
- Beyond that, you can go in any direction you want, depending on what you want to do online. For many people, the basic online activities include browsing the Web (Chapter 6), searching the Web (Chapters 8 and 9), and using e-mail (Chapters 10 and 11). Chat, too, is enormously popular (Chapter 12).

Chapter 3

Making AOL Work Your Way

IN THIS CHAPTER **PAGE**

Whenever you're on the Internet, remember that you're not doing anything magical; you're just using software. More precisely, you're using one or more software tools for visiting an online destination or doing something online, like ordering an airline ticket. Most of this software is provided to you by AOL. Some software products were created by AOL and made available to anyone on the Internet, including Netscape Navigator and AOL Instant Messenger. Some Net software was created by independent programmers or third-party companies for general use and, as such, is readily available to AOL members.

AOL 7.0 itself is software — a large, feature-packed application that comes in versions for the Windows and Macintosh operating systems. AOL 7.0 is simply software that makes Internet tools available and simplifies their use. As software, AOL can be personalized in many ways, so you can be make yourself at home even while online. This chapter shows you how to personalize AOL and AOL's Web sites to accommodate your preferences.

Many of AOL's customization features can be found on the toolbar's Settings menu.

Later chapters look at ways of customizing specific tools, such as the Web browser, e-mail, AOL Instant Messenger, and newsgroups.

Personalizing Your AOL Experience

This chapter takes a look at the most important ways you can customize AOL's features, including

- **My AOL:** This customizable information hub offers sports scores, stocks, horoscopes, weather information for any zip code, news on the subjects you care about, and more.
- **My Calendar:** This is your online and offline tool for keeping track of all the events, appointments, and goings-on in your life.
- **Favorite Places:** This feature lets you keep track of all your diverse destinations on AOL and the Internet so that you can readily revisit them in the future.
- **Your Buddy List and Address Book:** With these tools, you can keep track of all your friends and acquaintances, online and offline.
- **Your AOL account:** Access your monthly usage, change billing information, and learn about new membership plans.
- **Your Internet connection:** You can modify your account when you use a different kind of connection, such as a network, or dial into AOL from a different location.

AOL 7.0 lets you set almost all your online preferences in the Preferences window, shown in Figure 3-1. You can get there in two ways: from the address box (AOL Keyword: **Preferences**) or from the menu bar (Settings⇨Preferences). Preferences can be set offline or online.

To use all your sound and video files with the AOL Media Player, use the Multimedia link and check the box.

The Preferences window has three columns:

- **Organization:** These tools help you organize your e-mail messages and newsgroups postings (click Filing Cabinet), your downloaded files (click Download), and your browser (click Internet Properties).
- **Communications:** These controls relate to your use of e-mail and chat.

- **Account Controls:** Click Passwords to have your computer remember your password so that you don't have to type it every time you sign on. The Privacy controls let you set your Instant Message privacy controls.

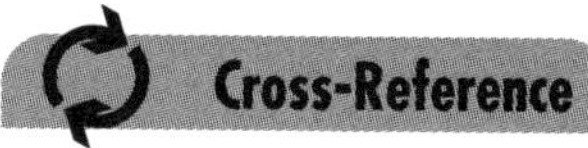

Chapters 10 and 11 are about e-mail, and Chapter 12 covers instant messaging.

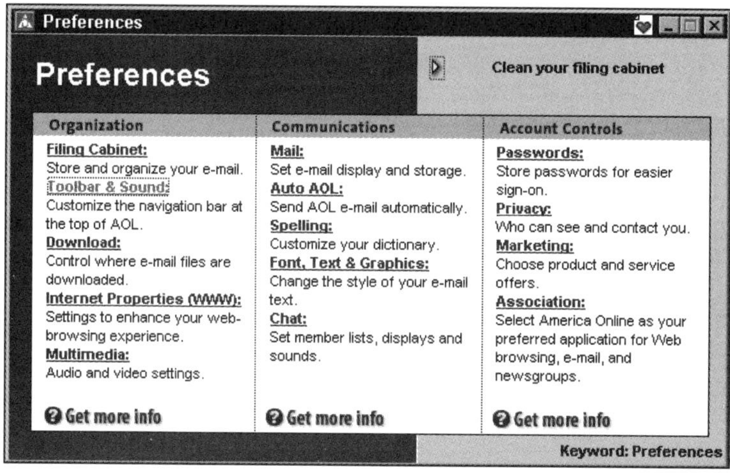

Figure 3-1. Use AOL's Preferences window whenever necessary to adjust the way AOL's tools work.

Your Own Information Service: My AOL

My AOL allows you to create a personalized Web newspaper consisting of the articles, sports scores, business stories, and other news items you want to read. But My AOL is much more than a newspaper. It helps you identify the information you want and then gives you the freedom to access it on AOL, on the Web, and with an AOL Anywhere device, such as a wireless phone, Mobile Communicator, and so on.

Both members and Internet users can use AOL Anywhere and the service is free for everyone. Figure 3-2 shows my personalized version of My AOL; yours will vary depending on your preferences. For more information, see AOL Keyword: **Anywhere**.

The idea is simple: You edit your own online newspaper, personalizing the sections you want to see. You can get news, sports scores, business updates, and entertainment news from a broad range of news sources. You can include international, national, and local news.

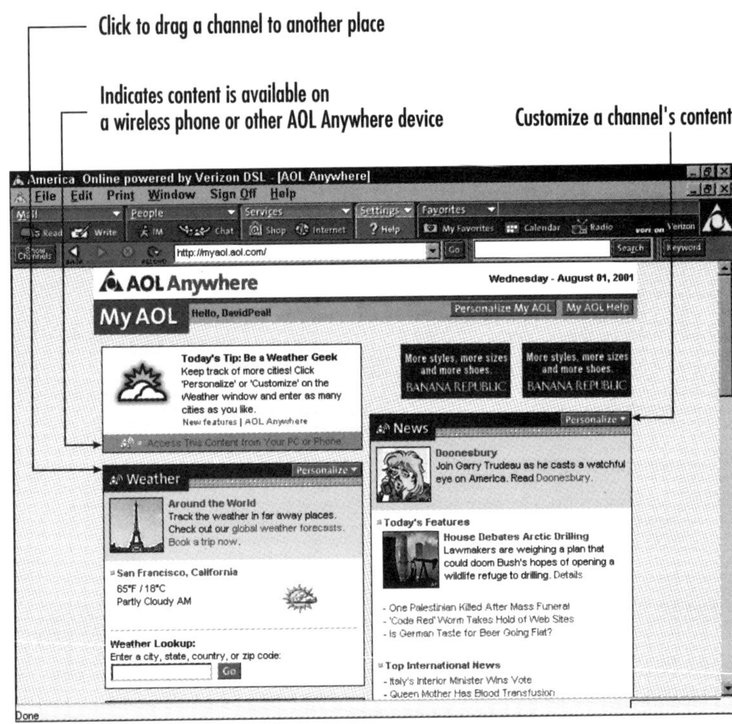

Figure 3-2. My AOL is your personal, always up-to-date Web information hub.

Here's how it works:

1. Use AOL Keyword: **My AOL**.
2. The first time you use My AOL, you need to register. Provide your zip code and screen name as instructed. You'll also be asked for your birthday (useful if you want a horoscope in My AOL) and other optional information. You have the opportunity to save your registration information on your computer. Read AOL's Private Policy (AOL Keyword: **Privacy**) if you have any concerns about the possible use of your personal information.

   After you register, you're ready to start customizing and reading My AOL. In the future, you won't have to log in; the page comes right up when you go to AOL Keyword: **My AOL**.

If you use My AOL on a computer without an AOL connection, all the content is on the Web. If you use My AOL when you are signed on to AOL, some of the content will be on the AOL service itself.

Like a newspaper, My AOL is arranged in columns — but only two columns, in this case. Each column has several channels. A *channel* is a window containing specific information, such as business headlines or weather forecasts.

If you want your weather report and horoscope personalized, use the My Preferences button to provide related personal information such as your birth date and zip code.

Personalizing My AOL takes only a few, simple steps:

1. From the My AOL opening page, click Personalize My AOL to bring up the Personalize My AOL window.
2. In the top section, called Add or Remove Content, choose the content you want (News, Calendar, Search, Portfolio, Weather, and so on) by clicking in the check boxes.
3. In the bottom section, indicate how often you want your information to be updated.
4. Click Save when you have made your selections.
5. Close the Personalize My AOL window when you are done.

Each separate bit of information (news, weather, portfolio, and so on) is called a *channel* and is displayed in a box within My AOL, as shown in Figure 3-2. You have several options in further refining a channel's position and content:

At My AOL, click Personalize at any time to add and drop content from My AOL.

- **To move a channel from one column to another:** Move your mouse arrow over the bumpy-looking part of the channel's title bar. The mouse arrow now shows a symbol with four arrows. Click now and drag the channel to another part of My AOL. When you see the red "Reposition Here?" pop-up, release the mouse button.
- **To remove a channel from My AOL:** Click the Personalize button in the upper-right corner of the channel box and select Remove. You are asked to confirm your decision; click OK.
- **To personalize the content of a channel:** Use the Personalize button and select Customize. (Not every channel can be personalized.) For some channels, such as My Calendar and Portfolio, choosing Customize takes you to the setup windows for the respective services. For other channels, such as News, you are taken to special My AOL screens, where you can determine what kind of news you want to read (Economy, People, and so on).

In My AOL (refer to Figure 3-2), you see the selections you made in the previous steps.

Using My Calendar

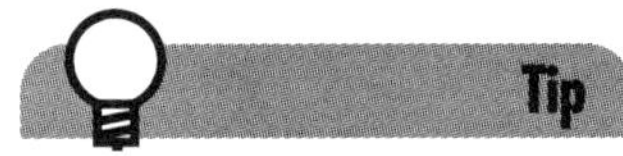

My Calendar lets you add and check appointments when you are offline. To access My Calendar on the Web with a non-AOL Internet provider, go to `calendar.aol.com`.

My Calendar enables you to create a schedule in the place where you may be spending many of your working hours nowadays — at the PC. With this easy-to-use but comprehensive calendar (see Figure 3-3), you can keep track of all your appointments, meetings, dates, business lunches, birthdays, anniversaries, favorite TV shows, classes, and the other important events.

Monthly appointments
Weekly appointments
View local events
Daily appointments
Print

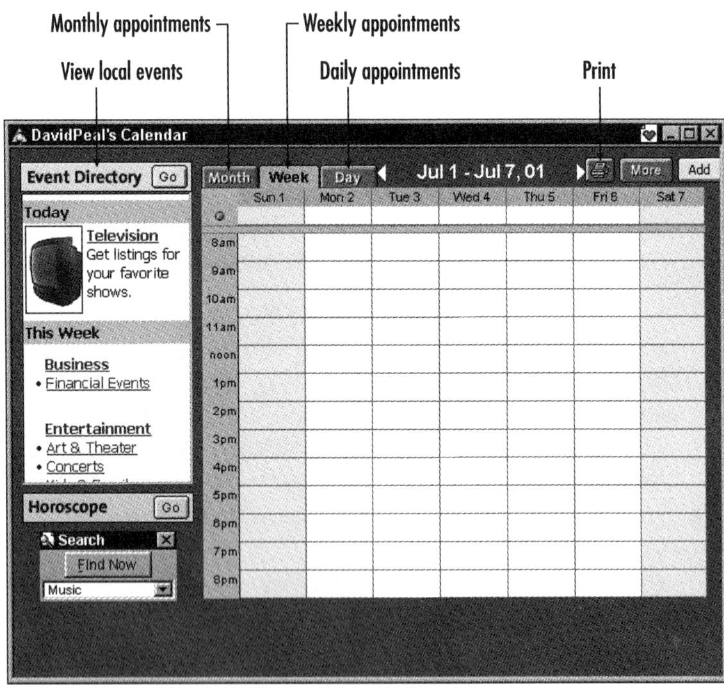

Figure 3-3. The My Calendar service helps you keep track of meetings, anniversaries, and all the events in your life.

Online, you can access My Calendar by clicking the Calendar button on the AOL toolbar or using AOL Keyword: **Calendar**. Offline, you can also use My Calendar by opening the AOL software without signing on. Then, click the Calendar button.

AOL's location-based services, Moviefone, MapQuest, and Local Guide, allow you to find a movie or event in your area, and add it to your calendar with all the specifics, including the date, filled in for you. All this information is at your fingertips in your calendar's Event Directory, on the left. Click the directory's Go button to browse for a concert, movie, or show of interest. The directory includes TV shows, trade conferences, book releases, and much more than you might expect.

For individual events, you usually get related information — synopses, trailers, reviews, and so on. Or, for a museum exhibit, get ticket information, dates for the show, directions to the museum, and hours. Spend some time exploring the Event Directory to appreciate how much you can do in your community. Then use the My Calendar service to start taking advantage of it all.

To add a show to your calendar with the Event Directory:

1. Find the specific event or movie, along with its time and place of showing (see Figure 3-4).
2. Click the Add to My Calendar link. A pop-up window confirms that the event and time was added to your calendar.

You are not restricted to adding scheduled public events to My Calendar. To add more detailed personal appointment details:

1. Display the calendar's Month view.
2. Click the event date in your calendar. The Appointment Details window comes up (see Figure 3-5).
3. Type a name for the appointment.
4. Use the buttons to type a note about the appointment or to make it a repeating event, as you might do for a favorite Wednesday night TV show. Repeating events can be repeated daily, weekly, or at other intervals.
5. Click OK to add the appointment to My Calendar.

In the future, click an event link to jog your memory about the details or add further details.

Click AOL Invitations in the Appointment Details dialog box to share time-and-place information with others interested in the same event (such as a weekly book club).

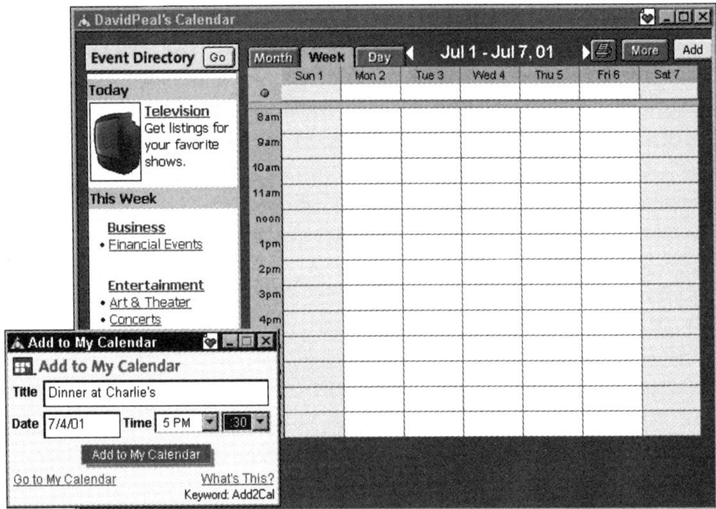

Figure 3-4. Press Ctrl+Y to jot down brief details for an appointment or event. Add the details in the box in the lower left, and the appointment is added to the correct date on the calendar (right).

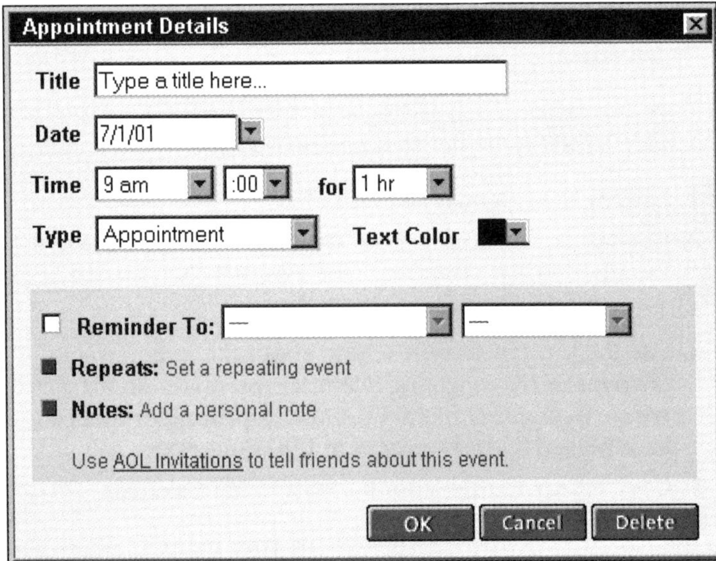

Figure 3-5. The Appointment Details window comes up when you (1) edit an existing event (click it) and (2) click a date to add a new event.

You can view the calendar in many ways — unlike the old drugstore calendars. Click the Month, Week, or Day tab to change the view. The monthly view provides a convenient overview of your appointments and times. Weekly and daily views show you blocks of time within a day. The weekly view, shown in Figure 3-3, helps you plan the week, which can be especially handy if you have family responsibilities or must travel regularly. The daily view gives hour-by-hour details. The daily view also gives you a monthly calendar without all the appointment details, which comes in very handy for any kind of planning. From either the monthly or daily view, you can scroll to the next month or day by clicking the left- and right-pointing triangles flanking the date.

Now that you have a calendar with all your events and appointments, how are you going to remember everything? With AOL's Reminder service, of course. You can set up the service to drop you an e-mail message (sort of like a wake-up call) at any point from 15 minutes to four hours before the meeting or whatever it happens to be.

To use the service, click the event to bring up the Appointment Details box. Place a check by Reminder. In the two drop-down boxes indicate how you want to be reminded (to which e-mail address) and how long before the event you wish to be reminded. Click Create Your Reminder to uses Reminders to prevent you from forgetting birthdays, anniversaries, and so on. You'll receive an e-mail message several days before the event.

Keeping Track of Favorite Online Destinations

AOL provides three ways of keeping track of favorite online destinations:

- Favorite Places takes you to any type of online resource on AOL or the Web.
- Hot Keys take you to AOL or Internet destinations, but only ten of them.
- My Places takes you to ten AOL destinations.

Each of these tools is described in the following three sections.

Using Favorite Places

One of the most useful ways of personalizing your online experience is to keep your own record of your favorite online destinations, in order to share them with others and to return to those places yourself. Your Favorite Places folder, available from the new AOL 7.0 Favorites menu, lets you keep a list of your favorite online destinations from AOL and the Internet.

You can view, edit, and visit your favorite places by choosing Favorites⇨Favorite Places.

You can use Favorite Places as a hot list of your favorite Web sites, but you can add much more than Web sites to your Favorite Places folder. You can also add the following:

- E-mail messages (for example, important job-related or personal messages)
- Newsgroups
- Your favorite AOL or Web message boards
- FTP sites you frequent
- AOL areas and individual windows within them, as long as they have a Favorite Places heart in the upper-right corner
- AOL channels

Chapter 14 focuses on newsgroups; Chapter 15 looks at FTP.

Creating Favorite Places

Using Favorite Places is a breeze. To add any page, message, site, or AOL area to your Favorite Places folder:

You cannot add an AOL area to your Favorite Places folder if it doesn't have a Favorite Places heart. Everything on the Web can be made into a favorite place, however.

1. Click the small heart in the window's upper right-hand corner, as shown in Figure 3-6.

   The Favorite Places heart is not visible if a window is maximized (made as large as possible), but you can still add the maximized window to your Favorite Places folder in one of two ways:

   - Reduce the window size (click the little picture, called the Restore box, showing two overlapping squares just below the AOL window's upper-right corner), and then click the heart. See Figure 3-2 to see the Restore box for My AOL. Try it to see how it works for any window.
   - Hold down the Ctrl and Shift keys and press the Plus key (to the left of the Backspace key).

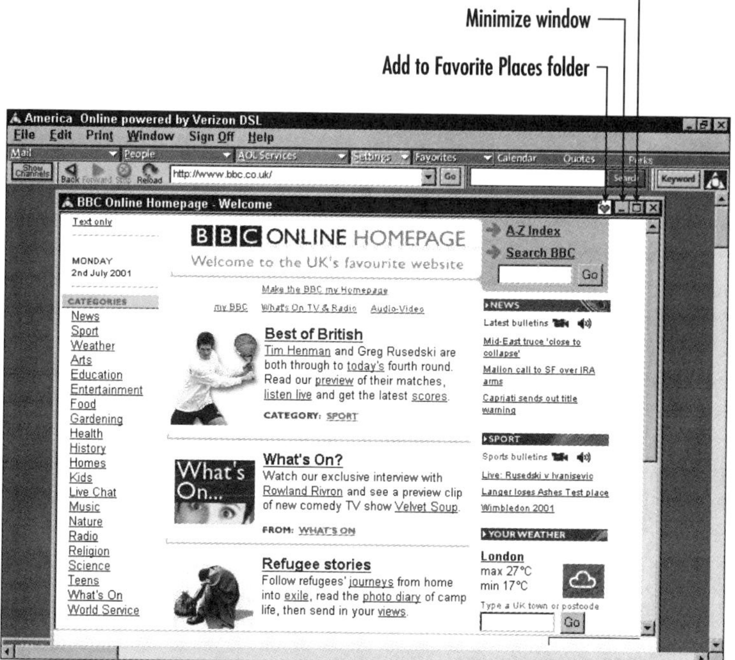

Figure 3-6. The BBC makes excellent use of multimedia throughout its site and offers several live radio stations around the clock.

2. A window like the one in Figure 3-7 pops up offering you four choices: Add to Favorites, Insert in Instant Message, Insert in Mail, and (new in AOL 7.0) Add to Toolbar. Click Add to Favorites. The new favorite will be in your Favorite Places folder.

To view your favorite places, just click the My Favorites button on the toolbar (or choose Favorites⇨Favorite Places). Your folder will differ from the one shown in Figure 3-8, depending on the favorites you choose.

On the AOL toolbar, the Favorites menu displays the first 20 items in your Favorite Places folder. As you can see in Figure 3-8, the first items consist of folders. On the menu, folders containing subfolders have little black triangles to the right. Move your mouse over the triangle to see a submenu of items in the folder. The submenu displays the first 20 items in a submenu, a sub-submenu, and so on. If you want to see more than the 20 displayed folders and items in any menu or submenu, click More Favorites from that menu or submenu to bring up the standard AOL Favorite Places folder (see Figure 3-8), where you have direct access to all your favorites.

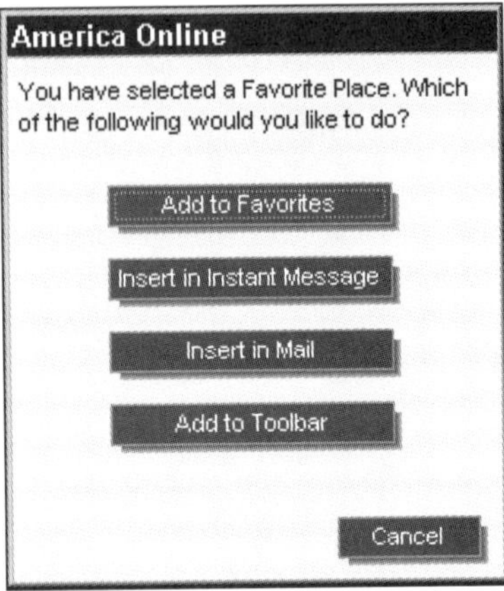

Figure 3-7. Store your favorites in the Favorite Places folder, or share them right away by inserting a live link to the destination into an e-mail message or instant message.

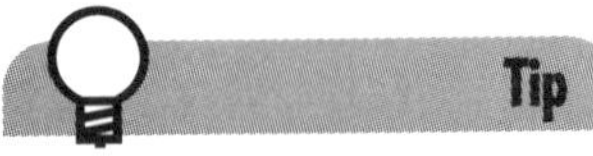

You can arrange the folders in your Favorite Places folder so that frequently used items are among the first 20 in the Favorite Places folder and thus displayed on the Favorites menu.

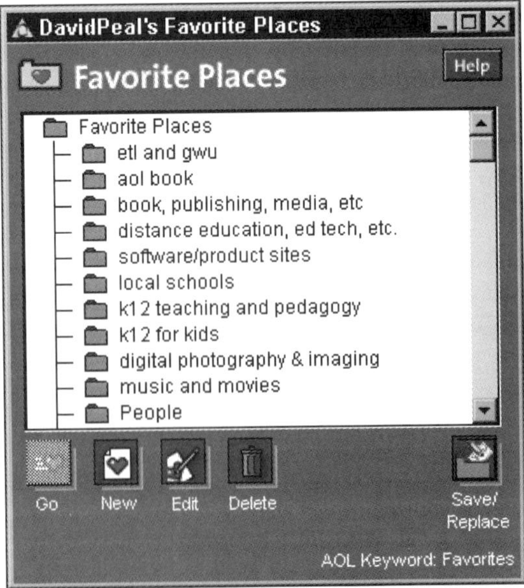

Figure 3-8. Use the Favorite Places folder to edit, delete, and rename your favorite AOL areas, message boards, and Web sites.

Adding a Favorite Place to the Toolbar

Before starting, your screen resolution must be set to 800 x 600 pixels or higher to make enough room on the toolbar for a new button.

To change your screen resolution, go to the Windows desktop. Right-click and choose Properties. In the Display Properties window, click Settings and, in the Screen Area section, drag the needle right or left until you're at 800 x 600 (or higher). Click OK.

AOL is optimized for 800 X 600 resolution. Anything higher may be difficult to read (too small) for some users. Windows XP's lowest resolution is 800 X 600, which is fine for adding toolbar buttons.

You can add up to three Favorite Places to the AOL toolbar, but you will need to remove buttons to do so. To add a Favorite Place to the toolbar:

1. Remove one of the three right-most buttons already on the toolbar, which will probably include Calendar and Radio, by right-clicking a button and choosing Remove from Toolbar.
2. Open the window you wish to make a Favorite Place.
3. Click the heart in the upper-right corner of the Favorite Place's window. In the window shown in Figure 3-7, click Add to Toolbar. You'll be prompted to select an icon to represent the Favorite Place on the toolbar and to give the new toolbar button a name. Click OK.

Managing Your Favorite Places

In no time, all sorts of links can crowd your Favorite Places folder, to the point where favorites become unrecognizable in weeks if you don't bring some order to them. Here are some tips for helping you cope with all your favorites:

To move folders within the Favorite Places folder, click a folder and drag it up or down. You can also move items around within a folder, or drop them into a folder. Again, just click and drag.

- **Create new folders.** Click the New button. When the Add New Folder/Favorite Place box pops up, choose New Folder. Choose a name and enter it. Click OK.
- **Move folders and Favorite Places.** To drag an item into a new folder (or any folder), simply click and drag it. You can move folders into folders, and you can move both folders and Favorite Places up and down the main list or the list of items in a folder. Note, however, that you can't alphabetize items.
- **Delete folders and old favorites.** Select any Favorite or folder and click the Delete button. Shift-click to select and delete more than one Favorite Places or folders in a row or Ctrl-click to select and delete items that aren't in a row.

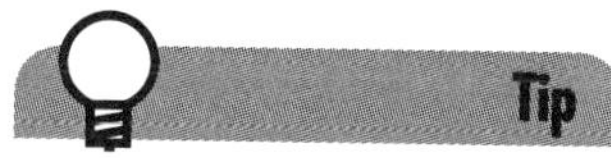

To Shift-click, hold down the Shift key before selecting several items in a row. Use Ctrl-click to select multiple items that do not appear next to each other.

Use Ctrl+F to find items in the Favorite Places folder. It also finds individual messages in your online mailbox and Filing Cabinet.

Save important e-mail messages in your Favorite Places folder.

Right-click a selected Favorite or a folder, and choose Delete to remove it, Edit to rename it, or another choice to insert it into an e-mail, an instant message, or even the AOL toobar.

Item names and folder names can be changed to clarify content or accommodate a changed online address.

- **Find lost favorites.** You can find and retrieve specific items using AOL's search feature. With the Favorite Places folder open, press Ctrl+F. Type a word to search for and click Find. You can make your searches case sensitive by clicking the Match Case box. (A case-sensitive search for *TCP/IP* would find *TCP/IP*, but not *tcp/ip*.) You can search only one folder at a time.
- **Order items within a folder.** The Favorite Places folder has its quirks. When you add an e-mail message to your Favorite Places folder, the message is automatically placed at the top of the list. When you add an AOL area or Web page, this new favorite goes to the bottom of the list. If you have several subfolders at the top of your favorites list, you can't drag an item *above* the top folder in the list — instead, the item falls into the folder! (This also means you can create a new folder and make it the first one.) To get around this problem, make any e-mail message you've received a Favorite Place by clicking the heart in the Read Mail window. You can now move an item or folder above the message. When you're done, you can delete the message.
- **Add Favorite Places.** You can create a favorite place from scratch by clicking New, choosing New Favorite Place, and supplying a name and a Web address (or URL for non-Web destinations). The name is what shows in the folder, while the URL tells AOL how to get to the actual destination.
- **Edit a Favorite Place.** Sooner or later, you will want to edit a favorite place. Just select it and click Edit to bring up the window shown in Figure 3-9. I use this feature all the time to rename an item with a name that I can remember. I also change a URL when a favorite place's URL changes. E-mail message names can't be edited, which is unfortunate because message names are usually long and don't identify a message's content.

Using Favorite Places on Several Computers

Each screen name on a master account has its own set of Favorite Places, and each of these folders can be used on any number of computers. If you use one screen name on many computers, you will soon discover that all your Favorite Places folders differ, because the Favorite Places chosen on one PC will exist only on that PC.

Figure 3-9. Edit your favorite places to give them meaningful names (Place Description) and update their URLs (Internet Address) if they change.

To use the same Favorite Places on several PCs:

1. From the copy of the AOL software with the most up-to-date Favorite Places folder, open Favorite Places and click the Save/Replace button in the lower right-hand corner (refer to Figure 3-8).
2. In the Save and Replace window, select Save the Favorite Places for Your Current Screen Name (if it's not already selected), and click OK.
3. Save your favorite places on a floppy disk (your floppy drive is usually the A: drive).
4. Remove the disk and put it in the other computer's floppy drive.
5. Open the Favorite Places folder on the other computer. Click the Save/Replace button. In the Save and Replace window, select Replace the Favorite Places for Your Current Screen Name. Follow the on-screen instructions.

Using Hot Keys to Access Your Favorites

Here's an older yet lesser-known way to personalize AOL. People who love keyboard equivalents, and the millions of people who cannot use a mouse because of a disability, will appreciate this technique. My Hot Keys lets you assign up to ten simple keystrokes to your favorite destinations on AOL and on the Web. To create shortcuts, choose Favorites⇨My Hot Keys⇨Edit My Hot Keys to display the editing window shown in Figure 3-10.

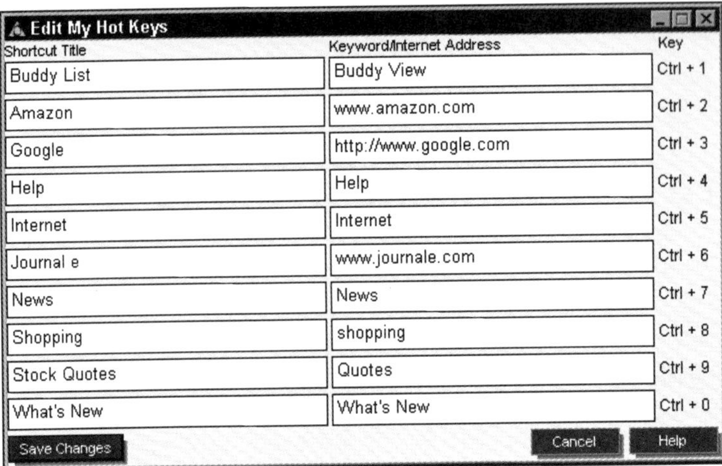

Figure 3-10. Type in the name of the Web site or AOL area, the Web address or keyword, and click save to edit your hot keys.

Notice that each row in the Edit My Hot Keys window has two boxes. In the first box, type a name you want to use to remember the area or site, for example, Amazon.com. I set up Amazon by simply typing **Amazon** over the existing selection. In the second box, to the right, type an AOL keyword or a Web address (URL) for a Web site, in this case, **www.amazon.com**. Click Save Changes when you're done adding your own shortcuts.

To visit a shortcut, you must be online. Hold down the Ctrl key and press a number from 0 to 9, corresponding to the keystroke assigned to your shortcut (for example, Ctrl+2, for Amazon).

Accessing Your Favorite AOL Destinations

With My Places, you can keep up to 12 AOL resources that you want at your fingertips — right on the Welcome Screen. (Remember that the Welcome Screen is always available when you're signed on. If you don't see it, select Window⇨Welcome Screen.)

You can also customize My Places at AOL Keyword: **My Places**.

To customize My Places

1. Type AOL Keyword: **My Places**. A small window called My Places appears.

2. Click the Change My Places button to bring up the Change My Places window.
3. You see 12 menu items. To replace any selected My Place item with a new choice of your own, click Choose New Place for that item and a menu of options pops up, as shown in Figure 3-11.
4. Make a choice from the menu. Continue making choices until you're done. Every menu has the same menu options, ranging from Computing to Travel. Some menus, such as People, Research, and Sports, have more than half a dozen selections you can choose from. In Sports, for example, your choices include Baseball, Basketball, and Golf.

The Welcome Screen displays your selections right away — and from now on, whenever you sign on. You can change My Places at any time.

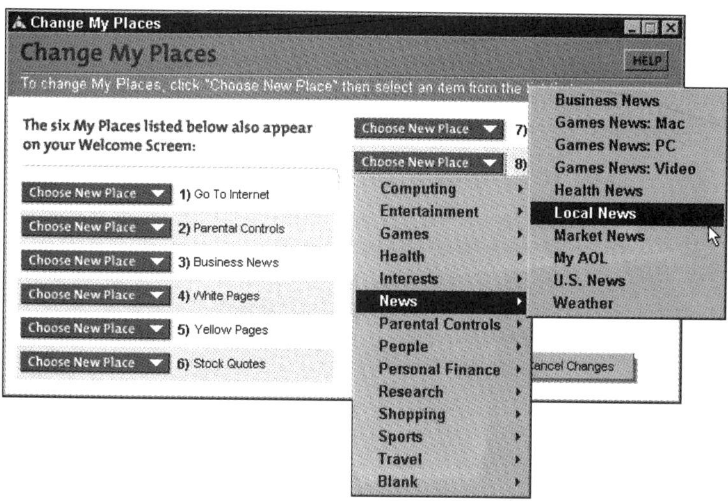

Figure 3-11. My Places puts your favorite AOL sites on the Welcome Screen for ready access whenever you are on AOL.

Keeping Track of Online Contacts

AOL provides many tools for both keeping up with your online friends and meeting new people online.

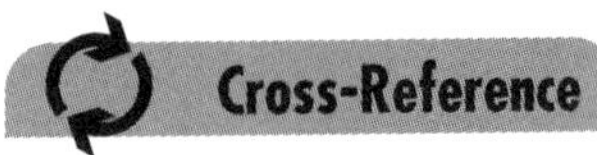

See Chapter 11 for info on the Address Book and Chapter12 for the Buddy List.

You can make changes to your Address Book even when you're not online. Start the AOL program but don't sign on. Then choose Mail⇨Address Book. Any changes you make will be saved for you the next time you sign on.

AOL provides two major ways of keeping track of your online buddies and other contacts, the Address Book and the Buddy List. Unlike Favorite Places, these two lists are kept on AOL's computers, not yours. That means that no matter how you access AOL (wireless phone, handheld computer, and so on), you will be able to use your latest Address Book and Buddy List.

- The Address Book, shown in Figure 3-12, gives you a way of keeping detailed information about all your friends, colleagues, relatives, and others. The Address Book is available from AOL's Mail menu whether or not you've signed on to AOL. Meant for use with e-mail, the Address Book can be used offline whenever you need a phone number or address. Use this feature to store people's fax numbers, multiple e-mail addresses, street addresses, birthdays, and so on.

- The Buddy List is an AOL feature that is now available in all versions of AOL Instant Messenger. Your Buddy List tells you which friends are online when you are so that you can send them messages and invite them to chats. You can set up your preferences to limit people's access to you, put out a message saying "I'm away from the computer" or something similar, or inform you of when certain buddies arrive online.

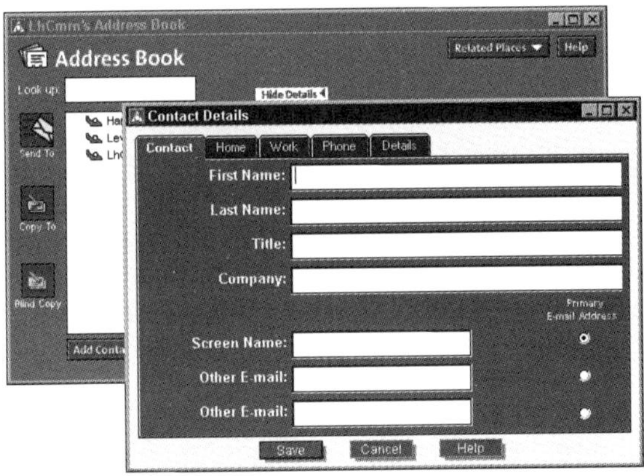

Figure 3-12. The AOL Address Book, plus the New Contact window, used to add people to your Address Book.

Personalizing Your AOL Account

Your account information consists of your screen name (used by others to recognize and communicate with you), your password (known only by you), and your billing information (known only by you and AOL). And for your ventures out on the Web, AOL offers a new Screen Name Service that extends the benefits of having a screen name (and associated information about you) as an online identity. You can customize and update screen names, passwords, Parental Controls, and Preferences by using the Preferences window, which I discuss in the beginning of this chapter.

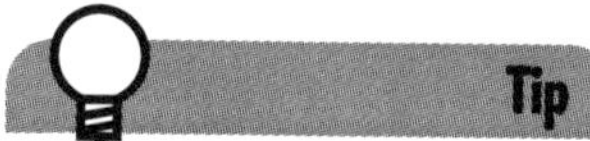

One way to customize your online experience is to create new screen names. Consider screen names for work, home, or for high-volume mailing lists (Chapter 13 is about lists).

Choosing Screen Names

Your screen name is how people recognize you online. It is your e-mail address on AOL, and your friends on the Internet can send you an e-mail message by adding `@aol.com` to your screen name. Your screen name shows up in other people's Buddy List (if they've added the screen name, of course); when they see your name in their Buddy List, they can send you instant messages.

Here are some guidelines to bear in mind in selecting a screen name:

- Every account can have up to seven screen names, including the screen name used to establish the account and provide billing information.
- You need a screen name when you sign on to AOL or use an AOL Web service, such as AOL Hometown, while using a non-AOL Internet connection.
- The first character of a screen name is capitalized automatically. Letters that you capitalize after the first character appear as capitals in the screen name. People e-mailing you don't have to bother with any capital letters, however.

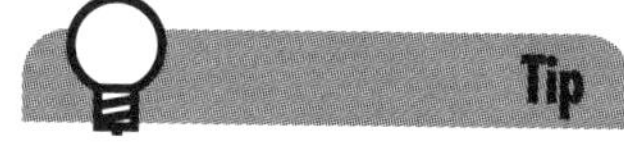

You can create as many as seven screen names for each master account. Each screen name can be between 3 and 16 characters, as opposed to 10 characters in the older versions of AOL.

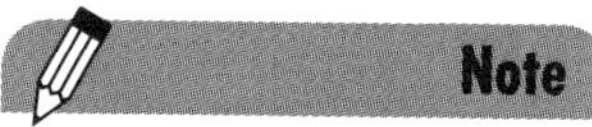

To use Parental Controls (see Chapter 4), a parent must first set up a screen name for a child, because the controls apply to screen names.

To create a screen name, go to AOL Keyword: **Names** and click Create a Screen Name. Use this area to delete screen names, too. Any screen name you want to use must be unique on AOL. If the name you prefer is not unique, AOL offers you a name that may include a string of numbers tacked on to the end of the name you wanted. Keep trying for a name of your

Using offensive words as screen names can lead to account termination (see AOL Keyword: **TOS**).

own choosing, perhaps by opting for more characters *and spaces*. Sixteen characters give you the scope for creativity but long screen names can tax your friends' memories. Remember, screen names are more for others than for you — it's the way they communicate with you.

Every screen name has its own password, and passwords can be changed at any time. Changing passwords adds security to your account by preventing others from accessing it. To change a password, sign on to AOL with the screen name whose password you want to change and then go to AOL Keyword: **Password**. Follow the instructions there. Remember to make passwords difficult to figure out. Here are some tips:

- Don't use familiar names, numbers, or dates.
- Use at least three characters.
- Try alternating numbers and letters.

AOL now stores a copy of all screen names for your account on its computers. When you add a new computer to your account, your screen names download and appear in the AOL Sign On window. You still have to enter the password for each screen name, but passwords can be stored on your PC so you don't have to enter them repeatedly:

1. Choose Settings⇨Preferences from the toolbar and then click Passwords.
2. In the Password box, simply type the password for the currently signed-on name. In the future, you won't have to enter the password when you sign on.

Using the Screen Name Service

Without a screen name, you can't sign on to AOL or use AOL Mail. With AOL's new Screen Name Service, you can do even more with your screen name. You can, for example, get access to online destinations such as CompuServe, Netscape, and a growing number of AOL and partner Web sites. The Screen Name Service can be very convenient for people on the go and for shopping online.

AOL's Screen Name Service can simplify access to many Web sites with e-commerce and other special services. With the new service, you do not have to enter your name and other information repeatedly. On AOL, for example, you can use your

AOL screen name to post and view digital photos at the "You've Got Pictures" Web site (`pictures.aol.com`), create a Web site at AOL Hometown (`hometown.aol.com`), and read e-mail on the Web (`aolmail.aol.com`). Other AOL and non-AOL Web sites are being added to the list of sites that can be accessed with the same screen name. The AOL Instant Messenger service lets you keep several different screen names, each with its own password.

When you visit a participating non-AOL or AOL Web site, just look for the official Screen Name Service (SNS) Sign In or Login button (see Figure 3-13). Click the button and, in the boxes provided, type your screen name and password. PetPlace.com (Figure 3-13) is an example of a site that lets you register for the service and then use your screen name to access the site's many features, including a personalized page. Other sites using the Screen Name Service include Kinko's, Monster.com, Stamps.com, and Rollingstone.com.

When you register for the Screen Name Service, you can create a profile containing personal information, such as your mailing address. This information is stored with AOL, and it is automatically used whenever you register at a participating site. Having a profile on record can speed up registration at other Web sites and simplify the shopping experience if you'll be buying things online.

The Screen Name Service is highly secure and protects both your transactions and the privacy of your information.

- If you have questions about confidentiality, go to AOL Keyword: **Privacy Policy**. Also, go to AOL Keyword: **SNS** and click Frequently Asked Questions.
- If you share your computer, be sure to log off when you finish a transaction using this service.

Updating Your Billing Information

When you initially became an AOL member, you provided an address, chose a billing method and price plan, and supplied some additional information. At any time, you can update all that information by going to AOL Keyword: **Billing**. There, you can view your current bill and payment data, change your contact information and payment method, and sign up for a different plan.

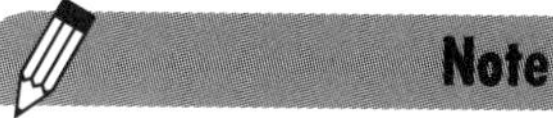

Internet users can use the Screen Name Service, too, by signing up at the Screen Name Service page (AOL Keyword: **SNS**) or any AOL or non-AOL Web site affiliated with the service.

Many AOL Web sites, such as AOL Search and Shop@AOL, can be viewed by anyone and do not require a screen name. Within Shop@AOL, the Quick Checkout service is available only for AOL members.

To modify your contact or billing information, visit AOL Keyword: **Change**.

Figure 3-13. PetPlace.com allows you to log on using the screen name established on AOL or an online destination using the Screen Name Service.

Personalizing Your Internet Connection

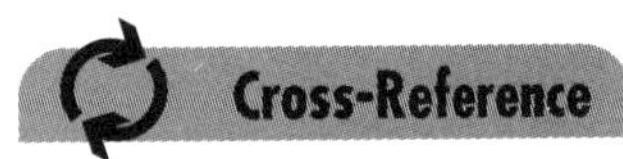

In Chapter 17, I look in more detail at high-speed connections, such as AOL PLUS for DSL and AOL PLUS for Satellite.

On AOL, you can choose the content you want, as you've seen with AOL's many services, including My AOL, My Calendar, and Favorite Places. Did you know that with AOL, your Internet connection itself can be customized? In the next few pages, I look at *networking,* the main alternative to modems, and at *locations,* the way you define how you are connecting and from where. Both can be changed as your situation changes.

Creating Locations for Use with a Network

The modem has been a popular access method since AOL's beginnings in 1985. In recent years, accessing AOL over a network has grown in popularity.

Network access can mean several things:

- **Accessing AOL through your local area network (LAN) at work**: Ask your systems administrator about the feasibility of accessing AOL at work.
- **Accessing AOL through your Internet service provider (ISP) by using AOL's Bring Your Own Access plan:** Unlike LANs, ISP-based access usually requires an analog modem, though more and more ISPs offer high-speed options such as DSL as well.
- **Accessing AOL through a cable Internet connection:** You can access AOL through the cable wires if your cable provider offers Internet services. You'll need to subscribe to those services and buy the proper equipment, including a splitter and a cable modem.

To run AOL over a network connection, you must first create an ISP/LAN location, as follows.

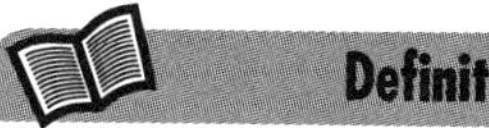
Definition

A *location* describes, minimally, *how* you access AOL. If you are using a regular modem, a location defines the area code you use to dial into AOL. If you use a network, physical location doesn't matter.

1. From the Sign On screen (or Goodbye screen if you've signed off AOL without closing the AOL application), click the Setup button to bring up the AOL Setup window (see Figure 3-14).

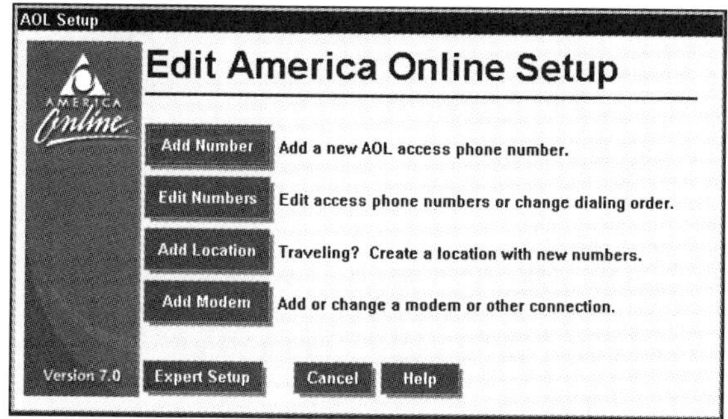

Figure 3-14. Click Add Location to create a new network connection or collect AOL access numbers for an area where you will be traveling.

2. Click the Add Location button to bring up the Add Location window (Figure 3-15).

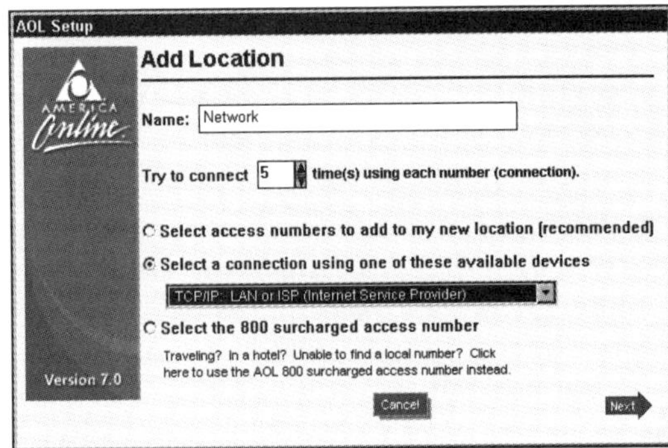

Figure 3-15. Create a network location so that you can use your ISP, cable modem, DSL, or other network connection.

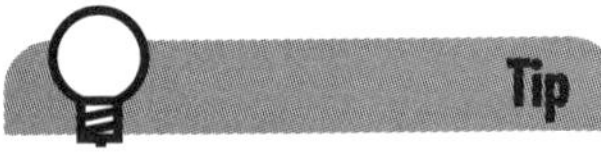

By switching locations in the Sign On or Goodbye Screen, you can alternate between a modem and a network connection.

3. In the Add Location window, you need to do three things:
   - Give your connection a Name, which you can later select from the Sign On window's Location box to use the new location. Choose a connection name that has meaning to you, such as *Cable*, *AOL PLUS, DSL*, or something else.
   - Leave the Try to Connect default as is.
   - Under Select a Connection Using One of These Available Devices, select *TCP/IP: LAN or ISP (Internet Service Provider)*.
4. Click Next. A window informs you that the location was created.

Now, to sign on to a network:

1. Establish the ISP, network, or cable connection.
2. Open the AOL software.
3. Choose the correct screen name and password, and from the Select Location drop-down menu, select the newly created network location.
4. Click Sign On.

Creating Locations for Use with a Modem

To access AOL when you're on the road with a laptop or someone else's PC, you need to use different access numbers to dial into the AOL service. Sure, you can dial your ordinary

Pittsburgh access numbers while visiting San Francisco, but do you want to pay the long-distance phone charges? Probably not. Instead, you simply create a new location, taking advantage of AOL's nationwide network of access numbers.

The following example shows how to create a new location for an upcoming visit to San Francisco, in the 415 area code:

1. Open the AOL software and, in the Sign On screen, click Setup.
2. In the AOL Setup window, click Add Location.
3. In the Add Location box (see Figure 3-15), do the following things:
   - Give the new location a name, such as *San Francisco.*
   - For the Try to Connect option, indicate how many times you want each number to be dialed. The default setting is 5.
   - Under Select a Connection Using One of These Available Devices, select Modem.

   Click Next when you're done.
4. In the Search for AOL Access Numbers window, type (in this example) 415 into the Area Code box.
5. From the list of phone numbers, select at least two local access numbers, following the on-screen instructions when prompted.

   In choosing access numbers, consider whether any of the numbers carry a toll charge, as many calls do within larger area codes. Sometimes adjacent area codes will be listed along with the area code you chose. Search for 415 in San Francisco, for example, and you'll also retrieve a list of 510 numbers in the East Bay.
6. After you have selected all the numbers you think you might need or use, click Next. Now you can modify the numbers as needed, depending on your phone's features. You may, for instance, want to indicate that you must dial 9 before placing an outgoing call.
7. Click Next and follow the instructions to confirm your numbers and complete setup.

You can have AOL automatically attempt to dial each access number up to 25 times.

Using AOL as Your Default Internet Software

When you open the AOL 7.0 software for the first time, you are asked (via a dialog box, with two check boxes) whether you want AOL to be your default Internet application for the Web and e-mail, and whether you want AOL to be your default CD Player.

What does this mean? Many applications let you embed Web links in documents. Microsoft Word and the other Microsoft Office applications, for example, let you link directly to Web sites, and you'll see links in e-mail and instant messages as well.

Where does the Microsoft Internet Explorer (MSIE) browser come from? As a Windows user, you probably have it preinstalled on your PC. Moreover, AOL's browser is based on MSIE and a full version of MSIE is installed and made available on your desktop when you install AOL.

What happens when you click such a link — in other words, a link *not* within AOL? Here's how the default Internet option works when you are online:

- If AOL is your default Internet application, the AOL software opens automatically and displays the page in the AOL browser.
- If AOL is *not* your default application, the Microsoft Internet Explorer browser opens and displays the page.

And here's how the default Internet option works *offline:*

- If AOL is your default Internet application, AOL opens, signs on automatically (you must type your password if you have not had it automatically stored), and then displays the page.
- If AOL is *not* your default Internet application, the Microsoft Internet Explorer browser opens, but does nothing unless you're on a network or signed on to AOL.

With audio CDs, it doesn't matter whether you are online or offline. Making AOL your default CD player just means that when you insert a CD, the AOL Media Player comes up to play it, as opposed to any other players that might be installed on your PC.

To make AOL your default Internet application, make sure that you're online and then follow these steps:

1. From the toolbar, choose Settings⇨Preferences. You can also use AOL Keyword: **Preferences**.
2. Click the Association link. Read the instructions and click OK to make AOL your Internet application. In practice, that means that whenever you try to visit a Web site or open the browser, AOL automatically opens and acts as your default Internet application even if you connect to the Internet through an ISP, LAN, or cable modem.

To make AOL your CD player after installation, use the same Preferences window. Click Multimedia, and make sure there's a check by the appropriate box. Click Save.

Where to Go from Here

AOL 7.0 greatly extends the ways in which you can customize AOL. This chapter has focused on the many ways you can create a personal Buddy List, Favorite Places folder, calendar, screen name(s), and a great deal more.

- Tool preferences are discussed in the chapters dealing with various tools, such as Chapter 6, which covers the AOL Web browser, and Chapters 10 and 11, the chapters on e-mail. For more about the Address Book in particular, see Chapter 11, and for more about the Buddy List, see Chapter 12.
- AOL's Help menu is available whether you're online or offline.
- For more about high-speed access, see Chapter 17.

Chapter 4

AOL for the Whole Family

IN THIS CHAPTER **PAGE**

The Net mirrors the real world. Sometimes the Net distorts, illuminates, and amplifies the real world, too. Just as you need to think of your family's safety and security when you are all walking down the street, so you should be mindful of their security when they are online.

Many parents and teachers worry unduly about online safety issues, maybe because they have heard exaggerated stories of the threats, without being familiar with the Net's countless opportunities for learning and fun.

This chapter looks at both sides of the picture:

- Simple tools for keeping kids safe
- Rich and readily accessible online resources for learning and fun

Online Safety for the Whole Family

With more than 400 million people around the world using the Internet "on a daily basis," according to CyberAtlas (www.cyberatlas.com), you can imagine that not everyone online is trustworthy. Online thieves may want your password, your address, or your credit card. Unscrupulous business people send unsolicited commercial e-mail messages to thousands of people. This is called *spamming*, and some spam may have explicit content that you don't want your children to see. Or you may receive links to X-rated Web sites.

No one from AOL will ever ask you for your password. Use AOL Keyword: **Notify AOL** to report anyone who asks for your password.

Another potential hazard is receiving and opening virus-infected files attached to e-mail messages. These files, when opened, can harm your system if you download and open them.

Against these threats, AOL offers you several options to help you maintain the level of security that is right for you and your family. AOL's Internet tools and services were designed, in fact, with safety in mind. AOL not only provides tools to keep unwanted and unsavory types at bay, but also pursues the worst offenders in court.

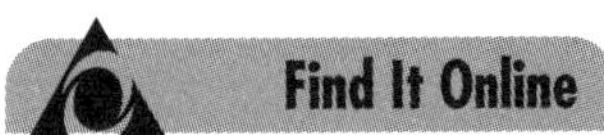

To find out more about protecting your computer from viruses, use AOL Keyword: **Virus**.

Parental Controls in particular were designed to help you keep your kids safe on both AOL and the Internet, regardless of the tool they are using. Use these controls to keep your children from accessing adult areas of the Internet and to prevent unsavory people from contacting your children. Use them, for example, to keep kids from inappropriate Web sites and to restrict the messages they can send and receive. Use AOL Keyword: **Parental Controls**.

The list of Web sites in Table 4-1 can help you better understand potential risks and the appropriate safety measures:

Table 4-1. Internet Safety Sites

Web site	*Web address*
GetNetWise	www.getnetwise.org/tools
Online Safety	www.aol.com/info/onlinesafety.html
Safe Surfing	www.safesurfin.com
Site Seeing on the Internet	www.ftc.gov/bcp/conline/pubs/online/sitesee

Web site	*Web address*
Family PC's Kids' Online SafetyGuide	`www.familypc.com/` (click Online Safety)
Safe Kids	`www.safekids.com`
Safe Kids' review of Internet filtering software	`www.safekids.com/filters.htm`
Safe Teens (specific advice for the risks teens might face)	`www.safeteens.com`
National Center for Missing and Exploited Children	`www.missingkids.com`

AOL also provides practical advice online that can help you keep your family safe. If anyone ever asks for your password or is otherwise unpleasant, use AOL Keyword: **Notify AOL** (Figure 4-1). You can also find a Notify AOL button in your Online Mailbox (in the New Mail and the Old Mail tabs).

Use Notify AOL to report obscene screen names, unwanted password solicitations, and other violations of AOL's Terms of Service (AOL Keyword: **TOS**). Everyone who uses AOL is expected to follow these guidelines. Every major Internet provider has similar, explicit guidelines. AOL Keyword: **Neighborhood Watch** pulls together diverse safety-related information available on AOL.

Figure 4-1. AOL Keywords: **Notify AOL** and **Neighborhood Watch** take you to places where you can find specific tips and effective tools for keeping kids safe.

Let kids know that if they are ever bothered online, they should report the incident immediately at AOL Keyword: **Kids Pager**. The incident will be followed up immediately by AOL staff.

Online Safety Tips

Online safety requires a bit of effort on everyone's part. If you are a parent, talk to your children about these simple guidelines, and make sure they understand and follow them:

- Never give out information that provides your address, phone number, or other personal information.
- Never provide your password to anyone online. If anyone asks for it for any reason, even if the reason sounds legitimate or if the person claims to work for AOL, immediately report the request to AOL Keyword: **Notify AOL** or **Kids Pager**.
- Never open files attached to e-mail messages when they're sent by someone you don't know. Even if the subject line seems friendly or makes you curious, remember that the attachment could contain a *virus,* a small program that can harm your computer and that you could inadvertently transmit to others.
- Report inappropriate comments in chat rooms and e-mail (AOL Keyword: **Notify AOL**). Some parents use Parental Controls to keep kids out of chat rooms altogether.
- Kids: Tell your parents if something happens online that makes you uncomfortable.
- Get to know the best of the Net, starting with a place like the American Librarians Association's Great Sites for Kids (`www.ala.org/parentspage/greatsites/amazing.html`). Baltimore's National Aquarium Web site, shown in the following figure, is one of the more than 700 sites to be found here.

Parental Controls can minimize dangers but can't create good online habits. That takes direct involvement. Know what your kids are doing online, and guide their attention to the kind of resources they can use for homework, fun, and family activities.

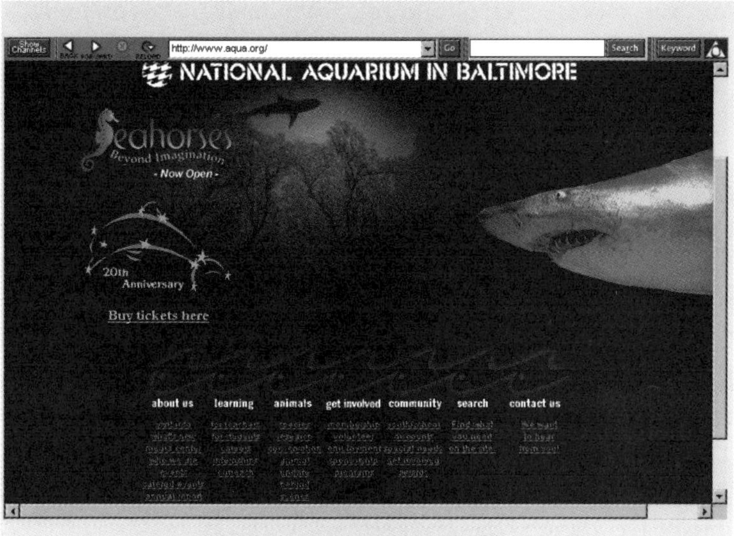

Using Parental Controls

If you are concerned about a child's online safety, use AOL's Parental Controls, shown in Figure 4-2 (AOL Keyword: **Parental Controls**). Parental Controls help you customize your family's access to online features and content.

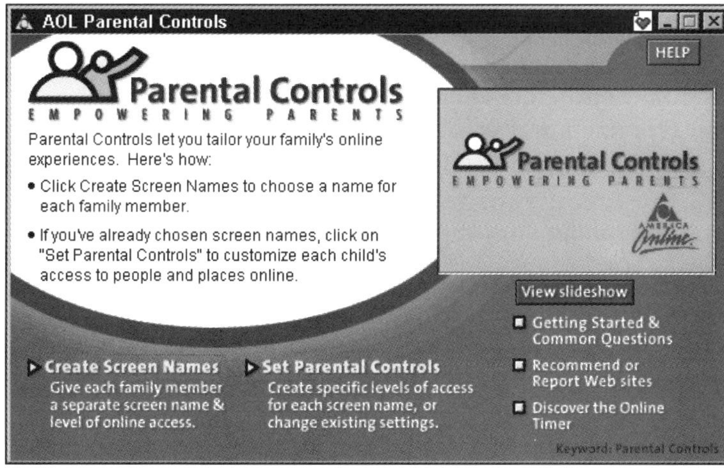

Figure 4-2. Parental Controls main window.

You can access Parental Controls from many places on AOL:

- ▶ Click the button in the lower-right corner on AOL's Welcome Screen.
- ▶ Select Parental Controls from the Settings menu on the toolbar.
- ▶ Use AOL Keyword: **Parental Controls**.
- ▶ Use AOL Keyword: **Neighborhood Watch**. Neighborhood Watch pulls together AOL's safety information in one place, including Parental Controls. You may want to make Neighborhood Watch a Favorite Place or assign it to a Hot Key for ready access in the future.

Use AOL Keyword: **Screen Names** to create and delete screen names.

It's important to realize that Parental Controls apply to screen names, not entire accounts. (Each account can have up to seven screen names.) To set controls for a child, that child must have a screen name.

When you create a new screen name at AOL Keyword: **Screen Names**, you are first asked whether the screen name is for a child. If you click Yes, you are presented with a document regarding AOL's safety policies. Click OK when you've read it. You are now walked through the process of choosing a screen name, choosing a password for that name, and using Parental Controls.

There are two steps in setting Parental Controls, each explained in the next few pages.

1. Assign a young person's screen name to one of the age brackets defined in the next section. Each age bracket is defined by a set of controls regulating access to various Internet and AOL tools and services.
2. Fine-tune the controls for Web, chat, downloading, and other tools. This step is optional, but I recommend it.

Assigning a Screen Name to an Age Bracket

Setting up a new, billed AOL account automatically puts the master account holder in the 18+, or General Access bracket, which entitles that person to unlimited access to AOL. Only the master account holder can create new screen names and set up Parental Controls for those screen names. The account holder can also create other master screen names among the seven possible screen names. Any master screen name (for example, a spouse) can add and remove screen names, set controls, and change billing information.

To assign an existing screen name to an age bracket, click Set Parental Controls in the opening Parental Controls window (see Figure 4-2) to bring up the window shown in Figure 4-3. There, you can assign screen names to one of several age brackets.

Some parents avoid giving children screen names that indicate their real names, gender, or contact information.

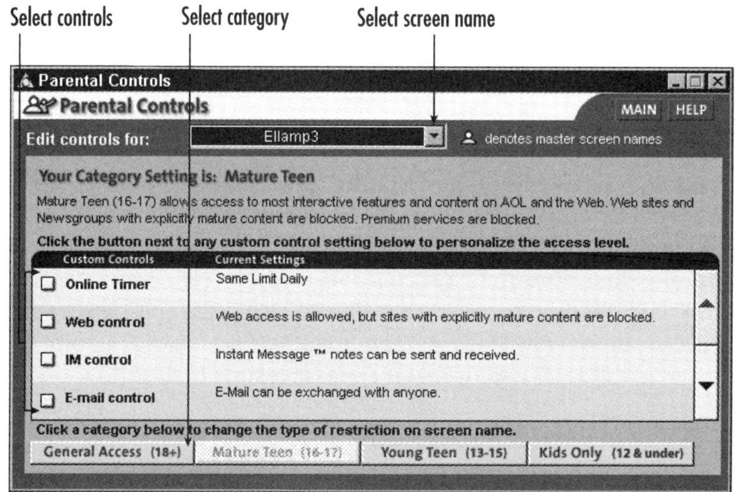

Figure 4-3. Click one of the four age categories along the bottom of the screen for the screen name (selected from the drop-down list). The grayed-out category is the one currently chosen.

1. Select the screen name from the drop-down list.
2. Choose from one of the following four options by clicking the appropriate button at the bottom of the window.
   - **Kids Only:** Restricts younger children to the Kids Only channel. A Kids Only account user can't send or receive instant messages (IMs), enter member-created chat rooms, or use premium services such as games, which are fee-based. (These games are safe enough, but also fun enough for kids to run up large bills!) A Kids Only user *can* send and receive text-based e-mail, which means no pictures are inserted or attached.
   - **Young Teen and Mature Teen:** Parents of teenagers may want to select the Young Teen (ages 13 to 15) or Mature Teen (ages 16 to 17) bracket. These levels of access provide more freedom than

The choice between Young and Mature Teen is a judgment call that depends on the child's maturity more than age. The choice also depends on an adult's readiness to unobtrusively monitor a child's online use.

the Kids Only level, but still prevent access to certain Web sites. Young Teens may visit some chat rooms. However, they may not visit member-created rooms. Young and mature teens may also use Web sites that are appropriate for their respective age groups, but they can neither download files from newsgroups nor use AOL's premium gaming services.

- **General Access:** The 18+ bracket provides unrestricted access to all features on AOL and the Internet.

Fine-Tuning a Child's Internet Access with Custom Controls

Use the Custom Controls area of Parental Controls to designate a second master account holder. That way, more than one adult can set Parental Controls for screen names on the account.

Assigning a child's screen name to an age bracket defines how much access and what kind of access the child has to various AOL and Internet services, such as chat, e-mail, the Web, and downloading. Parental Controls allow you to refine access level to individual tools so that you can, for example, assign a child to the overall Mature Teen level, but then use Custom Controls to block use of instant messages for that child.

To set Custom Controls

1. Use AOL Keyword: **Parental Controls** and click the Set Parental Controls button.
2. In the Parental Controls window (see Figure 4-3), use the Edit Controls For drop-down list to select a screen name.
3. Click the up and down arrows on the right side of the Parental Controls screen to scroll through the list of controls. To adjust any control, click the little square to the left of the control's name.
   - Online Timer
   - Web control
   - IM (instant message) control
   - E-mail control
   - Chat control
   - Additional Master (to give a screen name the authority to set Parental Controls)
   - Download control
   - Newsgroup
   - Premium Services

Because the Mail, Download, Web, Newsgroups, and Online Timer controls directly affect a child's access to the Internet, I will focus on them in the following sections. Figure 4-4 shows AOL chat controls set for a child. Similarly, a person setting up controls for instant messaging has the option for blocking them altogether.

Edward Willett's book, *Your Official America Online Guide to Internet Safety* (Hungry Minds, Inc.) goes into detail on Parental Controls, security software, and other ways to keep kids safe online.

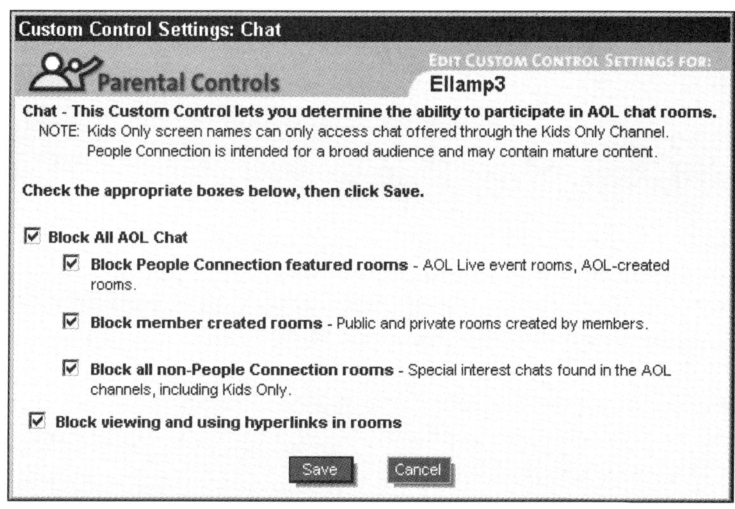

Figure 4-4. Chat controls can keep younger children out of trouble, if only by preventing others from learning of their screen name.

Setting E-Mail Controls

Many consider e-mail *the* essential Internet application. Unfortunately, abuse of e-mail has gone hand in hand with its growing popularity. Unsolicited mail can contain annoying or fraudulent offers or attempt to lure you (or a child) to offensive Web sites. Or you could receive unwanted file attachments. As annoying as junk mail can be, on AOL you have the power to control it. AOL itself does a good job of keeping unwanted mail away from members' mailboxes.

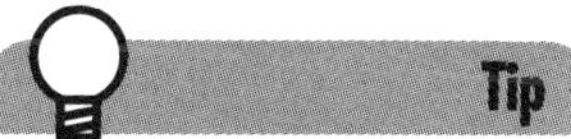

To find out more about curbing junk mail, also called *spam,* use AOL Keyword: **Junk Mail**.

The Mail Controls window (Figure 4-5) has been substantially redesigned for AOL 7.0. Along the screen's left are four clickable tabs:

- About Mail Controls
- General Controls
- People and Places
- Pictures and files

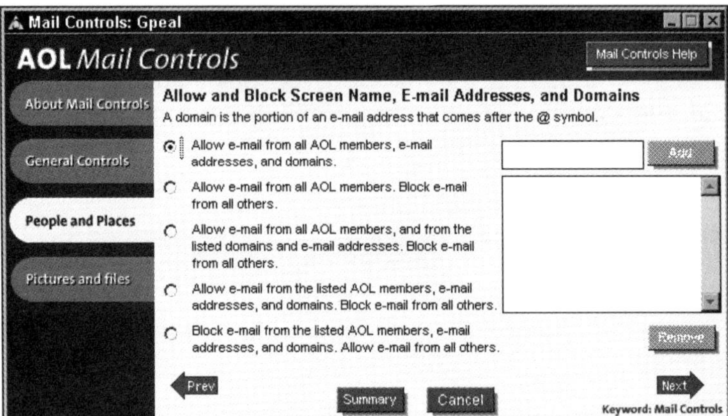

Figure 4-5. To restrict mail to and from certain addresses and domains (and from AOL or the Internet as a whole), read your options carefully. For options 3, 4, and 5, you need to use the Add box on the right. Type a domain or specific e-mail address into the box and click Add, and repeat until you are done.

Starting at the screen called About Mail Controls, read or follow each screen's instructions, pressing the Next button to move from screen to screen.

The General Controls screen pertains to whether the screen name for which the controls are being set should receive or not receive e-mail. If you want the screen name to receive mail, click the Allow All E-mail to Be Delivered to This Screen Name button. This is equivalent to setting no controls for the screen name. To set controls you must select Customize Mail Controls for This Screen Name and click Next.

The People and Places screen lets you further determine the specific addresses and domains from which the child can receive mail. When asked to indicate domains from which you don't want the screen name receiving mail, type in the part of an e-mail address that goes to the right of the at (@) symbol, as in `aol.com` or `netcom.com`.

Make your choices and click Next. The Pictures and Files screen lets you determine whether the screen name can receive pictures (image files) that are attached to an e-mail message.

At any point, click Summary to see all the Mail Controls set for this screen name. Click Save when you are satisfied.

Setting Download Controls

This control sets limits on the kinds of files young people can download. You and your family should be careful about downloadable files for all the same reasons you should be careful about files and photos attached to e-mail messages — they may contain viruses or material you don't want to see. More important in a day-to-day sense, they can clog up your hard drive and lead to longer online sessions that leave less time for other activities.

To *download* a file — whether it's an image file or software — means to copy it from an Internet computer to your computer. Chapters 15 and 16 are all about downloading.

You can set two controls for each screen name, specifying whether a child can download files:

- From AOL's software libraries.
- From the Internet's FTP (or *File Transfer Protocol*) sites. FTP is a tool for downloading files to and uploading them from your computer.

Parental Controls do not apply to third-party (non-AOL) software, such as FTP programs and stand-alone Web browsers, including the Internet Explorer browser.

AOL's software libraries are unlikely to represent any threat, but the same is not true for the Net's FTP archives. I have never had a problem with such files, but the risk is always there.

Setting Web Controls

Web controls appear to duplicate general Parental Controls in that they offer a set of four levels of access: Kids Only, Young Teen, Mature Teen, and General, corresponding to the four age brackets and four levels of Web access. Before custom controls can be set, a young person must be assigned to one of those four brackets.

Why set the Web Controls separately from setting the age bracket, which automatically also sets Web controls? Because you may want to consider giving a child broader Web access while keeping e-mail, downloading, and other controls at a lower level of access. Why broaden Web access? The Web offers extraordinarily rich educational resources, as you'll see later in this chapter. The Kids Only age bracket, for example, offers no Web access.

These controls are flexible. For teens drawn to inappropriate Web sites, you may want to set a level of Web access *lower* than the one created by assigning the teen to an age bracket.

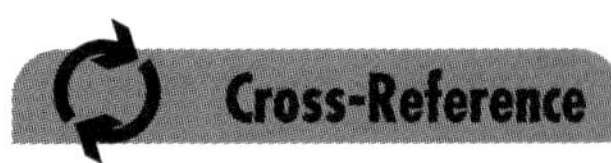

See Chapter 14 for more information about newsgroups. At AOL Keyword: **Newsgroups** you can set overall newsgroup preferences as well as newsgroup-by-newsgroup settings.

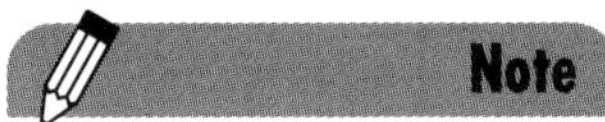

You can use the check boxes to activate more than one option in the Newsgroup Controls.

A *binary* is a complex file, such as an image, a sound, and a word-processing document.

Setting Newsgroup Controls

A *newsgroup* is an Internet discussion group focused on a specific subject. It's a publicly accessible, electronic bulletin board where you can read and post messages, from which you can sometimes download files.

You don't have to look hard for quality, specialized newsgroups on subjects of personal and professional interest. If you're convinced of the value of specific newsgroups, you need to do some research before making them available to a child.

Newsgroup controls offer six important choices:

- **Blocking all newsgroups:** The effect of this option is clear. Why block them all? Over the years, commercial, off-topic, and other inappropriate postings have flooded many newsgroups. If you're unfamiliar with newsgroups, it can be difficult to determine which groups are appropriate for kids and which ones have a minimal amount of junk. However, between the many good newsgroups and the stringent controls you can set on newsgroups, some parents may find blocking to be drastic.
- **Blocking expert add of newsgroups:** This option prevents a screen name from accessing newsgroups whose specific names kids happen to know. (A newsgroup name looks like this: `rec.cars.antique`.)
- **Blocking file downloads:** This option prohibits the downloading and viewing of inappropriate images. Parents who are concerned about kids violating copyright laws, seeing offensive pictures, or filling the family's hard drive with large music files may wish to block the downloading of binary files.
- **Blocking adult-oriented newsgroups:** You can block a screen name's access to potentially offensive newsgroups.
- **Blocking newsgroups with certain words in their names:** You can selectively prevent access to newsgroups with certain words in their titles. You can probably imagine the offending words; children of a certain age will know just what they are!

- **Block specific newsgroups:** This option (the last check box in window) lets you prevent a child from hanging out in certain newsgroups that, in your opinion, have no value or are inappropriate. You must know the full names of these newsgroups to use this control.

Using the Online Timer

If you're like me, your concerns about a child's access to the Internet isn't restricted to the sites and areas they visit online. Many parents express concern that their kids will spend more time online than doing homework or playing. Also, if the account is being charged on an hourly basis, parents might be concerned about the cost of all that time spent online.

AOL's Online Timer, shown in Figure 4-6, gives you the ability to limit the time kids spend online. To get there, go to AOL Keyword: **Parental Controls** and click Set Parental Controls. The timer is the first control listed in the main window. Click the square button to the left to bring up the screen shown in Figure 4-6. Click Next, and you will be stepped through four screens.

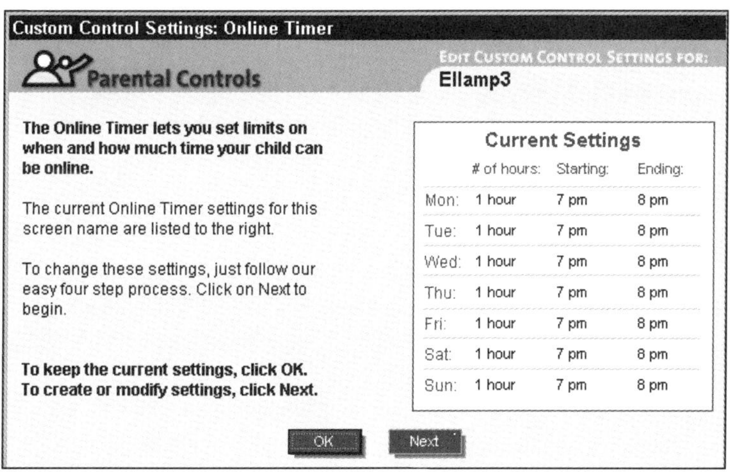

Figure 4-6. Use the Online Timer to limit the amount of time kids can spend online. From this opening screen, click Next to get started.

In the timer's screens, you indicate the following, clicking Next and Previous to move back and forth between screens:

- **The days during which the timer is to be in effect.** You can set the same hourly limits for every day, different limits for weekdays and weekends, or different limits for each day.
- **The number of hours.** For any day selected, you can set the number of hours that may be spent online, and the specific times of the day during which that time may be spent.
- **Your time zone.** AOL needs this information because members now live in time zones around the world. You want to make sure that your settings apply to your time zone.

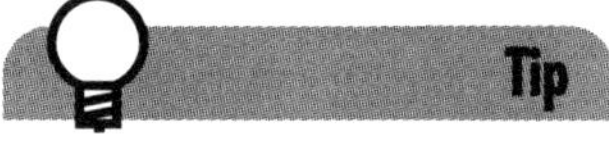

Use AOL Keyword: **Online Timer** to find out more about this feature and to set it up.

When the child's time runs out, the AOL connection is simply terminated. Parents can find out how much time has been used by signing onto the children's account and going to AOL Keyword: **Timer**.

When Parental Controls Are Not Available

Parental Controls apply to the AOL browser, the browser built into AOL (see Chapter 6). Other browsers you can use *with* AOL, such as Netscape Navigator (see Chapter 7) and Microsoft Internet Explorer, do *not* support AOL's Parental Controls.

For these occasions, Web *filtering* software can give parents and teachers some peace of mind that kids can't stray into dangerous areas or be approached by unsavory people online.

Valuable information about filtering software can be found at About's Family Internet site (`familyinternet.about.com/parenting/familyinternet/cs/internetfiltering`). FamilyPC magazine (`www.familypc.com`) has a section on online safety that regularly reviews filtering products.

Learning Anywhere, Anytime

It's not difficult to keep kids as safe as possible online, especially with AOL tools, such as Parental Controls. It can be a far greater challenger to use online resources in a positive way to help kids explore their interests and improve their schoolwork. In working with my own children and teaching educational technology, I have become convinced that much of the problem lies in knowing where to start; the rest lies in being clear about what you or your kids are trying to accomplish online.

The rest of this chapter provides some places to start to help kids with their education, both the classroom kind (for example, Civil War battles) and the everyday kind (for example, learning about fireflies in the summer). I leave it to you to use these and similar resources whenever it makes sense.

Using Homework Helpers

Homework helpers are online destinations that help students in all grades with either routine nightly homework oriented to the mastery of facts and skills, or with more complex school projects that require analysis, synthesis, and planning. A homework helper can guide students to encyclopedias, maps, calculators, problem sets, newspapers, almanacs, and similar materials.

AOL has offered an AOL-only service called Homework Help for many years (AOL Keyword: **Homework Help**). This area is especially appropriate for kids who do not have Web access. AOL recently launched an ambitious Web-based service, available to anyone on the Internet, called AOL@School. AOL@School and Homework Help have matured into invaluable homework helpers for kids, and are profiled in the next few pages.

AOL@School can be found on both AOL (AOL Keyword: **AOL@School**) and the Web (`www.school.aol.com`).

Homework Help on the Web: AOL@School

AOL@School is a kind of online service for teachers, parents, and students—a version of AOL that has been customized for use by schools (kindergarten through Grade 12) and schoolteachers. The AOL@School CD offers e-mail and chat as well as Web access.

Teachers can order a CD providing free access to e-mail, chat, and other tools by calling 888-708-0719. Using the software, students can connect only with sites "approved for their age group."

- **To start research for a paper or project:** Students should start by clicking Research a Topic. In the window that appears, click a level (such as Middle School), type in a search term (such as *Pearl Harbor*), and press Enter to begin your search.
- **To get routine help for daily homework in the traditional subjects:** Click Homework Help. You will be asked to choose a grade level and subject, and AOL@School comes back with a list of Web sites, vetted by educators. In addition to reliable content, you can find study aids, such as a dictionary, encyclopedia, and calculator (these tools are tailored to a student's grade level). Figure 4-7 shows a subject and level start page from AOL@School.

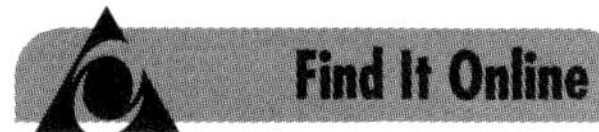

AOL@School's weekly newsletter alerts you to new educational Web sites. Subscribe from the opening page at AOL Keyword: **AOL@School**.

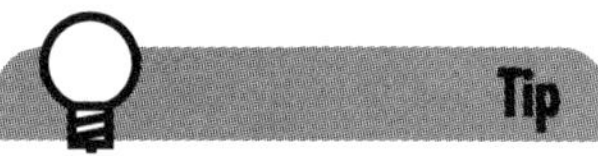

Much more than a way of answering specific questions, AOL@School provides opportunities for students to meet other students around the country (click Community) and to challenge themselves (click Brain Teasers).

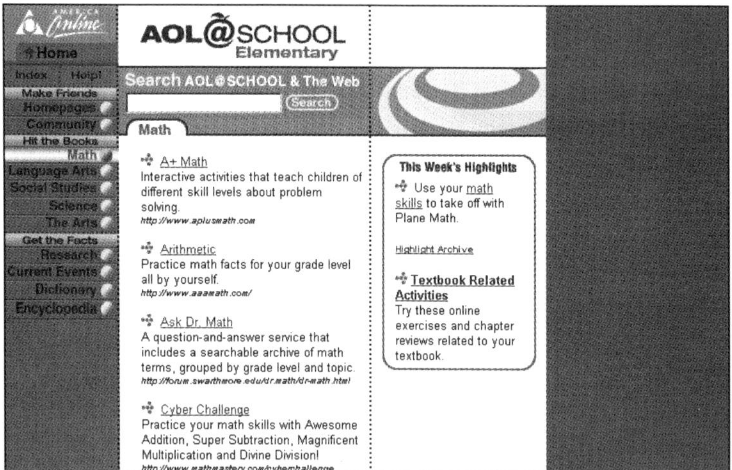

Figure 4-7. Go to AOL@School for homework help. This figure shows the kind of educational links you get when you select the elementary level and math.

Homework Help on the AOL Service

AOL's Knowledge Database, shown in Figure 4-8, is a well-used area where students can get help with concepts and answers to specific questions.

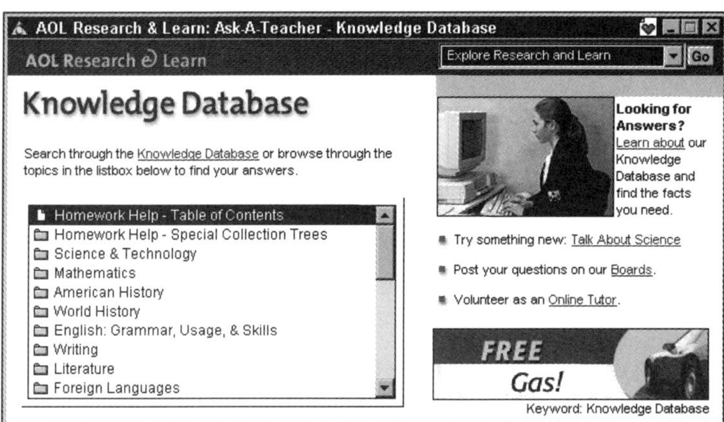

Figure 4-8. At AOL Keyword: **Homework Help**, click Look Up Answers to read the message boards in the Knowledge Database.

If you teach or want to teach, or have special expertise to share, consider volunteering your time and knowledge to help students. More information can be found at AOL Keyword: **Knowledge Database**.

- The Knowledge Database can be accessed from Homework Help and at AOL Keyword: **Knowledge Database**. This collection of more than 25,000 articles is arranged according to subject and grade level. The text articles were developed over many years by the AAC's large group of volunteer online tutors. The database can be browsed by general topic or searched for specific information. Within any Knowledge Database folder, you can find a Search the Database link.
- The message boards (click Post a Question in the appropriate school level) give you the opportunity to ask a volunteer for help with any concept, fact, or subject not covered in the Knowledge Database.

Because volunteer teachers' time is limited, make sure to try to find help on your own before asking a volunteer.

While AOL@School takes you "out" to the Net for homework guidance, Homework Help reflects an old AOL custom of members helping members, in this case, teachers helping students. These two resources cannot replace the hard work of practice and figuring things out, but they can simplify the process of finding the right information in the first place.

Discovering the World's Largest Reference Library

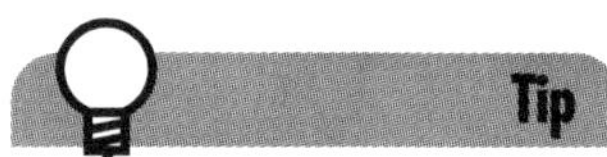

For any reference you discover, make sure to find out what organization or person is behind it. Is the information credible, authoritative, up-to-date, and usable?

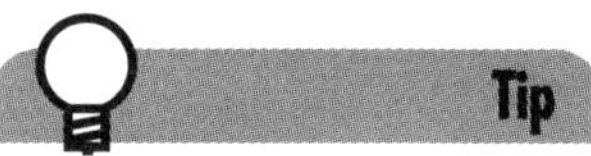

If you need additional reference materials, start at the Internet Public Library's Reference collection (`www.ipl.org/ref`).

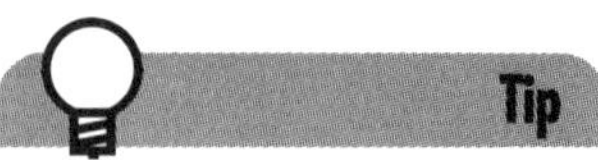

The complete Encyclopedia Britannica is available online at `www.britannica.com`. For a fee, useful learning tools can be accessed at `www.eb.com`. An advantage of online versions is that they can be kept up-to-date, unlike the print version. Many of the authoritative print encyclopedias, like the Columbia Encyclopedia, are available online, and you can also find Net-only resources, such as the Encyclopedia Mythica. The next few pages sample the Web's great encyclopedias.

Reference books seem right at home on the Internet. Their contents change quickly, but they can be readily updated online, unlike a printed reference book. Online, they can be searched and printed out. And you don't have to read more than a paragraph or a couple of pages at a time. The next few pages look at reliable, credible, and long-standing sources of facts.

Encyclopedias

It's a good idea to get comfortable with several general references, because between them, they cover much of the factual knowledge students are expected to know by the time they're ready for college. Sometimes, entries will have different perspectives or be more comprehensive.

World Book Online

`AOL Keyword:` **`Worldbook`**

In the past, students could not function in school without access to a nicely bound, multivolume encyclopedia, with World Book and Encyclopedia Britannica competing for the favor of students, parents, and teachers. Now AOL and CompuServe members have unlimited access to the searchable World Book Online.

World Book Online simplifies the search for specific information (on *tent caterpillars*, for example). The search results often supplement text articles with sounds, maps, tables, videos, and pictures whenever such content is available. Longer articles on subjects, such as photography, include a table of contents showing an article's sections as well as a set of links to related Web sites, articles, and study aids, all of which are usefully arranged on the Related Information tab. This is a resource for learners of all ages.

Columbia Encyclopedia

`www.bartleby.com/65`

For a somewhat more advanced perspective on any subject, high-school and older students may want to study some of the 57,000 or so entries in Columbia Encyclopedia. This tool is part of Bartleby.com, a collection of free, searchable classic reference resources, including the American Heritage dictionary and several editions of Roget's Thesaurus. Containing fewer multimedia references than the World Book Online, the Columbia Encyclopedia features concise and authoritative writing, with links to well-chosen related entries.

Encyclopedia of the Orient

www.i-cias.com/e.o

The old-fashioned term *Orient* used to refer to the East, back when the East meant northern Africa and the Middle East. Today, this area remains diverse and volatile yet still little-known. With so much political, cultural, and religious turmoil in that part of the world, students can find it difficult to find the reliable information they need in order to understand the forces at work there. This site was created by Norwegian scholars with precisely that intent. The content and format were designed for high-school students and adults. The concise articles often include timelines, maps, and photographs. Adults, too, can benefit from this encyclopedia to help make sense of the issues, people, and places mentioned in the headlines. Travelers can use this reference as one of the most thorough guides to this part of the world.

Encyclopedia Mythica

www.pantheon.org/mythica

At a certain age, many kids become fascinated with mythology. They like the cool stories and often identify with those not-quite-human figures who nonetheless exemplify human traits worth emulating or avoiding. The award-winning Encyclopedia Mythica covers the mythologies of Haiti, Persia, Japan, Norway, India, and Greece, among many other cultures, with definitions of almost 6,000 gods, goddesses, and supernatural beings. The encyclopedia's creator, M.F. Lindemans, modestly notes that his work is not exhaustive. However, you may not feel deprived to find, for example, a mere 66 articles on Voodoo, Haiti's religious folk cult.

The encyclopedia, shown in Figure 4-9, is fully searchable if your needs are specific and if you can spell what you're looking for. For general interest or deeper study, click Explore on the main page for a list of the major mythologies (Greek, Hindu, and so on). An A to Z index gives direct access to the encyclopedia's individual entries.

Students cramming for exams should not overlook the genealogies showing the principle lineages in Greek and Norse mythology. Younger children may enjoy having folktales read to them, especially the dozens of fairy tales collectively known as the Arabian Nights.

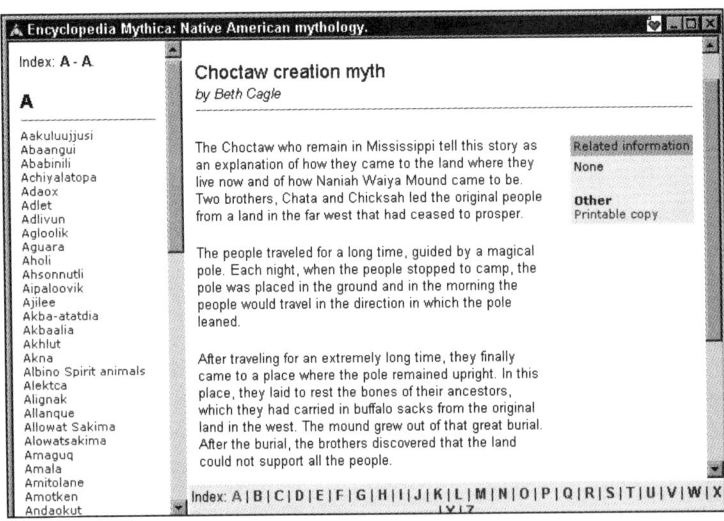

Figure 4-9. The Encyclopedia Mythica has plenty of fuel to fire the imagination, and some good bedtime stories (which can be printed out).

Infoplease

`www.infoplease.com`

Infoplease for Kids (`www.infoplease.com/kids`) offers a brightly designed homework center that includes an atlas, learning games, and in-depth features.

Infoplease (see Figure 4-10) attempts to be an all-encompassing reference work. The online version is part of the Family Education Network, an organization that participates in AOL@ School. Unlike the encyclopedias mentioned above, InfoPlease is appropriate for kids in elementary school.

Infoplease offers a variety of fact-finding resources, including dictionaries, encyclopedias, and assorted "almanacs," mini-encyclopedias that present general information on just about every subject. In addition, Infoplease has actual articles arranged for quick reading, including a timeline of world history, a list of the best-selling children's books, and the highest-circulation newspapers in the world.

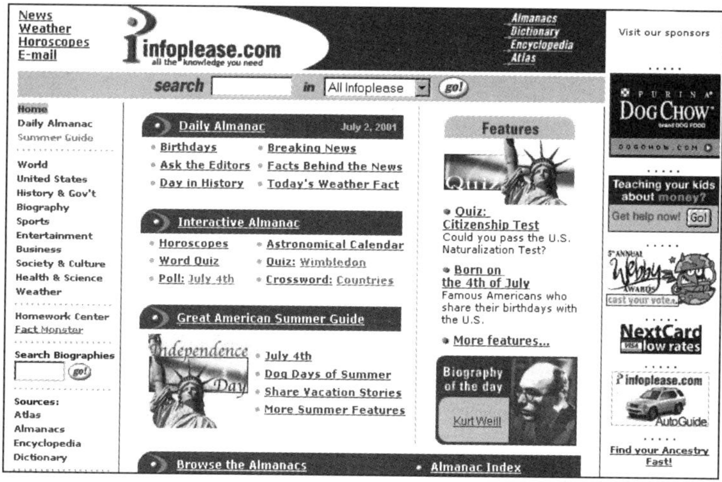

Figure 4-10. Infoplease strives to be the comprehensive online factbook.

Maps on the Net

Some of the encyclopedias mentioned in this section, such as World Book, include maps with their entries. Infoplease has a whole section called Atlas, showing maps for the world's countries.

At AOL Keyword: **Country Profiles**, you can find maps of continents and countries as well as U.S. states and many world cities. For more detail (for the U.S. at least), start at MapQuest (AOL Keyword: **Mapquest**). MapQuest can show you street-level maps when you're looking for a house or regional maps when you're planning a trip.

At AOL@School, go to the High School area and click through Social Studies and Geography to find an excellent collection of links to road maps, county maps, satellite images, and more.

Here's a map quiz: Where is Tuvalu (mentioned in Chapter 10), the country that owns the profitable TV domain?

Webopedia

AOL Keyword: **Webopedia**

This user-friendly guide provides encyclopedic depth in its coverage of computer and Internet terms and technologies. The encyclopedia is not comprehensive, but the depth of treatment for each entry makes the site indispensable, especially with its carefully selected links to supplementary information.

When You Need the Right Word

When you need to look up a word, you can't turn to a better place than the online world's many dictionaries and writers' tools. This section merely samples a few offerings.

Acronyms

www.acronymfinder.com

An *acronym* is the shorthand for a longer phrase. Instead of International Business Machines, most people say IBM. The problem with acronyms is that the listener or reader often has no idea what a writer or speaker is talking about. What does ADA mean, to choose an example in the news? To find out, use the Acronym Finder. (It stands for the landmark Americans with Disabilities Act of 1990, but also for Another Darned Acronym and the American Dental Association.)

AF's Systematic Buzz Phrase Projector generates important-sounding acronyms by randomly combining vogue business words. The acronym for the randomly generated *Optional Logistical Programming* would be OLP.

With the Acronym Finder (AF), you too can use acronyms that no one else can understand. Type an acronym (like **NATO**), and the AF searches for and displays the corresponding phrase. The AF contains more than 200,000 acronyms and abbreviations.

Bartlett's Familiar Quotations

www.bartleby.com/99

John Bartlett's *Familiar Quotations,* a collection of more than 11,000 great quotations, was published in 1901. The 10th edition is now available at a great reference site called Bartleby.com (www.bartleby.com). At the Bartleby.com site, you can also find searchable versions of the American Heritage Dictionary, Gray's Anatomy, the complete works of Shakespeare, and the complete 2000 Columbia Encyclopedia, profiled earlier in this chapter.

Bartlett's Familiar Quotations arranges authors both alphabetically and chronologically. Clicking any author's name in either listing brings up a page with collected quotes for that author.

You can search for quotes at Bartlett's opening page by using any word. Results from searches include a hyperlink from the author to a list of his or her famous quotes.

Web of Online Dictionaries

`www.yourdictionary.com`

The Web of Online Dictionaries (Figure 4-11) was created in the mid-1990s by Bucknell English professor Robert Beard. Today, this commercial site (run by a student of Prof. Beard's) brings together links to approximately 1,800 dictionaries of more than 250 languages. If you must write, like to read, want to travel, or just love words, Prof. Beard has created a destination that is well worth repeated visits.

Where to start? You can simply look up a word in English from the home page. Or, browse the Web of Online Dictionaries by language. For many languages, grammars are available. For English, specialty lexicons are available on dozens of subjects, including agriculture and medicine.

Figure 4-11. If you use the Web of Online Dictionaries to look up a word, you may come home with a hundred.

Every member of the family can find something useful. The Etymology of First Names dictionary can help parents decide on a suitably unique name for that baby-to-be. Kids might enjoy the word games, tongue twisters, crossword puzzles, and the chance to see their name in Egyptian hieroglyphics or Eskimo Inuktitut, the language of the Inuit people (Eskimos).

Your Daily Coordinates: Time, Weather, History

For U.S. weather in-depth — satellite photos, weather predictions, photos of historical weather disasters, fire weather forecasts, current weather, and forecasts up to ten days out — tune your browser to the official home of the National Weather Service (`www.noaa.gov/wx.html`). AOL Keyword: **Weather** brings you a continuously updated video weather forecast.

For time to the second, anywhere in the 50 states, set your watches at NIST's Official Time site (`www.time.gov`). Select a time zone, and a software clock downloads to your computer, where it runs until you get bored with clock-watching and close the browser window. Initially set to correspond to an atomic clock, the clock is accurate to within 0.3 seconds.

From its vast dusty holdings, the Library of Congress is constructing a place of multimedia wonders. The LOC's Today in History, for example, takes a few births, deaths, and events that happened on each date of the year, and documents them with pictures and original sources from the Library's fabulous collections (`lcweb2.loc.gov/ammem/today/today.html`).

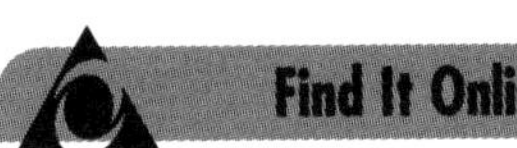

For global population statistics and policies, a useful place to start is the Population Reference Bureau (`www.prb.org`).

Uganda had a population of 23 million in 1990, but only 54,000 telephones, according to the 2000 CIA World Factbook.

The World in Numbers

The profiles of the two resources below only hint at the enormous wealth of statistical data available on the Web. You can find official and archival data on every subject from current country-by-country censuses to state-by-state slave demographics in the pre-Civil War South.

CIA World Factbook

`www.odci.gov/cia/publications/factbook`

The factual information in this classic online reference resource is always a year or so out of date because the print publication is not simultaneously published on the Web.

However, for about a decade now, savvy teachers and travelers have known the CIA World Factbook to be a thorough and reliable source of information about countries. For each country, you can find dozens of facts and statistics, including information about climate, geography, the economy, and political structure.

FedStats

www.fedstats.gov

More than 70 agencies in the U.S. government gather statistics of public interest. FedStats is an interagency Web site that collects these statistics and arranges them in useful and illuminating ways. You can find specific data by doing direct searches; browsing a state's data; and exploring categories, such as earnings, health, and housing. Among the highlights is following sites MapStats, a compact statistical profile of every state in the U.S. FedStats' Kids Page (see the following sidebar) links children to some of the fun and educational content being produced by these agencies.

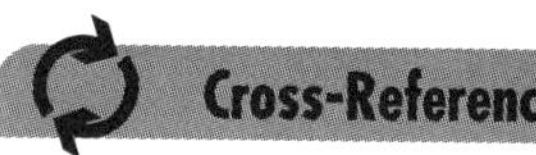

AOL's Government Guide (AOL Keyword: **Government Guide**), part of AOL Search, provides an easily browsable arrangement of the U.S. government's information storehouses. The U.S. government recently developed an official federal megasite called FirstGov (www.firstgov.gov).

FedStats' Kids Page

www.fedstats.gov/kids.html

Many U.S. government agencies do an amazing job educating students about what they do and why it's important, usually without sounding too pedantic. FedStats has gathered links to dozens of kids' sites created by these agencies.

- The Department of Health and Human Services, for example, has created their Girl Power site to help girls 8-14 "make the most of their lives" (www.girlpower.gov).
- The Environmental Protection Agency's Explorer Club uses games and graphics to teach elementary school students about recycling, water, and other subjects (www.epa.gov/kids). See the following figure.

(continued)

(continued)

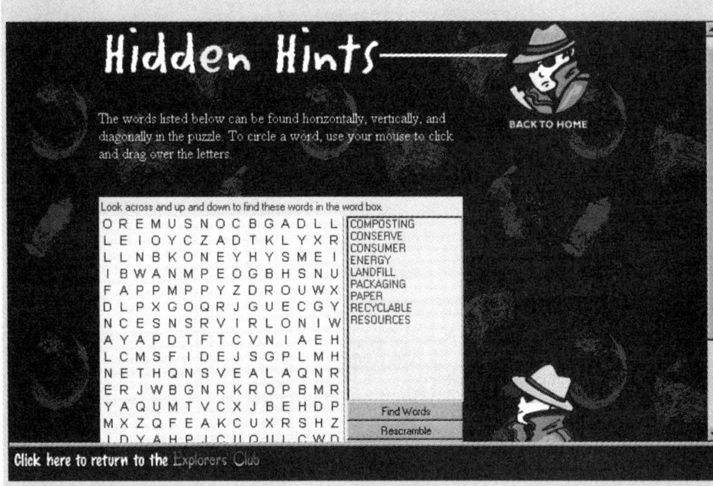

▶ The National Institute for Environmental Health Sciences (NIEHS) has a fantastic set of activities for young children: coloring pages to print, songs with lyrics to listen to on the computer, jokes, visual illusions, and more (`www.niehs.nih.gov/kids/home.htm`). Agencies that don't gather statistics have created outstanding resources for kids. Ben's Guide to the U.S. Government (`bensguide.gpo.gov`), created by the Government Printing Office, focuses on how the government works. The GPO site is organized by grade.

Online Newspapers, Magazines, and Books

`www.ipl.org/reading`

A classic Internet resource, the Internet Public Library (IPL) is broadly organized by age (Youth and Teen) and, within age, by subject (Homework, Health, and so on). Numerous collections of books, newspapers, magazines, and exhibits serve students of all ages. The beauty of the site lies in the quality of the selections, the clear organization, and the easy-to-use arrangement of materials.

There's nothing like reading a local newspaper to get a good first-take of a new place — weather, local concerns, perception of larger issues, and so on. The Internet Public Library's Online Newspapers area brings local realities to a global audience. The IPL provides a useful way to get the local information you need without relying on the little snippets that manage to pass through the cable and network news. Students can do research about their own community, or the U.S. as a whole, by reading foreign newspapers. What, for example, did people in Bangladesh and Vietnam think of the recent presidential election and its outcome? Reading different online newspapers about the same story can provide a reality check and, for students, a powerful form of learning. English-language papers are available around the world, by the way.

IPL's collection of online newspapers, magazines, and books can be found in the Reading Room (`www.ipl.org/reading`).

Like online newspapers, online magazines can be found in the IPL Reading Room. The more than 3,000 magazines are arranged by category for easy browsing. Browse the topical hierarchy to find publications of interest.

IPL's 17,000-item collection of books is arranged both alphabetically by author and title and in the Dewey system. The books tend to be older titles, including hundreds of classics and works by great authors whose copyright has lapsed. They're available here in text-only form. From the Online Text Collection page, links take you to many other digital libraries of this kind, with thousands of other books to read (`www.ipl.org/reading/books/other.html`).

Books are available in many ways online. Chapter 9 discusses digital libraries, and Chapter 18 has more to say about eBooks.

Onward to College and Life

High-school students and their parents can now plan every step of the road to college on the Web. Web-based services now support the whole process, including learning about SATs, choosing a college, applying, getting financial aid, moving in, getting adjusted to student life, and understanding distance-education options. An excellent source of information about every stage of the college-application process can be found at AOL Keyword: **Colleges**. The area includes a Decision Guide to help high-school students begin to think about what they want in a school and which schools appear to meet their needs.

A Web site that attempts to provide a comprehensive guide for students facing college is My College Guide (www.mycollegeguide.org). Here students can search for a college, apply for admission, learn about financial aid options, and read articles about college life.

Finally, to learn about the federal government's many college-planning, reserve, and financial-aid programs, visit Students.gov (www.students.gov), part of the official FirstGov site.

Where to Go from Here

This chapter provides an indication of the positive, educational, useful, and fun resources on the Net. Invariably, you (or your kids or parents) have information needs not covered in this chapter. What do you do?

- To get a thorough introduction to searching the Internet for anything you need to know or want to do, turn to Chapters 8 and 9.
- For a compact set of links to a vast amount of reference material, visit Refdesk.com (www.refdesk.com).
- Part of the attraction of the Net, for kids and parents alike, is the seemingly endless number of places devoted to fun and games. For every serious reference work or collection of books available on the Internet, you can find several fun destinations where kids can safely spend time, have fun, improve hand-eye coordination, and perhaps learn a thing or two. One place to start is AOL Keyword: **Kids Search** (click Fun Sites). For more games, go to AOL Keyword: **Learning Games**. On the Web, try MaMaMedia (www.mamamedia.com).

Chapter 5
Using the Web to Simplify Life

IN THIS CHAPTER **PAGE**

The World Wide Web can save you time and money when you make essential decisions, and it can simplify life when you go about your daily business. Consider, for example, AOL's My Calendar, discussed in Chapter 3. You can use the calendar to keep track of appointments, stay organized, and find concerts and movies in your community. Other Web tools can help you look for a job, book a vacation, check bank account balances, develop a savings plan, get a good piecrust recipe, and find a good deal on a new car. This chapter shows you how to use the Web to make short work of your daily routines.

Starting Out on the Web

The more you use the Web, the more starting points you'll find. You'll discover that with AOL, you don't have to know much about the browser itself to enjoy the Web. In Chapter 6, you'll also see that the more you know about the browser, the more you'll get from the experience.

Here are a few places to start:

- AOL's channels offer a place to start exploring the Web. Available from the channel window, which you can see in Figure 5-1, each channel points you to selected Web sites on its big themes. Start with one or two of AOL's 20 channels when you want the latest news and information in an area of personal or professional interest.
- If you hear about a Web site that sounds interesting, jot down the Web site's address, type it into the AOL address box, and click Go. If you like the site, you can save it as an AOL Favorite Place so that you can easily return there later without having to remember so many Ws and dots.
- If you're looking for a fact (like how many U.S. Presidents' sons have also been elected president) or an overview of a subject (such as basic chemistry concepts), you may want to conduct a search of the Internet. Any sites you discover can also become good candidates for favorite places.
- Use AOL's Internet Connection (AOL Keyword: **Internet Connection**), shown in Figure 5-1, to type a Web address or search the Web. This page is also available at AOL Keyword: **Internet** and by choosing Services⇨Internet⇨Internet Start Page. The Internet Connection combines a search box (using AOL Search) and a set of links to AOL's channels. In addition, it provides links to other essential Internet destinations.

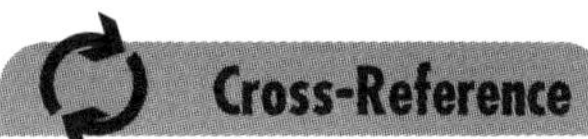

For more on Favorite Places, see Chapter 3. To find out about using AOL's Web browser, check out Chapter 6. If you want to know more about searching the Web, see Chapters 8 and 9.

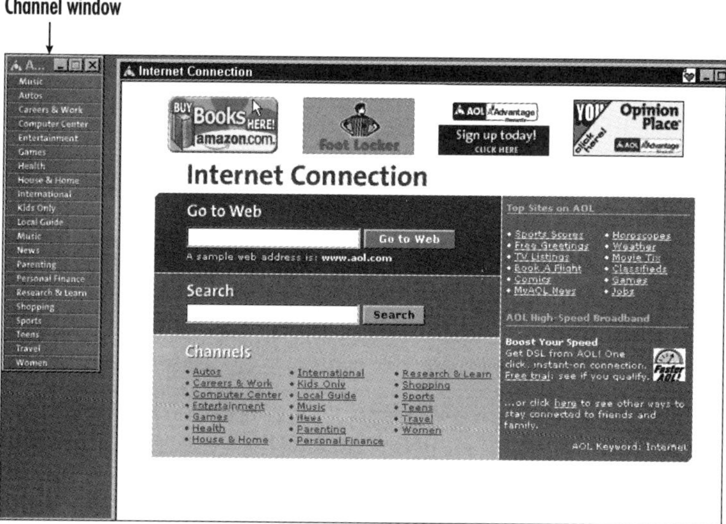

Figure 5-1. Use AOL's Internet Connection to explore useful Web destinations.

The rest of the chapter is devoted to some of the more practical reasons for going online. You will find starting points for each area of interest, but the paths you take from there depend entirely on your own situation.

Planning Your Financial Future

Creating a financial plan doesn't have to be intimidating or discouraging. In fact, when carried out online, the process has become much simpler than you might think. Bottom line: creating a plan online is simpler than doing it offline.

When you build a financial plan, you need to think about where you are now financially, where you want to be in the future, and what you must do to reach your goal. Your plan will include strategies for how much to save, how to invest, and how to handle the big events, like buying a house.

AOL gives you access to dozens of Web-based calculators for doing everything from developing a saving plan to figuring out the right mortgage or auto loan. To use one, you need to

Consider using the services of a financial adviser when making investment decisions, and watch out for "inside information" offered in chat rooms and message boards.

provide enough information for the Web-based tool to make its calculations. The calculators are quick, mistake-free, and easy to use.

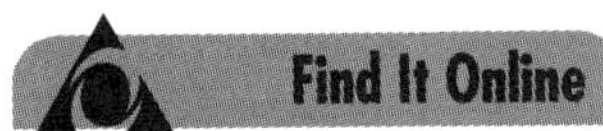

You can access many AOL Personal Finance calculators directly by using AOL Keyword: **Calculators**.

For example, the Debt Reduction Planner (Figure 5-2) at `quicken.aol.com/saving/debt/` lets you review your debts, savings, and income to generate a plan to reduce debt.

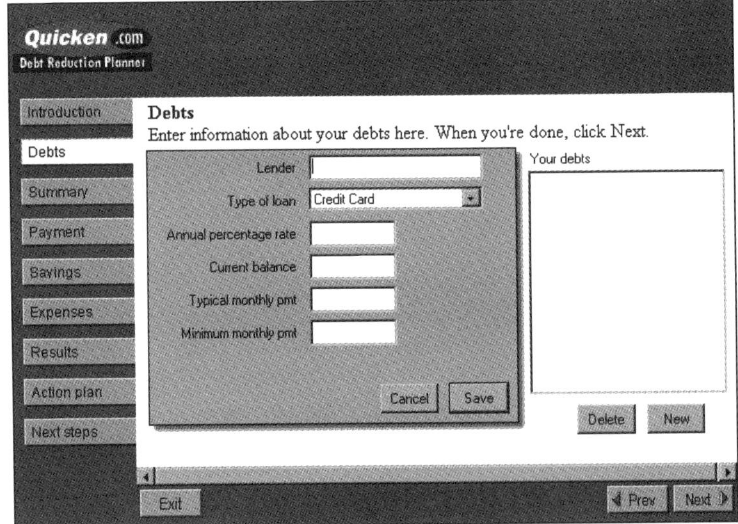

Figure 5-2. Debt Reduction Planner: Everything's easy except the action plan.

AOL's Personal Finance Channel (AOL Keyword: **Finance**) has grown into a comprehensive and clearly organized online destination. From the AOL Personal Finance Channel, click Saving & Planning to go to the Personal Finance home page shown in Figure 5-3. Note that this page has several big categories, each corresponding to a major theme — Business News, Stocks, Mutual Funds, Planning, Real Estate, and Banking & Loans. Each mini-site brings you information you can use; some have a lot more information than anyone could digest, so keep your goals in mind.

Saving and investing are an important part of any financial plan. On AOL and its Web sites, you have all the tools for making and tracking a portfolio of stocks, bonds, and funds. You can build a portfolio on the Personal Finance Channel's My Portfolio service (AOL Keyword: **My Portfolio**), where you can also keep up with market news, do research on companies and funds, and evaluate stocks' price performance over longer periods of time. Even if you choose not to invest right away, you can use the information at My Portfolio to create a model portfolio to practice selecting and following various types of assets. Also check out the handy news and research resource links.

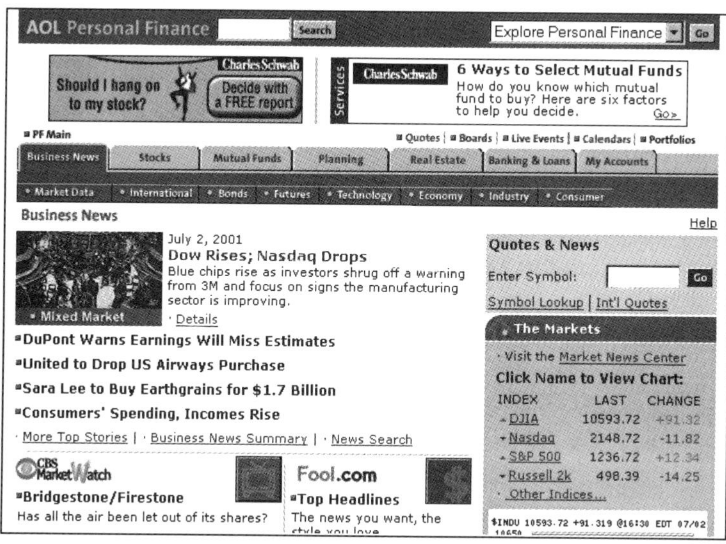

Figure 5-3. The Personal Finance Channel looks at all the key issues in your financial well being, such as saving for a house and planning for retirement.

To keep track of bank and investment accounts, the My Account Manager service (AOL Keyword: **My Account Manager**) lets you view up-to-the-minute numbers directly from the financial institutions where you keep your savings and investment accounts. On a single page, the My Account Manager service shows your current balances for accounts held in different institutions.

When you use My Account Manager, you will receive a notice (in a pop-up window) relating to the recently passed Gramm-Leach-Biley Privacy Act. This act requires that every company offering financial products must explain to customers exactly how their personal and financial information will be used by the company. In the case of My Account Manager, AOL's policy is to use such information strictly to provide the service itself. The information is closely safeguarded and disclosed to no one, except by subpoena or court order.

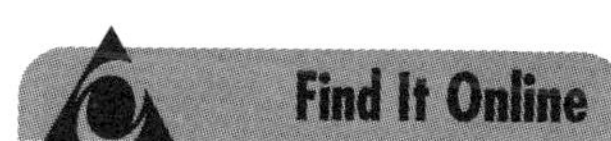

AOL Keyword: **Personal Finance** links you to many brokers who can help with the nitty-gritty of creating accounts, and buying and selling securities.

Find It Online

AOL's Benefits Checkup service is part of AOL's Government Guide. The service is available from the Services menu or at AOL Keyword: **Benefits & Assistance**. Find it on the Web at `www.benefits.checkup.com`.

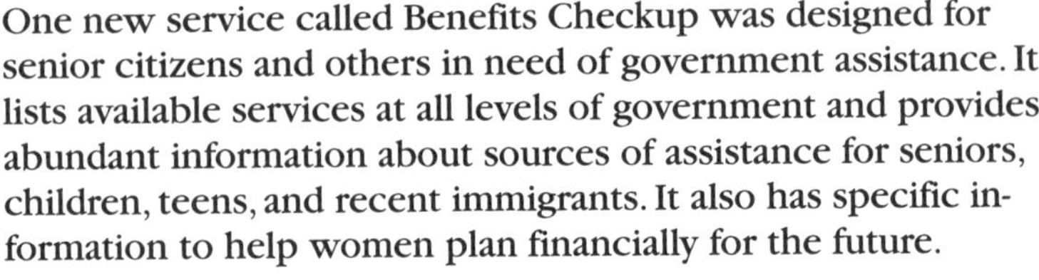

One new service called Benefits Checkup was designed for senior citizens and others in need of government assistance. It lists available services at all levels of government and provides abundant information about sources of assistance for seniors, children, teens, and recent immigrants. It also has specific information to help women plan financially for the future.

Banking Online

Home banking once required special software and a lot of patience. It never got people very excited — before the Web, that is. Now, more and more banks are making services available through the Web, and these banks seem to offer everything except the ability to use your PC as an ATM. My bank, for example, provides access to balances and allows transfers between accounts. I can tell which checks have cleared and which have bounced. If I wanted, the bank would be happy if I paid my monthly bills online, too.

Do a search for your bank by using AOL Search (Chapter 8), and you'll probably find many online services that you could be using too, perhaps for free.

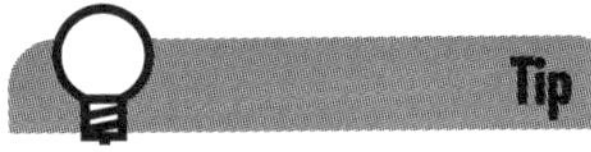

Tip

AOL's Online Banking Review lets you compare online banks in terms of their ease of use, customer confidence, and other factors. In the Personal Finance Channel, click Banking & Loans and Online Banking Review.

Buying a New Car

When I have had to buy a car, I have usually felt at a disadvantage simply because I was never quite sure who had the best price, what the car would cost to maintain, and how safe it would be to drive. Add to that the intimidation that results from not knowing whether the salesperson is telling you everything you need to know. And in shopping for used cars, it can be difficult to find out what a car has been through and what it's really worth.

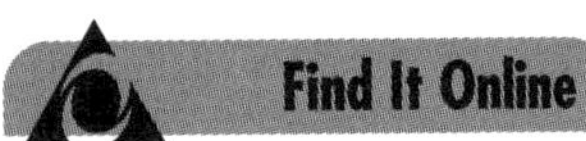

Find It Online

eBay has a special area (`www.ebaymotors.com`) where you can put used vehicles on the auction block or bid on them. See "Going Once, Going Twice," later in this chapter.

When you use the Autos Channel, you have all the tools you need to do your research, so you can walk into that showroom with confidence. Recently redesigned, AOL's Autos Channel is constructed to walk you through the basic steps:

- Find out the value of your current car.
- Identify a dealer where you can close the sale that you researched online. Search more than 11,000 dealers with a presence in AOL Local, AOL's collection of online city guides for large and medium-sized cities (AOL Keyword: **Local**).

- Get the specs and prices for any new car you've got your eye on. You can learn about price details, dealer incentives, size, customer complaint ratings, performance statistics, crash tests, closest competing autos, optional features, and more.
- Plug numbers into the calculators to find out what monthly payment you can expect to pay, given different interest rates and repayment periods.
- Find out how to change your car's oil, flush the radiator, jump-start an ailing battery, and install snow chains. You can even learn what's under the hood, so you can hold your own with the mechanic at the service station.
- Inform yourself by reading magazines, such as *Car and Driver* and *Road & Track* (from the channel's opening screen, click Enthusiasts).
- Register your car, a process that has gone online in many states.

Find It Online

At AOL Keyword: **ClassifiedPlus**, you can search more than a million ads and post your own. You can look for used cars in your community.

Looking for That Dream House?

A house is something too personal and too expensive to buy without walking through, inspecting, sizing up the back yard, and checking out the living room window's view. What you can do on the Web is learn *about* the house-buying process and then compare mortgage rates, prequalify for a loan, investigate a second mortgage, estimate your monthly payments, submit loan applications, compare offers, and plan each step of the relocation process. Recently, I was able to refinance with a national, online broker at a rate better than anything offered in my area. The real-world tasks were whittled down to several overnight-express deliveries, a brief visit by an appraiser, and a quick trip to a lawyer. Today, at AOL Keyword: **Mortgage**, you can create a table comparing rates for different types of mortgage in your area, then apply for the lowest rate on the spot.

The Real Estate section of the House & Home Channel can expedite a home search. Do a search for an apartment or house anywhere in the U.S., and you'll get descriptions, prices, and pictures, courtesy of Homestore.com, which carries online information about more than a million houses. Use the channel's mortgage area to search for an affordable mortgage once you find your dream house.

Tip

Any major expense is likely to involve at least two kinds of decision-making: You have to choose among the available products and vendors, and you have to figure out how to finance the product you decide on. Online resources support both processes.

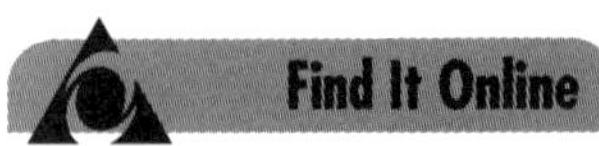

AOL Local guides often include a Real Estate section with information about neighborhoods, homes for sale, moving companies, and so on.

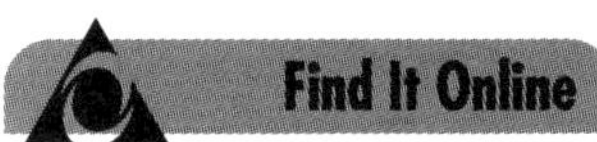

For more about Internet companies, go to AOL Keyword: **Internet Pros**. You can find out about new products and Internet-related jobs.

If you're serious about that new house, make sure you spend time using the many thoughtful services and inventive calculators available at Homefair.com, now part of the Homestore.com megasite (shown in Figure 5-4). Here you can investigate new communities based on schools, crime rates, taxes, and climate. This site can also help you do the following: find affordable and agreeable homes in the chosen community; select a mortgage and mortgager; and find a job in your new community. Buying one house is usually coupled with selling another one, and you can start that process here, too.

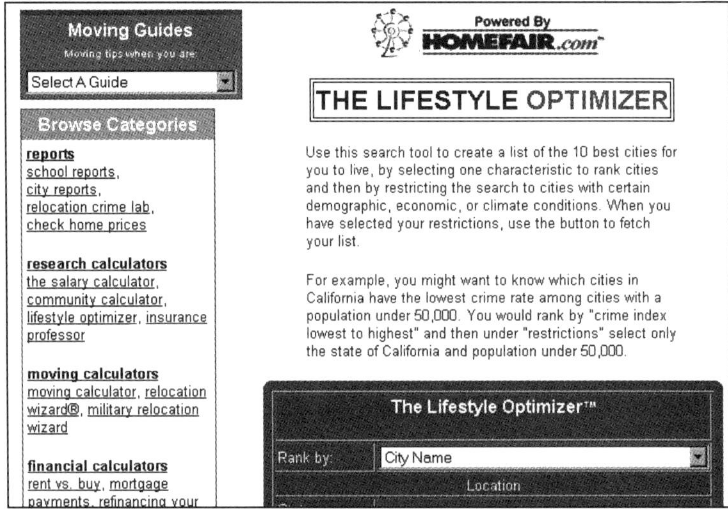

Figure 5-4. Homefair.com. Go ahead, optimize your lifestyle. Learn about a community before you move there.

Getting Ahead: Jobs and Careers

Right up there with planning for the future is finding the right job.

The place to start is your own community, if that's where you want to work. AOL Local (AOL Keyword: **Local**) offers more than 120,000 classified job listings that you can search or browse for jobs right in your hometown. AOL Local also offers job listings and employment agencies for other major U.S. cities, if you're doing a national job search.

On the Careers & Work Channel, a prominent Job Search button takes you to Monster.com's well-established Web service. Monster.com (AOL Keyword: **Monster**) brings together job seekers and employers. Currently, you can search more than 400,000 openings. Using the service (which is free, of course) is quite simple:

1. From the Monster.com site, type in your city or select your state, or both.
2. Select the kind of work you are seeking from the Select a Profession drop-down list.
3. If you want, in the Optional Keywords text box, you can type a word or two to narrow your search.
4. Click Search. Results of your search appear on a Web page; click a result for information about a particular job. Pay attention to the date for any opening. Not all online listings are up-to-date, but even older listings can indicate which companies are looking for what kind of skills.

If you register at the Monster.com Web site (using the AOL Screen Name Service), you can create a profile and have relevant job postings e-mailed to you instead of having to do a search every day, as outlined above. For more about the Screen Name Service, see Chapter 3.

From the Careers & Work Channel's opening window, you can research companies and make your résumé available online. Don't know what you want to do? Use the channel's Career Finder (AOL Keyword: **Career Finder**).

Don't miss the Careers & Work Channel's links to executive search agencies, résumé-writing advice, interviewing tips, and more. Everything counts when you're looking for that perfect job, and each step of the process is online — even, in some cases, the interview itself.

Staying Ahead of the Curve: News around the Clock

When you want up-to-the-moment details of a vote in Congress, a weather emergency in your hometown, developments in negotiations between two companies, or local college basketball scores, you want to be online, and you want to be at the right place online. AOL's News Channel

Find It Online

People looking for employment with the federal government might want to start at the Office of Personnel Management's useful, searchable USAJobs (`www.usajobs.opm.gov`).

Find It Online

AOL Keyword: **Workplace** (the AOL Careers & Work Channel) has direct links to many job-hunting services on AOL and the Web.

Find It Online

When you research a company that interests you, start with the company's Web site. In addition to finding out about its product line and organizational structure, you can learn about its culture and image.

shows you the latest international headlines and gives you the chance to find out more about current news in the worlds of business, health, sports, and politics. AOL Keyword: **News Search** lets you find specific stories and photos. AOL's news resources are based on its partner, CBS, and on wire-feeds such as Associated Press, Reuters, PRNewswire, and Bloomberg.

Just about every news organization has its own site dispensing information around the clock, every day of the year. Just type the name of a newspaper into the AOL browser and see what turns up. In addition, Web sites without a real-world presence, like Moreover.com (`www.moreover.com/news`), have gotten into the act. Moreover.com has quickly become one of the largest and best respected sources of information for every type and level of breaking news. Figure 5-5 shows the Moreover site. This free service extracts information from news resources considered timely and authoritative, and then makes it available to you, the user, as a series of categories, such as real estate news, online marketing news, and senior news. Open a category to see headlines, and click a headline to read a current article about a topic you are following. When searching Moreover, use focused, detailed queries to pull up highly specific stories with exactly the news reporting you want.

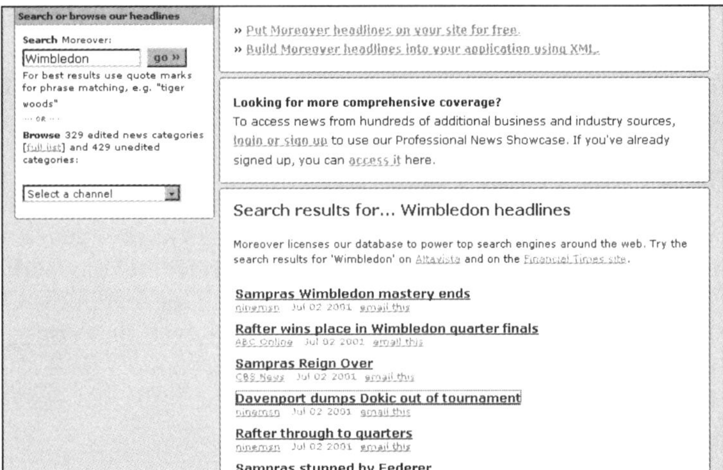

Figure 5-5. Moreover.com offers breadth of coverage and up-to-the-minute stories.

Stop Working So Hard

The information age drives everyone harder and gives many of us cause to grumble about sleeping less, working harder, putting in more hours, and thus not spending enough time with family and friends (which only adds to more stress). Not all the sages of the information economy appreciate the long-term toll on productivity caused by a hectic work pace.

Why not use the tools of the information age — especially the Web — to make the most of your free time? In the pages that follow, you can find ways to make more of leisure-time activities, from shopping to cooking.

Chapter 18 explores some of the newer, purely online pastimes, including alternative ways of listening to the radio, taking pictures, and watching TV.

Shopping Online at AOL

The convenience of shopping online goes beyond saved time, point-and-click ease, and the ability to search for the right gift. Shopping online can also save you money.

Today, just about every large retailer does substantial business on the Web, and thousands of smaller ones have gotten into the act. How do you find these retailers?

Shop@AOL (AOL Keyword: **Shopping**) brings together online vendors in a one-stop shopping experience. This experience surpasses what you could find in a physical store not just in the number of major vendors, but also in the kind of services — and cross-vendor services — that are provided. Say goodbye to long drives to look-alike malls, a confusing maze of displays, and difficulty finding the simplest item.

How do you get to Shop@AOL?

- AOL Keyword: **Shopping** takes you to Shop@AOL's main screen on AOL (Figure 5-6), from which you can search Shop@AOL. You can also start browsing Shop@AOL from this AOL screen.
- The Web address, `shop.aol.com`, takes you go straight to the Shop@AOL's opening page on the Web (Figure 5-7). Each time you visit, a different category appears, such as fashion or electronics.

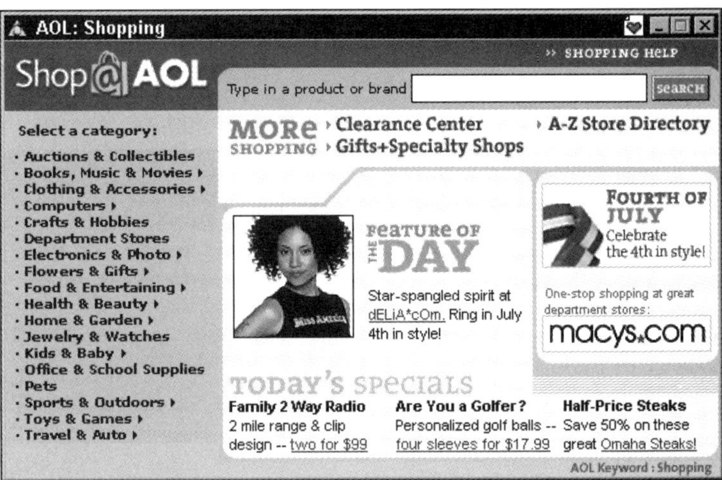

Figure 5-6. If you'd rather start searching or browsing from AOL, use this AOL screen (AOL Keyword: **Shopping**).

From the first page you see at Shop@AOL, you can click through categories until you find a store at which you can buy or price that baseball bat, garden hoe, or copper pot you're seeking.

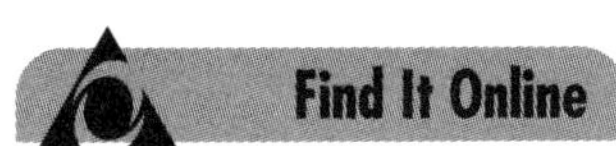

AOL NetMarket is an online-only department store where you must register and pay a fee to shop. As an AOL NetMarket member, you get a low-price guarantee, two-year warranties on items you buy, and special prices and discounts.

Use either of the search boxes shown in Figures 5-6 and 5-7 to search for a brand (such as *Canon*) or search by type of product (such as *digital camera*). In either case, your search results show which stores at Shop@AOL carry the item or product you're looking for, and at what price.

If you need to narrow your search (a search for *T-shirt*, for example, yields almost 9,000 search results!) use the drop-down lists at the top of the search results to sort results by relevance, brand, name, popularity, or price.

At Shop@AOL, you shop at your own pace in well-established "real" stores including department stores such as Target (AOL Keyword: **Target**), Wal-Mart (AOL Keyword: **Walmart**), and JCPenney (AOL Keyword: **Jcpenney**), as well as in stores that exist only online, like AOL NetMarket (AOL Keyword: **Netmarket**).

Figure 5-7. Search or browse, get customer service, comparison shop, make a purchase, find out about Quick Checkout . . . it's all here (`shop.aol.com`).

In addition to mall-wide searching, Shop@AOL features mall-wide customer service. Regardless of the type of store or store size, two levels of customer service protect you: the store's and AOL's. In fact, when you use Shop@AOL to shop for something, AOL's customer support is available at every point:

- While you're looking for products and choosing among brands and stores
- During transactions
- While waiting for your order to arrive
- After you receive your order

After you've found an item you like, AOL's Quick Checkout service expedites the transaction. This service allows you to enter credit-card information just once and then reuse that stored information later for express-line treatment when you buy something at Shop@AOL.

You can sign up at AOL Keyword: **Quick Checkout**. Once signed up, you can use Quick Checkout at sites using the Screen Name Service (Chapter 3) and when buying photo products through "You've Got Pictures" (Chapter 18).

When you do a search at Shop@AOL, you can readily find local (real) stores carrying the item. At the bottom of any results page, type your zip code into the Local Stores box and click Go!

Use AOL's Reminder service (AOL Keyword: **Reminder**) to receive an e-mail message reminding you to shop for birthdays and anniversaries.

Bargain hunters may want to receive the regularly published e-mail newsletter called *Deals and Steals*. They can subscribe at AOL Keyword: **Deals and Steals**.

If you are uncertain about buying things online, it's important to know that

- Shop@AOL's merchants must meet AOL's stringent standards for customer service, customer privacy, professional packaging, and product delivery.
- AOL provides its own round-the-clock customer services by e-mail, chat, phone, and message board. At AOL Keyword: **Shopping Help**, you can get answers to your questions about Quick Checkout, the Certified Merchant program, security, privacy, order status, store ratings, returns, and guarantees.
- Your purchases are backed up by the AOL Guarantee, which you can read about in the sidebar "Is It Safe to Buy Things Online?"

Shop@AOL is not just about buying things for yourself. Take advantage of the Shopping List feature (AOL Keyword: **Shopping List**) to create a list of items for a friend getting married, a family member having a baby shower, or a senior celebrating a big anniversary. Making wish lists public (following the instructions online) can simplify the gift-giving process and ensure that the celebrants get what they want. You can add your shopping list to My Calendar, mail it to someone, and even save it for later use if you're not ready to buy right now.

Provisioning Your Life

All the important things you buy from time to time can be bought online: computers, music, books, toys, and even wine (if you live in states where such purchases are legal). Shop@AOL is a good place to start your shopping trips, but if you don't find exactly what you are looking for, many alternatives remain.

Buying Computers and Computer Gear

Your computer hardware and software have a direct impact on what you can do online. Buying anything computer related, however, can be about as intimidating as buying a car. For starters, the jargon and terminology used to sell hardware and other devices can be confusing. At real-world stores, salespeople often encourage shoppers to buy the latest features without clarifying why people need them or what they do.

Is It Safe to Buy Things Online?

Yes. AOL Keyword: **AOL Guarantee** includes a limit on customer liability for fraud, a money-back guarantee, and several layers of customer support.

Consider also that the AOL browser is based on industry-standard technology for scrambling data so that it can't be intercepted or tampered with. In addition, AOL makes sure that all Certified Merchants provide a secure and safe environment for credit card purchases. Merchants must meet stringent criteria to be certified by AOL. They must, for example, ensure high standards in their packaging, their responsiveness to customers, and their online information about product availability. For more information, go to AOL Keyword: **Shopping Help**.

AOL's Computer Center, available from the channel window, is linked with CNET, the Web megasite produced by the CNET cable TV network (AOL Keyword: **CNET**). Together, AOL and CNET greatly simplify the process of getting background information, matching your needs to current products, and making informed decisions. The following list briefly describes some of the help available through the AOL Computer Center Channel and CNET:

- **Product Reviews:** After you identify a few products of possible interest, you can get background information and product reviews at AOL Keyword: **CNET**. From the opening page, click Hardware Reviews or Software Reviews and then browse to the product or type of product (or a vendor or price range). Look in particular for CNET's Buying Guides, which offer reviews and articles focused on particular subjects, such as digital cameras. Use the CNET search box to go right to the background articles and reviews you need to make an informed decision. However you get information about your product, you can then do comparison pricing to find out which online vendor has the lowest price (the list of vendors is large but not comprehensive).
- **Online Help and Support:** Need help using all that new computer gear? At AOL Keyword: **GetHelpNow** you can find live help from experts, message boards

Note

CNET's comparison shopping is separate from Shop@AOL and does not offer the same cross-vendor customer service policies. You can, however, find some good bargains for specialized items.

where you can ask other people questions, a new-user computer guide, and a technical dictionary. AOL also offers support through online lessons. At AOL Keyword: **Online Classrooms** or **Help Community**, you can take free classes on AOL, HTML, Paint Shop Pro, and office productivity applications.

If you have a printer and need to repeatedly purchase papers and cartridges, visit Printer Supplies (Print⇨Printer Supplies). This service can automatically detect the printer you are using and display products suitable for that printer. Enrolling in Quick Checkout can simplify such routine purchases.

Buying Books Online

Online bookselling has meant a big boost for many aspects of the book business, but consumers have gained the most. Amazon.com is famous for having challenged the chain stores, but these stores have countered with online ventures of their own. Meanwhile, smaller, independent bookstores are joining online cooperatives to stave off both aggressive brick-and-mortar superstores and new online-only superstores. Another change, discussed in Chapter 18, is that publishers are learning how to publish books in a secure, electronic online format, bringing existing books and new titles to a broader audience at a lower price. Figure 5-8 shows Barnes & Noble, AOL's official online bookstore. In addition to books, big stores like Barnes & Noble and Amazon offer movies, CDs, DVDs, and other items.

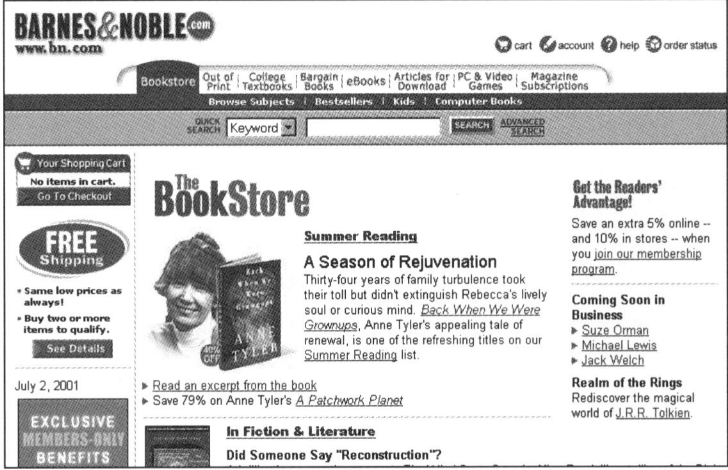

Figure 5-8. Barnes & Noble on the Web. Try buying an eBook.

Sites that compare book prices across Web-based booksellers include AddALL (www.addall.com) and BestBookBuys (www.bestbookbuys.com). At Shop@AOL, Half.com is a good way to get bargains on in-print titles. If you're in the market for an expensive, used, or out-of-print book, consider shopping at a specialized vendor. For used books, one good place to start is Bibliofind, which is now owned by Amazon (www.bibliofind.com).

Buying CDs Online

Like books, CDs lend themselves to online sales. Online shoppers can search for a specific CD in a fraction of the time it takes in a store (the kind with people in it), because they don't have to find a store that has their CD in stock, drive there, find a parking place, stand in line, and so on. Online CD stores can generally ship CDs anywhere. To top it off, most CD vendors let you listen to snippets from an audio CD before buying it, just so you're sure the CD has the piece or performance you really want.

AOL's Media Player makes hearing music snippets at places like CDNow easier and faster. The player plays RealAudio. On CDNow, you can find sound clips in various formats, including RealAudio and Windows Media Format.

CDNow (AOL Keyword: **CDNOW**) is AOL's official music store. At Shop@AOL, you can also buy CDs at other vendors; check the Books, Music, and Movies category at Shop@AOL's main screen. At Shop@AOL, you can buy DVDs from many stores in the Books, Music, and Movies department.

It's Showtime: Movie Times and Tickets

AOL's Moviefone (AOL Keyword: **Movie**) has become a comprehensive, interactive source of movie information. Moviefone is shown in Figure 5-9. More specifically, this is the place to go when you want to find out what movies are playing near you, when they're showing, and whether tickets are available for particular performances. Moviefone lets you buy tickets, too. To help you pick a movie to see, Moviefone provides trailers (video clips), critics' reviews, and users' reviews. When you buy tickets online, you must pick up the tickets when you arrive at the theater. Usually, all you have to do is provide a credit card showing the number used to place the order online. A small fee is added to your order.

Buying tickets online is a good way to make sure you get a seat at a first-run or popular movie.

For every new movie, Moviefone provides a plot synopsis, a rating, critics' and moviegoers' comments, nearby locations where it's showing, show times, and the chance to add the movie's name, place, and time to My Calendar with a click.

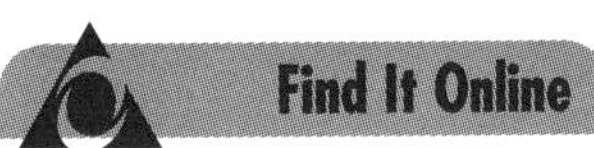

Chapter 18 has a section about watching movies online.

Figure 5-9. Moviefone: Why get movie info in the newspapers when you can find reviews, purchase the tickets, and get driving directions online.

Another place to get movie information is from AOL's Local Guide Channel (AOL Keyword: **Local**). Local Guides cover larger metropolitan areas (AOL Local) as well as smaller communities (Your Town); both can be accessed through AOL Anywhere (`aol.digitalcity.com`). For every community, an enormous range of information can be found not just about movies, but also about concerts, restaurants, weather, garage sales, and much more.

From House to Home

Find It Online

If you're not the do-it-yourself type and need a contractor, AOL Local offers a searchable guide at `aol.digitalcity.com/homeimprovement`.

After you've used online services to find a house or apartment, you can use the Net to make your new digs into a place where you want to live. Start with the House & Home Channel (AOL Keyword: **Home**) for comprehensive guidance in planning and carrying out those major projects. You can find step-by-step illustrated instructions for wiring, masonry, carpentry, painting, and other projects. Handy estimators (fill-in-the-blank calculators) help you figure out the amount of wallpaper or paint you need for those home projects. A guide to contractors is available in the channel's Home Improvement section.

For Cooks

Everything food-related has found a place on AOL or the Web, and a good place to find it all is AOL Keyword: **Food**, part of the House & Home Channel.

For everyday use, take advantage of the Food forum's searchable recipe finder (Services⇨Recipe Finder). Just type a pertinent word or two (**lobster** or **cobbler**, for example), and click Search. A page of results comes up after a few seconds. Click any recipes of interest. You can also browse categories of recipes to compare recipes by ingredients used, time involved, and so on.

The Food forum's shopping area provides a good variety of cookbooks and foods (through Shop@AOL). Vendors include Harry & David and AKA Gourmet. Geerlings and Wade is one of the vendors that sell wines online, though not to minors, of course, and only to people living in states where such shipments are legal. When shopping for wine on Shop@AOL, stores provide information on the states to which they cannot ship.

Hassle-free Vacation Planning

Vacations can take weeks of planning — where to go, where to stay, how to get there, what to see, what to bring, and so on. Planning online can cut the time and cost of your preparations. In the Travel Channel, you can start by booking your plane, lodging, and car rental.

Travel publisher Frommer's can help you create a travel itinerary that includes just the information you want: weather, hotels, attractions, and so on (AOL Keyword: **Frommers**). All you do is indicate where you want to travel and what kind of information you need (AOL Keyword: **Destinations**; click Frommer's Custom Mini-Guides).

While Frommer's covers the bigger and more popular destinations, use the Frommer's Destinations search box to find travel information about more out-of-the-way places. This information comes from the compact and informative *Rough Guide* travel books.

For planning a trip that involves driving, get to know MapQuest (AOL Keyword: **Mapquest**), an interactive mapping service that is closely integrated with Moviefone and AOL Local.

MapQuest can generate an overview map of just about every part of the world and a street map of just about any address in the U.S. MapQuest's turn-by-turn driving directions include driving times and explain how to go between any two addresses in the U.S. and Canada. I frequently use MapQuest for local trips and vacation planning. From MapQuest's opening page, you can reach the Road Trip Planner, which provides the planning tools you need to find out how to get to, and return from, your destination.

Going Once, Going Twice: Online Auctions

eBay does not sell goods, but instead provides the venue and services through which buyers and sellers can bid on and sell goods. You can find complete information at eBay.

Online auctions bring together people who need something with people who have that certain something. The idea is simple. Say that you have an 1891 Indian Head penny in mint condition. It might be worth something to others because it's beautiful, intrinsically valuable, or in good condition — or some combination of these reasons.

Online auction service eBay (AOL Keyword: **Ebay**), shown in Figure 5-10, provides a single venue where you can sell that old penny, find potential buyers, provide details (including a digital picture), manage bidding, and use online services for buying and selling. Listing items for sale is not free, but if you're buying, you don't have to pay a thing to register or bid.

Figure 5-10. eBay, a garage sale the size of Delaware.

The range of items peddled on eBay is amazing: cars, art, old books, used dolls, digital cameras, and all sorts of computer equipment. In looking for a doll for a child recently, I found more than 51,000 dolls in 38 categories — a lot more choice than my local toy superstore.

eBay provides full information about how to post pictures of something you want to sell online. The simplest way is to use a digital picture from "You've Got Pictures" (AOL Keyword: **Pictures**).

If you're interested in bidding on an item, you can limit your auction search to a region and a city if you want to meet the seller, see the item, and explore additional trading opportunities. Every item up for auction has a text description of the object, sometimes shows a picture, and as a rule provides information about the seller's reliability as reported by other eBay members. You can also see the item's bidding history, plus payment and shipping options.

Advice for Buyers and Sellers

If you're selling: Provide clear and explicit information about the thing you are selling and include a picture whenever possible. The winning bidder can use any such discrepancies to void the transaction. You must accept the winning bid. Bids can be submitted for a fixed amount of time, which you choose (3–10 days). If you want, you can end the auction early, but remember that many bids are submitted toward the end of the bidding process. eBay charges a variety of fees for specific services, all described in detail when you register to sell something.

If you're buying: Check the seller's feedback ratings (what other buyers thought of doing business with that person). A seller's rating can be found on the page where an item is being offered for sale. Do not place a bid thinking that you probably won't win. Acknowledge your responsibility to pay for *any* winning bid at the terms requested by the seller. Make sure you know what you are buying, from whom you are buying, and how you will pay for the item just in case you win the bid.

You can use AOL Mobile on your wireless phone to bid on eBay auctions while on the go. From the AOL menu, start at Shopping⇨Auctions. At the eBay window, first sign in if necessary and then search for an auction. You can bid on the featured auctions.

Where to Go from Here

In a matter of years, the Internet has become the place to start when pricing a computer, booking a cruise, finding an address, buying a house, and doing a hundred other things. Online services can cut the time and cost of doing tiresome day-to-day things, giving you more time for the things that count, online or off.

- For details about using the AOL Web browser, see Chapter 6.
- For an introduction to the Netscape Navigator browser, see Chapter 7.
- For more about activities that can be done entirely online — as opposed to the real-life activities that can be supported online — see Chapter 18.

Chapter 6

Behind the Wheel: Using AOL's Web Browser

IN THIS CHAPTER **PAGE**

The World Wide Web, or *Web* as most people call it, has become a part of daily life for millions of people. To use the Web, you need some software called a *browser*. AOL includes a browser that is always at your fingertips.

The Web is just a part of the Internet — the "visual" and interactive part. But your AOL browser is not just a way of viewing Web pages. It's becoming a way to do everything on the Internet, as you'll see in this chapter.

Why You Need a Browser to Use the Internet

The basic unit of the Web is the *page*. A Web browser is, put simply, a tool for using pages. Pages can contain just about anything from words to 3-D games that can be played by several people (in different places) at the same time.

Most pages have hyperlinks, also called *links,* which make your Web-surfing experience interactive. Click a link on one page, and the browser downloads and displays a new page that may contain text, graphics, animation, musical accompaniment, and all the glitz and wonder people have come to expect on the Web.

Every page has a Web address, which you can read about in the "What You Need to Know about Web Addresses" sidebar later in this chapter.

When you type a Web address into the browser software on your computer, the browser asks a computer (called a *server*) on the Internet to send a copy of the Web page you requested to your computer. The server then turns the requested page into little packets of data, which the browser puts back together again so that you can experience the page.

Browsers do the following things:

- Make it possible to see and experience sounds, pictures, video, animations, and much more.
- Simplify navigation, thanks to links; click links to move from one page to another.
- Allow anyone with access to the Internet to publish on the Web.

Understanding Today's Web

In the future, historians may consider the year 1989 as the end of the 20th century: The Berlin Wall fell, closed societies started opening borders, and the World Wide Web was invented. By freeing the flow of the world's information, the Web has been one factor in breaking down the monopoly of information on which closed societies depended.

Since the establishment of the Internet as a project of the U.S. government in the 1970s, scientists could see the need for tools to access the rapidly growing body of knowledge on the network. Tim Berners-Lee, a young English physicist working in Geneva, developed an ingeniously simple way of publishing and linking documents across computer networks. In the late 1980s, Mr. Berners-Lee developed both the first Web browser and HTML, the computer language used to create Web pages.

Tip

Tim Berners-Lee tells the inside story of the Web's conception and development in *Weaving the Web* (Harper, San Francisco, 1999).

A Tool for Browsing the Web

You'll probably spend most of your time on the Web browsing — reading one page with text and pictures, and then clicking links to see related Web pages. The process is so simple you can get the hang of it by simply clicking and looking. Figure 6-1 shows one of AOL Local's Web pages. AOL Local is an AOL service on the Web that provides information for just about every large town and big city across the U.S. As you can see, AOL Local offers a ton of choices, including words and pictures to click for related information.

Browsing just means going from one Web page to another by clicking links.

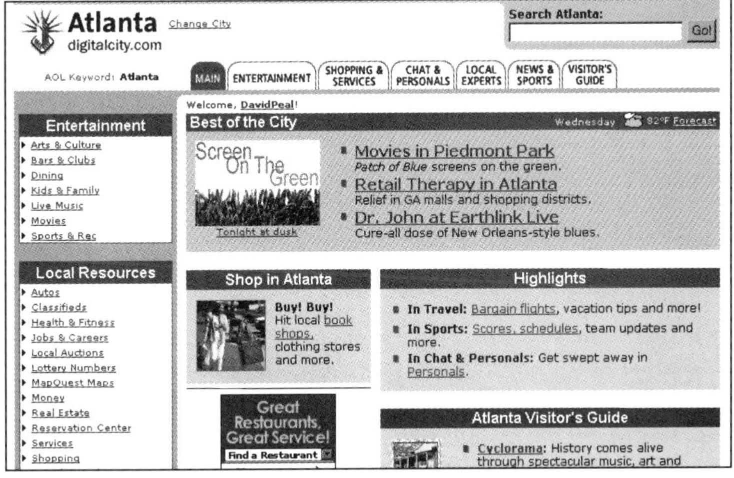

Figure 6-1. One page of a billion, linked to others, linked to still others. This particular page is a hub, guiding you in a few clicks to hundreds of pages about the city of Atlanta.

A Tool for Using Other Tools

The browser was invented with simple formats in mind: text and eventually pictures. In addition to Web pages, early browsers were meant to provide access to other Internet services, such as e-mail.

The browser remains an amazing all-purpose tool and can be used to read e-mail, take part in newsgroups, and download files using FTP:

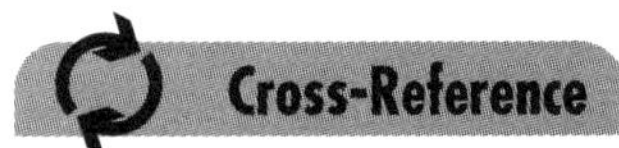

Cross-Reference

Find out how to use AOL Mail on the Web in Chapter 10. For information on using the browser for newsgroups and FTP, see Chapters 14–15.

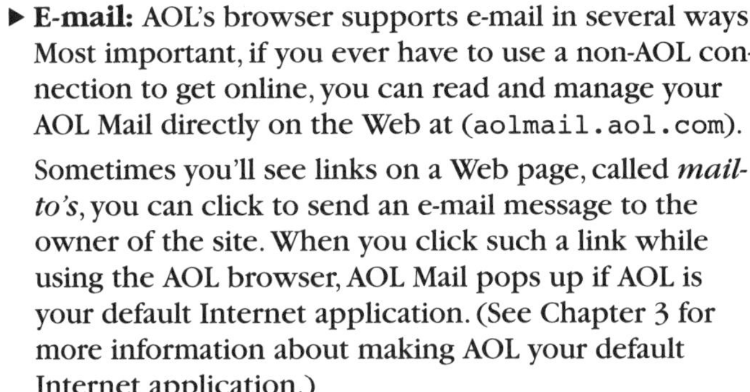

- **E-mail:** AOL's browser supports e-mail in several ways. Most important, if you ever have to use a non-AOL connection to get online, you can read and manage your AOL Mail directly on the Web at (`aolmail.aol.com`).

  Sometimes you'll see links on a Web page, called *mail-to's*, you can click to send an e-mail message to the owner of the site. When you click such a link while using the AOL browser, AOL Mail pops up if AOL is your default Internet application. (See Chapter 3 for more information about making AOL your default Internet application.)

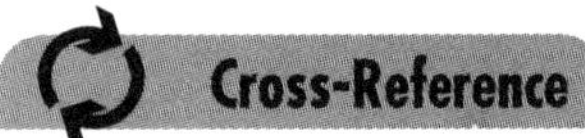

Cross-Reference

For more on newsgroups, the Google Groups service, and message boards, see Chapter 14.

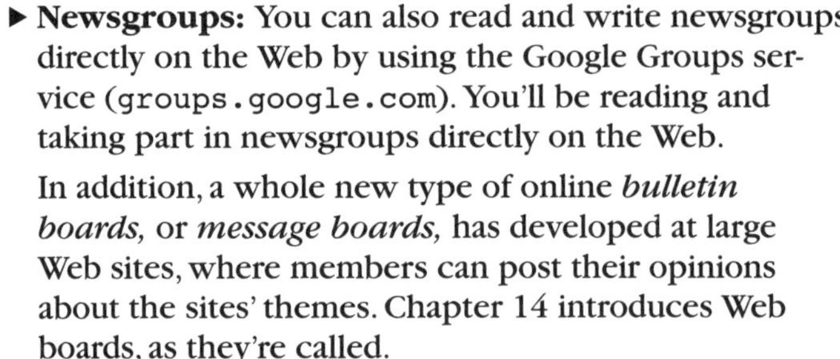

- **Newsgroups:** You can also read and write newsgroups directly on the Web by using the Google Groups service (`groups.google.com`). You'll be reading and taking part in newsgroups directly on the Web.

  In addition, a whole new type of online *bulletin boards,* or *message boards,* has developed at large Web sites, where members can post their opinions about the sites' themes. Chapter 14 introduces Web boards, as they're called.

Note

You can have several copies of the AOL browser open at the same time, downloading in one, searching in another, viewing a site in another, and more. Just enter new addresses into the address box to bring up a new browser window.

- **FTP:** The *File Transfer Protocol* is a powerful way of moving files across the Internet. Think of an FTP site as a publicly available hard drive, from which you can help yourself to software, music, and other files. As you'll see in Chapter 15, you can use the AOL browser to download files from an FTP site or from any Web site that has files that can be downloaded.

More Than a Tool . . . a New Medium

Today's Web has gone beyond its original vision. More than a constellation of static information pages that are linked to each other, more than a simple way of using traditional

Internet tools, the Web also supports on-screen movie theaters, basketball courts, shopping malls, and online classrooms with message boards, links, and video-taped instructors. Such sites require additional software, which AOL either provides or makes easy to get. See "Multimedia Madness" later in this chapter.

With such a diversity of content, today's Web can be difficult for people with visual impairments or other disabilities to access. AOL members with disabilities can use AOL's voice recognition software to write e-mail and send instant messages.

See AOL Keyword: **Voice Center** for more information about voice-recognition software.

Web Pages and Their Elements

As you explore the World Wide Web, you see an amazing variety of Web pages, ranging from pages with simple text to multimedia creations that feature animation, video, 3-D effects, and interactive games. In the next few pages, I outline some of the page elements that you'll probably see as you browse the Web.

Creating Your Own Web Pages

Over the years, creating Web pages has become a popular way for people with shared interests to find each other. At AOL Hometown (AOL Keyword: **Hometown**), AOL provides tools for quickly creating and sharing Web pages with friends and family. If you prefer to do things from scratch, all you need is a word processor to make a page. Microsoft Office applications let you create a Web page by simply saving a Word, Excel, PowerPoint, Publish, or other Office document as an HTML document. (HTML is the language used to create Web pages.)

Chapter 16 describes Web tools you can use to develop pages from scratch, including Netscape Composer and HTML-Kit.

For complete information about creating Web pages, see *Your Official America Online Guide to Creating Cool Web Pages,* 2nd Edition, by Edward Willett (Hungry Minds, Inc.).

On the AOL service, use the News Channel and AOL Keyword: **CBS** for the latest news.

Washingtonpost.com, whose opening page is shown in Figure 6-2, uses every standard Web element to deliver news around the clock to people who don't happen to live anywhere near the Beltway. It underscores the Web's importance in making local papers readily available to anyone.

Figure 6-2. The online edition of a great city newspaper uses a variety of media, including audio, video, words, photos, and message boards.

Here's a list of common Web page elements and media:

- **Words (or *text*):** Words constitute the basic page element because they convey the most complex information. On today's Web, everything is visual, including text. Web designers can vary font type, color, and size. They can create graphics files consisting of words. And they can use something called style sheets to create elegant color, type, and link designs. If you create pages yourself, you can take advantage of these effects, too.
- **Pictures (or *graphics*):** Pictures enrich words on the Web and provide visual interest. Kids expect illustrations, scientists expect diagrams, sports fans expect to see action shots, and so on. The use of digital photographs can add to any page's immediacy. If you're reading the Washington Post online, for example, you can expect to see pictures of either politicians or bumper-to-bumper traffic.

- **Links (or *hyperlinks*):** Links are the threads that connect pages on the Web; they make documents available with a single click. Click a link such as Investors Hold Their Breath in Figure 6-2 to get more information about this story.

  Clicking a link can take you to another part of the Web page, to another page on the same Web site, or to a whole new Web site altogether. The rule is that a link takes you somewhere else, whether it's near or far.

  The most common kinds of links are words and pictures (or parts of pictures). Links in text are usually highlighted in a different color and underlined; links in pictures can sometimes be harder to find.

- **Video and audio:** Many sites today use video and audio. Newspapers and radio stations in particular make aggressive use of audio and video, round the clock. You'll encounter two main kinds of video and audio: streaming and non-streaming, both explained in more detail in Chapter 15. Figure 6-3 shows the AOL Media Player being used to listen to BBC radio.

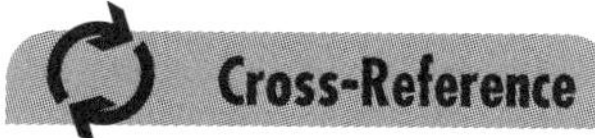

Streaming and nonstreaming video are explained in Chapter 16. Chapter 18 profiles some sites that use streaming video.

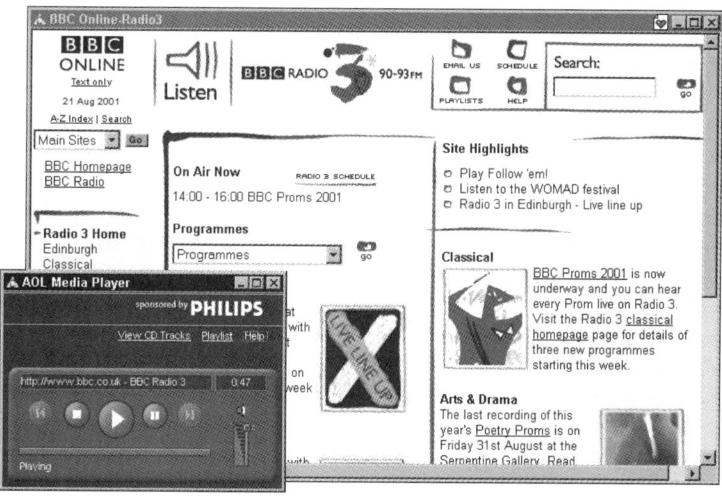

Figure 6-3. AOL Media Player can play your favorite radio stations.

- **Java and JavaScript:** Java is a programming language that is used to write applets. *Applets* are little programs that run from a Web browser and enable you to view and use such things as games, mortgage calculators,

Web *interactivity* may mean that a Web page uses buttons and fill-in-the-blank boxes for you to express preferences and add information. Or it may mean that people can communicate with each other in real time, as in Groups@AOL (AOL Keyword: **Groups**), which I discuss in Chapter 18.

Web-based chat programs, and scrolling news windows. For a wonderful example of how Java can be used, go to `prominence.com/java/poetry` to create your own refrigerator poetry — just drag the words around with your mouse until you've completed your very own poetic masterpiece. Figure 6-4 shows AOL's Java-based Easy Designer, a mini-application you can use to create and illustrate Web pages (AOL Keyword: **Easy Designer**).

JavaScript is different from Java. You need to know about JavaScript because some pages have *bad* JavaScript, which the AOL browser will not be able to display. A message (Internet Explorer Script Error) informs you of this fact. When prompted, you should choose not to continue using scripts on the page.

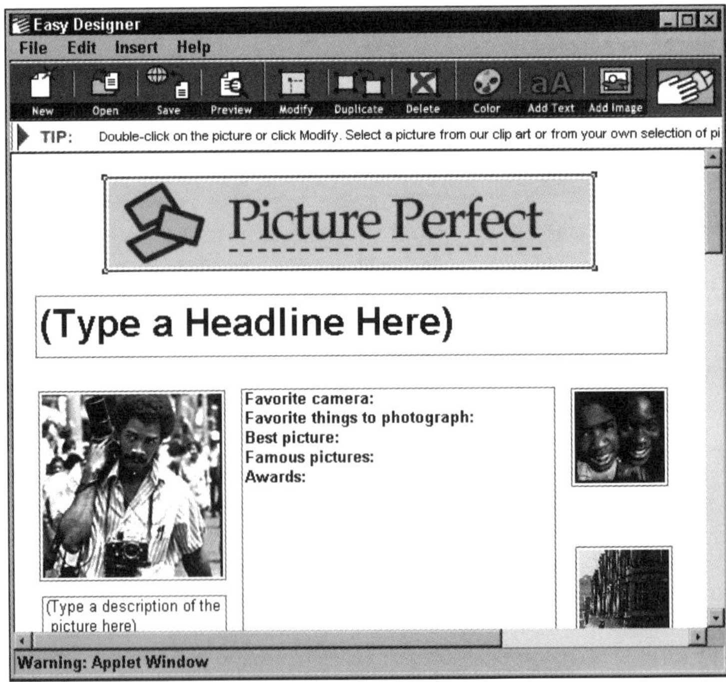

Figure 6-4. You can use Easy Designer, a Java application, to build Web pages at AOL Hometown.

What You Need to Know about Web Addresses

A Web address, or URL (short for Universal Resource Locator), identifies every document on the Internet. A Web address such as `http://www.aol.com` has several parts:

- **Protocol:** Tells your browser what kind of information you want. The best-known protocol is `http://`, which tells your browser that this is a Web page. You don't have to type **http://** when you type an address into the address box.
- **Domain name:** The next part of a URL identifies the network and specific computer where content can be found. In `www.hungryminds.com`, for example, the computer is called www and the domain is called `hungryminds.com`.
- **Filename:** If you're visiting a specific page of a Web site, you see a specific filename, such as `beach.htm` or `baby.html`. If a URL doesn't explicitly contain a filename, as in `www.hungryminds.com`, you're visiting the main page, called a *home page*.

When you display a page, its URL appears in the AOL address box. Sometimes these URLs appear with a URL vastly more complex than what you originally typed. Don't worry about the apparent complexity. At the very beginning of the URL, you can usually find an ordinary address, which you can use to revisit the site or make it a favorite place. It's best not to use huge URLs as favorite places; they may not be there next time.

The AOL Browser in Action

The AOL browser window is where you do almost everything on the Web. Because it's so important (and despite the fact that it seems so easy to use), I will be spending the next few sections on showing you how to make the most of this simple yet powerful tool.

The browser is like any window. In Windows, the browser window has buttons in the upper-right corner to make the window smaller or larger and to close it. Like other windows, you can click the browser's title bar to drag it around the screen as you see fit. To resize it, click any border and drag it into a new position. In the upper-left side of the window are AOL's navigation buttons, shown in Figure 6-5. If a browser window is larger than the AOL display, a vertical or horizontal scroll bar (or both) will appear, so you can see the whole browser.

To increase the amount of the AOL display that can be used by the browser, choose Settings⇨Preferences. Click Toolbar & Sounds. In the preferences box, click Text Only and then click Save.

Telling Your Browser Where to Go: The Address Box

The address box is just a box in which you type the address of the page you want to visit. After you type the address, such as **www.hungryminds.com**, click Go or press Enter.

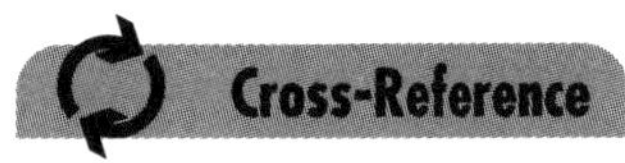

Chapter 5 explores the essentials of accessing Web sites, and Chapter 8 is all about AOL Search, AOL's comprehensive Web-based search service.

Don't confuse the address box (in the center of the toolbar) with the search box (the yellow-framed box on the right). Use the address box to go to a specific Web address. Use the search box to find specific Web addresses.

AOL 7.0 has an autocomplete feature in its address box that makes typing URLs easy. Visit a Web page once, and the next time you want to go back to the page, you have to type only enough of the address for the browser to recognize it and do the rest. The address box also remembers AOL keywords; in fact, it remembers the last 25 keywords or URLs thay you type. To turn the feature on, choose Settings⇨Preferences from the AOL toolbar. In the Preferences window, click Toolbar & Sound. Make sure a check is by the Auto-complete Keyword and Web Address Entries option.

Telling the Browser How to Get There: Navigation Buttons

The navigation buttons, shown in Figure 6-5, work quite simply. These buttons keep track of AOL screens as well as Web pages, and the trail backward and forward extends to 25 different online places.

AOL Anywhere and the Web

The idea behind AOL Anywhere is simple. You can't always be in the same place as your PC, and you may find yourself at a PC without AOL installed. But why should that stop you from enjoying the benefits of AOL?

With a handheld computer, wireless phone, or other device — or with *any* browser and *any* non-AOL connection — you can still use your favorite AOL features wherever you happen to be, thanks to AOL Anywhere.

It's important to mention that the AOL Anywhere devices differ in the extent to which they offer Web services. Instant AOL offers a fairly full Web experience. When you use AOL Anywhere over a wireless phone, handheld computer, or AOLbyPhone, however, you get smaller chunks of Web content, based on the weather, stocks, news, and other preferences you set up with My AOL, covered in Chapter 2. These restrictions have to do with the simple fact that AOL Anywhere devices often have small screens and limited memory or processing power.

The Web's inventors dreamed of "device independence," so that the same content would be available on any type of machine. Look for much more Web content — everywhere — in the years ahead.

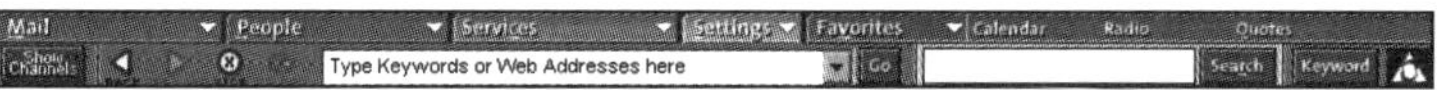

Figure 6-5. At least one of the four navigation buttons is usually grayed out (not usable) in a particular circumstance.

- **Back:** This button takes you to the last page or AOL area you've viewed. Using your keyboard, you can do the same thing as clicking Back by pressing the Alt key and then the left arrow key.
- **Forward:** After you've backtracked, if you want to move forward again, click this button. The button is active only if you've already used the Back button. The keyboard alternative is Alt+→ (the right arrow).

Some pages have their own, built-in navigational buttons showing arrows or words, such as *next*.

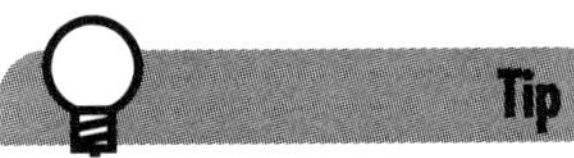

If downloading a page from the Web seems to take too long, the page may have encountered some Net turbulence along the way. Clicking Reload can sometimes make it download more quickly.

- **Stop:** Whether you type a URL or click a link to a new page, you can click the Stop button if the page takes a long time to appear in your browser. You can also use this button if you change your mind about viewing a page before it's finished loading.

  If some of the page has already loaded, you see a partial page. The keyboard alternative for clicking Stop is pressing the Esc key.
- **Reload:** This button downloads the current page again. Usually, you reload a page that didn't completely download, was stalled, or timed out.

Understanding Your Compass: The Status Bar

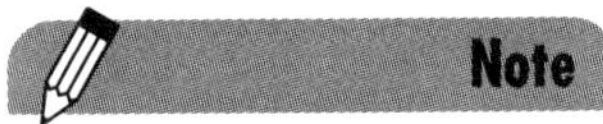

You can open several AOL browsers at the same time. Back, Forward, and other commands apply only to the active browser.

At the bottom of the browser window, the status bar tells you what's going on as you're downloading a Web page (see Figure 6-6). Move your mouse arrow over a Web link until the arrow turns into a finger and the status bar at the bottom of the browser shows the page's Web address. Click the link, and the status bar shows you:

- Whether you've successfully connected with the computer where the page is sitting.
- How much of the page has been transferred (using a blue bar meter in the lower-right corner). The blue bar represents the downloaded parts of a page. There is no guarantee that a page will continue downloading at the same pace at which it started.

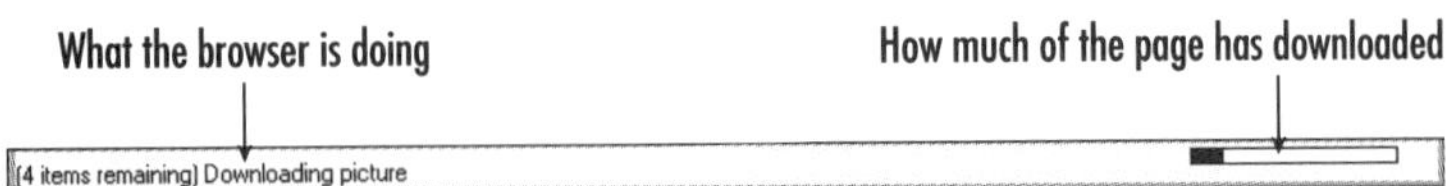

Figure 6-6. The status bar keeps tabs on whatever task you've asked the browser to do. It visually estimates the time it will take for a Web page to download. After the requested page arrives, the word *Done* appears on the far left.

Keeping an eye on the status bar may not ease your frustration when the browser seems to be taking forever to download a page, but at least the status bar will show you what the browser is trying to do. If it's not doing anything, you may want to click the Stop button and then the Reload button.

The History of Browsers

For its first few years, the Web consisted of words and only words. The content consisted of words, so that's all the browsers could handle.

In the early 1990s, a college student at the University of Illinois named Marc Andreessen, with a small group influenced by the work of Berners-Lee and others, developed a browser called Mosaic, which could display pictures as well as words. In 1994, Andreessen helped create both Netscape (the company) and Netscape Navigator (the browser). This simple, visual tool helped to change the world.

Software giant Microsoft got its start in the browser business by licensing a version of Mosaic, and Microsoft quickly managed to catch up with Netscape. Both companies gave their software away, fueling the Web's popularity.

The heated competition of these two companies, in combination with the Web's popularity and freely available browsers, led to the dramatic improvement in both browsers. Today they display everything from old-fashioned text articles to live concerts, with video, audio, and interactive features.

AOL members have benefited from the white-hot browser wars of the mid-1990s. The AOL browser is based on Microsoft's Internet Explorer browser (version 5.5) and AOL now owns the Netscape browser, the subject of Chapter 7. Within the AOL software, you use the AOL browser.

AOL can be used to run any Windows-based Internet software, hence all Windows browsers. As a result, you can use lesser-known browsers such as Opera (`www.opera.com`), which often have specific benefits worth exploring. The visually impaired might want to look into a speaking browser such as IBM's Home Page Reader (`www.ibm.com/able/hpr.html`).

Right-Clicking Text, Links, and Graphics

If you're familiar with Windows software, you probably already know that many programs let you click the right mouse button to see a context-specific menu of options. AOL's browser is no exception.

Right-clicking anywhere on a Web page in the AOL browser offers you many useful ways of using the page. The options offered to you when you right-click vary, depending on where you click a page. This material might seem a little obscure, but you'll find many ways to control pages by right-clicking them.

- If you right-click blank space on the page, you can perform actions on the page as a whole.
- Select text and then right-click, and you see a short menu that includes Copy.
- Right-click a graphic, and you see a menu that includes Save Picture As.
- Right-click text, and your first menu option is Select All (select all Web elements on the page, that is). Once selected, the page can be saved to your hard drive.

Right-Clicking Text

Right-clicking any text (nongraphical) part of a page gives you the following options, most of which pertain to the page as a whole:

Copying from a Web site is a fast way of grabbing addresses and product information from a Web page. If you use content from a Web site for any other purpose without permission, you may be infringing on the owner's copyright. AOL Keyword: **Copyright** has information on this hot subject.

- **Select All:** Selects every element on the page. (Web elements are discussed earlier in this chapter.) Once selected, these elements can be copied or saved.
- **Copy:** Lets you copy anything selected — a few words or the entire page — to the clipboard. You can paste stuff from the clipboard into a word processing document or elsewhere.
- **Print:** Prints the entire page.

Right-clicking nonselected text gives you additional choices:

- **Create Shortcut:** Creates a shortcut to this Web page on your desktop. To visit the page again, all you have to do is double-click the shortcut. (If you are not online, AOL will come up and let you sign on to view the page.) This is a great way to set up a link to a valuable

Web site. It can function as a second home page — a sort of beach cottage on the Web. When you click the desktop shortcut, your default browser opens and displays the page.

- **Add to Favorites:** Adds the page to the list of favorite sites maintained in the Windows Start Menu. Be aware that this list is *not* the same as Favorite Places on AOL. The AOL Favorite Places folder is available only when you're using AOL. The Microsoft Favorites are available from the MSIE browser as well as the Start menu. Both systems have benefits, but maintaining two such lists can get confusing. The advantage of AOL's Favorite Places is that it can hold any kind of information, not just Web pages.

If AOL is your default Internet application (for more, see Chapter 3), the AOL browser opens when you select an MSIE Favorite.

- **View Source:** Displays the HTML skeleton of the page. If you're interested in creating your own Web page, this is a tremendous way to learn the ins and outs of HTML and to find out how certain effects are achieved. Using View Source can help you troubleshoot problems with your own page.
- **Print:** Sends the current page to your default printer. Pressing Ctrl+P does exactly the same thing.
- **Refresh:** Reloads the page, which, in the case of pages that change frequently, ensures you're looking at the latest version, not the earlier version that your browser stored in its *cache* (see "Managing Your Temporary Internet Files" later in this chapter).
- **Properties:** Provides you with basic information about the page, such as its exact address. Sometimes, on AOL, a Web page is displayed as an AOL keyword but doesn't show a URL. To get the URL and explore the site on your own, you can copy the URL from the Properties box (Ctrl+C), and paste it in the address box (Ctrl+V) — even though it looks like it can't!

Right-Clicking a Link

Right-clicking a picture or text link in a Web page brings up a short menu that gives you several options. You can open the link in a new window — a good way of keeping the original window open so that you can return there easily. You can also choose Copy Shortcut to copy the linked-to page's URL, which you can then paste into a word-processed document or use while editing a favorite place.

Right-clicking a linked graphic gives you the same choices, plus a few extras. You can, for example, save a copy of the picture on your hard drive.

Other options when right-clicking a link include:

- **Open:** Means just that. Select the link and open it in place of the current page.
- **Open in New Window:** Lets you keep the current page open and open the linked-page in a new browser.
- **Save Target As:** Saves the pointed-to page on your hard drive. You may do this to study others' pages or to troubleshoot your own page if you don't have the original file handy. Note that this saves only a page's HTML, not any embedded graphics. I have used this option to save large movie files and prevent a movie player from coming up automatically. At the Internet Archive (`www.archive.org/movies`), the historical movies from the 30s, 40s, and 50s can't be played until the movies have been downloaded and the player has been modified.
- **Print Target:** Prints the pointed-to page.
- **Copy Shortcut:** Copies the pointed-to page's Web address so that you can then paste it into an e-mail message, instant message, or word-processed document.
- **Add to Favorites:** Adds the pointed-to page to the Microsoft Internet Explorer Favorites folder.
- **Properties:** Displays the URL of the pointed-to page.

Right-Clicking a Graphic

Right-clicking a nonlinked graphic (that is, a simple picture that doesn't do anything or link to anything) gives you options that include:

AOL's screens do not have selectable text or pictures, and right-clicking doesn't do anything.

- **Save Picture As:** Saves the picture to your hard drive. Watch out for those copyright infringements.
- **Set as Wallpaper:** Makes the picture your desktop wallpaper.
- **Copy:** Sends the image picture to the clipboard. From there, you can paste a picture into other programs.

- **Add to Favorites:** Puts a link to a picture in your list of favorites. Again, this is Microsoft's Favorites, not AOL's Favorite Places.

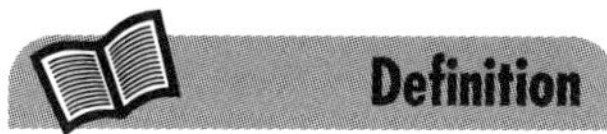

Windows *wallpaper* is a picture that appears on your Windows desktop.

Saving a Page on Your Hard Drive

To save a copy of a single page or entire site, make sure the browser window is active by clicking it.

From the AOL menu, choose File⇨Save As. A Save As dialog box appears. You have two major options for saving the document.

- Web Page, Complete and Web Archive for E-mail have a similar result: They save the page and all of its associated graphics and other elements for viewing offline. Links will not work when you are offline.
- Web Page, HTML Only, and Text also have a similar effect: The HTML (text and markup) is saved, but not the graphics. A saved page is available when you are not online and can be read in the browser. Studying other people's HTML is a great way to learn it.

When saving, make sure to put the saved pages in a place where you can find them later! It is easy to lose track of such things.

Closing a Browser

Like most browsers, AOL lets you open as many copies of the browser at the same time as you want. Sometimes you wind up with a lot of open browser windows, even if you don't want them all. Why? Some links are set to open new browser windows. When you have a browser window open and type a different URL into the address box, a new browser opens. To close open browsers, click the X box in the far upper-right corner. Or, press Ctrl+F4.

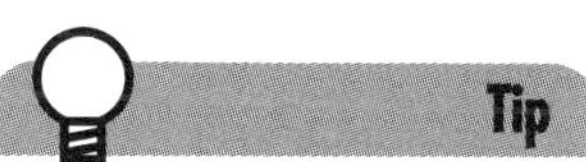

You can also right-click the button for the minimized browser in the Windows taskbar and choose Close.

When You Can't Access a Page: Error Messages

You used to get errors all the time when trying to access Web sites. These days, errors seem to be fewer in number. For the record, an error can be anything that prevents you from viewing a Web page that you're trying to access, regardless of the reason for this difficulty.

Problems you may encounter include the following:

- The page has disappeared into thin air, which happens when a page is deleted from a server or a server discontinues operation.
- The page just isn't downloading. It may be in high demand, or the server may be simply too slow for the traffic. Try again later, as in a few seconds later. Net traffic varies by the second. Just click the Reload button on the navigation bar.
- The page is password protected, is accessible only to the Webmaster, or can be viewed only by members of some organization. There is not much you can do in this case.
- The page is trying to set cookies, and your browser's privacy settings are too high to allow it. Check your privacy settings.
- Maybe you just got the address all wrong. Go to AOL Keyword: **AOL Search** and do a search for the Web site.

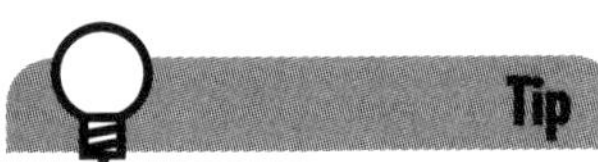

Sometimes you get to your destination faster by including less information in your URL, leaving off the filename or the last parts of the address.

Often, you have the right site but the wrong page. In this case, you might try climbing up the site, one directory at a time, until you find a working page. To go up, delete the URL's last named folder or filename. For example, you would change the (fictitious) Web page `www.aol.com/Africa/travel/kilimanjaro.html` to `www.aol.com/Africa/travel`.

If that doesn't work, go to `www.aol.com/Africa` and finally to `www.aol.com`. At this top-level page, do a site search for *Kilimanjaro*.

The good news is that the AOL browser displays a message letting you know why you can't access a page and what to do about it. Another bit of news: More and more sites are posting friendly error messages that indicate, for example, when the server address is correct but the page requested is incorrect (such as when a page maintained by a college student disappears because the student has graduated). Other sites automatically redirect you to pages whose addresses have changed, posting helpful messages along the way.

For a simple explanation of various error messages, go to the NetHelp Web site (`www.aol.com/nethelp`) and click Internet Error Messages.

Making the AOL Browser Work Your Way

You have many ways to customize AOL's browser so that it works the way you like. To make these changes, you need to tinker with the underlying Microsoft browser by resetting the preferences listed in the Internet Properties box. The box is available at Settings⇨Preferences; in the Preferences box, click Internet Properties (WWW).

You can customize many of your browser's features. The most important features include the following:

- Maintaining your history list (addresses of recently visited pages).
- Managing your *cache,* the folder on your hard drive where Web pages and their elements are stored to enable faster future downloading of those pages.
- Adjusting the appearance of pages to improve your ability to see or experience them.

Tracing Your History Trail

Your browser keeps track of your *history,* the addresses of sites you've recently visited. This list makes it possible for AOL's Back and Forward buttons to know which pages were previously viewed.

The idea is that if you've visited a site once, you may want to go back again. Sometimes remembering a Web address (or 20) can be difficult, and many sites that are useful at one moment aren't necessarily worth keeping in your Favorite Places folder.

AOL keeps track of the past 25 places you've visited. This includes windows you open on AOL, pages you view on the Web, and pages you view within a Web site. It also includes things you might not have selected (like the AOL Welcome Screen and Buddy List), but which are open anyway on AOL. You can view this list, your *history trail*, by clicking the down arrow to the right of the address box (Figure 6-7).

To have AOL clear your history trail whenever you sign off AOL, follow these steps:

1. Choose Settings⇨Preferences.
2. In the Preferences window, click Toolbar & Sound.
3. Check the Clear History Trail and Auto-Complete option. Or remove the check to let the history trail span several online sessions, which can be a good way of picking up your browsing where you left off.

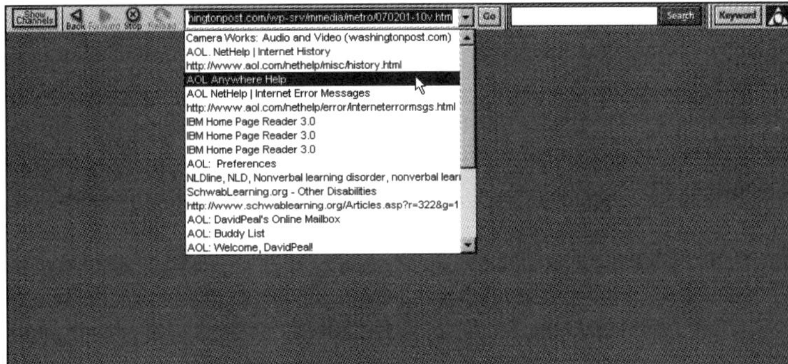

Figure 6-7. AOL's browser lets you return to sites you've visited recently by checking your history trail.

Managing Your Temporary Internet Files

You may notice that when you return to some sites, they load (display) more quickly than when you first visited them. That's because your browser has stored the HTML and the graphics in its *cache,* a folder on your hard drive. (I use the default folder, `C:/Windows/Local Settings/Temporary Internet Files`.) When you visit a page again, your browser uses the cached images instead of the images on the Internet. Fetching files from the cache on your hard drive is much faster than downloading them from some distant Internet computer. These cached items are called *Temporary Internet Files.*

All those stored files take up disk space, and if hard-drive space is at a premium, you may want to get rid of cached items or at least limit the amount of space devoted to them. Another reason to clear your cache from time to time is that cached page elements (pictures and so on) can become out of date, because Web pages change over time. When you revisit a site on the Internet, you don't want to see an old version stored on your hard drive.

The following procedures can help you manage your cache to avoid wasting space or displaying old pages. First, you need to open the Internet Properties box by choosing Settings➪Preferences. In the Preferences screen, click Internet Properties (WWW). Alternatively, you can right-click the Internet Explorer icon on the desktop and choose Properties.

Then consider how up-to-date the pages that you frequent need to be. If you're reading the Odyssey or Shakespeare's plays online, you may not want the cache refreshed; the pages never change. But if you're a stockbroker, you may not want to cache anything, because your data must always be fresh.

As in other things, wisdom lies somewhere between always and never.

To change the way your browser deals with temporary files

1. Click the Settings button in the Internet Properties dialog box. This opens the Settings dialog box shown in Figure 6-8.

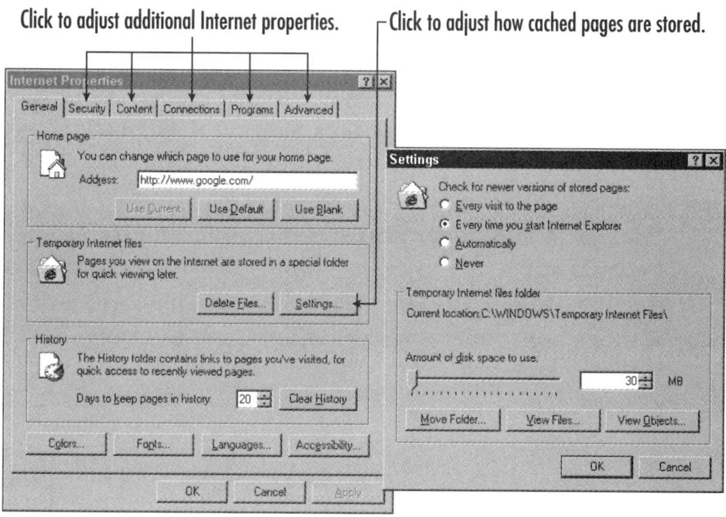

Figure 6-8. Customize the way your browser deals with temporary files by using the Settings box.

2. At the top of the dialog box, select how often you want the browser to check for updated versions of pages stored on your hard drive. Your options range from updating a page every time you request it (not using the cache) to using the cache exclusively.

   In between, if you refresh a page *automatically,* the browser will check the Web page more or less frequently, depending on how frequently the page changes.

At any time, you can update a page by displaying it and then clicking the Reload button.

3. Still in the Settings box, you can specify how much disk space you want to use for storing temporary Internet files, click the Settings button once again.

4. In the Temporary Internet Files Folder section of the Settings box, you see a slider that you can drag right and left to increase and decrease the number of megabytes devoted to your cache.

   Click the spinner's up and down arrows (to the right of the slider) for more precise control.

   How much space to devote to your cache? With high-speed access, you should be able to decrease your cache size since it doesn't take that long to download a fresh copy of any page. Dial-up accounts with slower connections may want to increase their size to speed up their Web rambling. If you spend time with multi-media and gaming sites, a larger cache size may let you store larger files for quicker access later.

5. To delete your temporary files, stay in the General tab of the Internet Options box. In the Temporary Internet Files section, click Delete Files.

   You'll be asked to confirm your desire to remove all cached files.

6. Click OK when you are done making changes in the Settings box. You can always return here to change your preferences.

The Web Is for Everyone

Millions of visually impaired people may need to adjust the size and colors of text and backgrounds to make browsing possible. They're the ones who benefit most from the accessibility features described in this section. For them, the legibility of text depends on factors like line length, letter size, and the color contrast between the text and the background. Between Windows' accessibility settings and the style sheets you can create, all these text variables can be adjusted.

The WWW Consortium, consisting of all the major vendors, recently created guidelines for designing Web pages so that the broadest possible audience can access them. If you create pages, you can find these guidelines at `www.w3.org/WAI`. The consortium's director, Tim Berners-Lee (yes, the same guy who invented the Web), summarizes why the W3 Consortium is creating accessibility standards: "The power of the Web is in its universality."

Seeing pages is only part of the problem of Web accessibility. Some people have limited use of their hands because of a disability, accident, or carpal tunnel syndrome. But with voice-recognition software, they can enter text and thus use e-mail and messaging tools. You can find out more about using such software at AOL Keyword: **Voice Center**.

Customizing Page Appearance

In the AOL browser, you can specify what colors and fonts are used to display the pages that you view on the Web. The color and font preferences have more than cosmetic value. They can make pages more accessible, especially to the millions of people with a visual impairment.

To improve readability by sharpening the color contrast between the text and background color and by enlarging the font, follow these steps:

1. Click the Colors button on the General tab of the Internet Properties dialog box (Figure 6-8) to open the Colors box. The choices in this box determine what

Note

HTML supports three kinds of links: Links that haven't been clicked (unvisited), links that have been clicked (visited), and links that your mouse pointer is touching but that you haven't clicked yet. You can set the color of each type of link by using the Accessibility settings.

colors appear on a page if the page's designer has not specified the colors.

2. In the Colors section, uncheck the Use Windows Colors check box to activate the Text and Background colors buttons. Use those buttons to adjust text and background colors (maximizing the contrast between the colors can make pages easier to read). Click OK.
3. Likewise, clicking the Fonts button on the General tab lets you adjust font type on Web pages.

To change the font *size,* which is essential for the hard-of-seeing or for people working on a laptop outdoors, you need to open up the Microsoft Internet Explorer browser, which is installed for you when you install AOL (and it probably came with your computer, too). Follow these steps:

1. On your Windows desktop, double-click the MSIE "blue e icon," labeled Internet Explorer.
2. From the browser's menu bar, choose View⇨Text Size and then choose one of the text sizes, from Largest to Smallest, as shown in Figure 6-9.
3. Back in AOL, open any page, and you can see the enlarged text size.

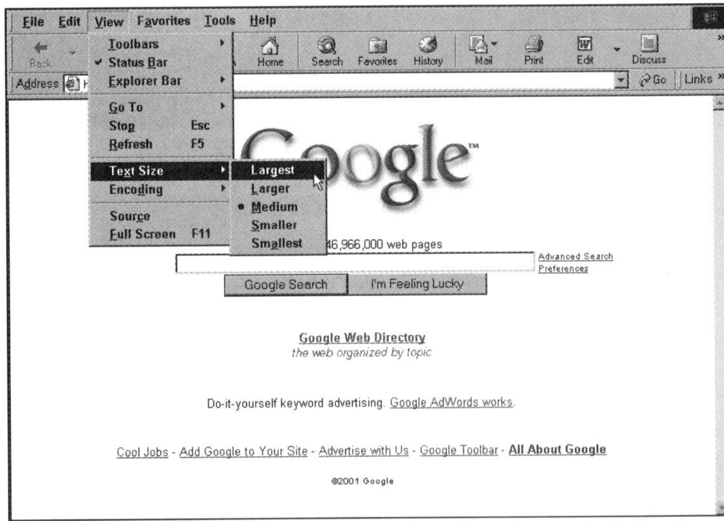

Figure 6-9. Enlarging text can make a site viewable by people with difficulties seeing. You need to use the Microsoft Internet Explorer browser to change the size of the text in the AOL browser.

Multimedia Madness

On today's Web you can listen to interviews with celebrities, watch old movies and music videos, tune in to radio stations, get a graduate degree, and much more. The AOL browser makes it all possible.

The AOL Media Player has been enhanced for the latest version of AOL and will automatically play most of the sound and video you'll encounter on the Web. To make the player your standard way of hearing music and watching video, select Settings⇨Preferences. Click Multimedia. If it's not already checked, click the box next to "Use the AOL Media Player for supported media types," and click Save.

AOL 7.0 also uses *plug-ins,* small programs that automatically open and play the other types of multimedia content. You will encounter such content on the Web. Some plug-ins are embedded in pages, and others run in a new window. All plug-ins work automatically. AOL includes, or makes easily accessible, all the major plug-ins.

- **Shockwave:** Shockwave is used for everything from complex 3-D simulations of real-world processes to imaginative interactive games.
- **Flash:** Similar to Shockwave, the Flash player brings you interactive games and quick-loading, elegant animations. Art museums use it to put their exhibits on display, and artists make their work available in the new format. Hundreds of bright, interactive, occasionally educational games are available in Flash, too, and countless companies are marketing their products with Flash demonstrations.
- **RealPlayer:** RealPlayer is provided free with AOL 7.0. It is used for music, video, or both. Audio "streams" are called RealAudio; video streams are called RealVideo. (*Stream* just means it plays right away; you don't have to download it first.) Many news and sports organizations use RealPlayer for online broadcasting.

  On AOL, the AOL Media Player comes up automatically when you listen to RealAudio radio stations and watch RealVideo movies. However, if the video or music is part of a page (with a player that appears on the page), the AOL Media Player won't appear.

If it's fireworks you want, watch the year-round July 4th display at Happy 4th of July (`www.aristotle.net/july4th/fireworks/show.html`).

Multimedia can best be enjoyed with a high-speed DSL, cable, or satellite connection. Chapter 17 explains your options.

Chapter 15 has much more on using sound and video files.

Find It Online

Another popular video player you may see is QuickTime, which you can get from the Browser Plug-Ins page (`multimedia.aol.com`).

Where to Get Plug-ins

Looking for new plug-ins and exciting new content? Here are some places where you can find many plug-ins to download and use:

- AOL's Browser Plug-Ins page (`multimedia.aol.com/`) has links to places where you can get the latest plug-ins, and it also takes you to examples of new multimedia content.
- For plug-ins of every type, look at the Plugin Site (`www.thepluginsite.com`).

- **Acrobat Reader:** AOL does not include the Acrobat Reader software for viewing pages in PDF format, but you can download it from the Browser Plug-ins Page (`multimedia.aol.com`). PDF documents are highly formatted, attractive documents that have the feel of something printed, with page numbers and a precise layout.

  Making Acrobat (PDF) files requires additional Adobe software, which is not free but can be purchased through Shop@AOL or CNET.

Whenever you encounter content requiring a plug-in that you don't have, your browser can usually do most of the work of getting it for you. Pages with such content usually have a Get Player link or something similar. If you click the link, the software is usually downloaded and automatically installed with no cost and minimal bother.

Bringing Music and Video to the Web with AOL Media Player

Probably more than any technology, RealAudio and RealVideo have made audio and video an everyday part of the Web experience, making it possible to seamlessly experience radio concerts, interviews, news documentaries, and music videos. RealPlayer works its magic thanks to something called *streaming*. On AOL, when you click a link for streaming audio or video based on the Real standard, the AOL Media Player comes up. Figure 6-10 shows the player, with the standard controls. In general, when you have a choice of player in which to view or listen to something, select RealPlayer.

Figure 6-10. AOL Media Player serves most of your audio and video needs on the Web.

RealNetworks (the maker of RealPlayer) has created a large collection of radio, TV, and entertainment links to services that use its player (`www.realguide.com`). Figure 6-11 shows the Real Guide. The selections you make here will play in the AOL Media Player.

Note

Creating Real music and video for RealPlayer (and the AOL Media Player) requires the RealSystem Producer software. A basic, free version of RealSystem is available at `www.real.com`.

Here are some other places to find Real media:

- When you shop at CDNOW on the Web, you can usually sample CD tracks by listening to RealAudio snippets. Listening to snippets is a great way of learning about new music. The clips play in the AOL Media Player.

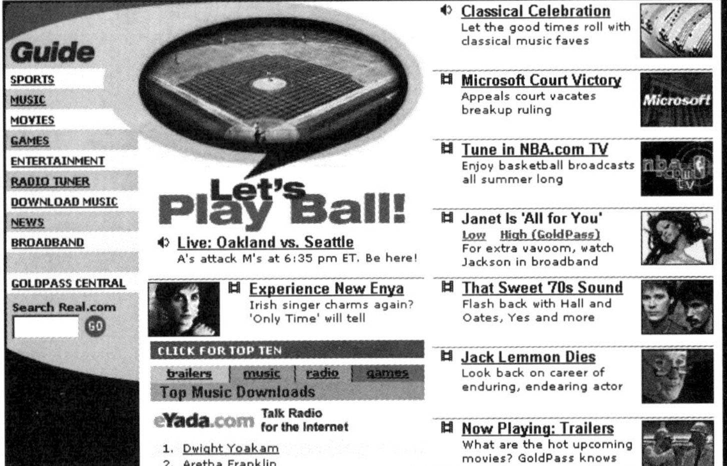

Figure 6-11. The Real Guide provides a directory of Real content that includes baseball games, radio stations, music videos, news programs, and a great deal more.

- BBC Online makes heavy use of RealAudio and RealVideo in its day-to-day news reporting (`www.bbc.com`), as do hundreds of radio and TV sites around the world. BBC radio stations are available around the clock in RealAudio format. The player is embedded unless you select the BBC from the Real Guide (Figure 6-11), in which case it will play in the AOL Media Player (Figure 6-10).
- National Public Radio makes available RealAudio versions of its daily programs, including *All Things Considered* and more than three dozen other shows (`www.npr.com`).

Animating the Web with Shockwave and Flash

Macromedia's Shockwave adds movement and animation to a Web site without making you download gigantic files. And you can use a file without waiting for the entire file to download. Figure 6-12 shows a Shockwave jigsaw puzzle found at Macromedia's Shockwave page (`www.shockwave.com`) in the Games section. Macromedia is the company that developed both Shockwave and Flash.

The Library of Congress has also created a set of jigsaw puzzles, with historical themes of course. Check out Rosie the Riveter. The URL: `memory.loc.gov/ammem/ndlpedu/activity/puzzle/puzintro.html`.

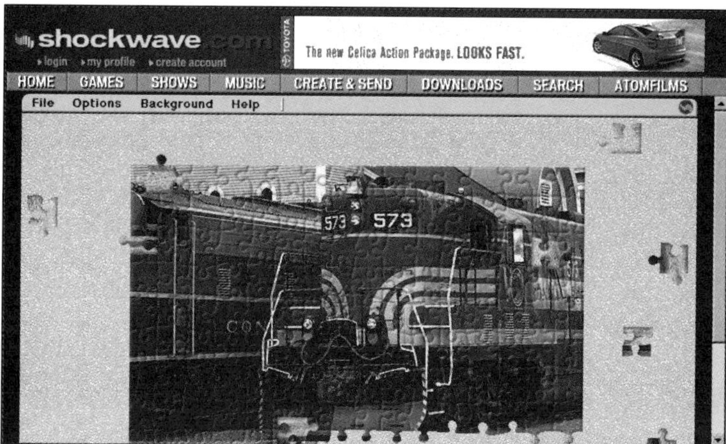

Figure 6-12. At Shockwave.com, drag around the pieces of an online jigsaw puzzle. Make the puzzle as hard as you want, and don't forget about the hints.

Shocked pages bring you games, Dilbert cartoons, physics experiments, and simulations of every sort. I have seen Shocked pages that help students understand the Doppler effect and visualize how a very small change can effect planetary orbits.

Macromedia's Flash, also from Macromedia, is derived from Shockwave and is designed to make fast-downloading animations for the Web. Creative people love Flash's abilities to transform text, images, and sound, without the jerky pace and bitmapped look of traditional video on the Web. I'll be profiling a few Flash sites in the next section.

What's on the Web Tonight?

If reading about multimedia doesn't do much for you, try experiencing it. Make sure your computer's speakers are working, and be prepared for some short waits while the presentations load, especially if you have a dial-up connection.

Use AOL Search (covered in Chapter 8) to find multimedia content in areas of interest to you.

120 Seconds

www.120seconds.com

Part of Canada's CBCRadio 3, 120 Seconds hosts edgy, experimental, often hilarious RealPlayer and Flash short movies and animations. Much of this site's content is wonderfully child-appropriate; some of it less so.

Alien Empire

www.pbs.org/wnet/nature/alienempire

This Flash-powered PBS site is devoted to insects. It teaches kids about them through a series of educational (but cool) presentations and fun puzzles. Kids move through these creations at their own pace.

AtomFilms

www.atomfilms.com

The Animations section includes many Flash and Shockwave short movies, often of high quality. Some of the movies are hosted on Shockwave.com.

Becoming Human

www.becominghuman.org

Later chapters look at other aspects of Internet multimedia. Chapter 16 includes a section on Winamp, which allows you to listen to individual music files. Chapter 18 lists numerous sites where you can find still more videos, movies, and radio stations on the Net.

Produced by the Institute for Human Origins, Becoming Human includes a five-part overview of the evolutionary process. Parts of the overview are narrated animations. You can view other parts of this site at your own pace, a screen at a time, by clicking. Click Resources for a mini-encyclopedia of key terms in archaeology and human evolution.

Flash Film Festival

www.flashfilmfestival.com

The real-world Flash conference features speakers and a competition featuring the industry's most creative online work in a dozen categories. Contestants' Flash creations can be enjoyed year round at this Web site. Spend time exploring sites in different categories, which range from experimental to commercial. Figure 6-13 shows a festival entry called *smallblueprinter.*

With this program, you can drag the elements of an architectural blueprint onto the screen and move them around to make a house or the floor of a building. Then, by clicking the Isometric View and 3-D Walkthrough tabs, you can see the blueprint rendered in 3-D and move through it to experience the space you created.

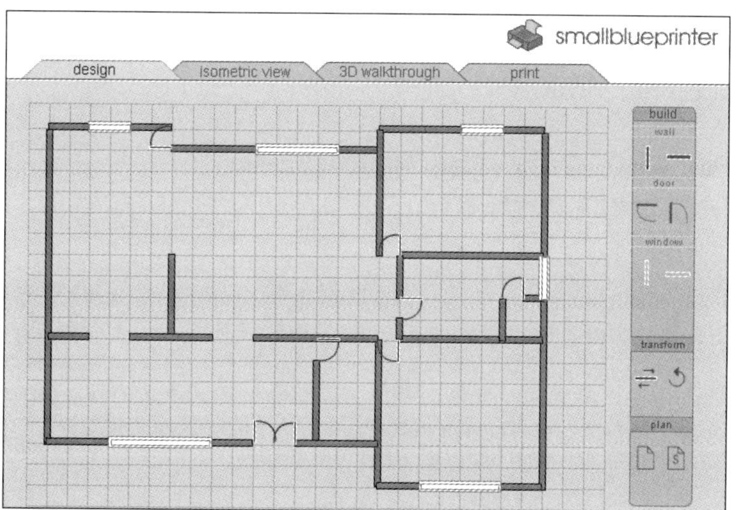

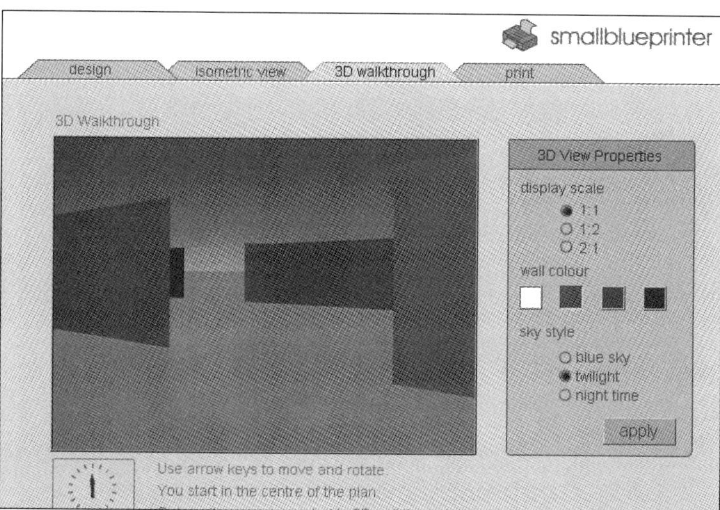

Figure 6-13. From the Flash Film Festival, smallblueprinter lets you create simple architectural blueprints (top) and then move through the space you created (bottom).

Flash Kit Arcade

www.flashkit.com/arcade

Know a teenager with homework to do? Don't even think of telling him (or her) about The Arcade, which has hundreds of interactive games to play: action games, adventure games, classic games, you name it. It forms part of Internet.com's Flashkit.com site, created for the community of Flash developers. (If you make Web pages, check out the large collection of Flash tutorials.)

For Kids Only: The Nickelodeon Channel's Nick Jr.

www.nickjr.com

Many multimedia sites cater to kids in elementary school. This one includes games, stories, music, and art for fans of Franklin the Turtle, Blues Clues, Little Bear, and other popular characters (check out AOL Keyword: **Nick**, too). Figure 6-14 shows a Blues Clues story book that speaks the words and gives kids as much time as they want to read and linger.

Figure 6-14. Blue online.

For Kids Only: Sesame Workshop

AOL Keyword: **Sesame**

Sesame Workshop has tons of games and music for kids, with opportunities for writing and making art as well. Sesame is part of PBS, of course, and its characters, including Clifford and Arthur, have interactive online personae as well as online fan clubs. Start at AOL Keyword: **Character Index**.

h.i.p. Pocket Change

`www.usmint.gov/kids`

Your federal tax dollars have been used, among other things, to create some amazing Web content, such as the U.S. Mint's Flash-powered collection of games for kids. The Puzzle Maker gives kids three minutes to put together a jigsaw puzzle of any of the U.S. state quarters. The Making Sense of Cents animation has a step-by-step cartoon, with sound, that shows children how coins are made and circulated.

History Wired

`historywired.si.edu`

The Smithsonian's National Museum of American History uses this site to make its holdings more available, but it has re-created the museum experience in the process. It's based on new technologies (not Flash or Shockwave) and lets you move through the museum strictly according to your interests, not according to how the rooms are laid out.

National Geographic Online's Sights & Sounds

`www.nationalgeographic.com/ngm`

Start here, at the home of the interactive version of *National Geographic Magazine*. Click Sights & Sounds for National Geographic stories that have been transformed through sounds, videos, text, and images. One Sights & Sounds feature, for example, called "Phantoms in the Night," creatively blends video, Flash, voice-over narration, and the compelling photographs for which National Geographic is famous. As part of the feature, you can listen to jaguar calls.

Poems That Go

www.poemsthatgo.com

In this online poetry gallery, each poem starts with words, of course, but transforms them by adding colors, images, moving letters, voices, and music. If you want to create Flash animations, you can find many ideas here. If you like poetry, you may read poetry differently in the future.

Shockwave.com

www.shockwave.com

Shockwave.com shows off some of the games, puzzles, and entertainment products made with Shockwave. Like sports? Shockwave.com lets you play solitaire and baseball, and the pool game recreates the feel, action, and sounds of playing on a real pool table.

Where to Go from Here

The homely browser began as a way of creating and reading simple text pages. Soon, pictures were added. In a few years, the browser has delivered a whole new medium, with live radio, colorful games, more.

- AOL's Computer Center Channel has a huge amount of information about the Web and browsers.
- This book doesn't really go into making Web pages, but AOL Keyword: **Web Page** can provide everything you need to create your own page.
- For help with your browser, use AOL Keyword: **Nethelp**, and click the World Wide Web subject.
- Chapter 7 is all about Netscape Navigator, an innovative, full-featured, free browser.

Chapter 7

All-Purpose Vehicle: Netscape Navigator

IN THIS CHAPTER **PAGE**

Netscape was the first graphical World Wide Web browser to go mainstream. This chapter introduces the essential features of the latest and best version of Netscape. It has come a long way since it was first released in late 1994, and there are many good reasons for using it:

- **You enjoy the view.** Some sites look best when viewed with a particular browser — that's just how they were designed. For pages tailored to Netscape, you'll want to have the Netscape browser handy. Netscape also has the advantage of complying closely with the Web's standards. On the other side, you may have to use the Microsoft Internet Explorer browser (and the AOL browser, which is based on it) to view some pages that work best with MSIE-tailored Web design.
- **You already know how it works.** You may want to use Netscape simply because you're familiar with it. If you use Netscape at work or school, for instance,

you may find that using Netscape at home is more convenient.

- **You like specific features.** If you do a lot of messaging, for example, you'll like the fact that Netscape Messenger (pretty much the same as AOL Instant Messenger) is built right into the browser. So are path-breaking browser innovations such as My Sidebars and a powerful search capability.

Getting and Installing Netscape 6

In general, Netscape is more like an application than a mere browser, and that alone is a reason to use it when you're not using the AOL browser.

When signed on to AOL, you can run several Internet applications at the same time. For example, you can run Netscape while using the AOL browser.

As an application, Netscape must be downloaded and installed. As an *Internet* application, Netscape requires an Internet connection. That means you must sign on to AOL before opening and using Netscape. If you are away or at work and don't have the AOL software, Netscape runs just fine with any Internet connection, for example, a network or someone else's Internet service provider.

You can download Netscape from the Netscape home page (`www.netscape.com`). Bear in mind that specific download procedures can vary over time, although the overall process remains the same. The following steps can give you a good idea of what to do:

1. Look for the Download button at the top of the page and click it. The Download button looks like a downward-pointing arrow. You are taken to a page where you start the process.
2. In the next page, click Netscape Browsers, one of the several areas from which you can download different kinds of software at Netscape. On the next page that comes up, click Netscape 6 (or the most current version). On separate pages, you may be asked to indicate your language, your operating system, and the specific version of Netscape you wish to download.
3. On the next page, click the Download (or similarly labeled) button. A standard Windows dialog box appears and asks where you want to save the file.

4. Find the directory on your hard drive where you want to save it (for example, the Windows desktop or default Download directory specific in the Download Manager) and then click OK. Be sure to remember where you save the Setup file on your computer.

   The download starts. At this point you are downloading just a small setup program called N6Setup.exe, *not Netscape itself*.

   A dialog box briefly appears on-screen, indicating that the download is taking place. After a short period of time, the download finishes, and the dialog box disappears. At this point in the process, you have downloaded only an installation program called N6setup.exe, not the actual Netscape software.

5. Find and double-click the downloaded file. The setup program now automatically downloads and installs Netscape itself.

   From this point on, follow the on-screen instructions. Agree to the licensing agreement by clicking Accept. When prompted for type of installation, choose Recommended.

6. When you are done, the Netscape program folder appears, with the new icons, and your new browser opens up automatically.

7. The Netscape Activation window prompts you to enter a screen name so that you can access My Netscape, the calendar (essentially the same as My Calendar in AOL), the Instant Messenger software (again, essentially the same as AOL Instant Messenger), and other personal features. You can use the screen name and password you use with AOL or AOL Instant Messenger (Chapter 12).

Getting Familiar with Netscape 6

Netscape 6 (or later) looks involved, because it has so many features. Figure 7-1 can help you sort out the major screen sections and their purposes. Just about everything on-screen can be modified so that you can see more of the actual browser window (on the right). For example, you can reduce the amount of space taken up by My Sidebar (on the left) and the toolbars (at the top).

Maximize Netscape to view the small taskbar buttons (in the lower-left corner) as clearly as possible.

You can start Netscape 6 in several ways. In each case, you must first be signed on to AOL or another Internet service provider. A work, college, or school network would all be fine.

- From the Start menu, choose Programs⇨Netscape 6⇨ Netscape 6.
- On the desktop, double-click the Netscape 6 shortcut icon, which was created during installation.
- Click the taskbar icon. If you don't have a taskbar icon, you can drag the Netscape 6 icon from your desktop to your Windows taskbar, which is ordinarily at the bottom of your Windows desktop. Dragging to the taskbar, by the way, doesn't remove the icon from the desktop. You wind up, instead, with two icons, one on the desktop and the other on the taskbar.

After a moment, Netscape appears, and you can begin to explore the Internet. Figure 7-1 shows Netscape.

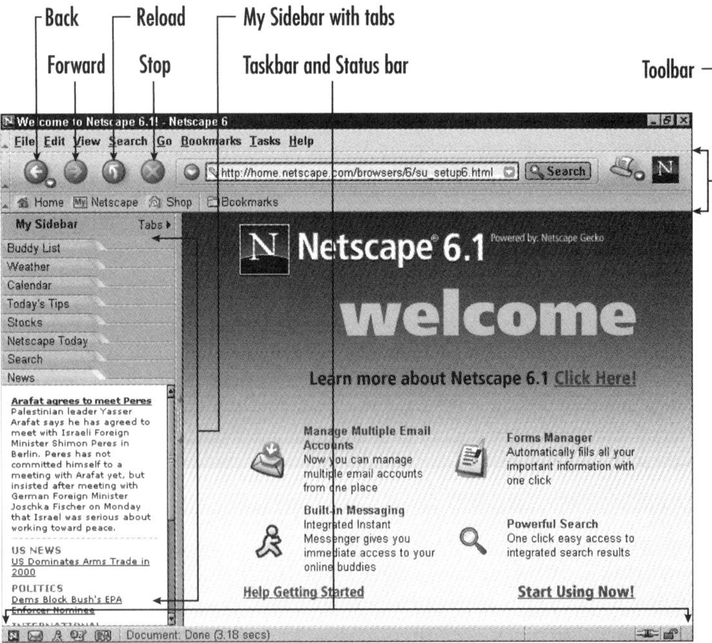

Figure 7-1. In Netscape 6, you'll probably be mostly interested in the browser window. The toolbar and status bar support your activities in the browser window.

Netscape 6's main window has four main parts:

- **Toolbar:** At the top of the Netscape window, you have the toolbar, with three horizontal strips of icons or clickable menu names. Use these bars to control Netscape (the menu bar), navigate the Web (the navigation bar), and visit your favorite online destinations (the personal toolbar). The next section discusses the toolbar in more detail.
- **My Sidebar:** On the left is My Sidebar, which allows you to get customized information without using the browser window.
- **Browser window:** The browser window, which displays any Web site you choose, takes up the main part of the screen.
- **Taskbar and status bar:** At the bottom of the window is a thin strip (a bar) that includes the taskbar on the left and the status bar on the right. The taskbar is used to access Netscape's additional tools, including Netscape Messenger (similar to AOL Instant Messenger) and the Composer page-building tool (described at the end of the chapter). The status bar is part of the browser and displays the progress of pages as they download.

Using Netscape's Toolbar

You use toolbars to tell applications what you want them to do. The Netscape people organized the most commonly used commands so that you can easily see and use them at the top of the Netscape window. Figure 7-2 shows the three toolbars — the menu bar, the navigation toolbar, and the personal toolbar.

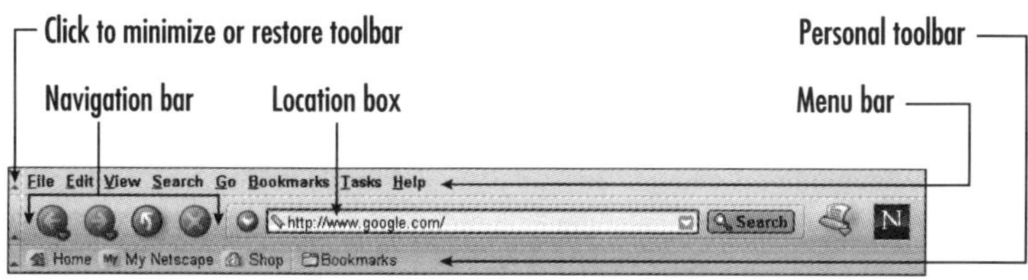

Figure 7-2. Netscape's toolbars are your online dashboard.

You control the buttons on the Personal toolbar, which comes with some likely favorites: your bookmarks, My Netscape, and Shopping.

Choosing File⇨Edit Page is useful if you want to view your own page and edit the HTML.

If you come across a Web page that's in a language you don't understand, Netscape 6 can translate it. Choose View⇨Translate.

These three toolbars can take up a lot of room, especially the navigation bar. To remove them temporarily from view, click the upward-pointing triangle at the far left of any bar. Restore the particular toolbar to view by clicking the now downward-pointing triangle.

Using the Menu Bar

The menu bar groups Netscape commands into eight menus. That's a lot of choices, and sometimes it can be easy to forget what menu command can be found in what menu. As with most programs, it's a good idea to familiarize yourself with all the menus. That way, you know where to find the important commands, such as your preferences (Edit menu) and bookmarks (Bookmarks menu). Many of these commands duplicate actions that you can take by using the sidebar, toolbar, and taskbar.

- **File:** Among the File menu's key commands are those that allow you to open new windows, save files, create Web pages in Netscape Composer (described later), and print a displayed page. You can choose File⇨Open to go to a Web page (HTML file) located on your hard drive. The Print Plus command has a drop-down menu consisting of three choices identical to those in AOL's Print menu (Print Central), described in Chapter 2.
- **Edit:** The Edit menu is principally helpful in editing text. Here also is the home of your preferences, which give you the ability to customize many Netscape features.
- **View:** View⇨Page Source lets you see the HTML (Web code) used to create the displayed page. This feature is useful for people who want to see how someone achieved a particular Web effect. From this menu, you can also make a page's text smaller or larger. View also lets you see (or not see) My Sidebar.
- **Search:** The Search menu provides handy access to various kinds of searches. For example, you can search for a Web page, a word *on* a Web page, and the Internet White and Yellow Pages.
- **Go:** The Go menu gives you access to the essential navigational actions of going backward, forward, and home. Like the AOL Window menu, the Netscape Go menu

includes a list of open pages and recently visited pages for quick backtracking. If you use voice-recognition software that lets you activate menu commands by speaking them, you can use keyboard shortcuts. People who prefer a keyboard to a mouse will appreciate keyboard shortcuts as well.

Like AOL's history trail, the Go menu also includes a list of recently visited pages; choose a page to visit it. The Back and Forward buttons (described later in this chapter) have their own drop-down history trails!

- **Bookmarks:** The Bookmarks menu allows you to add, file, manage, and visit *bookmarks* (favorite Web pages). See "Using Netscape 6's Bookmarks" in this chapter.
- **Tasks:** Use the Tasks menu to carry out Internet-related activities in Netscape 6, such as using the Instant Messenger software (Ctrl+3) and creating a Web page with Composer (Ctrl+4)
- **Help:** This menu can assist you in mastering any of Netscape's myriad features. If a technical support person asks you which version of Netscape you're using, you can find out by choosing Help⇨About Netscape 6. Unlike AOL's Help menu, Netscape's is available only when you are online.

 **Note**

While using Netscape, your Favorite Places, Parental Control settings, and other AOL preferences are *not* available.

Open the Print button's drop-down list and choose Print Plus to access Print Central, Printer Supplies, and Printing Services. Print Plus is the same as Print Central, described in Chapter 2.

Using the Navigation Bar

The four big buttons on the left side of the navigation bar are fairly intuitive. You use them when browsing from page to page, and back, on the Web. See "Navigating with Netscape" for details. They are similar to AOL's four navigation buttons, described in Chapter 6.

The Location box in the middle of the navigation bar is Netscape's equivalent of AOL's address box. Use this box to do one of the following:

- **Go to a specific Web address.** Simply type the address in the box and press Enter.
- **Do a Web search.** Type a search term (such as **ferrets**) that describes what you want to find out about and click Search.

Using the Personal Toolbar

A *bookmark* in Netscape is like a Favorite Place in AOL, which are fully covered in Chapter 3.

Your personal toolbar is a set of buttons, each linked to an online destination that you frequently visit. You can add and remove buttons whenever you want.

First, you might want to remove buttons to make room for new ones:

1. Choose Edit⇨Preferences.
2. In Netscape's Preferences box, click Navigator.
3. In the Select the Buttons You Want to See in the Toolbars box in the lower left, uncheck the items that you don't want to appear.
4. Click OK.

To add a button to the personal toolbar, see the instructions in the "Using Netscape 6's Bookmarks" section of this chapter.

Using My Sidebar

Netscape 6 has an information-packed feature called My Sidebar, which is essentially a window that slides out from the left side of the Netscape browser window. If you don't see the sidebar, press the F9 key or simply click My Sidebar's handle. You can always drag the sidebar right and left to adjust the amount of space it uses. Click the handle again to close it.

The sidebar is organized in what is called a *tabbed* interface, as shown in Figure 7-3. Each tab is like a filing-cabinet drawer that slides open when you click it. When you open a tab, its contents appear in a folder-shaped area. When you're done using a tab, you can click the top to close it again. The layering of the tabs allows many panels to fit into My Sidebar and creates a clean, compact interface; it's there when you need but can be closed when you don't.

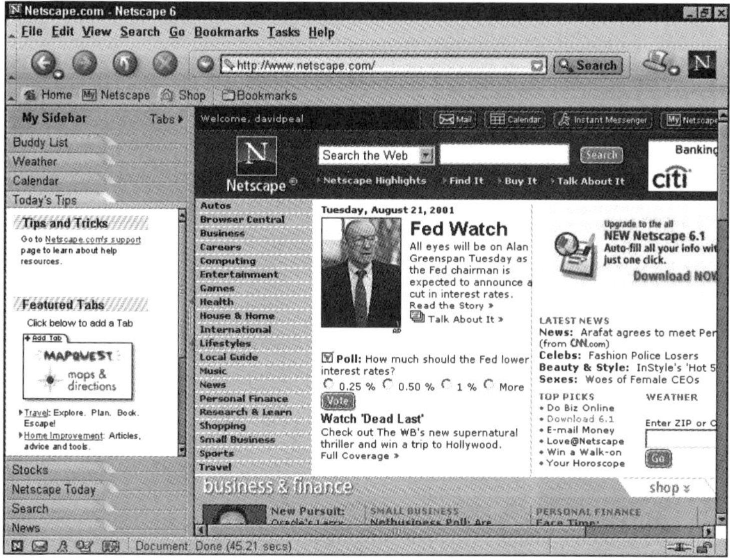

Figure 7-3. The Today's Tips tab on My Sidebar.

Among the tabs that come with Netscape are

- **What's Related:** Open this tab to see a list of pages related to the page that you're viewing in the browser window. What's Related collects information on the browsing habits of many people. If you don't want your browsing behavior recorded, remove the What's Related panel, as explained in "Adding and Deleting Tabs."
- **Buddy List:** AOL Instant Messenger has been a huge hit. A version of it is fully integrated into Netscape Navigator and can be accessed from the Buddy List panel. To use AIM on Netscape, you can use the screen name and password that you used to register AIM. After you're registered, the same Buddy List you see in AOL and AIM appears in the Buddy List panel in My Sidebar. Double-click any of your buddies on the list to summon up a Netscape-version of AOL Instant Messenger, with familiar features (see Chapter 12) but a slightly different look.

The Search tab uses the same list and tools as AOL Search (see Chapter 8).

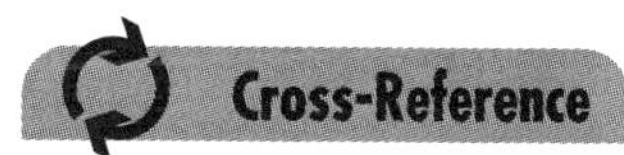

Chapter 12 is devoted to AIM.

To send an instant message, open the Buddy List tab and click the Sign On button. When signed on, your Buddy List appears. Right-click an online buddy and choose Send Instant Message. To send a message to someone not on your list, click the Send an Instant Message button above the list (see Figure 7-4). The button's icon shows a small arrow and a message.

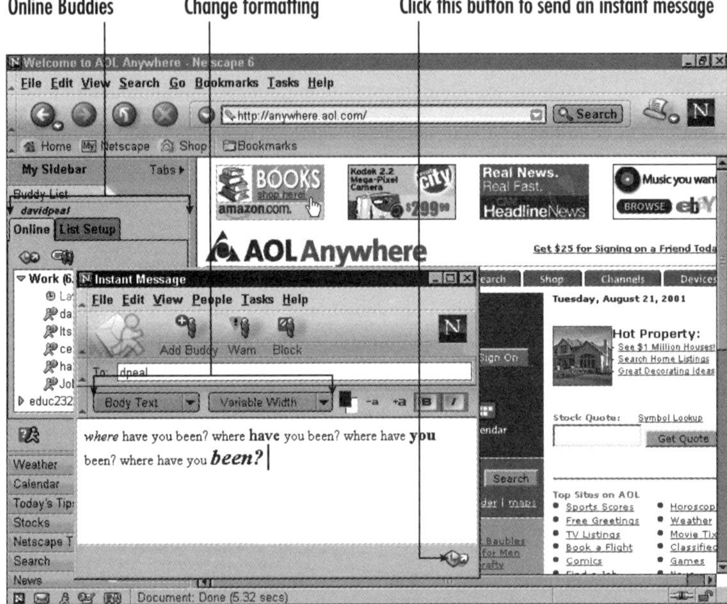

Figure 7-4. Netscape Messenger works like AOL Instant Messenger, but in an even more compact space.

- **Stocks:** This tab displays any stocks you have entered into a personal stock portfolio. If you've never modified your portfolio, then you see the default display of the major market indexes. To create your own portfolio, click View Portfolio Manager to open the Portfolio window in the browser. Look for a Customize link. Follow the on-screen instructions to add information about individual stocks and funds.
- **News:** Click this tab to see headlines from CNN.com, AP, Sportsline, and other news services. Headlines that you click on the tab appear in the browser window on the right.

Adding and Deleting Tabs

You can remove any of the tabs that come with My Sidebar and add others. Note that removing a tab merely removes it from view; the tab isn't deleted entirely. You can always restore it later.

Here are the steps for adding and deleting Sidebar tabs:

1. Open Netscape 6. If your sidebar isn't showing, choose View➪My Sidebar or press the F9 key.
2. On the sidebar's top-right corner is a Tabs button (See Figure 7-5). Click it to reveal the Tabs menu.
3. Choose any checked item to deselect it. Likewise, choose an unchecked item to select it and add that tab to My Sidebar.
4. To choose from a larger set of tabs, use the Tabs menu again and choose Customize Sidebar. The Customize My Sidebar window appears. On the left is a list of available tabs, arranged in categories (NetBusiness, International, and so on); click a category to see the tabs available. On the right is a list of tabs currently in your sidebar.

For even more tabs, click the Find More Tabs button at the bottom of the Customize My Sidebar window.

To change the position of a tab in My Sidebar, choose it from the list on the right in the Customizing My Sidebar window, and click the Up or Down button.

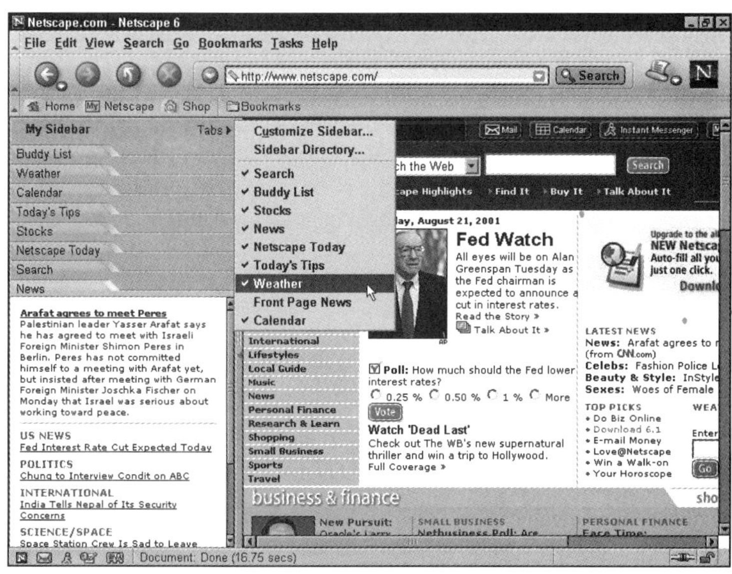

Figure 7-5. Use the Tabs menu to manage tabs you see in My Sidebar.

- To add a tab to your sidebar, click the arrow to see the tabs in a category, skim the available tabs, choose the one you want, and click Add. If you want to know what's inside a tab, select it and click the Preview button at the bottom of the window. Another window displays the contents that would appear in your sidebar. Close the window when you're done.

  At the bottom of the window, the Find More Tabs button takes you to many additional tabs, including WebCalendar, which picks up event and appointment information from AOL's My Calendar.
- To remove a tab from My Sidebar, click it once in the right panel of the Customize My Sidebar window and click the Remove button. (This is another way of removing tabs, in addition to the one described in Step 3.)

5. After you're done adding and removing tabs, click OK.

Customizing Content

You can customize the content of some tabs. For example, you can build a News tab that shows local and national news, the weather, and other features of interest to you.

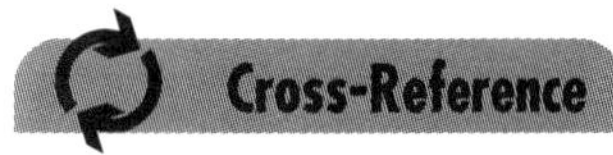

My AOL and My Netscape are intended to provide the one place on the Web where you can receive customized information — weather, stocks, news, horoscope, and so on. For more, see Chapter 3.

How does this work? Just as AOL has My AOL, Netscape has My Netscape — a Web page whose content and layout you customize. The two pages differ in content and purpose: My Netscape is a page you use to customize content in My Sidebar. My AOL is a page you use to identify the content you want to appear either on the Web (when you're away from the PC where you use AOL) or on an AOL Anywhere device.

To customize the tab content, you must first customize the My Netscape content, as follows:

1. Choose Tabs⇨Customize Sidebar. The Customize My Sidebar box opens.
2. Click a tab from the list on the right. If the Customize Tab button lights up at the bottom of the window (*lights up* means becomes legible and thus clickable), you can modify the panel's content. (If Stocks is selected, for example, and the button is clickable.)
3. You'll be taken to My Netscape page. Scroll to the section of My Netscape you wish to modify, and click the

Edit button in the section's upper-right corner. Instructions in the edit window walk you through the process. While using My Newscape, you can customize other sections, too. If tabs are based on those sections, their content will reflect your customizations.

4. Click Save when you are done with your modifications to My Netscape and close the My Netscape window. Click OK to close the Customize My Sidebar window.

Navigating with Netscape

Shown in Figure 7-1 and Figure 7-3, the browser window is simply the place where you view Web pages. That is, it's where just about everything happens in Netscape. A Web page is the basic unit on Netscape — as on every browser — and each page has its own address.

If you want to visit a Web page on Netscape and you know its address, follow these steps:

1. Type its Web address (such as **www.aol.com**) into the Location box (refer to Figure 7-2). As with AOL, you can leave off the `http://` part of an address.
2. Press Enter, and Netscape takes you to the page you requested. *Don't click the Search button — you'll do a search for the URL.*

You can also visit a page without knowing its address, by

- Choosing it from your personal toolbar, discussed earlier in this chapter, or your Bookmarks menu, described later.
- Clicking any link on any displayed page. As in AOL's browser, you can tell a link by the shape of your mouse cursor. Just move your cursor over the link, and it changes from an arrow into a pointing finger.

When you browse from page to page, you create a sort of *trail*, or list, consisting of the page names and addresses you visited, one page after another. Like all browsers, Netscape lets you go backward along the trail to revisit pages you've seen, and then forward to return to the page where you left off. You follow your trail of pages by using the big Back and Forward buttons

Caution

Netscape 6 has no equivalent of AOL's Parental Controls. To restrict the sites children can access or the amount of time they can spend online with Netscape, parents must use filtering software (see Chapter 4).

The keyboard alternative for typing in a specific URL to visit is Ctrl+L, which brings up the Open Web Location box.

on the left side of Netscape's navigation bar. Figure 7-6 shows these two buttons, as well as Reload and Stop. (It's useful to think of these buttons as two pairs.)

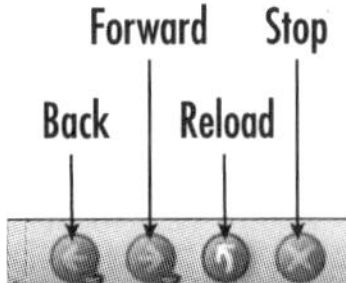

Figure 7-6. Back displays the previously viewed page; Forward displays the next page. Reload downloads a page again; Stop prevents a page from downloading.

The two other buttons have to do with the page you are currently viewing. Remember that browsing the Web means downloading a Web page to your computer, where your browser displays it. The Reload and Stop buttons give you some control of the process of retrieving individual Web pages:

- ▶ The Reload button lets you redisplay a page that has either not completely downloaded (parts are missing) or not downloaded at all (the browser window is empty, and nothing is happening).
- ▶ The Stop button lets you stop a page from downloading if it's taking too long or you changed your mind. You can also stop a page by pressing the Esc key, as in AOL. After you stop a page, try refreshing it to see if it downloads correctly.

Netscape, like the AOL browser, keeps track of the pages that you've visited, so you can revisit them.

- ▶ The drop-down menu in the Location box shows only the specific sites you've seen, not the individual pages within them. It shows *site names*.
- ▶ For revisiting specific pages, click the small arrow just under either the Back or Forward button. You see a history of previous pages seen and (if you've backtracked) subsequent pages. These lists show actual Web addresses.

Like the AOL browser, the Netscape browser lets you right-click a displayed Web page to copy text and images, view HTML, open links in new windows, and so on. As in AOL, the choices vary, depending on which element you right-click.

Searching the Web

Netscape 6 offers two major ways to do a Web search: using the Search sidebar to manage a search and searching exclusively within the browser window.

To find out more about doing Web searches, see Chapter 8 (on AOL Search) and Chapter 9 (on using other search tools).

Searching the Web (1): My Sidebar

One of the major uses of any browser is to conduct searches for specific information. If you want to look for something on the Web and you're using Netscape 6, My Sidebar's Search tab offers a key advantage. That is, you can see your search results and actual retrieved pages at the same time (the results are in the sidebar tab, on the left, and the pages are in the browser window, on the right). You don't have to use the Back button to go from back and forth from your results page to the pages retrieved by the search.

To do a search using the Search tab:

1. Open the Search tab.
2. Type the word or words that you're looking for in the field at the top of the tab.
3. Select the search engine to use. You can choose more than one search tool if you want.
4. Click the Search button.

   The results appear in the browser window on the right, with a summary list of the same results in the Search tab itself. If you use several search engines, each result has an icon indicating the search engine that retrieved it. Not surprisingly, different engines retrieve the same pages, though each engine has its quirks and will return pages the other one missed. Figure 7-7 shows the results of a simultaneous search using all search engines.
5. Click any promising link in the Search tab to view a page in the browser window to the right.
6. To save the results of a search, click Bookmark This Search button on the Search tab. To return to the list later, open the Bookmarks menu. You will find the search results in a folder at the bottom of the Bookmarks menu.

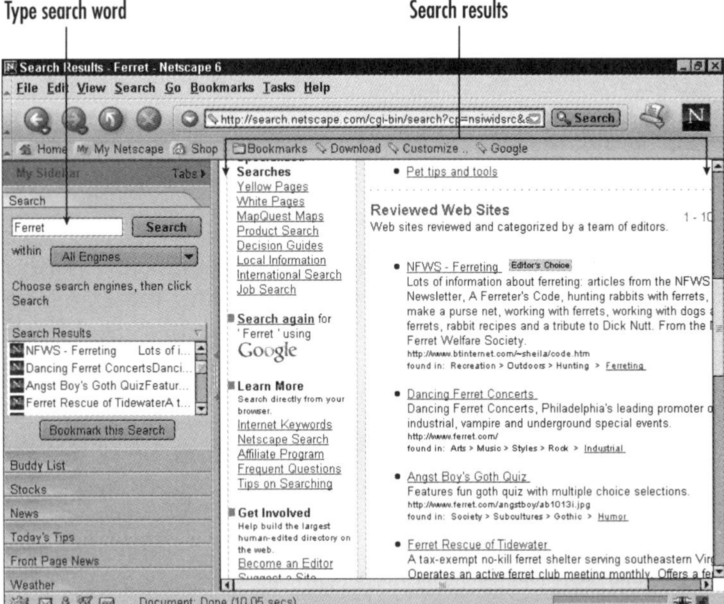

Figure 7-7. Click a result from the search results in My Sidebar (left) and see the results in the browser window (right).

Searching the Web (2): Location Box

The Location box does more than provide a place to type in a Web address. It is also a search box where you can type search terms describing what you are looking for. Using the Location box puts search capabilities at your fingertips, since you don't have to use a special search interface.

As with AOL Search, your Netscape searches from the Location box and Search tab begin with the Netscape Open Directory, a directory of hand-selected Web sites, discussed in Chapter 8.

For example, suppose you want to find information about ferrets, the curious creatures that like to burrow (sort of like a good search engine):

1. Type **ferret** into Netscape's Location box and click Search (*don't press Enter*).
2. The results appear in the browser window and also in the Search tab, just as when you started from the Search tab in the previous section. You can use the tab to save the search results as a bookmark for later retrieval.

Searching the Web (3): Netscape Search Page

Using either the Search tab or Location box to do a search has the advantage that your results in either case appear in the Search tab. This means that you can click results on the left and view the retrieved pages on the right. If you want to use the entire browser window (with My Sidebar closed), you can use the Netscape Search Page, shown in Figure 7-8.

To get there, you can either

- Click Netscape's Search button on the navigation bar.

  or

- Choose Search⇨Search the Web.

In the Netscape Search Page, select a search page for this search. If you want to use one of the engines offered (which currently include Netscape, Google, Lycos, GoTo, and others), put a check next to Keep *Name of Search Engine* as My Search Engine. To do the actual search, simply type in the search term(s) or phrase(s) into the Search the Web or Ask a Question box, and click the button to the right. (The name of the button changes with the engine chosen.)

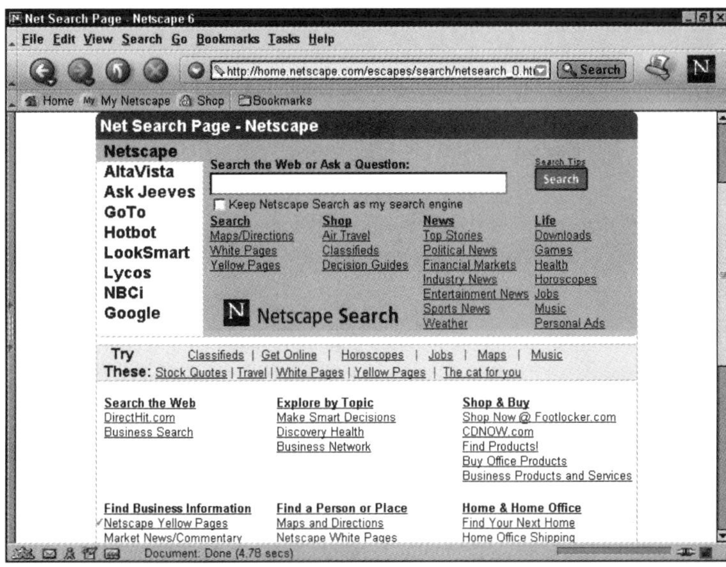

Figure 7-8. From Netscape to Google, choose any search engine listed here to run your searches.

Finding Words on a Page

Sometimes when you do a search and click a page to see what you found, you have no idea why the page was returned. It often helps to look for the search term on the page itself, to find out the context in which the term or terms are used. On long pages, searching for a specific word is often essential.

To find a word on a page:

1. Choose Search⇨Find in This Page (or just press Ctrl+F).
2. In the Find in This Page box, type the word, phrase, or other characters (in a row) that you want to find.
3. Choose from the search options, such as matching upper or lower case.
4. Click Find or press Enter to begin the search. Press Enter repeatedly to run the search again to see how often and in what contexts the word appears.

Setting Up a New Home Page

A *home page* is the Web page that you see when you open the browser program. You can have Netscape open to any page — the Netscape home page (the default), your company site, your personal favorite site, a search engine (which I do), or something else. If there's a specific page with a complex address to use as your home page, display the page before starting.

1. Choose Edit⇨Preferences. The Preferences window appears. With Navigator selected on the left, your home-page options appear on the right.
2. In the When Navigator Starts Up section, you have three choices: making your home page a blank page, opening to a specific home page, or opening to the page displayed when you quit Netscape the last time. Make a selection.

If you select Home Page, you must complete the Home Page section (Step 3). If you select something other than Home Page, you're done; click OK.

3. In the Home Page section, type the Web address of the desired home page. Or, with the page of your intended home page displayed, click the Use Current Page button.
4. Click OK. Now, every time you start Netscape 6 or click the Home button on the navigation bar, you'll return to your newly selected page.

Using Netscape 6's Bookmarks

Bookmarks are Netscape's way of helping you keep track of your favorite sites on the Web. After you bookmark a site, you can return to it by choosing the site from the Bookmarks menu.

Although you can bookmark any number of pages in a site, lower-level pages are more likely to disappear or change address than top-level pages.

Adding Bookmarks

To bookmark a Web page so that you can easily go back to it later, follow these steps:

1. Display the page that you want to bookmark. Right-click and select Bookmark this Page from the pop-up menu that appears.
2. The Add Bookmark window appears, as shown in Figure 7-9. Select the folder where you want to put the new bookmark. The default folders include the Personal Toolbar Folder and Best of the Web.
3. To create a new folder, click the New Folder button. In the resulting Create New Folder window, type in a name for the folder and click OK. The new folder appears, selected, in the Add Bookmark window. Leave it selected if you want to put the new bookmark in this folder.
4. Click OK.

To bookmark, you can also press Ctrl+B to add the page to the bottom of the actual Bookmark folder.

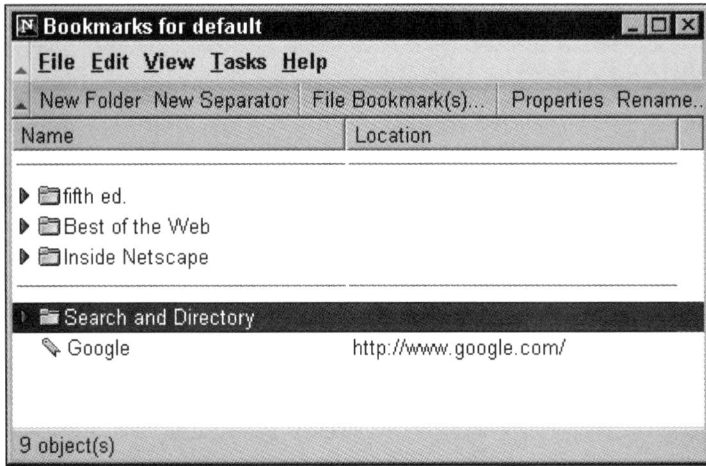

Figure 7-9. The Add Bookmarks window allows you to assign a bookmark to a folder when you first save it.

Arranging Your Bookmarks for Easy Access

Over time, you may want to add new folders and groups of folders to your Bookmark list, move bookmarks between folders, and delete both folders and bookmarks. You can easily accomplish these tasks in the main Bookmark window, which is always available by pressing Ctrl+B or choosing Bookmarks⇨Manage Bookmarks.

To delete or rename bookmarks and folders, right-click the item and select Delete or Rename.

Adding Folders to Manage Your Bookmarks

To start managing your bookmarks, it usually makes sense to create folders for the specific types of bookmarks you are saving (possible new folders include *vacation*, *music sites*, *baseball*, and so on).

1. Choose Bookmarks⇨Manage Bookmarks (same as Ctrl+B). The Bookmarks window appears, showing you a list of existing folders and bookmarks.
2. Select the bookmark *after which* you want the new folder to appear.

   Or, to create a folder within a folder, *double-click* the folder within which you want the new folder to appear.

3. Click the New Folder button on the Bookmark window's toolbar. The Create New Folder box comes up.

4. Type the name of the new folder and click OK. A small folder appears in the place identified in Step 2, with the name you typed in this step.

Placing a Bookmark into a Folder

To place an existing bookmark in a folder for easy retrieval later:

1. Open the Bookmarks window (Ctrl+B).
2. Click and drag the bookmark into a folder. To put more than one bookmark in the same folder, hold down the Ctrl and click each bookmark to be moved. Then drag them into the folder.

   If you have a long or complex set of bookmarks and folders to move, dragging them through the Bookmark window can be difficult. Instead, select the bookmarks and then click File Bookmark(s) on the window's toolbar. In the Choose Folder window (otherwise identical to the Add Bookmark window shown in Figure 7-9), you see a list of existing folders. Select the folder into which to move the bookmark(s). Click OK.

A *divider* or *separator* (File⇨New Separator) is a horizontal line. This line provides a visual cue used to group related bookmarks and folders.

If you use the Microsoft Internet Explorer browser, your MSIE Favorites are imported as a folder into the Bookmarks window (Imported IE Favorites).

Visiting a Bookmarked Web Site

The Netscape 6 Bookmarks menu operates in the same way as the AOL 7.0 Favorites menu. Each Favorite Places folder corresponds to an item in the AOL Favorites menu. Likewise, each folder in your Bookmark window corresponds to a menu item in the Bookmarks menu. Each subfolder is a submenu, and so on. In both AOL and Netscape, uncategorized Favorite Places/bookmarks will be separately listed in the menu and can be directly selected.

To visit a bookmark in Netscape, select it from the appropriate menu or submenu of the Bookmarks menu. Highlighting a folder displays a submenu showing the individual bookmarks in the folder.

Using Netscape Composer

Composer is a visual tool for building Web pages, available free with every copy of Netscape 6. This page-design software is available by clicking the icon on the lower-left corner of the Netscape window. The Composer icon looks like a pad of paper with a pencil positioned above it. Chapter 16 profiles Composer and includes an illustration of this powerful software.

Where to Go From Here

This chapter covers the core functions of Netscape 6 — browsing, searching, using My Sidebar, and managing bookmarks.

- ▶ If you can't find the answer to a question about Netscape 6 in this chapter, use the Help menu for assistance with Netscape, Composer, and the Internet in general.
- ▶ If you're technically inclined, you can find out more about the Mozilla project, upon which Netscape 6 is based (`www.mozilla.org`).
- ▶ Entire books have been devoted to Netscape over the years, including *Netscape and Communicator Bible* (Hungry Minds, Inc).

Chapter 8

Internet Searching Made Easy with AOL

Everything is searchable these days. You can search for files on your computer and for words in your files. You can search for definitions in online dictionaries and for books to buy online. You can search the holdings of the Library of Congress, and of course, you can search the Web. But the Web's so big, and there are so many types of content to search for. Where do you start?

This chapter introduces AOL Search, AOL's comprehensive solution to online searching. AOL Search features a topical directory of about three million handpicked Web sites. You can also do a broader search, using AOL Search's list of (currently) about half a billion pages. In one place, AOL Search provides the tools for searching the Web, searching AOL, *and* searching non-Web content such as maps, e-mail addresses, and White and Yellow Page listings.

The AOL Search Solution

Until recently, there seemed to be more search engines than Web pages worth searching. Rather than focus on accuracy and simplicity, these search engines tried to distinguish themselves by collecting as many sites as possible and then adding all sorts of stores, information kiosks, and advanced search features of interest to few. AOL Search, however, focuses on search in its many forms, and provides a single site for all your searches.

At its core, AOL Search is based on a hand-selected and carefully organized directory of Web sites. The directory's goal is not to collect *all* pages, but to collect the most informative and reliable ones for any subject. Over twenty thousand volunteer editors have helped AOL's effort in this area for several years. The effort of creating the directory grew from the Netscape Open Directory Project (`www.dmoz.org`). Many other Web search services, such as Google, Netscape, and Lycos, rely on this directory. The directory organizes its sites into intuitive, meaningful categories that correspond to the way people actually think about a subject. You can see these categories on the opening page of AOL Search (AOL Keyword: **Search**), shown in Figure 8-1.

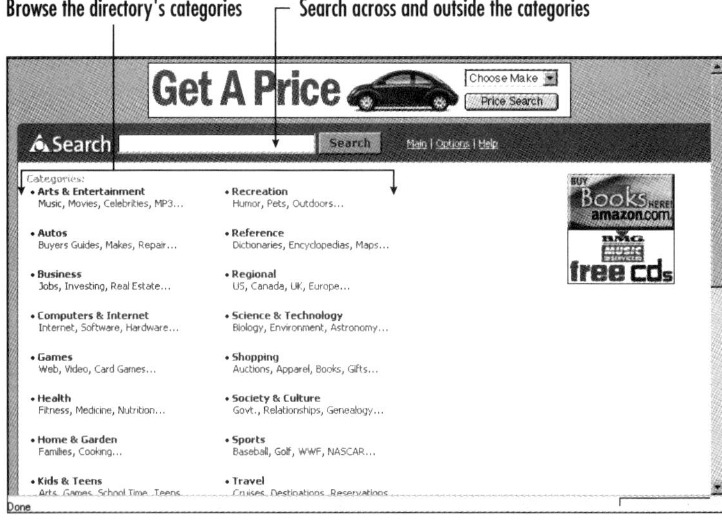

Figure 8-1. AOL Search's opening page. Start clicking categories to browse the directory or type a search term into the text box to search a larger, unfiltered group of Web sites.

When you use AOL Search, you can start by browsing this directory of hand-selected sites. You can also start by doing a search for specific information. The next section looks at the difference between searching and browsing.

Browsing or Searching?

Let's say you want to buy a dog.

If you don't know much about dogs, you probably want some general information. To get that information, you can *browse* through the categories of AOL Search's directory. You might start at the most general, relevant category (Recreation, in this case) and then move from the Pets category to the even narrower category of Dogs. Here you can find general-purpose Web sites, such as the Dog Owner's Guide and online areas available only on AOL. You will also find even narrower categories, such as Grooming, Health, and Training. Eventually you find the specific sites — and you may need to consult several — with the sort of information you need.

Browsing categories guarantees that you'll find sites about the topic of interest, but sometimes such sites can be sprinkled through many categories. How do you find all of them? And how do you find information that is so specific that it could be buried in sites that might not seem relevant through simple browsing?

Do a *search*! Searching the Web — with the help of a *search engine* — gives you access to a much larger database than does a directory. But searching is a different thing than browsing. In the dog search, you might search specifically for breeders, pet stores, and vets in your community.

Definition

A *search engine* is online software that maintains a huge list of Web sites. You type in a *search term* that indicates what you want to find (such as, **vacation rentals Oregon**), and the engine searches its lists for pages containing those words.

The results can be more satisfying, but in return, you'll need to

- Think of search terms — words and phrases — that convey what you are looking for. Sometimes, reworking a search term is required to get the results you want.
- Evaluate the large number of pages that most searches retrieve when you use a large engine like AOL Search.

Ultimately, browsing and searching reward you with answers to questions you care about. The next section focuses on the process of searching.

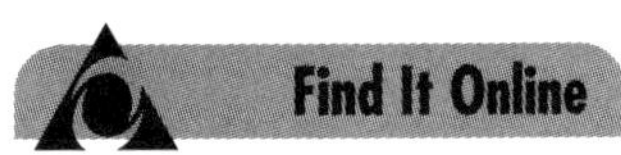

For help using AOL Search, go to AOL Keyword: **Search**.

Using AOL Search

To browse and search, you start at AOL Search. You can go to the opening page for AOL Search (see Figure 8-1) in several ways:

- Go to AOL Keyword: **Search**.
- Click the Search button on the AOL navigation bar.
- Visit `search.aol.com` with any browser at your disposal if you're away from home and don't have access to the AOL software.
- On the AOL navigation bar, type a word or words in the search box, which is next to the Search button, and click the Search button.
- From the AOL Services menu, choose Internet⇨Internet Start Page. The Internet Connection page includes a prominently labeled text box in which you can do searches.
- While using AOL Instant Messenger, type in some search terms where it says Search the Web and click Go. AOL Search opens up and displays your search results.

A *search term* or *search query* contains the words you choose to describe what you are looking for. *Search results* are the Web pages that include your search term.

A Sample Search: Basset Hounds

Searching the Net doesn't take much more training than searching the cereal section of the supermarket, and can be comparably successful. Both require that you try to keep your purpose in mind despite the distractions everywhere you turn.

To do an effective search, just do two simple things:

1. Start with an ordinary question, such as "Do I really want a basset hound as a pet?"
2. Identify the key words that describe your interest and order them from specific to general. Key words in this case are *basset*, *hound*, and *pet*. The rest of the words are too general and have nothing to do with your search.

Voilà, you have a query (*basset hound pet*) that you can use in AOL Search. A *query* consists of a word or words that sum up what you want to find. It's a fancy word for *search term*.

In the search box on the navigation bar, type **basset hound pet** and click Search. After the search query is run through both the AOL Search directory and the larger list of Web sites in AOL's search engine, the results appear, as shown in Figure 8-2.

For more information on wording and refining queries, read the tips for asking good questions in Chapter 9.

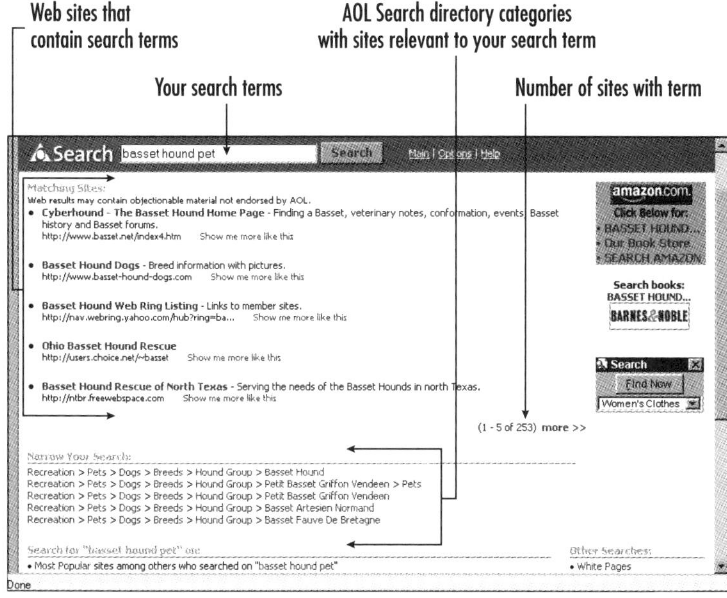

Figure 8-2. Use the results from AOL Search to find out about basset hounds as pets.

Interpreting Your Search Results

Doing a search can make you aware of the size of the Web. Often all the *hits* (or individual search results) don't fit on one page; often they require dozens or hundreds of pages. Generally, the first few pages of results will be the most relevant.

Your search will include AOL content only if you are signed on to the AOL service at the time. Otherwise, your search will be Web only.

AOL Search shows you a handful of sites at a time. At the bottom of the page, there's a More link that you can click to see the next page of sites. Click the Back link to revisit previously viewed pages of results. You can see the More link in Figure 8-2. The Back link appears only on subsequent pages.

Your results page(s) has sections that include

- **Recommended Sites.** AOL Search sometimes (but not in every case) presents a Recommended Sites section at the top of your results list. These are usually AOL sites or Official Sites related to your search.
- **Matching Sites.** These are Web pages found not only in the Open Directory, but in a search using AOL's search engine. AOL includes a warning about the possible inappropriateness of the search results. Some sites are not in the AOL Search directory and may have content that doesn't meet AOL's Terms of Service.
- **Narrow Your Search.** This section includes Open Directory subcategories that you can click to find groups of sites of likely relevance to your search terms.

In the Matching Sites section, each search result, such as the one shown in Figure 8-3, has several parts. Each part can provide useful information to help you decide whether to click the link and visit the site. Each AOL Search result includes the following:

- **The Web page's title.** For example, *Cyberhound — The Basset Hound Home Page*.
- **A description of the page or site.**
- **The Web address (URL) of the linked page.** You may find the Web address useful if you print the AOL Search results for reference. The address can give you information about the content, too. The address, `basset.net`, suggests that the site is devoted to basset hounds.
- **A Show Me More Like This link.** If you see this link and think that the search results list is especially good, click the link to find more such pages.

• **Cyberhound - The Basset Hound Home Page** - Finding a Basset, veterinary notes, conformation, events, Basset history and Basset forums.
http://www.basset.net/index4.htm Show me more like this

Figure 8-3. Each search result includes several elements.

Extending Your Search

After you check out the search results for your first query, you can run it through other search tools and look for other kinds of information. Try using the handy links in the Search for . . . On section, which is at the bottom of your search results page (see Figure 8-4).

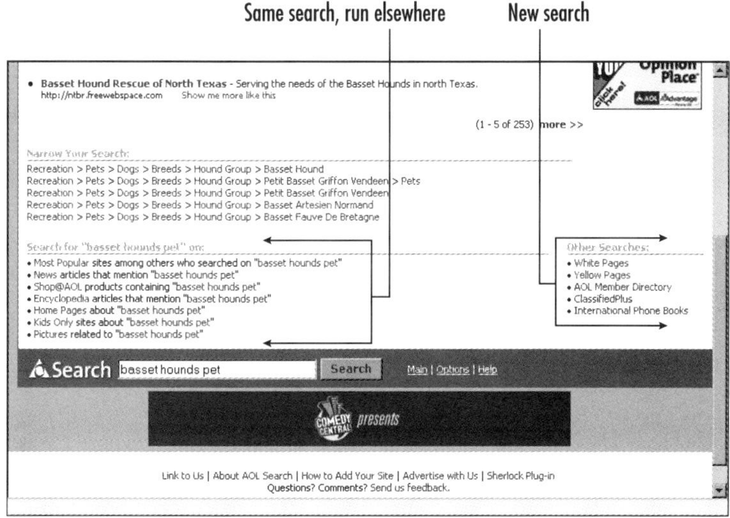

Figure 8-4. Extend your search by searching for non-Web content, such as news stories and home pages.

When you use AOL Search, you can find the following useful links in the Search for . . . On section:

- **Most Popular:** Click this link to check out the results of related queries asked by other AOL Search users.
- **News:** Click this link to look for news articles that relate to basset hounds. These articles are drawn from the major news feeds and archived at AOL. (Don't be surprised if you don't retrieve too many stories about basset hounds.)
- **Shop@AOL:** Click here to buy a basset hound T-shirt, brooch, sign, coffee cup, statue, etc. (Not a bad idea if you need a gift for a hound enthusiast!)

- **Encyclopedia:** This link takes you to articles in the World Book Online that are about or that mention basset hounds. For information searches, the Encyclopedia link often produces the most useful results.
- **Home Pages:** See who has created personal pages mentioning basset hounds and made them available at AOL Hometown.
- **Kids Only:** Look for basset hound sites on AOL Search for Kids. As it turns out, a basset hound site isn't available, but broadening the search to *hounds* or *dogs* produces a rich yield of sites.
- **Pictures:** This link takes you to pictures that relate to your search topic. In the basset hound search, the images seem to come from pictures that appear on Web sites about basset hounds.

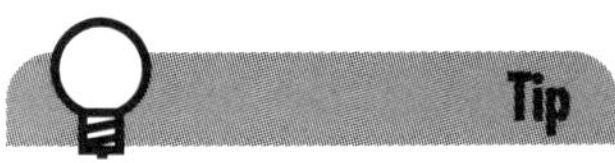

A new service from AOL (`images.google.com`) also lets you use Google to search for pictures.

Finally, the Other Searches list, which is on the right of the page shown in Figure 8-4, lets you start a new search for specific data, such as phone numbers and online classifieds.

Refining Your Search

You can refine your query by adding or editing words to make your search term more precise or more accurate, or both. For example, you can

- Search for a specific phrase by enclosing the phrase in quotation marks. For example, you can type the phrase **"four score and seven years ago"** as the search term.
- Changing a word to a related word. For example, I changed *dogs* to *hounds*. Search engines often look for variations of *hound* (such as *hounds*), while a search for *hounds* will retrieve only pages with that word. Bottom line: Plural words are more specific than singular ones.

You can also refine your query using the Search Options page on AOL Search. These options let you create precise queries without worrying about those pesky ANDs and ORs, the dreaded *Boolean operators* that once plagued Web searchers.

From AOL Search's home page, click the Options link to bring up the page shown in Figure 8-5. Using this page helps you quickly put together complex searches that can yield better results.

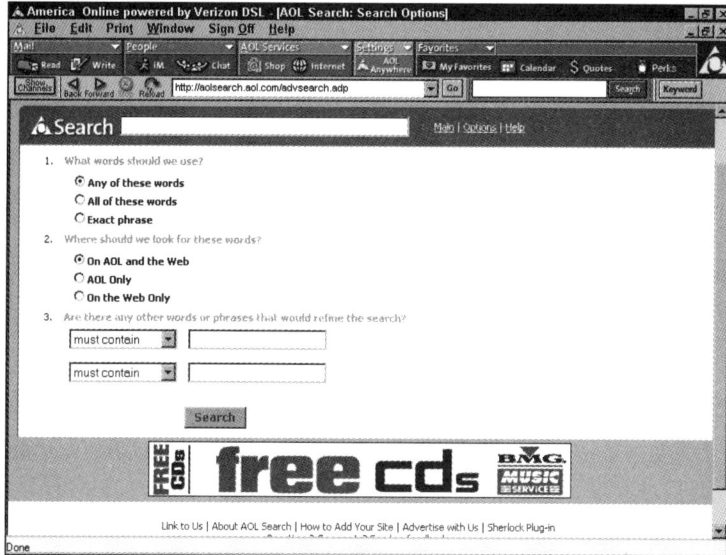

Figure 8-5. Powerful queries without fuss.

To use the fill-in-the-blank form, you first type your search terms in the text box at the top. Before clicking the Search button at the bottom of the page, take a look at how your search words are related to each other. Which are essential? Which belong in a certain order? Which additional words do you not want to appear? For example, in a search for information about the *peach*, you might want to exclude the words *Peach State*.

The Search Options page helps you beef up your query by indicating

- **How to weigh the words in a query.** You can look for any or all of the words, or even search for all the words in order. Words that must go in a certain order make up a phrase. A *phrase* is simply a string of words you're looking for, in a specific order.
- **Where AOL Search should look for the words.** You can search AOL and the Web or limit the search to one of the two areas. AOL's resources are reliably family-friendly. The Web's resources are broader but also more uneven, and you may find a few that are less family-friendly.

- **Which additional words you want to add to further refine your search.** Here you specify any other words that must be included or *not* included. Use the drop-down list to choose between Must Contain, Must Not Contain, and Exact Phrase (if you are adding two or more words in the box).

Refining Your Search with Power Operators

The Search Options page creates precise queries for you by adding all the quotes, ANDs, parentheses, and symbols that power searchers use. When you're just not getting the results you wanted, you may need to take the extra step of writing in the Boolean operators, such as AND, OR, NOT, and NEAR. When used between search terms, these operators tell AOL Search how you want the words in your search term to be related to each other on returned Web pages.

Note, however, that these operators can be tricky to use, and AOL Search's Help section should be read closely to ensure that you get the best results. For more about search operators and their usage, click Help at AOL Search and then click Advanced Search Techniques.

Useful operators include AND, OR, NOT, NEAR, ADJ, and the question mark (?), which is a wildcard, meaning it can stand for anything. The least obvious of these operators are probably the following:

- NEAR asks AOL Search to find words near each other, such as *apples near oranges*.
- ADJ is short for *adjacent*, which means that you can specify which of several words you want to find close to another word. Using ADJ lets you construct *flexible phrases*, with one term constant and the others variable. The example given online in AOL Search's Help area is: *(president or george or george w.) adj bush.* This search would return President Bush, George Bush, and George W. Bush.
- A *wildcard* is a character that stands for another character or characters. For example, if *feed?* is your search term, then AOL Search looks for *feed, feeder, feeding,* and every result beginning with *feed*. You can use wildcards in searches to represent unknown characters in your search.

You can't use wildcards in phrases, because phrases look for exact (not flexible) matches of words within the quotation marks.

Doing Family-Friendly Web Searches

Many schools and parents teach kids how to recognize and analyze the difference between opinion and fact. They are also teaching kids how to evaluate sites. And kids are learning to tell an adult if anything online makes them uncomfortable.

The Internet industry uses technology to grapple with the problem of restricting Internet content without denying kids access to riches of the Internet. The industry's strategies include

- Controlling what children can retrieve from search engines and filtering out apparently offensive sites. The problem is that the screens are rarely more than adequate.
- Creating handpicked directories of kid-appropriate sites, so kids can't access anything that's inappropriate. This solution prevents access to some sites, but also limits kids' ability to link or explore.
- Devising technologies for offline browsing, such as WebWhacker, from Blue Squirrel (`www.bluesquirrel.com`). In the controlled offline environment, parents and teachers can focus on content. Being offline prevents kids from doing searches and following links in unwanted directions. However, being offline also deprives kids from all the valuable resources available there.

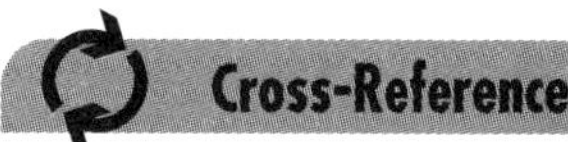

Parental Controls give parents several tools for safeguarding their children while using the Web. See Chapter 4 for more about this essential AOL service.

A special version of AOL Search, which is called Kids Only Search, is available from the Kids Only Channel and at AOL Keyword: **KO Search**. KO Search is strictly based on a *directory* of kid-appropriate sites.

For kids using AOL Search, searches can be made family-safe. After your child does a search on AOL Search, scroll to the bottom of the results page. In the Search for . . . On section, click Kids Only. This tells AOL Search to run the search term through Kids Only. Figure 8-6 shows the Kids Only Search page.

For What It's Worth: Evaluating Web Sites

What makes a site good? How do you know whether your search was useful?

Reasons to visit a Web site vary, and so do criteria for evaluating sites. If you were looking for information about the ratio of boy babies to girl babies in China, you would have different criteria for what makes a page useful than if you were looking for the lowest airfare from Singapore to Charlotte, North Carolina. If you're doing genealogical research, the site with the most accurate and abundant information about your family probably wins out; pure information is what counts in this case.

Graphics and design elements rarely make one site's content better than another site's, unless you love interactive gaming, online art, Web design, and what designers call eye candy. Sites that meet your needs, look great, and are easy to read belong in your Favorite Places folder.

If you simply need accurate and reliable information, here are AOL@School's recommendations for evaluating Web content:

- Who is the publisher? (In other words, what is the source of the information? Is the source reliable? Does it have a bias?)
- Does the site's address (URL) indicate that the site resides on the server of an organization with a political or philosophical stake in the issue being addressed?
- Is the site's language scholarly, formal, or informal?
- Is the information detailed?
- Does the site contain spelling and grammar mistakes?
- Does the site identify the author of its content and provide his or her credentials?
- Does the writer seem objective, or does he or she have a point of view or product to promote?
- When was the Web site last updated?
- Does the site have a bibliography?

Figure 8-6. The place where kids can start searching for online content.

Here are some other ways to do kid-friendly searches:

- Searchopolis (`www.searchopolis.com`) is a full-blown kids search community with its own directory.
- Several general-purpose search engines let parents filter search results by merely clicking a link. The services are called Family Filter in AltaVista, SafeSearch in Google, and Search Guard in Lycos.
- Information Please for Kids has a wide variety of reference-related destinations for kids. Although the site focuses on homework, the service provides many opportunities for fun, too (`kids.infoplease.com`).

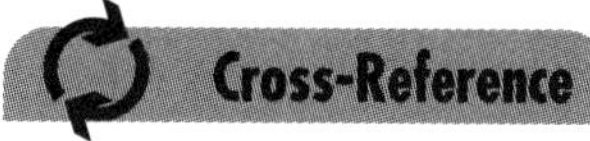

In Chapter 9, you can find more details about Google and Lycos. Also, I cover Information Please for Kids in Chapter 4.

AOL's White Pages, Yellow Pages, and E-Mail Finder

AOL Search is just the start. AOL's other search tools let you look for phone numbers, e-mail addresses, street maps, and more.

The idea of online White and Yellow Pages is simple: Why search for someone's street address or your drugstore's phone number with the old-fashioned Yellow Pages, when larger and more current listings are available online? White Pages and Yellow Pages on the Net consist of searchable electronic databases with millions of names. As in familiar phone books, White Pages provide listings of individuals, and Yellow Pages provide listings of businesses. Unlike the phone books, however, the Web gives you access to national and international addresses, not just your city or county. Online listings are also updated more often than paper listings — approximately four times a year. In addition, there are no pages to tear or get ripped out.

Finding Residential Addresses (White Pages)

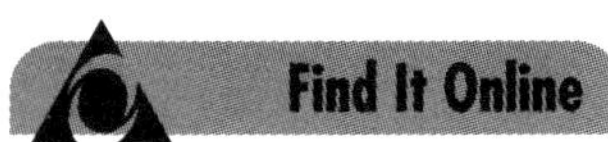

The AOL White Pages are available from the People menu; the AOL Yellow Pages from the Services menu.

To do a White Pages search for someone's street address or phone number, use AOL Keyword: **White Pages**. The only piece of information you must provide is a last name, but any additional information can significantly improve your chances of uncovering the correct address.

You can modify or remove information about your own listing on the AOL White Pages. For instructions, click the Help link.

A simple search yields the same information as flipping through the White Pages book: name, address, and phone number. On the Web, additional information is only a link away: driving directions to the person's house, a neighborhood map, and a local or state guidebook. You can also search for the person's e-mail address or send that person an American Greetings card. Figure 8-7 shows you the White Pages.

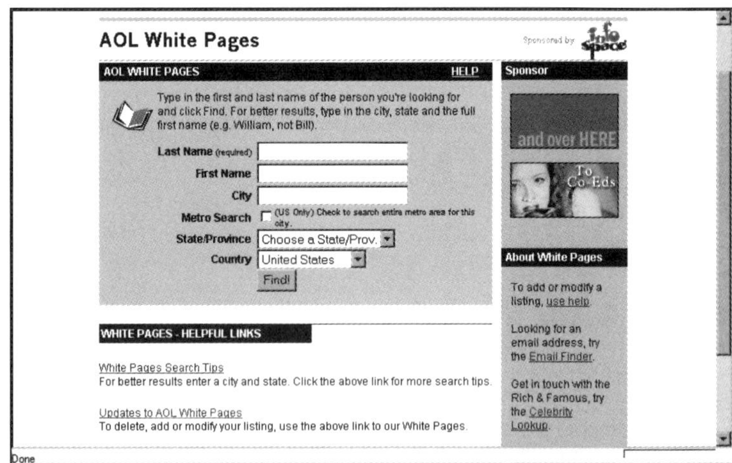

Figure 8-7. Find a residential address with this simple form.

When you find someone's street address with the AOL White Pages, you can click his or her name to see a list of hot spots and businesses near that address. You also get a neighborhood map, driving directions, and more.

Use the White Pages' neighborhood services if you need to help an elderly person but can't be there yourself.

Finding E-Mail Addresses

You can find AOL's E-Mail Finder at AOL Keyword: **Email Finder**. Unlike the White and Yellow Pages, the E-Mail Finder is not based on publicly available data. Instead, it works by collecting e-mail addresses from Internet service providers and from people who voluntarily provide the information.

It is important to realize that when you look for e-mail addresses through the E-Mail Finder, you might uncover old or inaccurate information. After all, the database has no way of knowing which e-mail addresses are current — unless individuals make an effort to update their information.

As with the White Pages, you can modify or hide your own e-mail address; just click Revise E-Mail Listing. To delete or modify your information, search for yourself, and click Delete or Update.

As a result, you may have less luck finding someone's e-mail address than searching for the same person's real address. Remember, the best way to find someone's personal information is to ask that person.

Finding Business Addresses (Yellow Pages)

AOL's Yellow Page service (AOL Keyword: **Yellow Pages**) works like AOL's White Pages but goes further in the searches you can do and in the results you will get. White Pages are alphabetized by name, but with the Yellow Pages, you can search for businesses by name and by category (insurance, pets, and so on). You can also limit your search to businesses that are a certain distance from your home or workplace. As for your results, they include whatever the Yellow Pages service can find, including a phone number, a street address, and a link to a business Web site, if the business has one.

Ten national directories are currently available from the Country drop-down list when you use the AOL White Pages. For more choices, scroll down to the International Directories, which include business or residential listings, or both, for 50 countries.

You can do precision searches by using the Yellow Pages' tabs, which include the following:

- **Detailed Search:** Zero in on businesses by zip code or (if you know it) by phone number.
- **Distance Search:** Find a business within a certain distance from you or that's in a specific location. Use the Search Within menu to tell the Yellow Pages *how* close you want the business to be.

- **Canada Search:** Find businesses in a specific city or province.

For any business that you find by using the Yellow Pages, you can get a map, driving directions, and the ability to choose the fastest route.

Getting Maps and Directions: MapQuest

For driving conditions in more than 60 cities, use MapQuest's traffic tab. The maps are usually updated every two minutes.

If you're into maps or want more than driving directions, become familiar with AOL's complete mapping service, MapQuest, shown in Figure 8-8 (AOL Keyword: **MapQuest**). MapQuest is closely integrated with AOL's two other major local-information services, Moviefone and the AOL Local Guide Channel, and you will find MapQuest services whenever you need driving directions to movie theaters and local events. The MapQuest store stocks more than 10,000 maps, atlases, books, and travel-related items.

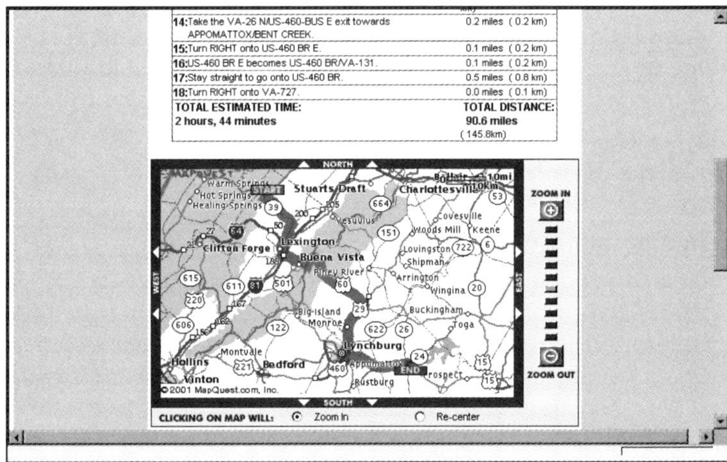

Figure 8-8. Using MapQuest to get driving instructions from Goshen to Appomattox (both in Virginia).

When you get driving instructions, you can print them out for use in the car. Or, if you have a Palm-compatible computer, you can download the directions. From the results page, scroll down to the map, click Download to PDA, and save the file. The next time you HotSynch your handheld device, you retrieve the directions and can use them in the car. Finally, you can have the directions e-mailed to you (or someone else) by clicking the E-Mail button next to the Download to PDA button.

Where to Go from Here

AOL Search offers a strong solution to the built-in problems of searching the Web. Starting with a handpicked, well-organized directory of choice Web sites, AOL Search gives you the choice of browsing the directory or searching a much larger list of Web sites on AOL's search engine. With AOL Search, you can easily extend your search to an encyclopedia, child-friendly sites, news archives, and other resources.

- The next chapter introduces some of the Internet tools that you can use to do special-purpose searches. All these tools are available through AOL.
- Searching for mailing lists and newsgroups is handled in more detail in Chapters 13 and 14, respectively.
- Searching for files to download? See Chapter 15.

Chapter 9

From Breadth to Depth: Doing Specialized Searches

IN THIS CHAPTER | PAGE

Sometimes you need a search tool that

- Focuses on a specific type of information, such as images.
- Draws on an authoritative resource, such as articles in medical journals or from government sources.
- Restricts the search to a single Web site.
- Uses more than one search engine at the same time.
- Finds data that *can't* be retrieved by even the best Web search engines.

This chapter provides guidance in using search engines and other tools you can use in all these situations.

Exploring Search Engines

Three search services — Google, Lycos, and Northern Light — offer special features focusing on *types* of information, such as full-text articles, newsgroup postings, images, and multimedia. All three do Web searches as well, and two of them offer unusual approaches to searching that can produce consistently good results.

- Google pioneered the idea of ranking Web sites partly according to whether other people find them useful. In addition, Google recently started offering specialty searches of newsgroups, government sources, and images.
- Lycos offers searches for images, sounds, and video, and also hosts a tool for searching 100 million downloadable files.
- Northern Light searches full-text documents, newswires, and other non-Web resources. It is also unique in *presenting* its results by subject categories, simplifying the work of evaluating results.

Google

A *googol* is the number 1 followed by 100 zeroes. The Web site, Google, claims to have indexed more than a billion Web pages. *Search engines* keep track of millions of Web pages and their addresses. To find out how search engines work, check out `www.howstuffworks.com/search-engine.htm`.

What singles out Google is how it searches. Some engines collect pages more or less indiscriminately, indexing one page and then all linked pages, and so on. In contrast, the search engine used by Google (`www.google.com`) ranks the sites it collects according to the number of pages linked to them. If a page is linked-to by pages that are themselves popular, then that page is ranked even higher. In a nutshell, the more pages linking to a page, the higher that page will appear in your results page. Google's premise is that if a page is linked by other pages, it is probably pretty good, and probably of interest to you.

Google tends to be highly reliable. Figure 9-1 shows the results of a Google search for information about the recent discovery of a complete dinosaur skeleton by scientists from the University of Chicago. Without the Web, retrieving these pages through library research would take hours; this search took half a second.

With Google, you use quotes to indicate exact phrases, but you don't have to use *AND, OR,* plus signs, or any other Boolean operators. In fact Google always assumes that you're using *AND*, the simplest and most powerful of the operators.

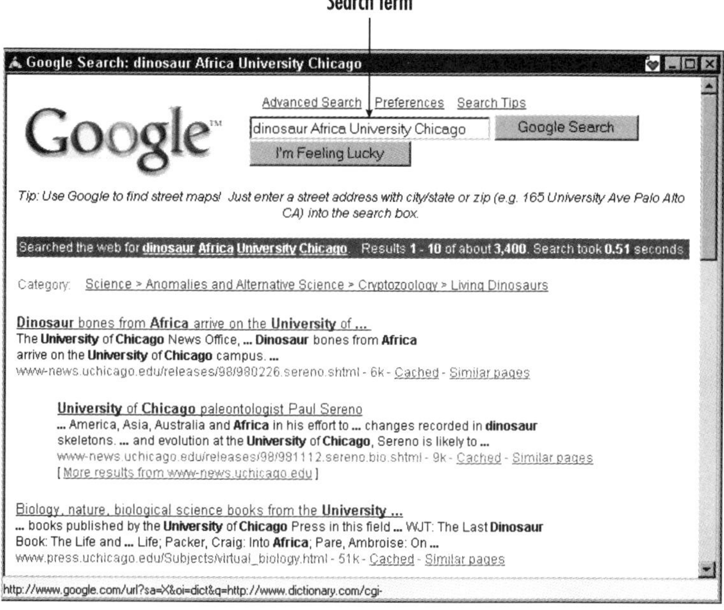

Figure 9-1. Your search terms appear in **boldface** in Google's search results.

A Google search can be restricted to pages in one or more languages. In addition, Google's messages and help pages can also be displayed in different languages. Look for the Advanced Search link on the top of every Google page.

Click I'm Feeling Lucky to go directly to the first item Google returns in response to your query.

When you use some search engines, your search results can leave you shrugging. "What does this page have to do with my query?" you might wonder. With Google, you can retrieve the *cached* (saved) page for any search result. Such a page is the snapshot of the page as it looked when Google most recently indexed it. Just click *Cached*, the last word of every search result (see Figure 9-1).

To appreciate this feature, consider all the reasons why that snapshot might differ from what's available right now: A page could add new content, get a new address, or just disappear. So, if Google can't find a page after you click a link, try the cached page instead. The information may be old, but it could still be useful for you.

Parents: Use Google's SafeSearch to filter. From the Google home page, this option is available by clicking Preferences.

Search with a Human Face

The first generation of search engines indexed Web sites automatically, making the search process hit or miss, at best. AOL uses Inktomi technology and the Open Directory Project to replace automatic indexing with human selection — directories built by people who care about a particular subject.

Major search services on the Internet — including Google and Lycos — have adopted the Open Directory. Directories in general opt for quality over size, but the Open Directory Project has enough editors to offer size as well as quality. Currently approximately 40,000 editors contribute site reviews to Open Directory's numerous categories, and approximately 3 million sites have been added to date. Editors exercise their judgment in choosing sites, placing them in one or more categories, and describing them in a few words. This human touch adds enormous value, setting the Open Directory apart from the mechanically compiled search engines.

The Open Directory (`dmoz.org`) has a deep hierarchy of sites. That means that every new site is likely to fit well into an existing subcategory of sites. As a result, when you browse the directory, you can count on finding clusters of sites germane to your interests. When using the directory, the at symbol (@) indicates a subcategory of sites, and a plain link indicates a link to an actual site.

For any good pages returned by your search, click Similar Pages to see more of the same.

Recently, Google has added several important types of content to search. Each of these search types requires you to type in a search word or words describing what you are looking for.

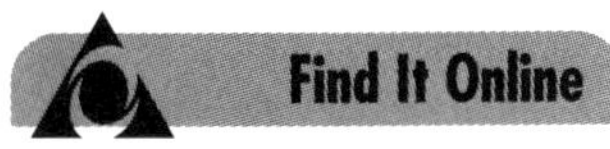

AOL has created a highly usable guide to official information. The Government Guide is available from the Services menu.

- **U.S. government sites:** You can do a search (for information about koalas, for example) and choose to have the results narrowed down to pages on official U.S. sites. Click Advanced Search, scroll down to Topic-Specific Search, and click U.S. Government. This search restricts its scope to government sites (of every level, branch, and agency).
- **Newsgroup postings:** Search for newsgroup postings written since the mid-1990s, and then read them and post to the newsgroups, using the Web instead of a

special newsgroup reader. You read individual newsgroup threads, and search across all newsgroups for all information about (for example) *measles* or *fish sauce.*

- **Images:** To search for images, go to `images.google.com`. A search for *frogs* retrieves more than 11,000 images containing *frog* in their filenames. The search page shows small pictures; click one to visit the page containing the pictures. Be wary of copyright violations in your use of anything you find (see AOL Keyword: **Copyright**).

I discuss newsgroup searches in detail in Chapter 14.

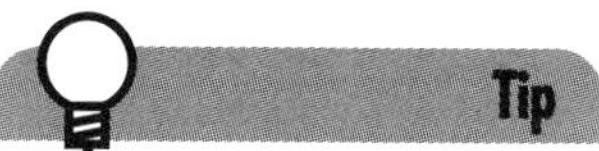

Many parents use the Lycos Search Scrub feature to filter out unwanted images and music when children do searches.

Lycos

One of the Net's earliest general-purpose search engines, Lycos now focuses its searches on a directory created by the Open Directory Project, the same one used by AOL Search.

So why use Lycos? Lycos features a set of specialized media searches. When you use Lycos's Multimedia area (`multimedia.lycos.com`, shown in Figure 9-2), you can also search for image, video, and sound files, including a million MP3 music files. Lycos also provides the opportunity to download the players and plug-ins required for playing these files, many of which you already have on AOL. Finally, Lycos offers a huge archive of over 100 million downloadable files.

The Multimedia service includes a file-search tool that is discussed in Chapter 15.

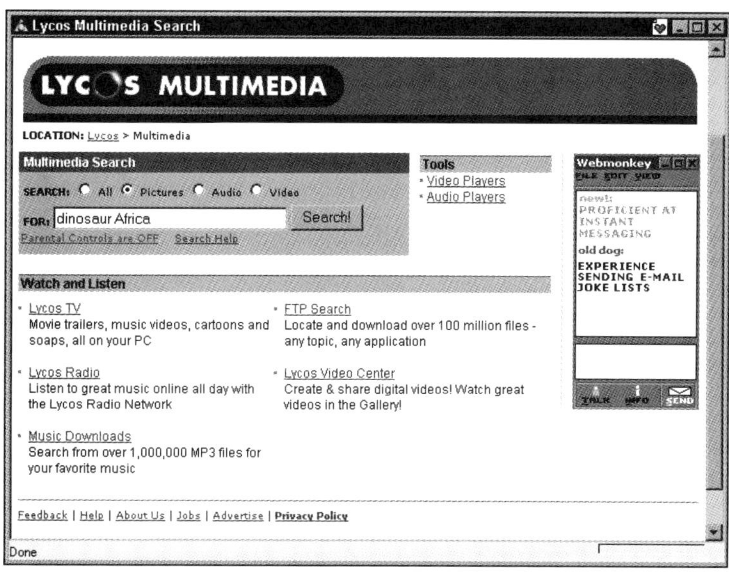

Figure 9-2. Lycos is a good choice for multimedia searches for MP3 music files, FTP files, JPG images, sounds, and video.

Northern Light

Northern Light (`www.northernlight.com`), shown in Figure 9-3, is highly respected among professional researchers and people who require up-to-date information, including business people, teachers, and librarians.

Tip

Northern Light boasts a large index, and it returns fewer dead links than other engines.

Northern Lights consists of a core list of Web sites that you can search for free and a library of non-Web resources called the Special Collections, with more than 25 million full-text documents in more than 7,500 "full-text journals, books, magazines, newswires, and reference sources." To these Special Collections, it adds approximately 250 print and electronic sources each month. The Web searches are free, and the full-text articles cost $1-4 per article.

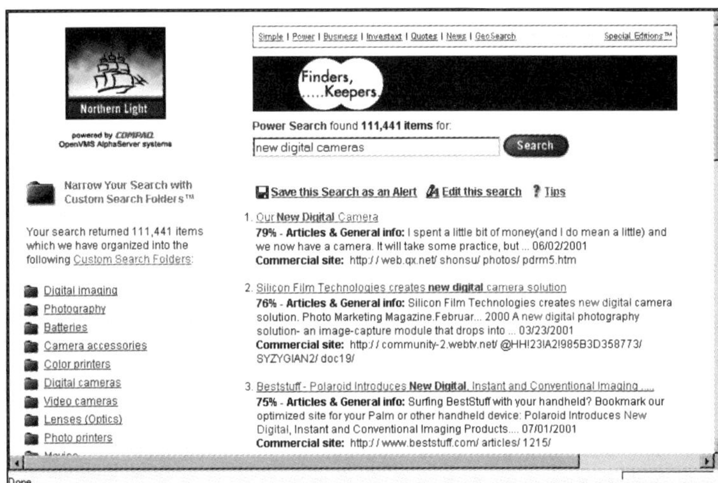

Figure 9-3. Using the Power Search, I limited this Northern Light search to commercial sites published in the last six months.

On Northern Light, Web queries can be made in everyday language (*What is the capital of Sweden?* would be fine). Northern Light also supports highly complex queries. Northern Light's Power Search option allows you to use text boxes and check boxes to specify the scope, publication date, and source of the information you seek. Scope can include any of 15 or so subjects — from the arts to travel (that is, you can search within these subjects). You can also restrict your searches to documents in a certain language and from a certain type of source (official, commercial, college newspaper, job listing, and so on).

Northern Light displays search results in the center of the page, as shown in Figure 9-3. On the left are a list of blue Custom Search folders, arranging the results by data type (such as press release), source (the Web, for example), and language. Different folders are generated for each new query. This usable format gives you an overview of your results and allows you to focus on specific results by their type or source. Among your results you may find some items from Northern Light's full-text archives, which are available in a folder called Special Collection documents. You will see the article's title, source, and summary; to read the whole article, you will need to purchase the article for (currently) around $2.95.

Other free services include the GeoSearch, which can restrict a Web search to services within a certain distance of your home or other location. In researching local services and businesses, this service can be indispensable.

Special Editions are professionally compiled, in-depth overviews of topical issues, such as e-commerce, computer viruses, wireless technology, and autism. Each is a mini-directory with carefully chosen and well-annotated resources, combined with hard-wired live queries that you can run to see the very latest information on topics of interest. A *live query* is a ready-made search term that you can run to see the up-to-the-moment search results.

Tips for Asking Good Questions

At the heart of every search is a query, whether you are searching a directory, a multimedia archive, or Northern Light Special Collections. A query translates what you want to find out into terms that a computer can use to retrieve what you're looking for. Your success with any search can depend on putting your query in just the right way. Here are some general guidelines for turning your questions into effective queries:

- **Be clear about what you want to know and whether the Web is the best place to start.** If you want to tap opinions and expertise (to get advice on buying a piano, for example), searching for specific AOL message boards may make more sense. On these boards, you can ask people questions and then ask follow-up questions. If your question is news-related, consider using AOL's News Search or White Pages.

- **Think of specific words that convey what you want to find out.** In your query, use only the most relevant words and order them from most important to least important.
- **Use a search tool's preferences.** Preferences can help you specify whether your words form a phrase (words that belong together, as in "London bridge is falling down") or whether some of the words must appear on the page and others don't.
- **Check your spelling.** Some engines give you latitude if you misspell something; others take you at your word and give you just what you asked for. If your search turned up nothing useful, check your spelling. If a wild-card is available, as in AOL Search and Northern Light, you might want to learn to use it.
- **Refine your query and run it again.** When you finally start to turn up valuable sites, use a Show More Like This link if it's available (as in AOL Search and Google). If your search didn't turn up anything at all or anything relevant, think of synonyms, additional words, or specific words.

Special-Purpose Search Collections

Sometimes you want a human guide to help you figure out which sites to visit for any area of interest. Open Directory performs this task on a very large scale, with many editors laboring away in every category (Business, Health, and so on). The following services have a different approach: They bring experts' insights into a topic's most valuable sites. If you or someone you know is developing a new interest in plants, travel, music, photography, the outdoors, or other subject, pay a visit to some of the following destinations.

The WWW Virtual Library (VLIB)

The Virtual Library, or VLIB calls itself "the oldest catalog of the Web." Tim Berners-Lee, who created the World Wide Web, also created VLIB. The VLIB actually consists of 300 or so virtual libraries, centrally cataloged and searchable at `www.vlib.org`, are widely recognized as some of the most reliable guides to online resources.

The Virtual Library is especially strong for academic subjects, so college students may find it helpful.

Each library in the VLIB consists of choice, well-arranged links in the subject area in question. Some libraries have original content and go very deep into their subjects. The Web Developers Virtual Library, for example, has instructional material on every level and facet of developing pages (`www.wdvl.com`). The Virtual Library provides you the one point from which you can search all the libraries.

The VLIB's libraries really are *virtual* — available only online. Each library has a volunteer librarian who's responsible for the content. The site provides each librarian's name, e-mail address, and affiliation.

Argus Clearinghouse: Librarians Rate the Net

The Argus Clearinghouse (`www.clearinghouse.net`) grew out of a collective project undertaken in the early 1990s by Lou Rosenfeld's information-science students at the University of Michigan. Rosenfeld's design firm, Argus Associates, continues to maintain the site.

Like the Virtual Library, the Clearinghouse directory consists of guides to Internet resources about well-defined subjects, such as disabilities or distance education. Unlike the Virtual Library, the Clearinghouse chooses only those resource guides that meet its content and design standards. Therefore, you can be assured that the resources are well chosen, described, and evaluated.

Clearinghouse recognizes the best guides with its regular Digital Librarian Award. One recent winner, Senior Women Web, shown in Figure 9-4, features information and interactive resources for older women.

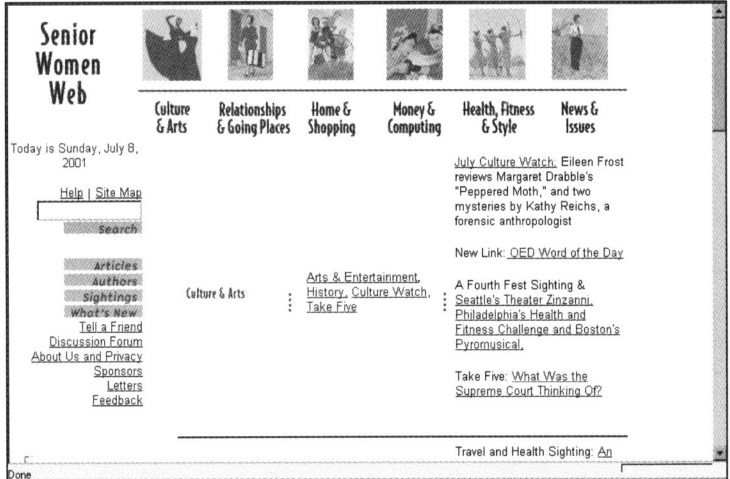

Figure 9-4. Senior Women Web recently won Argus Clearinghouse's Digital Librarian Award.

About.com

Some directories specialize in a locality or region, such as Germany or Africa. From About.com's `websearch.about.com/cs/regionalsearch/`, click Regional for links to these search sites.

About.com has 700 specialized sites — comparable to VLIB's libraries and Argus's guides — but is less academic in feel. Each site is created and maintained by one or more subject-matter guides and includes community features like chat and message boards. The expert guides put together focused collections of Web sites, write lengthy articles, and provide interactive opportunities. Unlike other search services, About.com seeks to create new content and build communities of people with a strong interest in certain subjects.

One useful feature is the ability to search About.com both within the individual sites and across all sites. I have found this search feature useful on numerous occasions when using the crafts, disability, education, and photography sites. Especially useful, for me, are the full-length, original articles.

Figure 9-5 shows the kind of specialized community you can find at About.com. This one helps you do searches for information about specific regions.

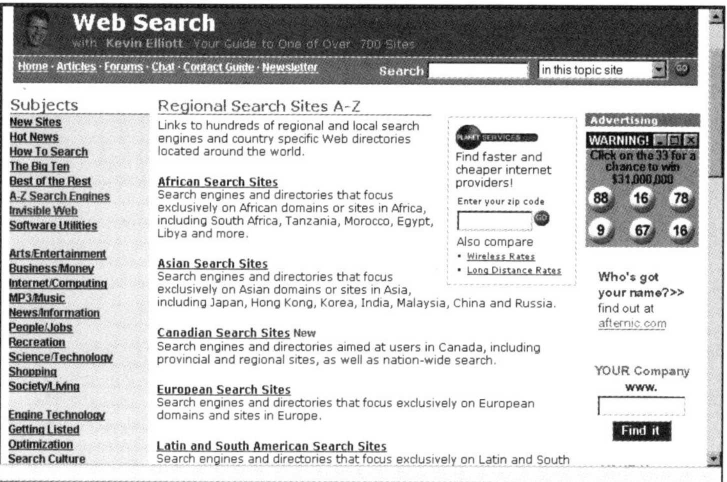

Figure 9-5. About.com can help you discover search engines devoted to specific world regions for use in travel, business, and research.

Digital Librarian

Digital Librarian is the one-woman work of Margaret Vail Anderson, a librarian in Cortland, New York (`www.digital-librarian.com`). While Argus and About.com look at big areas from the perspective of one or a few human guides, Vail Anderson gathers choice sites in approximately 100 categories and arranges them in a conveniently compact interface. I never fail to make a discovery while browsing this collection of high-quality sites.

For each category, you can find a long alphabetized list of resources (it can be difficult to find things, though). Almost every individual listing is sufficiently annotated to give you a sense of what you will find at the site when you click the link. Ms. Vail Anderson uses a special icon to denote new resources as she adds them and keeps the site up-to-date.

Ms. Vail Anderson's category, Internet subject directories, takes you to dozens of other quality directories (`www.digital-librarian.com/subject.html`).

Searching Individual Web Sites

Some Web sites, such as IBM.com in the business world and Megasoccer.com in the sports world, have become so big that they require their own internal search engines. CNET's Search.com brings together some 800 searchable Web sites, grouped into categories, such as movies, news, sports, gaming, and many others.

Search.com offers two important features:

- **Metasearching:** Metasearching enables Search.com to search more than one huge site at the same time. In a metasearch, the results are grouped by source. Figure 9-6 shows results of a metasearch in Health sites for information about colic.
- **Specialty searching:** Use this feature to restrict your search to individual sites. In the Television category, for example, you can currently choose from ten sites to search, including TV Guide and the Internet Movie Database. You can search one at a time or several at a time.

  In the Breaking News category, you'll find about a dozen searchable sites, including the BBC, CNN, and US News & World Reports.

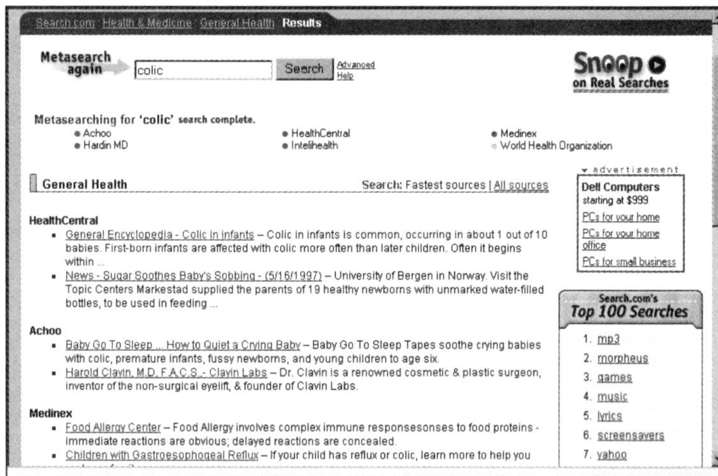

Figure 9-6. Search.com did a metasearch of six sites looking for information about colic.

Invisible Web Searches

For Gary Price, a librarian at George Washington University, some of the most informative and useful data on the Web cannot be retrieved by using a traditional search engine. This "invisible" information is locked away in many places on the Web, including databases, compilations of companies, audio recordings of speeches, articles buried in online journals, and obscure government publications. These sites are not published on their own Web page, and hence are not indexed by search engines. However, they are part of larger sites that are indexed. Price and others have manually collected these indexable pages through which large data collections can be indexed.

Price has brought together hundreds of invisible Web resources and published them in Price's List of Lists (`gwis2.circ.gwu.edu/~gprice/listof.htm`). One section is call the Current Awareness Resources via Streaming Audio & Video, a continuous multimedia view of political and business news as they unfold country by country, around the world.

Finding Authoritative Resources

Your health and your rights. Here are two areas of life where *not* having authoritative and reliable information can be very expensive. After all, do you want your doctor making a decision based on literature that is not peer-reviewed? Or your lawyer engaging in fanciful speculation about your legal rights? Why should you be less well informed?

To be informed, you need access to experts and people with experience. Net resources on health and the law can also help you choose the doctors and lawyers who make the most sense given your needs and budget. Without the Net, choosing the right professionals can take luck and time. After you find a professional, you can ask good questions and do the research that enables you to think through any advice you get.

Health: Specialized Resources

Most people have concerns about their health or the health of their kids, spouses, and parents. If you don't now, it's safe to say that you will one day. One of your first considerations should be to find information that you can understand and trust. Authoritative information you can't understand doesn't do a bit of good and may lead to misunderstandings with medical professionals. Fortunately, popular medical resources are cropping up on the Web, and you can start looking for them on AOL.

Through AOL you have access to health-related information of every type: traditional and alternative, professional and consumer, mental and physical, and so on. Here are general places to start your search for hard medical information on AOL and the Web:

- The Health channel (AOL Keyword: **Health** or Services⇨Medical References)
- Medical Resources & References (AOL Keyword: **Medical Search**)
- The Health Web Center (`www.aol.com/webcenters/health`)

The following specific resources take you to information about conditions and treatments:

Even the Mayo Clinic's site is no replacement for consulting a doctor. Use such sites to gather the information that you need to ask your doctors questions.

- **Mayo Clinic's Conditions & Treatments:** The Mayo Clinic's Conditions & Treatments service (AOL Keyword: **Conditions**) is devoted to hundreds of specific conditions. For any condition, you can find information about the likely diagnosis and treatments, as well as nutritional advice. You can also find links to related, authoritative sites and community support resources, such as message boards. Mayo pages include links to relevant information about approximately 8,000 medications. Another medication database is available from the Health Channel's main window.

  Owing to the human and financial importance of preventive medicine, the Mayo Clinic also provides a series of Healthy Living Centers, with reliable information about aging, eating, working out, and other subjects for men and women.

- **MEDLINEplus Health Information:** A new service of the National Library of Medicine, MEDLINEplus Health Information was developed for consumers of medical services (just about everyone, in other words). It includes a searchable directory of consumer-friendly Web sites and a guide to medications. Each drug entry includes a readable description and a discussion of side effects and interactions. Also useful are the many medical dictionaries and encyclopedias, directories of physicians by specialty, and information about clinical trials (courtesy of ClinicalTrials.gov). Figure 9-7 shows MEDLINEplus's opening page (`medlineplus.gov`).

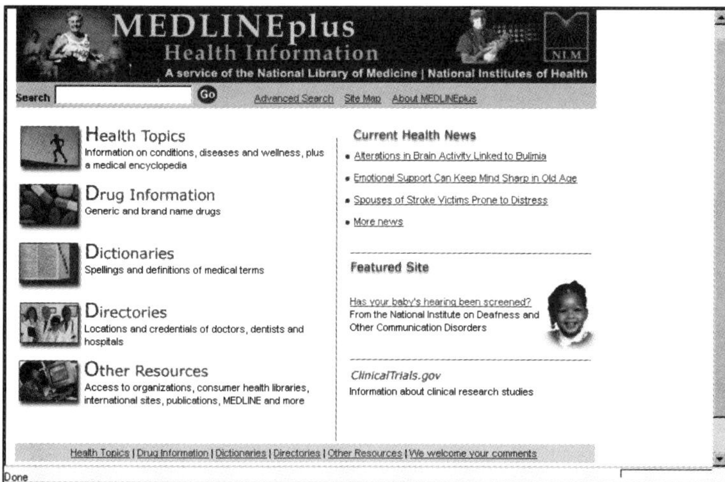

Figure 9-7. MEDLINEplus is authoritative and easy-to-use.

- **WebMD:** A newer, commercial service is WebMD (AOL Keyword: **WebMD**). The scope of information is comparable to Mayo and MEDLINEplus, but what distinguishes WebMD are the many opportunities to talk with others in condition-focused message boards and chat rooms. When I visited recently, the Back Pain Support Group boards alone had more than 6,000 messages to read. WebMD includes many tools for finding a doctor, assessing your community's air quality, identifying health risks, and more.

Need a lawyer? Start at AOL Keyword: **Law** and look for the Find a Lawyer link.

AOL recently announced a broad agreement with legal publishers Martindale-Hubbell to provide law information throughout AOL's online areas.

Law: Specialized Resources

Law, like medicine, is one of these areas where expertise is often well rewarded and where professional service can be unavoidable and expensive. You'll benefit in many ways from being an educated consumer of legal services.

- **Nolo:** Nolo, a publisher of self-help law books for nonlawyers, has brought its no-nonsense approach to the Web at Nolo: Law for All (`www.nolo.com`), shown in Figure 9-8. Of special value is the Plain-English Law Center. There, you can find the Nolo Law Dictionary and a legal encyclopedia organized by day-to-day subjects, such as buying a house and responding to traffic tickets. The articles are written in a direct and often witty style. The Statutes & Cases area gives clear instructions for doing your own research into case law at different levels, through the Supreme Court.

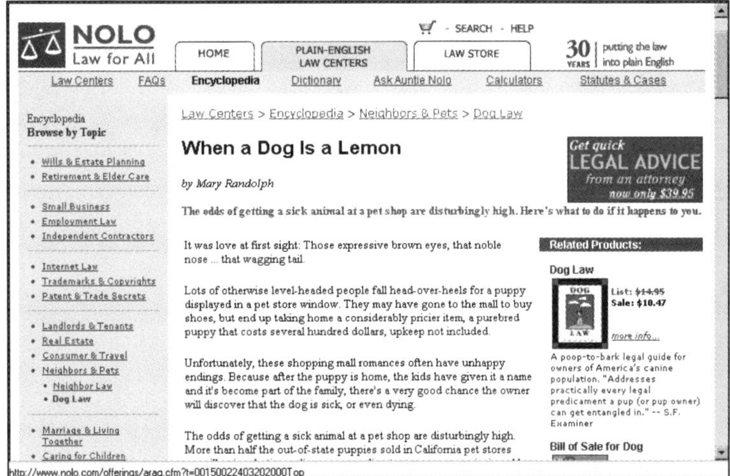

Figure 9-8. Use Nolo.com to understand your rights, and your dog's.

- **FindLaw:** Some consider FindLaw — a winner of Argus Clearinghouse's Digital Librarian Award — the best place to start looking for law information (`www.findlaw.com`). Because FindLaw has grown so big, so fast, it serves a broad range of users, including consumers, law students, businesses, lawyers, and paralegals of every specialty. The scope of the service can make it a little overwhelming, but you can be comforted by the fact that, if something is law-related, it is probably on FindLaw.

At FindLaw, consumers can locate guidelines for finding and interviewing a lawyer as well as formalizing an agreement. Of special value are a series of online guides from the American Bar Association on consumer law, family law, home ownership, and other subjects, all readable and useful.

If you own a small business, you will find articles on employee benefits, intellectual property, credit and collections, unfair practices, and dealing with the government, often specific to your state.

From Libraries on the Web to Digital Libraries

The search for the most reliable information has traditionally led straight to the library stacks. Many researchers still consider the Web less reliable than the library, because Web sites don't go through a screening and review process; anyone can publish on the Web. Much of this distrust is unfounded, however. Many major publishers are making books available as *eBooks*, books in electronic format. More and more, libraries themselves are putting parts of their collections online.

Cross-Reference

Chapter 18 introduces the subject of electronic books and summarizes the tools for reading these *eBooks*.

Find It Online

Adobe Acrobat (PDF) files offer a polished look and are sometimes authoritative. You can now search for any of more than a million PDF files at `searchpdf.adobe.com`. Chapter 6 introduces Acrobat.

For now you can get access to libraries on the Web in two ways:

- Through libraries' searchable catalogs, which provide information *about* books.
- Through the growing collections of traditional books, pictures, music, and other library holdings that are being digitized.

Although thousands of libraries can be searched, only a small portion of their holdings is now available online. The number is constantly growing.

Discovering Library Catalogs on the Web

LIBWEB gives you access to libraries with searchable online catalogs in over 100 countries (`sunsite.berkeley.edu/Libweb/`).

Even when you can't retrieve books and documents online, LIBWEB can make short work of library searches in your hometown or anywhere. You can't actually take out books yet, but you can

- Create a bibliography for school or work.
- Find out what's current in any field and then use other Web resources to get reviews of the work. Or go to your local library to get books through interlibrary loan.
- Find out who wrote what and when, and who published it.
- Find out which branch of your public library has a particular book (if your library system is online) and whether anyone has checked it out. Or find out which books are overdue and renew them online.
- If you have access to a university library, you can often use its online databases, such as ERIC, Books in Print, and LexisNexis.

Digital Libraries

Around the world, thousands of libraries and museums are digitizing their collections as a way of preserving them and making them available to a larger audience. University libraries are leading huge projects to put millions of old documents online, and major museums are creating digital versions of their permanent collections.

You can read the story of Project Gutenberg and find out how to volunteer for the ongoing project at `promo.net/pg/`.

The first online publishing ventures on the Internet involved the republication of the textual versions of out-of-print, public domain books. Back in 1971, Project Gutenberg grew out of a community-minded project launched by computer scientist Michael Hart. For thirty years now, the project's purpose has been to publish online versions of classic books in their original languages, including works by Herman Melville, Edith Wharton, Anton Chekhov, Agatha Christie, and Omar Khayyam. Mr. Hart has made more than 3,500 classics available and adds to them every month, with the help of volunteer transcribers and proofreaders. Many of these texts are finding their way into new formats suitable for use with a portable reading device or Palm-compatible handheld.

Two other collections link to thousands of online books:

- The University of Pennsylvania's Online Book Page, with 14,000 titles in electronic format (`digital.library.upenn.edu/books`).
- Tufts University's Project Perseus makes available the text from online classics dating from the ancient world through the English Renaissance. Included are modern English translations, maps, glossaries, and other useful tools (`www.perseus.tufts.edu`).

The Smithsonian Institution has created a long list of public libraries that are digitizing their rare holdings and making them available on the Web (`www.sil.si.edu/SILPublications/Online-Exhibitions`).

Other libraries and archives aim to make older documents available in their original form, as well as in text and other (PDF) formats. The University of Michigan's Making of America (MOA) digital archive, for example, currently holds more than 2 million individually scanned pages of nineteenth-century American magazines and books. Access to original documents can bring the excitement of discovery to students and history buffs who otherwise lack access to archives.

Major libraries like the Library of Congress are beginning to create digital versions of their holdings. Best known is the LOC's American Memory project (`memory.loc.gov`), which consists of more than 70 online exhibitions that depict daily life in American history. To assemble the collections, the LOC has digitized original sounds, motion pictures, photographs, and original documents to create the experience of a specific moment in the past. Figure 9-9 shows an image from the LOC's American Memory collection called "The Emergence of Advertising in America."

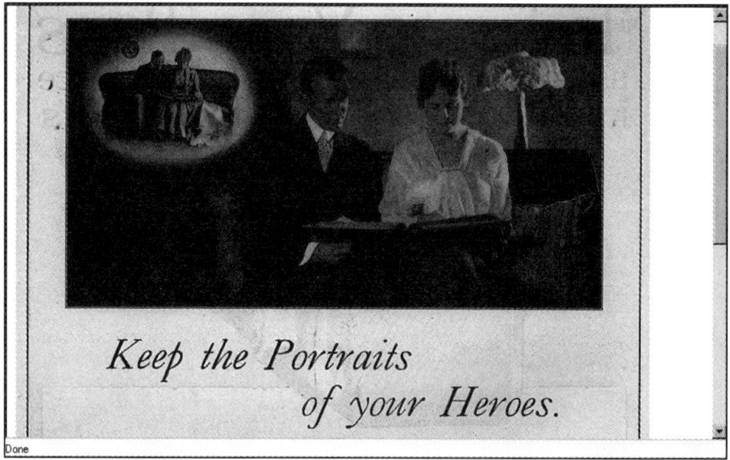

Figure 9-9. This Kodak ad from 1917 urges parents to keep a portrait album of sons who have gone to fight in France.

Where to Go from Here

Information is locked up in all sorts of places on the Web, and this chapter introduced a few of the keys you can use to unlock it.

- Chapter 8 guides you through AOL Search, a comprehensive, general-purpose search service. Make sure to start your searches here, especially in the browsable AOL Search directory.
- For help finding mailing lists, see Chapter 13.
- For help finding newsgroup postings, see Chapter 14.
- For help finding files to download via FTP, which is an Internet tool for downloading files, see Chapter 15.

Chapter 10

You've Got Mail: Handling the E-Mail You Receive

Electronic mail, or *e-mail*, or just plain *mail* lets you stay in touch with colleagues, family, friends, and anyone you care about or who counts in your life. The most obvious advantages of electronic mail over paper letters are speed, cost, and convenience. An e-mail message gets to its destination in seconds, so that a message meant for someone in Australia won't take significantly longer to arrive than a message meant for your next-door neighbor. As for convenience, you can send the same message to many people at the same time, you can search old mail for specific information, and you can even unsend messages — something you certainly can't do with old-fashioned letters.

This chapter looks at all aspects of receiving and managing your mail on AOL. It also introduces the AOL Anywhere service and devices, including handheld computers and wireless phones, which extend the usefulness of e-mail even further.

Understanding E-Mail Addresses

The ability to *unsend* mail is a feature that's unique to AOL Mail.

On AOL, your screen name is your e-mail address. All screen names on an account have their own password-protected mailboxes. Each AOL account can have up to seven screen names.

To receive mail, you must make sure that people know your e-mail address. To other AOL members, your e-mail address is your screen name. Internet users can also send you e-mail. They just have to add a bit of information to your screen name to make sure that you get the message: the @ symbol, plus **aol.com**.

Figure 10-1 shows an e-mail message with e-mail addresses and screen names showing.

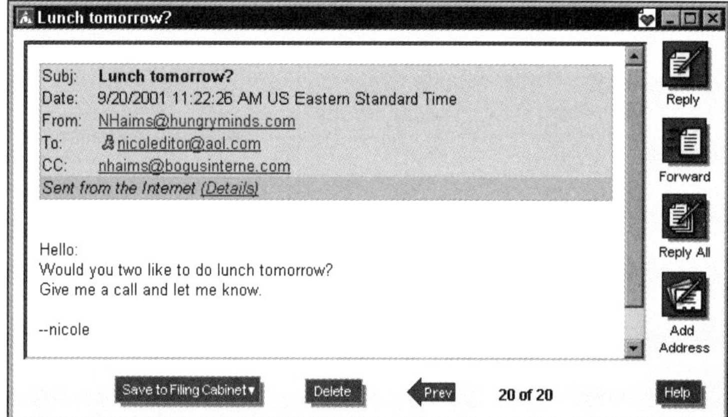

Figure 10-1. Every e-mail includes the address of the sender and recipients.

You'll see e-mail addresses in many contexts and use them in many ways. An e-mail address identifies both a person sending the message and the *domain* (a company or institution, usually) through which the person accesses the Internet. Take this made-up example: `verne20000leagues@aol.com`. The sender's screen name is `verne20000leagues`, and `aol.com` is the *domain*. The domain tells you, if you're interested, something about how the sender connects to the Internet (through AOL, in this case).

Domain names have several parts, indicating the *name* of the domain and the *type* of the domain. The first part, `aol`, is, of course, AOL's domain; `com` means that AOL is a commercial entity. Each part of a domain name is separated by a period (the famous *dot*). The major global domains — `.edu`, `.com`, `.net`, `.mil`, and `.org` — have three letters. National domains often have two letters, as in `.jp` for Japan, `.au` for Australia, `.ru` for Russia, and `.tv` for Tuvalu. The domain type, on the right, can have two parts, as in `co.uk` (a company in the United Kingdom) or `ky.us` (the State of Kentucky in the United States).

In the near future, you can expect to see new domains such as `.info`, which can be used by anyone, for any purpose, and `.biz`, for businesses around the world. If you ever buy your own domain name (which isn't very expensive), it may be in one of these new categories.

Note

The `.tv` domain is worth a lot of money, and Tuvalu has been licensing it to such non-Tuvalu interests as *The Economist* magazine, whose video site (`www.economist.tv`) is shown in Chapter 1).

Getting E-Mail Help

E-mail seems so simple. Why would you ever need help? Because you can do so much with e-mail, from working with diverse types of attachments to taking part in mailing lists. Any time you use AOL's e-mail services, click Help for ideas and tips.

- While writing a message, click the Help button in the bottom right-hand corner for how-to procedures on approximately 50 basic tasks.
- While using your mailbox, click the Help button.
- AOL Keyword: **Mail Center**, shown in Figure 10-2, offers how-to help, useful links to mail-related destinations online, and direct access to AOL's mail tools and services.

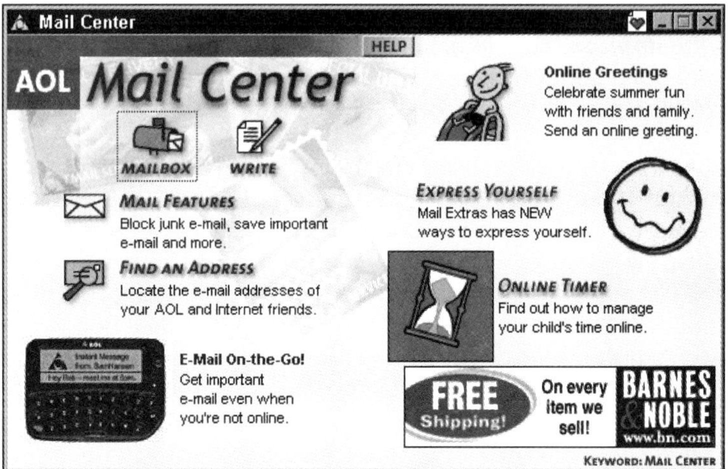

Figure 10-2. Find out how many things you can do with e-mail at AOL's Mail Center (AOL Keyword: **Mail Center**).

Using Your AOL Mailbox

The first thing millions of people do on AOL each day is read their mail. AOL's You've Got Mail icon and the famous voice telling you that "You've Got Mail" were already imprinted in many minds before Meg Ryan and Tom Hanks made a movie about electronic romance.

If the You've Got Mail icon on the Welcome Screen shows a raised flag, then you've got mail. If you've read a message and used the Keep As New option, explained later in this chapter, then you still see the flag.

E-mail messages, like letters, are delivered in a mailbox. How do you get to your AOL mailbox? Here are three ways:

- Click the You've Got Mail icon on AOL's Welcome Screen.
- Click the Read icon on the AOL 7.0 toolbar.
- Use the keyboard shortcut Ctrl+R.

Your Online Mailbox appears on-screen. However you retrieve your mail from your Online Mailbox, up comes an electronic mailbox like the one shown in Figure 10-3.

Your Online Mailbox has three tabs. Click a tab to see the three mailboxes in your Online Mailbox: New Mail, Old Mail, and Sent Mail. Each tab has the same four columns, or pieces of information, for each message (type, date, e-mail address, and subject). Here's how the tabs work:

- **New Mail:** This mailbox contains both the truly new messages (ones you have not read yet) and the messages you have read and decided to keep as new. Keeping a message as new can be a helpful way of reminding you that you need to follow up on the message in some way. To keep a message as new, select it and click the Keep As New button.

  Messages stay on the New tab for up to about four weeks.
- **Old Mail:** Here, you find the messages you have read but haven't kept as new. By default, messages stay here for three or four days, but you can keep them for up to a week by adjusting your preferences. After that, old mail is automatically deleted from your Online Mailbox, meaning you won't be able to access it again. Don't worry, though. You can set your preferences to save old mail messages on your hard drive. (See "Managing Your Filing Cabinet.") Or, click Save As New to hang on to old mail for about a month.
- **Sent Mail:** This mailbox keeps copies of the messages you sent in the past four weeks.

To adjust how long to store your old mail (up to seven days), choose Settings⇨Preferences. In the Preferences box, click Mail and click the up and down arrows to adjust the number of days.

To save messages permanently, see "Managing Your Filing Cabinet," later in this chapter.

File attached

Picture inserted

Figure 10-3. AOL's Online Mailbox, filled with unread messages.

You can sort messages by date, file type, sender, or subject. Just click the appropriate column head. Click again to see the reverse order. To restore the default, click Date.

Message Types

Message *type* is indicated by an icon on the far left of each message line in the mailbox.

- **Envelope icon:** The message consists of words only — no inserted images or file attachments.
- **Computer disk fastened to the back of the envelope:** A file is attached to the message. See "Handling File Attachments."
- **Envelope icon with a check through it:** You've already read the message. Unless you select this message and click the Keep As New button, the message is transferred from the New Mail tab to the Old Mail tab when you close the mailbox window.
- **Small square in the lower-left corner of the envelope icon:** The message contains an inserted picture or HTML-formatted text and images. Anyone on the Internet can send you HTML-formatted messages, but only AOL members can insert and receive messages with pictures.
- **A blue message icon (not shown in Figure 10-3):** Official AOL mail, such as the message you receive when you join AOL.

Sizing Up Your Messages Before Reading Them

When you open your mailbox, notice that each message is on its own line. For each message you can see four pieces of information that describe the message. Scan this information to identify important and personal messages, as well as messages of less interest and the occasional unsolicited message.

The four pieces of information, from left to right, are listed in Table 10-1. Refer to Figure 10-3.

Table 10-1. Sizing Up Your Messages

Type of information	*Indicates*
Type	Whether this is a simple text message or something more complex. I describe message types in more detail in this section.
Date	Date that you received the message. Open the message to find out the exact time the message was sent.
E-Mail Address	Sender's e-mail address (screen name or Internet e-mail address). Long e-mail addresses are chopped off at about 16 characters.
Subject	Message's subject, as typed by the person who sent the message.

Reading Your Mail

To open a message, either double-click it or select the message and click the Read button.

When you open any message in your mailbox, the first thing you see is the message header at the top of the message, which repeats information from the mailbox (date, subject, and so on). This header includes the underlined screen names and e-mail addresses of the message's sender and recipients (including people who received a courtesy copy, or CC). The Running Man icon appears next to AOL screen names. (Refer to Figure 10-1.) You also see the name and size of any attached file.

If an Internet friend sent the message, you can get more complex information by clicking Details.

You're likely to receive e-mail that contains blue underlined links, also called hyperlinks, in the message body. A link may take you to AOL content (if the link is in an AOL channel newsletter, for example) or to another location on the Web. Pass your mouse over a link to see the actual Web address (URL).

Caution

Unsolicited mail can contain links that you think are unsuitable for children. Use Mail Controls, covered in Chapter 4, to restrict who can send mail to a child's mailbox, and be sure to report e-mail that violates AOL's Terms of Service by clicking the Notify AOL button in the Online Mailbox.

AOL's Online Presence Indicator

New in AOL 7.0 is AOL's Online Presence indicator, or OLP. The Online Presence indicator allows you to get instant information about your AOL buddies and Internet friends. (That's because the OLP works with AIM-registered Internet e-mail addresses, too.) You can also use OLP to help organize your Address Book and Buddy List.

When you receive an e-mail or instant message from an AOL member or AIM user, the person's screen name appears in the message header next to the AOL Running Man icon. (The following figure shows you what the OLP indicator looks like in the header of an e-mail message.)

Just click the screen name (which is formatted like a hyperlink) to find out if the member is online. In the box that appears, you can choose to do any (or all) of the following:

- Send new mail to the member
- Send an instant message to the member
- Add the member's screen name to your online Address Book
- Add the member's screen name to your Buddy List
- View the member's profile
- View the member's Web page at AOL Hometown

Click to find info

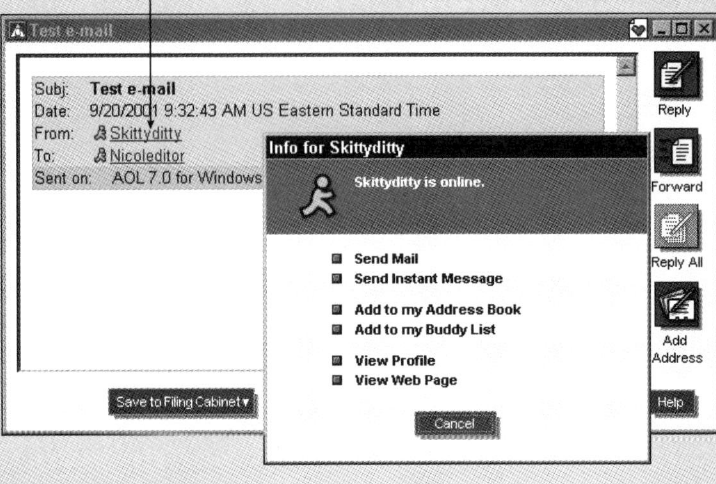

Managing Your Mail

Managing your e-mail doesn't involve more thinking than sorting through your postal mail and deciding what is for you, what is for others you live with, what must be taken seriously, and what can be tossed in the garbage.

You can do any or all of the following to any message you receive:

- Reply to the person sending the message.
- Reply to the sender and to all the other people who received the message.
- Forward the message and any file attachment to someone else or several other people.
- Move the message to your Filing Cabinet, where you now have the option of storing it in named folders.
- Leave the message in your Online Mailbox and click Keep As New. (See "Using Your AOL Mailbox," earlier in this chapter.)
- Use AOL's new Online Presence indicator to find out if the AOL member who sent you the e-mail is online or to add the person's screen name to your Buddy List or Address Book. See the sidebar, "AOL's Online Presence Indicator," in this chapter, for more information.
- Save the message as a text file or Web page for use in other programs, such as a word processor, or for viewing in a browser.
- Delete the message.

Replying to a Message

E-mail messages have a conversational feel; some people consider messages closer to talking than writing. Even if you lavish care on making your messages unique, they can still be part of larger conversations. To reply to a message:

1. With a message displayed, decide if you want to quote the original message. Then, decide *what* you want to reply to.
   - To include all or part of a message in your reply, use your mouse to select the part of the text that you want and click the Reply button. The selected text appears at the top of the new Write Mail window.

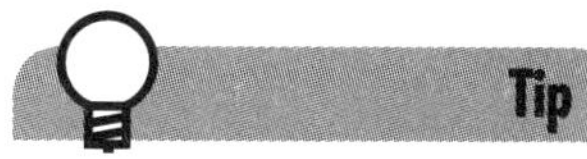

Use your keyboard to manage mail. After opening the first of your new messages, simply use the right/left arrow keys and to work through your messages.

- If you'd rather not quote anything, leave all the text unselected, and click Reply. Nothing will appear in the new Write Mail window. In this case, the only indication that you are replying is the Subject line, which will have *Re:* and the same Subject line that the sender of the original message used.

2. Decide who to reply to:
   - To reply to a message someone sent just to you, click the Reply button in the upper-right hand corner of the Read Mail window.
   - If you were one of many recipients of the message, as in an informal mailing list for your bowling team, click the Reply All button instead of Reply. If you choose to exclude some recipients from your reply, select the addresses you don't want and delete them.

   In either case, if you first selected some text, it appears to the right of a vertical blue bar in your Reply window, as shown in Figure 10-4.

With a message displayed, add the sender's e-mail address or screen name to your Address Book. Just click the Add Address button, edit the Address Book entry for that person, and click OK. Chapter 11 has all the details.

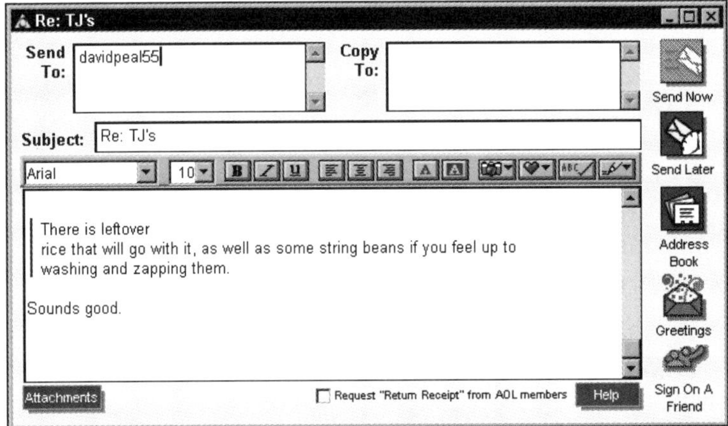

Figure 10-4. In this figure, the reply follows the quoted text.

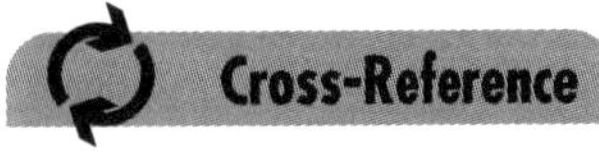

Chapter 11 discusses formatting effects and other e-mail options.

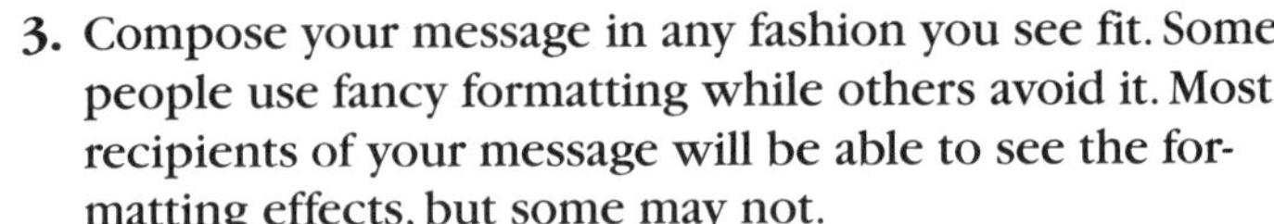

3. Compose your message in any fashion you see fit. Some people use fancy formatting while others avoid it. Most recipients of your message will be able to see the formatting effects, but some may not.
4. All done? Click Send Now. Want to send the reply later? Click Send Later.

Forwarding a Message

Forwarding a message means passing the message on to someone who was not a direct or indirect recipient. You forward when you think a message will interest someone else.

To forward a message, first display it and then:

1. Select nothing if you want to forward the entire message without emphasizing anything in particular.

   Select part of the message to highlight just that part, while also sending along the original message in its entirety.
2. Click Forward. Your new message picks up the original message's Subject line, preceded by *Fwd:* and a space. In the body of the message, you see *nothing* if you forward the entire message, or just a few words if that's all you want to forward. In either case, the entire message is forwarded.
3. Optionally, add some words of your own, if you wish, to provide context for the entire forwarded message or the message fragment. Click Send Now.

You can't select discontinuous parts of a message to highlight in a forward, but you can select the whole message and delete what you don't want.

Saving a Message

To save a message, display it and choose File⇨Save As. Give the message a name in the File Name field of the Save As dialog box that appears. Then find a folder in which to keep it. The Save In field identifies the drive (hard drive, Zip drive, and so on) and the main folders window identifies the folder in which to keep the file. In the Save as Type box, you can choose to save the message as text or HTML. The HTML option makes the most sense for HTML-formatted messages (with links and styling), such as AOL's channel newsletters (which I describe in Chapter 13). Click Save when you're done; you can now retrieve the saved message at any time while on AOL by choosing File⇨Open and navigating to the folder in which you saved the message.

Printing a Message

To print from your mailbox, you must be online. To print from your Filing Cabinet, which holds your archived messages, you can be online or off. To print any displayed message, use Print⇨Print or Ctrl+P.

Deleting a Message

Deleting old or unwanted messages is a good way of preventing your mailbox from becoming unmanageable. To delete a *displayed* message, simply click the Delete button. The next message appears in its place. To delete a message from the mailbox, select it and click Delete.

To delete several messages, press Shift and then click the first and last of a series of messages to delete. Press Ctrl and then click to select messages scattered throughout your mailbox for deletion. Then click Delete.

You can restore deleted messages for a day after you delete them by choosing Mail⇨Recently Deleted Mail. Select the message you want to keep and click Keep As New.

Change your mind about a message you've deleted? You can *restore,* or undelete, messages for about a day after deleting them. From the AOL toolbar, choose Mail⇨Recently Deleted Mail. From the list of deleted messages, select the message and click the Keep As New button. Click Read first if you want to verify that you've found the right message. The next time you open your Online Mailbox, find your salvaged messages by scanning message dates for the date when the message was originally received.

Handling File Attachments

What's a *file attachment*? It's a document, picture, or sound file that is sent to you along with the message you received. It's called an attachment because it is sent together with the e-mail; its mailbox icon shows an envelope with a disk attached to it (refer to Figure 10-3). When you open a message with an attached file, the header shows you

- The name of the attached file, including the all-important file extension, which tells you what program you need to use the file.
- The size of the file.
- The approximate amount of time needed to download the file (DL), given your connection type and modem speed. In Figure 10-5, you can see in the header that the message has a file attached.

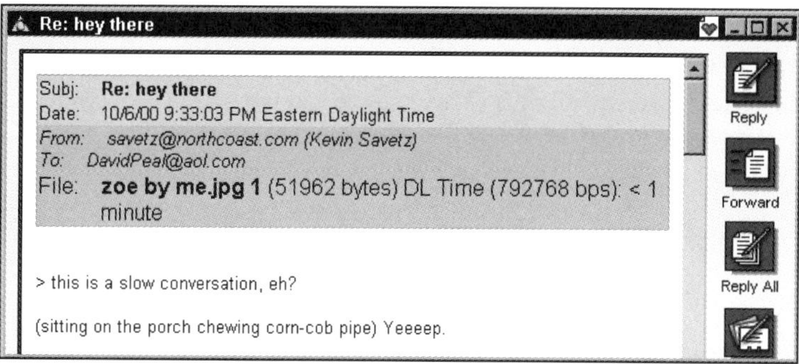

Figure 10-5. This picture, whose file size is 52K (***51962 bytes***), will take less than a minute (***< 1 minute***) to download (***DL Time***).

Downloading Attached Files

The longer you're on AOL, the higher the likelihood that someone you know will send you a file attachment. AOL makes downloading attached files easy.

1. With the message displayed, click the Download button. From the drop-down menu, choose Download Now. Use Download Later if you want to save all your downloading for the end of a session or for a time specified in Automatic AOL (see "Getting Your Mail Automatically").
2. A standard AOL window comes up warning you about the dangers of downloading files from unknown sources. When you're done reading it, click Yes to proceed if you have some idea who sent you the message.

   If you have downloaded the file before (which can happen for many reasons), a message asks whether you want to do so again. If you're unsure that you still have the file or ever saw it, use Download Manager to look for the file. Choose File⇨Download Manager and click the Show Files Downloaded button. If you don't see the file in the Download Manager window, look for it by pressing Ctrl+F.

   - If you have in fact downloaded the file, select it and click Locate to find out where it is and whether it is still available.
   - If you haven't downloaded the file, download it from the open message.

Don't download files if you don't know who sent them — and even if you do know who sent them always scan attachments for viruses before downloading. Unless you're expecting the file and know exactly what it is, never download attachments ending in EXE or VBS — they can be dangerous. Find more information at AOL Keyword: **Virus**.

Keeping downloaded files in a folder is the best way to avoid losing them. To change the default download folder, use the Download Manager as described in Chapter 15.

3. Confirm where you want to save the file and what you want to call it.
4. Retrieve the file and use it as you wish.

Using Downloaded Files

Anything can be attached to a message: a picture (JPG or GIF), a word-processed document (DOC, RTF, or TXT), a compressed file (ZIP), an entire software application (ZIP or EXE), or something else.

- Image and sound files are pretty easy to handle. Usually, AOL automatically displays images and plays sounds as they are being downloaded.
- If the file doesn't play or display, or if it is a word-processed document, you see the following message box after the file has downloaded:

  ```
  The file has been downloaded.
  Would you like to locate the file now?
  ```

  Click Yes, and you are taken to the open folder where the file was downloaded. You may need to scroll through folders to find highlighted files.

  Note: To see the Download Complete box, you must right-click the Internet Explorer icon on the Windows desktop. Choose Properties. Click the Advanced tab. In the Browsing category, find the Notify When Downloads Complete option and make sure a check is in the check box.
- Opening DOC and TXT (text) files automatically opens an application in which to view and edit them. If your PC doesn't know which program to use to open the file (no program has been *associated* with it), you are asked (in a window) to identify the program you want to use for the file. For text files, you can choose AOL itself, because text files can be opened by choosing File⇨Open.
- You'll frequently see zipped files attached to messages; these files are reduced in size and combined into a single file for speedier downloading. You download such files, as normal. AOL automatically unzips compressed files immediately after they've been downloaded or when you sign off. You can decide when to unzip them and whether to delete the ZIP file afterward at Settings⇨Preferences. Click Download and use the buttons on the right to make your choices.

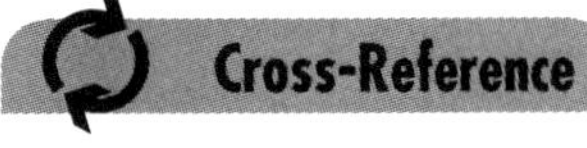

Chapter 16 introduces software that gives you more control over zipped files and the ability to zip your own files.

Managing Your Filing Cabinet

Your Filing Cabinet is the set of folders on your hard drive where you can automatically store, for as long as you want, all your messages — the ones you've read, the ones you've sent, and the ones you've written but not yet sent. AOL provides you with a set of folders for your sent, received, and to-be-sent messages. You can also create folders to store messages on a similar subject or from the same person, as I did in the window shown in Figure 10-6.

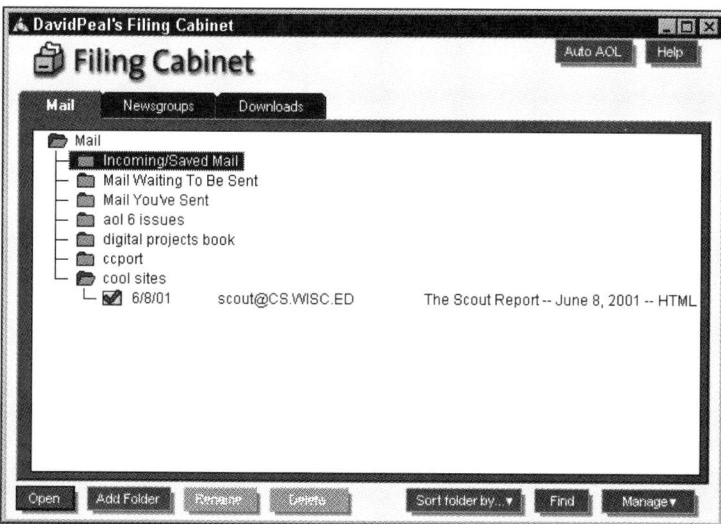

Figure 10-6. Your Filing Cabinet keeps all your messages, files, and postings on your hard drive. AOL supplies the first three folders, but you can create new folders like I did.

You can also set up your Filing Cabinet to keep track of downloaded files and the newsgroup postings you've downloaded with Automatic AOL, described in the next section. Your Filing Cabinet is always available, online or offline, at Mail➪Filing Cabinet. Online, you can learn about your Filing Cabinet at AOL Keyword: **PFC**.

To have AOL save *all* your messages in your Filing Cabinet, you need to adjust your preferences. Choose Settings➪Preferences. In the Preferences windows, click Filing Cabinet. In Figure 10-7, the bottom two preferences let you decide which messages to save in your Filing Cabinet automatically. Make sure a check appears in the boxes, and click OK. You can also tell the AOL software how much space on your hard drive to devote to the Filing Cabinet, and how frequently to back it up. Backups are discussed later in the chapter.

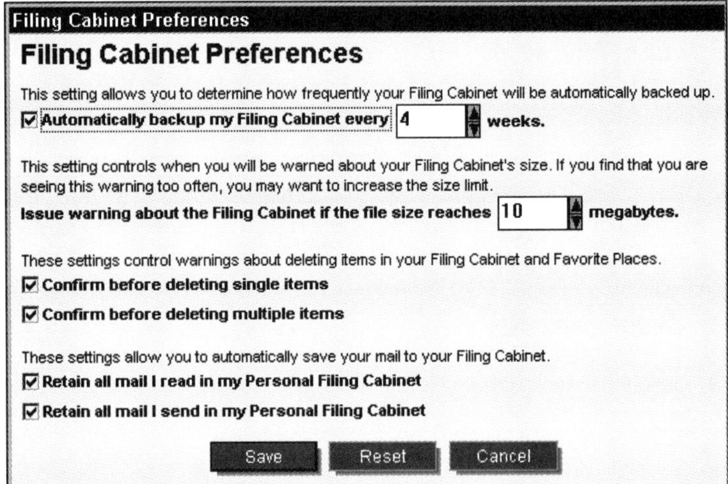

Figure 10-7. Your Filing Cabinet preferences.

Using Your Filing Cabinet

When you read a message stored in your Filing Cabinet, it comes up in the same Read Mail window that you use for your daily mail. From this window, all the buttons work, so you can reply, delete, or forward a message or add the sender's address to your Address Book.

- To delete one or more messages, select them and click Delete. You can Shift-click or Ctrl-click to select groups of messages to delete.
- To find a message tucked away in some obscure corner of your Filing Cabinet, open the folder and then click Find or press Ctrl+F. Bear in mind that Ctrl+F looks only through message headers. Your Filing Cabinet's Find button is slightly more complex: It gives you the ability to search the content of messages, as well as their headers. Searching content can be slower, but retrieves the information you specify.

- You can now create a subfolder in any Filing Cabinet folder and a subfolder within any subfolder. Then, sort your messages and drag messages into the folder.
- To sort a folder, simply select the folder and click the Sort Folder By button. Then, select how you want to sort the folders.

You can sort Filing Cabinet folders as well as your mailbox. Sorting folders helps you see all the messages from the same person or on the same subject.

Creating Folders for Your Filing Cabinet

Having AOL store your messages automatically is a good way to avoid misplacing or losing them. It is also a good way to create a gigantic Filing Cabinet that can slow AOL's start-up performance and become difficult to use.

The alternative lets you save only the messages you want to save, and also lets you create folders in which to save them. You can add folders to your Filing Cabinet in two ways:

- In your Filing Cabinet, open the folder and click Add Folder. Give the folder a name. You can drag the folder to a new position, or folder, and drag messages into it.
- With an e-mail message displayed, click Save to Filing Cabinet. From the bottom of the menu that comes up (shown in Figure 10-8), choose Create Folder. In the little Create a Folder box, give your new folder a name and click OK.

The Save To Filing Cabinet menu has separator lines. Any new folders you manually add to your Filing Cabinet appear between these lines in alphabetical order.

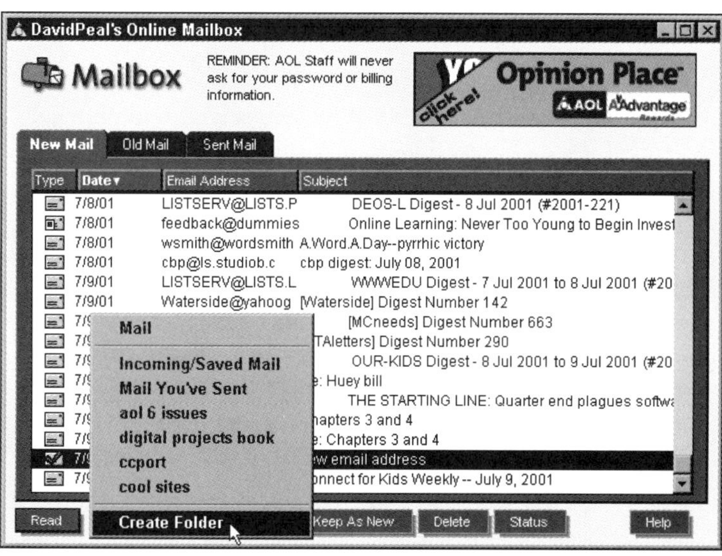

Figure 10-8. Use this menu to save messages in folders created by AOL or by you.

From now on, you can save other messages in your new folders.

You can save messages in your Filing Cabinet while viewing the mailbox or when you have an individual message open:

- Looking at your mailbox, you can add several messages at the same time to the Filing Cabinet (hold down the Shift or Ctrl key while clicking); then click Save to Filing Cabinet.
- Looking at an individual message, click the Save to Filing Cabinet button.

You now indicate the folder where you want to save the message:

- **Mail:** Sends the message(s) to the top-level Mail folder of your Filing Cabinet. These extra-special messages appear in your Filing Cabinet at the same level as the major mail folders.
- **Incoming/Saved Mail:** Sends a selected or open message to the folder that contains all the mail you receive, regardless of subject or sender.
- **Mail You've Sent:** Sends a selected or open message to the Mail You've Sent folder, which is designated for the messages you've sent.
- **Folders you have created yourself:** In addition to the standard menu options, any folder you created appears on this menu as well (as in *cool sites* in Figure 10-8).
- **Create Folder:** If you want to save selected mail in a new folder, choose this item. A small dialog box appears where you type the name of the new folder. In the future, you can save messages in your new folder.

Saving manually requires daily vigilance. If you forget to save your sent or incoming messages, AOL automatically deletes them after a specified amount of time.

Backing Up Your Filing Cabinet

Your Filing Cabinet includes the e-mail messages you've recently sent and received, whether you've been storing automatically or manually. It also includes any organizational scheme you've created by saving messages in special folders. And it includes downloaded files and newsgroup postings.

Too Many Filing Cabinets?

The messages in your Online Mailbox are stored on AOL's computers and are thus available from any copy of AOL on any computer.

By contrast, your Filing Cabinet saves mail on the hard drive of the computer where the copy of PC is installed. That means you will have a separate Filing Cabinet, and separate Filing Cabinet preferences for *each* screen name and for *each* upgraded version of the AOL software. As a result, your old messages can be distributed across several Filing Cabinets, making it difficult to remember where to find a specific message.

To get around the problem, you can copy your Filing Cabinet file from one copy of AOL to another. You can do this because the Filing Cabinet is stored as one file for each screen name. That file has the same name as your screen name, and it is located in your America Online 7.0/ Organize folder. Because of its size, a file may require a Zip disk when you transfer it.

Be careful, though. When you copy a Filing Cabinet from one AOL folder to another, you are copying over an existing Filing Cabinet. To avoid this, first rename the existing Filing Cabinet file (for example, from `dpeal` to `dpeal01`).

Copying and transferring your Filing Cabinet comes in handy if you have just installed AOL on a different computer.

Upgrade AOL at AOL Keyword: **Upgrade**.

In your Filing Cabinet preferences (Settings⇨Preferences), you can have your Filing Cabinet backed up automatically.

The default setting is for backups to occur once every four weeks when you sign off. You can decrease or increase the frequency of backups by clicking the arrows in the Filing Cabinet Preferences dialog box.

From time to time, you may want to protect your valuable information by creating a back-up copy of your Filing Cabinet.

To change your Filing Cabinet preferences, follow these steps:

1. Choose Settings⇨Preferences and select Filing Cabinet.
2. Place a checkmark in the checkbox to automatically back up the Filing Cabinet. Click the arrows to indicate how often you want the backups to take place.

3. You can also adjust the settings to have AOL warn you if your Filing Cabinet becomes too big or to warn you if you delete files or Favorite Places. If you're not sure if you want to change these settings, leave the defaults in place.
4. To restore the backed-up Filing Cabinet, click Manage⇨Restore.

To manually back up your Filing Cabinet, follow these steps:

1. In AOL, choose File⇨Filing Cabinet.
2. In the Filing Cabinet window, click Manage. In the pop-up menu, choose Backup.
3. In the Backup Your Filing Cabinet window, click Backup Now.

To restore your Filing Cabinet from a backup copy:

1. In AOL, choose File⇨Filing Cabinet.
2. In the Filing Cabinet window, click Manage. In the pop-up menu, choose Restore.
3. In the Restore Your Filing Cabinet window, click Yes. Your Filing Cabinet will be restored as of the date the last backup was made. Any information saved to your Filing Cabinet since the date of the last backup will be lost, however.

Don't delete messages you read on your handheld or wireless phone. AOL Anywhere devices can't yet be synchronized with a desktop Filing Cabinet.

Getting Your Mail Automatically

Automatic AOL lets you download e-mail messages, as well as message board and newsgroup postings, either on demand or on a set schedule. This is a useful option because it enables you to always get your mail whenever you want it — and store it on your home computer. If you do the downloading automatically, AOL automatically signs on for you, fetches messages, and signs off. To set up this feature, just follow these steps:

For Automatic AOL to work, your computer must be turned on, the AOL software must be open, and your modem or other connection device needs to be set up. But you need not be signed on to AOL.

1. Choose Mail⇨Automatic AOL and use the check boxes to tell AOL *what* to download or send during an automatic session: e-mail messages waiting to be sent, new mail, newsgroup postings, and so on. Figure 10-9 shows the Automatic AOL window.

2. To indicate which screen names will receive the messages and files, click the Select Names button and put a check by the appropriate screen name or names. You also need to enter the corresponding passwords so that AOL can sign on automatically and perform tasks for those people.

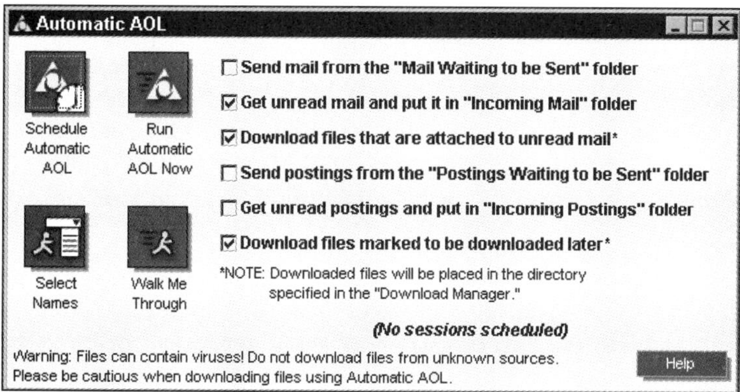

Figure 10-9. Tell AOL to retrieve messages, files, and postings automatically for offline use.

3. Tell AOL when to download messages for the screen names selected in Step 3. Click the Schedule Automatic AOL button to open the scheduling window. In the window, you
   - Check Enable Scheduler.
   - Set the frequency for message pick-ups. You can have your mail downloaded from every half hour to every day.
   - Specify the days when you want automatic pickups and deliveries.

   You don't have to schedule a session if you'll be running ad-hoc sessions (see the Tip).
4. Close the Automatic AOL window to set your new schedule.

You can read your automatically downloaded mail by opening your Filing Cabinet. Choose Mail⇨Filing Cabinet, and open the Incoming/Saved Mail folder.

Tip

If you don't need the regular pickups, just run Automatic AOL whenever you need it. From the Automatic AOL window, click the Run Automatic AOL Now button.

Find It Online

For tips and advice for avoiding junk mail, start at AOL Keyword: **Spam**. From there you link to Parental Controls and use the Mail Controls (Chapter 4) to restrict the kinds and sources of mail that minors can receive.

Managing Junk Mail

At home, I get so much paper junk mail that I usually sort the day's mail at the garbage can, throwing away much more than I keep. That's an example of managing mail. Fortunately, you can stop most junk e-mail on AOL, too.

Start at AOL Keyword **Neighborhood Watch** for guidelines on keeping kids safe and avoiding unwanted mail.

Unsolicited messages, otherwise known as *spam*, plague all Internet subscribers. Although AOL uses advanced technology and legal action to stop spam, you might get unwanted messages from time to time. Such mail includes make-money-fast schemes, advertisements of adult Web sites, barely credible business offers, and the occasional annoying chain letter.

Here are some guidelines for managing unsolicited mail:

Your AOL mailbox now has a Notify AOL button you can use to report offensive and unsolicited messages.

- Whenever you see a message from someone whose address you don't recognize or whose Subject line contains a pitch or a teaser, consider simply deleting the message right away. (Or, right-click the message in your mailbox and choose Ignore. When you close the mailbox, the message goes into the Old Mail box, from which it will disappear in a few days.)
- Never download files attached to messages from unknown senders. If you make the mistake of downloading such a file, never open it! It could contain a virus, worm, or other nasty critter and do serious harm to your computer.
- You often find *links* (blue, underlined words or phrases that link you to Web sites) in unsolicited messages. These links can direct you to offensive sites or fake pages meant to look like AOL. The e-mails and Web pages may claim that you've won a prize or encourage you to type in your password. Ignore these bogus messages and links.

Spam e-mail addresses are often faked, but you can often decode the domains from which they are sent (AOL Keyword: **Learn Domains** explains how).

Here's AOL's advice: "To play it safe, you can display the destination of the links before you click them. Simply position the cursor over the link. The destination (Web address) appears in a small box. Links to Web pages show the Web address or URL. Links to areas on AOL say *On AOL Only*. Displaying the destination, before clicking a link, is helpful if you're not sure if you should follow the link."

You can report inappropriate or unsolicited e-mail messages from within your Online Mailbox. If you're not sure if an e-mail message violates AOL's Terms of Service, use AOL Keyword: **Notify AOL** to find out more on handling offensive mail, message board postings, and instant messages.

Use Mail Controls, as explained in Chapter 4, to block mail from certain domains. For children, use Parental Controls (AOL Keyword: **Parental Controls**) to ensure that children don't receive messages you find inappropriate.

AOL Anywhere: New Ways to Do Mail

You don't spend all of your time sitting in front of a PC with AOL installed. At work or at school, on the road or at the playground, the AOL software is often not available, and few people travel or take vacations with their PC in tow.

AOL has created new ways of using AOL features in exactly those situations. The growing collection of AOL Anywhere services can be used from *any* connected PC, regardless of whether the AOL software is installed. You can now read your mail and use other features with gadgets like handheld computers and wireless phones. Finally, new gadgets, such as Mobile Communicator and Instant AOL, bring the convenience of AOL Anywhere into the home. The following sections provide an overview of what's involved in using mail anywhere.

Here are some handy AOL Anywhere tools:

- **AOL Mail on the Web** gives you access to your AOL mail when you're using a Web browser but don't have the AOL software. This means you can do your mail on anyone's computer, as long as the computer has an Internet connection.
- **AOL Mail for PDAs** lets you read and send mail using a handheld computer, such as a Palm or Pocket PC.

Find It Online

For more about AOL Anywhere services, go to AOL Keyword: **Anywhere** or choose Settings⇨AOL Devices.

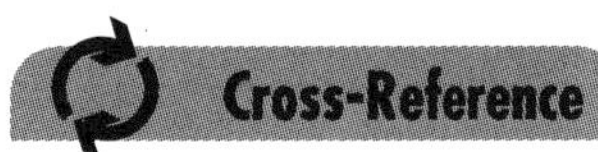

AOLTV is covered in Chapter 18.

- **AOL Mobile Communicator** lets you get mail and AOL services, such as shopping and weather, from wireless phones.
- **AOLTV** gives you many AOL features, including chat, browsing, and e-mail. While you watch a show, you can use AOL on your TV via a set-top box.
- **AOL Mail Alerts** allow you to receive notifications on your pager or cell phone whenever you get new e-mail; the service can be set up to display only the messages that you really want to read.
- **AOLbyPhone** allows you to hear your e-mail messages, news, restaurant reviews, and other AOL services, over the phone.

Using AOL Mail on the Web

AOL Mail on the Web is just like the AOL Mail described so far in this chapter, except that instead of doing your mail using the AOL software, you use the Web and an Internet connection. If you're traveling, at a friends house, or at work, you can check your mail. Here's what to do:

1. Connect to the Internet through a network or Internet service provider. If you're using someone else's computer, ask that person how he or she connects to the Internet.
2. Open the browser, if it isn't open already.
3. Type **aolmail.aol.com** into the browser's address box and press Enter.
4. Enter your screen name and password in the boxes provided. If you use a current copy of the Netscape or Internet Explorer browser, your password can be stored so it won't have to be reentered. (Whether you want someone else accessing your account is another question.) When your screen name has been accepted, you see a final button that you can click to access your e-mail.

Figure 10-10 shows AOL Mail on the Web. Notice the similarities to your ordinary Online Mailbox, including the three tabs (New Mail, Old Mail, and Sent Mail). Also, Download Now, Close, Keep As New, and Delete are available at the top as well as bottom of the Web page when you open a message.

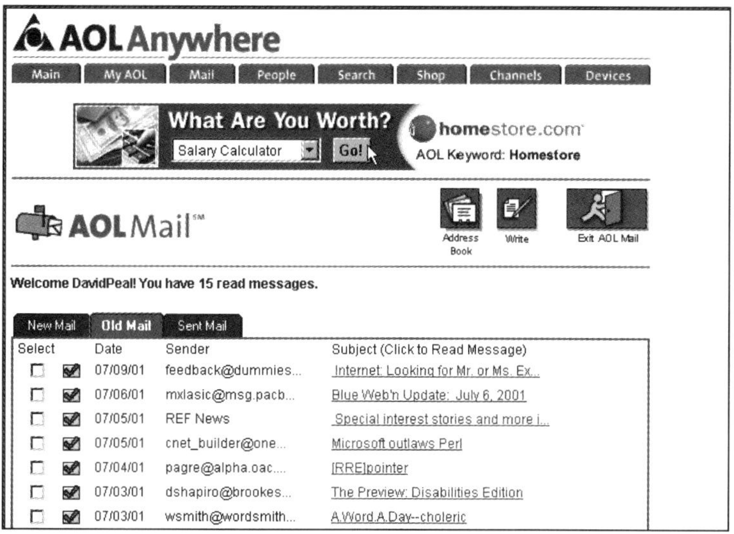

Figure 10-10. AOL Mail on the Web.

You may also notice some differences, including the following:

- You can't sort your mail on the Web.
- You don't have access to your Filing Cabinet because your Filing Cabinet is stored on your hard drive, not AOL's computers.
- AOL Mail on the Web may be slower than your regular AOL mail service because you're subject to Web traffic jams.
- Check boxes before each message give you the ability to select a *group* of messages (by clicking in the boxes) that you want to delete or keep as new.
- New messages are linked (underlined and blue) and thus clickable. To read a message, click it. If a file is attached to a message, the file is also linked.
- You can reply and forward messages, but you can't Send Later (for replies) or Download Later (for attached files).
- You can't yet quote selectively, but you can quote the entire original message by clicking the Include Entire Original Text in Reply check box, which is above the Reply button in the original message.

Be wary of deleting messages when you use AOL Mail on the Web. You don't have access to your recently deleted mail and thus can't later retrieve a message you've read and deleted until you sign on from home.

To quote selectively, you can copy and paste text from the original message (using Ctrl+C and Ctrl+V) into the Write window. Use the Review Original Message button in the window where you're replying.

You can attach only one file per message.

To write a new message, click the Write button in the main AOL Mail window (see Figure 10-11). To attach a file, click Browse and find the file on your floppy, zip, or other disk.

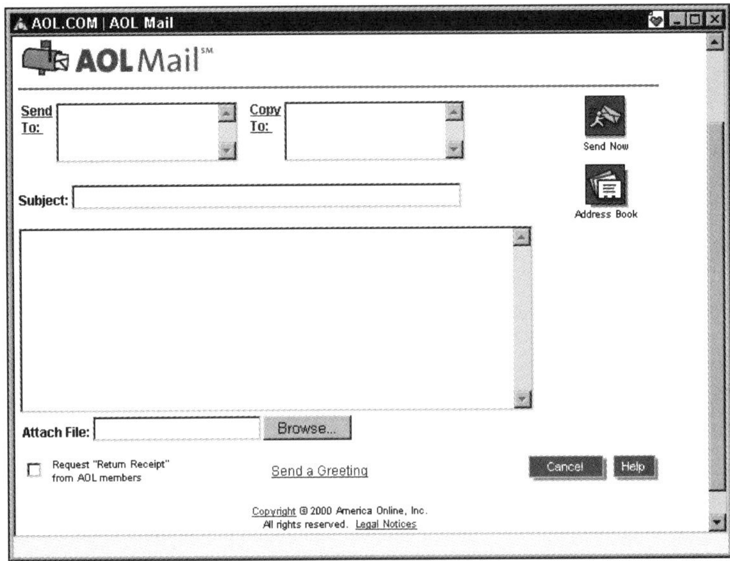

Figure 10-11. Writing a message in AOL Mail on the Web.

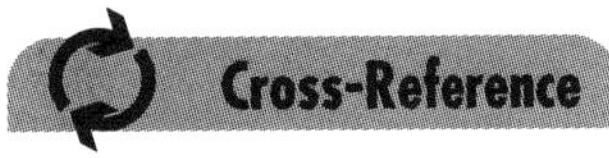

For more on creating and using a Buddy List, see Chapter 12. For more on using the Address Book, see Chapter 11.

Increasingly, AOL Anywhere devices can display more and more personalized content, which you set up by using My AOL, as explained in Chapter 3. For example, your Buddy List, Address Book, and My AOL content preferences are popping up on AOL Mail on the Web, Mobile AOL, AOLTV, and elsewhere. Maintenance of all this information on AOL's computers enables you to use it from any device, anywhere.

When writing a message from the Web, notice that the Send To and Copy To boxes are linked, which means that they can be clicked. These are the boxes where you put the recipients' e-mail address(es). Clicking either link brings up a copy of your Buddy List, the list you use to keep track of the screen names and addresses of online acquaintances. You can also see an Address Book button. Click it to select addresses to use in the Send To and Copy To boxes. From the Web view of your Address Book, you can add a new contact to your Address Book that will appear no matter where you use AOL.

To leave AOL Mail, click the Exit AOL Mail button in the upper-right corner of the AOL Mail window.

Using Your Handheld Computer for Mail and Messaging

AOL now lets you read, save, and send e-mail on a handheld organizer. Palm is the world's most popular PDA (personal digital assistant), but you can use similar devices with AOL as well, including Windows CE devices and Pocket PCs, and Palm-compatibles like the Handspring Visor.

On any of these AOL Anywhere services you can do the following:

- See your new, old, and sent mail.
- Write and send messages.
- Reply to, delete, and forward mail.
- Use Automatic AOL.
- Keep a File Cabinet, similar to the Filing Cabinet you have for each copy of AOL on a PC or Mac. File Cabinets, however, are not currently synchronized with Filing Cabinets.

All your messages on the New, Old, and Sent tabs are maintained on AOL's computers, so you can access them on your handheld device. If you delete a message from your PDA, the message won't be available on your home computer.

To find out what you need to access your mail on your handheld computer, see Table 10-2. All the software you need is free. From AOL Keyword: **Anywhere**, select Handheld from the drop-down list, and click Go. In the AOL for PDAs window, click Palm for both the wired and wireless versions of the AOL Mail software.

Table 10-2. Using AOL on Your Handheld Computer

Type of Handheld	*What You Need*
Palm 3.0 or higher, including all Handsprings	AOL for Palm OS, Palm modem (not wireless), and a phone jack
Wireless Palm (series VII)	The wireless version of AOL for Palm OS and a subscription to a wireless service provider, such as OmniSky

(continued)

Table 10-2. *(continued)*

Type of Handheld	*What You Need*
A Pocket PC device from Hewlett-Packard, Casio, Compaq, and others	AOL Mail for PocketPC, PocketPC modem (not wireless), phone jack
A Windows CE device from Hewlett-Packard, Casio, Compaq, Philips, and others	Windows CE 2.11 or higher, AOL Mail, working modem, phone jack

The PDA Community (AOL Keyword: **PDA**) has a highly informative newsletter called Pocket Press. At this keyword, you can also find message boards, Palm software, software reviews, and PDA-related chat and links.

AOL Keyword: **Shop@AOL** carries all major PDAs.

Getting and Installing AOL for Palm OS

Because of the Palm's (and Palm compatibles') enormous popularity and the higher cost of Pocket PCs and wireless services, this section takes a closer look at AOL for the Palm OS. Installation and usage instructions for all versions of AOL for handheld devices are available online at AOL Keyword: **PDA**.

With AOL for Palm OS, you'll find many familiar AOL elements on the screen, including the look of the mailbox and the layout of individual messages.

To get AOL for Palm OS:

1. Go to AOL Keyword: **Anywhere**. From the All Services drop-down list, select Handhelds and click Go.
2. Under AOL for Palm OS, click the Download button. On the next page, select the kind of Palm you have (wireless or wired).
3. On the next page, click Windows Download. You are prompted to save the file; save it in the default directory specific in Download Manager (File⇨Download Manger). The file's name is `aol30.prc` or something similar.
4. When the file has downloaded, double-click it. The Palm software is placed in your Palm desktop software's Install Tool. Next time you synchronize your Palm, the AOL software will be transferred from your desktop to your handheld. After synchronization, you are ready to go.

Getting Started with AOL for Palm OS

To start AOL on your Palm handheld, you first need to open your launcher, the screen showing all your applications. Tap the Home icon in the upper-left corner of the Palm's Graffiti writing area. If AOL for Palm has been installed correctly, the familiar triangular AOL icon appears on the screen along with a group of other icons.

Follow these steps for signing on:

1. Tap the AOL icon to get started. AOL for Palm is actually a series of mini-applications, whose icons you can see after you tap the AOL icon. These applications include Mailbox, File Cabinet, Instant Message, Buddy List, Write, and Auto AOL.
2. Tap the Sign On icon in the upper-right corner of the AOL Mail display with your stylus. All your screen names have been automatically downloaded to your Palm. Choose a screen name and enter the corresponding password. If you want to save the password so that you don't have to enter it again, tap the Store Password check box.

   From the Sign On screen (like the AOL Welcome Screen) you can click either Sign On or Setup. Use Setup to create a new location (set up local access phone numbers) as described in Chapter 3.

   To edit your location (where you store your local access numbers), click Setup and follow the on-screen prompts.
3. Tap the small Sign On button after you have entered a password and selected a Location (phone number). When you're signed on, the screen is identical, but Sign Off replaces Sign On.
4. After you're signed on, you can read and write e-mail:
   - To read your mail, tap Mailbox. Your mail now downloads, probably more slowly than when you use AOL on your PC. Just the same, it's your familiar AOL mail. Just as with your ordinary mail, you have three tabs: New, Old, and Sent, though you can't sort them by date or sender as you can on your PC. Messages you've read can be kept as new by returning to the AOL opening screen and tapping AutoAOL; click the appropriate box, and click Run AOL now.

This procedure is based on my use of a prerelease version of AOL 3 for the Palm, using a Handspring Visor. Your PDA may require slightly different steps.

The latest version of AOL lets you synchronize your PDA's Address Book with the one on your desktop computer.

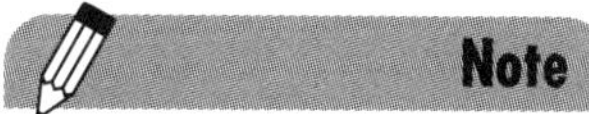

Although you can use AOL Mail on the Web while you are signed on to the AOL service from another computer, if you are signed on to the service when connecting with a Palm, you will be disconnected.

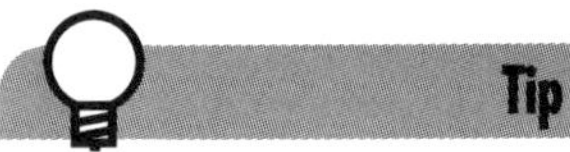

Click Send IM to exchange messages (yes, your Buddy List is available on the AOL opening screen).

Seeing your My AOL news, sports, and weather requires Palm OS version 3.5 or higher.

Currently *not* supported on AOL for PDAs are more advanced mail functions, such as embedding graphics, inserting links, attaching files, and so on.

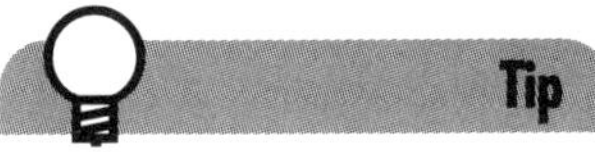

With AvantGo, you can download MapQuest maps for use on your Palm whenever you're in a new neighborhood and need a map at your fingertips.

- To write a message, tap Write from the opening AOL screen. Your Write screen looks entirely different from AOL's Write Mail window. You see a To line, a CC line, and a Subject area. You need to use Graffiti or a Palm keyboard to fill in these lines. Click Send Now or Send Later (or Cancel). For messages to be sent later, click AutoAOL at the mail AOL window, check the appropriate box, and click Run AOL now.

Managing messages on a Palm means replying, forwarding, deleting, and moving them to your File Cabinet. Clicking Save places a copy of any open message in your File Cabinet Saved tab, where it will be available only when you are using the same handheld device.

With your Buddy List, you can tell who's online at any moment.

Using AOL for Palm OS, you can now use the AvantGo software and service to download Web content from hundreds of journals, including *The New York Times, The Wall Street Journal, The Onion* (a satirical online daily), and *Englishtown* (daily English lessons).

AvantGo is free. You download the software from the AvantGo site (`www.avantgo.com`), install it on your PC, and install it on your Palm the next time you do a HotSync. At the Web site, you can register and select the content you want to download. This content is transferred to your Palm when you do a HotSync. Tap the AvantGo icon on your Palm launcher to read the day's articles from the selected newspapers.

Getting Mail Notifications on Your Pager or Wireless Phone

With the AOL Mail Alert Service, you can receive notifications on your pager or wireless phone when your AOL account receives important e-mail messages. The service works with any device that has an LCD window and displays text messages. The notification informs you of the sender and subject line, and shows as much of a message as your display will allow. Using a filter, you can specify which messages are sent to your device — all messages, all AOL messages, or messages from certain people. Use AOL Keyword: **Mail Alerts** for more information.

Mobile Communicator: E-Mail and IM Machine

The Mobile Communicator device was created for people who love to stay in touch by e-mail and messaging. As with all the AOL Anywhere devices, your regular AOL screen name can be used on Mobile Communicator. People talking to you can tell from the way you're listed in their Buddy List whether you're at your PC or at the playground with your Mobile Communicator. The rest of the family will appreciate the fact that, with AOL Mobile Communicator, multiple screen names on one account can use AOL at the same time.

As with Instant AOL (see the following sidebar), any privacy preferences set on AOL apply to your use of the Mobile Communicator, and any changes made to your preferences on the communicator update your desktop version of AOL.

You need to buy the Mobile Communicator and sign up for the monthly service. For prices and an online user guide, see AOL Keyword: **Mobile Communicator**.

Note that the AOL Mail Alert Service does not permit you to receive and send actual messages. Like a pager, the incoming message tells you that someone is trying to communicate with you and that you need to use another device (a computer or connected telephone) to read the entire message and reply. The received messages aren't forwarded mail, but just notify you of incoming mail. The service costs nothing beyond your existing AOL account and any monthly fees you pay for your paging or cell phone service.

Using AOLbyPhone

The new AOLbyPhone service enables you to receive your e-mail by telephone, which (unlike pagers and cell phones) is ubiquitous, at least in the developed world. The service works as follows. You pay a monthly fee (currently $4.95), in addition to any ongoing AOL subscription fees. To use the service, you dial 1-800-574-1779 (you use the same number to sign up for the service). You need an account number (use your phone number to simplify things) and a personal identification

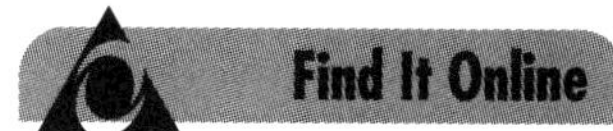

For more information, go to AOL Keyword: **AOLbyPhone**.

number (PIN); both can be changed online at AOL Keywords: **AOLbyPhone** and **AOLbyPhone PIN**, respectively.

To use the service, you need to identify yourself by voice; the system can actually recognize you by your voice. As in a recorded message, the recorded voice gives you a series of menu choices, from which you can choose e-mail, news, movie times, stock quotes, and so on.

Using AOL Over a Wireless Phone

Definition

Wireless technology consists of devices that connect with the Internet through radio waves. Wireless requires no cables to use the Internet connection, thus you can use wireless devices anywhere.

What's so special about wireless technology? It cuts you loose from the desktop and its tangle of plugs and cords. The AOL Anywhere family of services includes two fully wireless devices: Mobile Communicator and the AOL Mobile service for cell phones. Instant AOL and AOLTV use a *wireless keyboard,* allowing you to type anywhere in the room.

When you use AOL on a cell phone all you see is a little text window, making wireless technology perfect for situations when you need to check your latest e-mail, get the forecast or a movie time, or do similar tasks.

How do you get text into a wireless phone to write e-mail? For all such questions, start at AOL Keyword: **Wireless**.

Using AOL on a wireless phone requires that you subscribe to one of the two wireless services through which AOL is now being offered: Sprint PCS Wireless Web and AT&T Digital PocketNet. You also need to buy one of the supported wireless phones. For more information about rates and benefits (number of minutes per month, free minutes, roaming charges, and so on), visit AOL Keyword: **Wireless** and check out links for cell phones.

The way you turn the wireless connection on and navigate the menus varies based on the type of phone you use. AOL's menu structure doesn't vary, so the demo at AOL Keyword: **Wireless** offers a good idea of the AOL features available, as well as how to access them.

The information at your fingertips when you use Mobile AOL on a cell phone comes from several sources:

- Your AOL mailbox, together with your Buddy List.
- The information preferences you set up at My AOL. These preferences, covered in Chapter 3, give you wireless access to your stock portfolio, weather forecasts, and political, sports, and entertainment headlines.

▶ AOL's location-based Web services. You can access MapQuest to get directions, and AOL's Local Guide Channel can help you find restaurant recommendations, concert times, and more. And you can use MovieFone to find movie times and locations.

Where to Go from Here

E-mail can quickly become central to everything you do on the Internet. AOL has long offered the simplest e-mail service to use, and now AOL Mail has come to the Web, the handheld computer, new devices like the Mobile Communicator, and old devices like the TV and wireless phone.

▶ Chapter 11 looks at sending messages, styling them, using the new Address Book, following netiquette, adding signatures, and more.

▶ Chapter 13 is all about *mailing lists,* which are communities based on e-mail.

▶ Chapter 18, which profiles AOLTV and AOL by cell phone, picks up the story of AOL Anywhere where this chapter left off.

Chapter 11

Sending Mail

IN THIS CHAPTER **PAGE**

Sending messages gives you the ability to take an active part in the world of the Internet. In this chapter, you can find out how easy it is to send someone a message. I also show you how to jazz up your messages with links, pictures, signatures, smileys, and more.

To create a new message, start by clicking the AOL toolbar's Write button. Up comes the Write Mail window, shown in Figure 11-1. Your basic message has three parts: the e-mail address or addresses of your recipient(s); the subject line; and the message itself. The next three sections look at each of these three message parts.

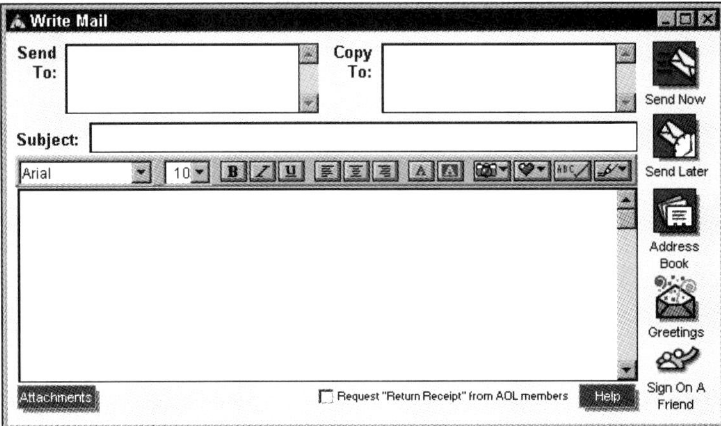

Figure 11-1. A clean slate: Here's where you make your mark.

Who's the Message For?

Cross-Reference

See Chapter 10 for information about the components of an address.

Tip

When writing e-mail, you may want to add the address last to avoid inadvertently sending a message before you're done.

Tip

AOL automatically completes e-mail addresses for you—if the person you're writing to is listed in your Address Book.

Sending a message requires at least one piece of information — an e-mail address. In the Send To box, enter an AOL screen name (without the `@aol.com` part). For friends not on AOL, a full Internet e-mail address is required (for example, `friend@suchandsuch.com` or `mypal@thisandthat.net`).

If you want to send your message to several people at once, you can easily do so. Whether the addresses are on AOL or the Internet, simply separate them with commas. Or, press Enter after each address. Don't worry if the addresses break (are automatically split) in weird places, such as between the *co* and the *m*. Maximizing your Write Mail window usually displays the addresses properly, and the computer sees the names as complete in any case.

The following list shows the types of e-mail recipients that you can address in your messages:

- The direct recipient of your message is the person (or persons) whose e-mail address goes in the Send To box. This is the person for whom your message is primarily intended.
- The indirect recipient is a person whom you want to be aware of a message or its contents. You can have more than one such recipient, but remember to

separate the addresses by commas. The addresses go in the Copy To box. Such messages are sometimes called *courtesy copies* (CCs).

Direct and indirect recipients can see each others' screen names or e-mail addresses in the message header, the descriptive lines at the top of every message.

- If you don't want the message's direct recipient (in the Send To box) to know that someone else is reading the message, send a *blind courtesy copy* (BCC) to the indirect recipient. You do this by enclosing the screen name or e-mail address in parentheses in the Copy To box. For multiple BCCs, separate the enclosed addresses with commas, as in `(helen@troy.mil, bismarck@prussia.gov)`.

  BCCs do make sense in some circumstances, for instance when sending mail to a very large group of people who don't want or need each other's addresses. To send a BCC to a large group, address the e-mail to yourself and BCC everyone else.

BCCs can be risky. If the direct recipient finds out that someone else was privy to an exchange, it can seem sneaky, a breach of confidentiality.

You don't have to be signed on to AOL to write a message, only to send it. You can draft messages offline and then click Send Later to store them. Online, retrieve your message by choosing Mail⇨Mail Waiting to be Sent and send it by selecting the message and then clicking Send Now.

What's the Message About?

You can help the people who receive your messages by letting them know at a glance, when they scan their mailbox, what a message is about. In the Subject line, you describe what's in the message and characterize the message's attitude as well.

People get so much mail these days that unless your Subject line is clear, your recipients may delete your message without bothering to open it. A short, punchy, communicative, and descriptive Subject line is likely to get positive attention.

Some people, like me, make the mistake of asking several questions in one message. Often, parts of my multisubject messages are never read. One subject per message can help ensure that the recipient doesn't overlook anything.

Exercise the same care in the messages you send as you expect from the messages you receive. AOL Keyword: **Neighborhood Watch** covers all angles of e-mail responsibility.

Writing Effective Messages

In an e-mail message as in a phone call, you are communicating from a distance. Although you can't hear the grain of someone's voice in an e-mail, you can lavish as much time as you want on your messages and responses. The next few sections offer suggestions for making the most of e-mail communications.

Keep Your Voice Down

Some message writers feel the need to do the equivalent of shouting in their messages. They press the Caps Lock key and type everything in ALL CAPITAL LETTERS. People who send out unsolicited commercial messages use this technique all the time. Messages in all capital letters are difficult to read, because the reader cannot identify a word (as in ordinary writing) by its shapely pattern of short and tall letters:

```
BE THE FIRST TO INVEST IN THIS SURE-FIRE
WINNER!!!
```

So, how *do* you emphasize certain words? In messages you send to someone on AOL, you can use italics, as you'll see in "Embellishing Messages" later in this chapter. In messages sent to people on the Internet, the reader may see only plain text and no styles, italics or otherwise—although rich text from AOL does work with most recipients' mail. Instead, you can use asterisks on either side of the word to get some *attention* or underscores to indicate a title, such as _War and Peace_. The best way to get attention and emphasize words is to write concisely, directly, and respectfully.

Avoid Needless Provocation

Messages sent to the Internet or those addressed with a combination of AOL and Internet recipients cannot be unsent, unlike messages sent to people on AOL. (See "Unsending a Message" later in this chapter.) That's a good reason to avoid sending any message you might later regret. Messages are easily misunderstood because you can't use body language to clarify your context. Because the other person isn't standing in front of you, it's easier to write hotheaded and intemperate messages than it might be to say something like that in person.

What to do? Don't even bother counting to ten. Click the Send Later button to give yourself a chance to calm down. (I discuss this button in "Sending That Message on Its Way" later in this chapter.) Review your letter later. It's just too easy to say something by e-mail that you will regret later.

Brevity

Brevity can help in the competition for the world's scarcest resource — other people's attention. Excessive brevity, however, can easily sound clipped. To avoid sounding short-tempered, try personalizing your messages. Begin with the recipient's name on a separate line, for example.

Quote Aptly

When you reply to someone's message, you can save people from having to read through an entire string just to get to the one sentence you're referring to if you quote only the most relevant parts of the message sent to you. In mailing lists in particular, no one wants to see the same message repeated in its entirety. To quote part of a message, use your mouse to select only the most pertinent words in the original and then click Reply or Reply All.

Signal Your Feelings

Words on paper can't convey intention and emotion the way a raised eyebrow or wrinkled nose can; that's what e-mail *emoticons* (also called *smileys*) are for. At AOL Keyword: **LOL Online**, you can find lists of abbreviations to help you signal your feelings. Here are some common smileys:

:-(	Frown
:-)	Smile
:P	Sticking out tongue

Tilt your head to the left to see the effect.

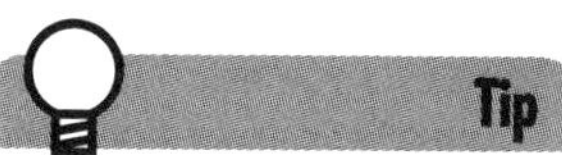

For graphical smileys, click the Greetings icon on the right side of the Write Mail window and then click Smileys.

Another way to signal emotion is through common online shortcuts that clarify intentions, explain gaps in the communication, and provide a bit of shared meaning:

Btw	By the way
Lol	Laughing out loud
Ttyl	Talk to you later

Rewrite Again and Again

The single most frequent reason why I unsend a message (something you'll learn how to do in a few pages) is that I discover a glaring and embarrassing typo. If you take the time to reread your messages before you click Send Now, you can spare yourself the consequences of hasty comments and silly misspellings. The more important the message, the greater the consequences of sending too hastily.

On AOL you can spell-check your message by clicking the little ABC button in the Write Mail toolbar (Figure 11-1). The spell checker compares each of your words to its own list of words. For each word it can't recognize, the spell checker provides a list of choices. You can tell the spell checker to add the unrecognized word to its list, learn the word because it is correctly spelled, or skip the word just this time or all the time. Sometimes, you'll want to replace your chosen word with the spell checker's recommended word.

Talking Back

E-mail works best if it's two-way. Not answering mail from someone you know, especially if a reply is reasonably expected, can be rude. You shouldn't, of course, answer unsolicited mail from strangers; in fact, doing so can even be against your interests, because it just confirms the validity of your mail address.

If you can't respond when a response is expected, a short acknowledgment with promise of follow-up is often the right thing to do.

Make It Easy on Your Reader

Here are tips to help recipients read your message:

- Add a blank line between paragraphs. This visual cue says that one discrete paragraph is done and another is coming up. The space also gives people a chance to take in what you have written.
- If you want to include items in list form, keep each item short. Use asterisks (*) for unnumbered lists (items that don't have a necessary sequence, as in a grocery list). Use numbers (1, 2, 3...) for numbered lists (steps that have an order, as in a recipe or any procedure).

- Warn people in the Subject line if the message is long by adding *(long)* to the end of the subject. They'll at least know to read the whole thing before responding.

Just Say No to E-Mail

Some people don't like to write. Some busy people don't answer their mail quickly, or at all. If your message matters and your recipient may not be the writing type, give the message in person or call the person on the phone. If you're sending the same message to many people with whom you work, the overhead of everyone reading and responding to your message may be greater than the trouble it takes to walk door-to-door to get a response. A face-to-face (*F2F*) conversation can consist of more replies, counter-replies, and nuances of tone and body language in a minute than an e-mail exchange can accommodate in an hour. Talking F2F is a good way to schmooze and offers the chance to put out small fires before they become flames.

Sending Your Message on Its Way

Just before you send a message to an AOL member, you can request a *return receipt* — a message that is automatically sent to you when the recipient opens your message. Click the Return Receipt box at the bottom of the Write Mail window so that it has a check mark in it. Note that the return receipt merely registers a message being opened — not being read, or read in its entirety.

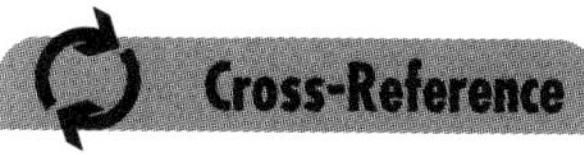

Click Send Later if you have a reason for not sending your message right away. (See the "Sending Mail Later" sidebar.)

After you have typed your recipients' screen names or e-mail addresses in the Send To box and Copy To boxes, given the message a subject, written a message, and (optionally) requested a return receipt (for AOL addresses only), click Send Now.

Sending Mail: Preferences

Your mail preferences give you several ways of customizing the way AOL sends your messages. These preferences are available at Mail⇨Mail Preferences; Figure 11-2 shows your Mail Preferences window.

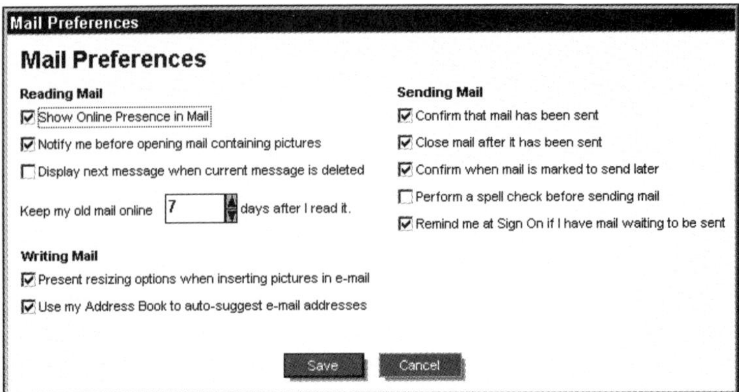

Figure 11-2. Set your Mail preferences using this window.

- **Confirm that mail has been sent** causes a little box to pop up when a message has been successfully sent; click OK to close it. Having the box appear can be useful when you've sent a large file and aren't quite sure if the file was completely uploaded and the message sent.
- **Close mail after it has been sent** automatically closes the mail window after the message is sent. You may prefer to de-select this preference and keep a message *open* after it's sent so that you can modify and re-send it to other people. For example, you can send the same message to ten people you want to invite to a party. For each guest, add a personal comment and change the name in the Send To box.
- **Confirm when mail is marked to send later** serves to remind you that you clicked Send Later (see the "Sending Mail Later" sidebar) and that the message *wasn't* yet sent. You can still retrieve the message from your Filing Cabinet, edit it, and then send it.

After the Message Is Out the Door

After you've sent that message, you can keep track of it in ways not possible with an old-fashioned paper letter.

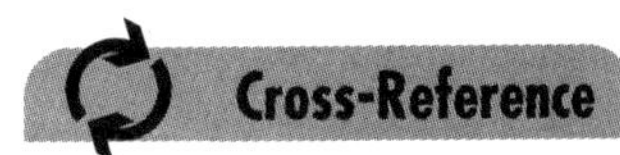

Your Filing Cabinet and Sent mailbox are discussed in Chapter 10.

- Reread mail you've sent. Your Sent mailbox has all your recent e-mail messages for the last month or so (Mail⇨Read Mail⇨Sent Mail). In your Filing Cabinet (FC), available from AOL's File menu, you can maintain an archive extending back as far as you want.

Sending Mail Later

The Send Later button often comes in handy. For example, you might choose to send mail later when the message is particularly sensitive or has been written in the heat of the moment. Draft the letter as usual, but instead of clicking Send Now, click Send Later to let it sit for a while — give yourself time to cool off, have dinner, change your mind.

Or use Send Later to send a message to a high-volume mailing list (see Chapter 13), so you can clarify your message before having others poke it full of holes.

Just to make sure the message *still* doesn't inadvertently get sent, I often put a 1-2 letter fake screen name in the Send To box. You can't actually send the message unless all e-mail addresses in the Send To box are valid. (AOL screen names must have three or more characters to be valid.)

You can edit your Send Later messages whether you're online or offline. They're maintained by selecting Mail⇨Mail Waiting to Be Sent, a folder within your Filing Cabinet, which I discuss more generally in Chapter 10. To receive an automatic reminder when you sign off AOL, use the preference shown in the Mail Preferences window (refer to Figure 11-2), under Sending Mail.

- Get notification of mail you've sent. Click the Return Receipt box at the bottom of your Write Mail window, and you can find out automatically whether any of your AOL recipients got your message.
- Find out whether your message (for AOL recipients only) has been read. In Sent Mail, you can find out when your message was read (at least, when it was opened) by any of your recipients who are AOL members. Right-click any message to someone on AOL and choose Status. You'll see a little window that provides the Subject line of your message in the title bar (after *Status of*), who read it, at what exact time. Finding the status does the same thing as getting a return receipt. Use return receipts for those special messages and message status for other messages.

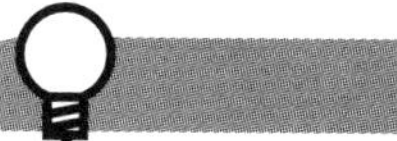

You can even check the status of mail you received, in the New mailbox, to find out when you read your messages. Select the message and click Status.

Unsending a Message

Messages to friends on the Internet can't be unsent. If you send an e-mail to several AOL members and just one Internet e-mail address, the message can't be unsent.

With a real letter, you can't change your mind after you've dropped it into the mailbox. By contrast, you can unsend — retrieve a sent message before it's read. How do you find out if it's been opened? Select the message in Sent Mail, click Status, read the status, and close the window. If the message hasn't been read, select it, click Unsend, and click Yes to confirm that, yes indeed, you want to remove all traces of it.

Using the Address Book

The Address Book, shown in Figure 11-3, does much more than a traditional address book, with its street addresses and scribbles up the side of the page. And it's much more than a simple list of friends' e-mail addresses. It's both, and more.

For each person, the AOL Address Book lets you keep a great deal of useful information:

- First and last name
- Up to three e-mail addresses, with the ability to check a default if there are more than two addresses for one person
- Home and work street addresses
- Phone, fax, pager, cell, and work numbers
- Birthday and anniversary
- Web address (for your acquaintances' personal, business, and organizational pages)
- Spouse's name
- Free-form notes

Online, the Address Book is available in AOL devices, such as AOL for Palm OS, AOL Mail on the Web, and Instant AOL, all of which are covered in Chapter 10. Offline, the Address Book is available on your desktop copy of AOL (Mail⇨Address Book), where you can get addresses and add contact information. I use the offline Address Book all the time to get phone numbers as the need arises.

The contacts in your Address Book can also be grouped to create *mailing lists* — that is, groups of e-mail addresses, each with its own name. When you send a message to the group, the message goes out to everyone on the list. Chapter 13 has complete procedures for creating your own mailing list.

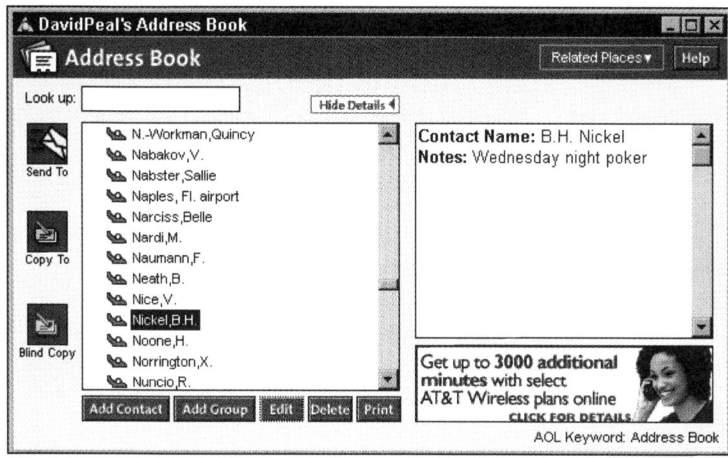

Figure 11-3. The AOL Address Book.

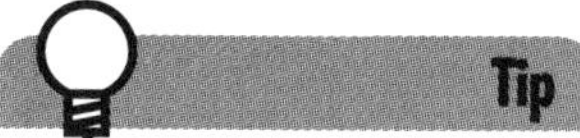

Your Address Book is available offline or online, at Mail⇨Address Book. While online, it is available to you from any AOL Anywhere device or PC.

Adding a Name to the Address Book

You can add a new address to your Address Book in three ways.

- Display a message and click the screen name or e-mail address that appears in the header. An information screen appears, offering various options. Click Add to My Address Book. The Contact Details window of your Address Book, shown in Figure 11-4, appears. See the sidebar, "Using AOL's New Address Book Features."

  This window will automatically be filled in with name and e-mail address information from the message header, and you can provide a proper first and last name. On the other tabs are places for any notes, phone numbers, and other information you want to add. You can always add information later by selecting a contact or group from your Address Book and clicking the Edit button.

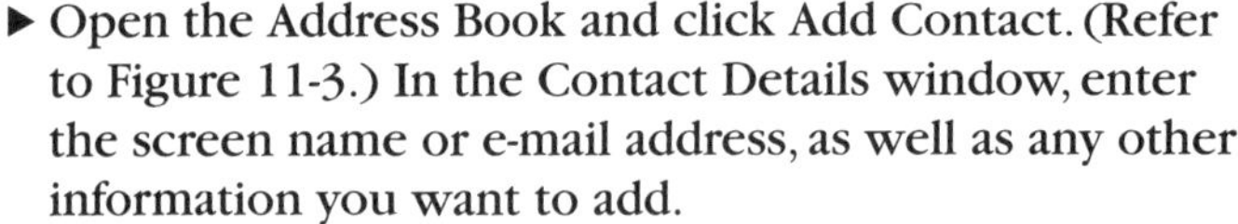

- Open the Address Book and click Add Contact. (Refer to Figure 11-3.) In the Contact Details window, enter the screen name or e-mail address, as well as any other information you want to add.
- If a friend sends you a mutual buddy's e-mail address, you can copy the address from the e-mail message and paste it into the Address Book. Select the text with your mouse, right click, and select Copy; open the Address Book and click Add Contact. Move to the place where you want the text to appear, right-click, and select Paste. In the Details tab, you can type in anything about the contact.

Tip

You don't have to enter an e-mail address if you just need to add someone's postal address or other information.

To have names appear next to each other in your Address Book, add the same series of letters before each last name. For example, to display all of your Chicago relatives' names one after the other, type in *Chi* before each last name. (Why before? Because entries are ordered by last name.) All names with *Chi* now appear grouped together with each name on a separate line in your Address Book.

Note

The AOL Address Book orders items by whatever it finds in the Last Name field. If you use *only* the First Name field, as you might for a sibling, friend, or Madonna, the person is ordered by first name.

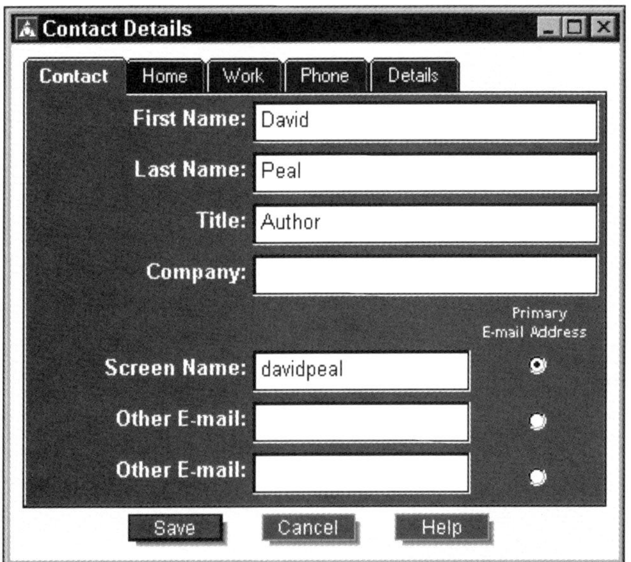

Figure 11-4. Adding a new person to your Address Book, with room for birth dates, spouse's names, and fax numbers, as well as e-mail addresses.

Using AOL's New Address Book Features

The Address Book in AOL 7.0 makes it easy to keep up with both your e-mail and instant messages. With the Address Book's automatic features, you no longer have to worry about typing an AOL screen name wrong or remembering an Internet friend's long e-mail address.

One new feature makes adding the screen names to the Address Book as easy as pointing and clicking. Every time you get an e-mail message from an AOL member, the person's address or screen name appears as a clickable link in the message header. This Online Presence (OLP) indicator also lets you check to see if AOL buddies are online.

To add the screen name to your Address Book, click the screen name and click Add to My Address Book. Add information about the person (such as his name and street address) and click Save. Of course, you can add the e-mail addresses of your Internet contacts, as well.

The Address Book is capable of suggesting names and automatically completing your entries in the Send To box, which makes sending mail that much simpler. Just start typing a contact's name in the Send To box, and a drop-down list (shown in the following figure) with matching suggestions from your Address Book appears below. Choose an entry from this list for a quick way to finish addressing your message.

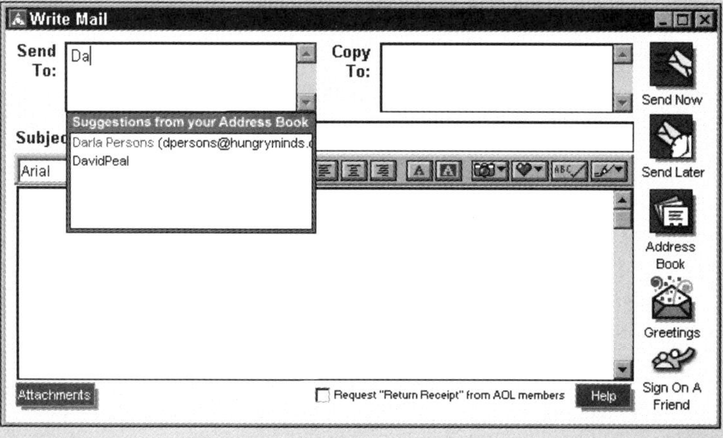

Using Address Book Entries in E-Mail

Using the Address Book when writing a message can save you time and prevent errors. It also greatly simplifies the process of sending the same message to many people (creating simple lists is discussed in Chapter 13).

To quickly access the Address Book when you're composing an e-mail message

1. Open the Write Mail window. Click the Address Book, which is on the right. The Address Book appears.
2. Select a name from the Address Book. You can select several names by pressing Shift or Ctrl before clicking the names.
3. Still in the Address Book, click the Send To, Copy To, or Blind Copy button to move the selected addresses into either the Send To or Copy To box of the Write Mail window. Double-clicking a selected contact adds it to the Send To box.
4. Write your message and click Send Now or Send Later.

When you start typing someone's name in the Send To box of the Write Mail window, AOL automatically searches your Address Book and suggests a name from a drop-down list. Select a name and press Enter to have AOL automatically complete the entry for you.

Attaching Files to Messages

Attaching a file to a message is like sending a gift in one of those padded envelopes, which can includes a letter along with a book, photographs, a CD, newspaper clippings, or anything else. I also use attachments all the time to share proposals, communicate with students in a course I teach, send my mother-in-law pictures of the kids, and so on. Attachments make e-mail a true workhorse.

To attach files:

1. Open the Write Mail window and click Attachments.
2. In the window that appears, click Attach. By default, a window appears that shows you all the files in your default Download folder. Use Download Manager (File⇨Download Manager) to change the default. Click the Preferences button and choose a new Download folder at the bottom of the page.

   You may need to *navigate* to another folder on your hard drive to find a specific file. In Figure 11-5, I'm navigating (moving from folder to folder) looking for a file to attach to an e-mail message.

When you reply to a message that has a file attached, the reply doesn't include the originally attached file. When you forward a message that has a file attached, the file *is* forwarded along with the message.

3. When you find the file you want to attach, select it and click Open. An Attachments window appears.
4. Click Attach again if you want to attach additional files and repeat the steps. If you inadvertently add a file you don't want to send, select the file and click Detach.

   Click OK when you're done making attachments.
5. Complete and send the message, with the files attached. Attachments take a bit longer than ordinary messages. A progress box tracks the upload.

2. Click Attach
5. Click open
1. Click Attachments
4. Click file
3. Locate Folder

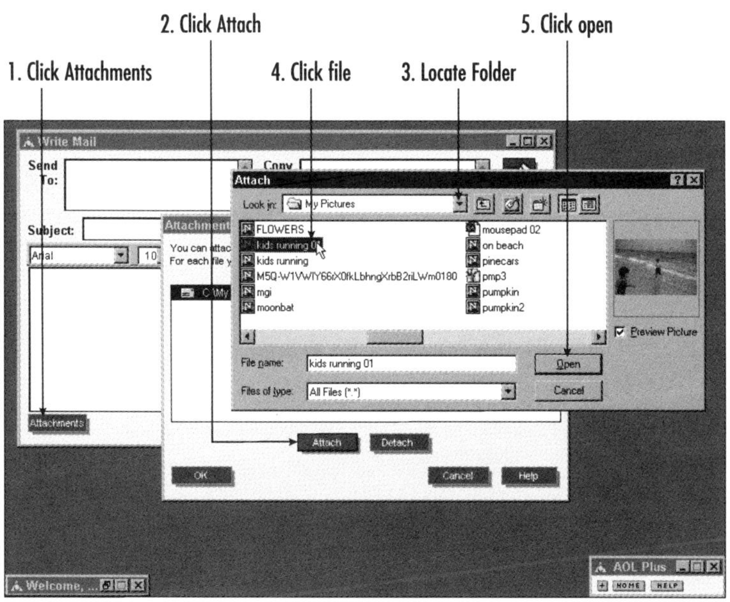

Figure 11-5. One document has been attached, and a second file (the image shown in the preview box) is being added.

Cross-Reference

Sending multiple attachments causes them to be compressed into a single ZIP file. See Chapters 15 and 16 for more about making and using ZIP files.

Embellishing Messages

Embellishing messages means changing

- The way they look (fonts and styles)
- The kind of content they contain (images, backgrounds, links, and HTML)

These effects are at your fingertips in the Write Mail window. To add smileys, banners, and fancy stationery, use the Greetings button.

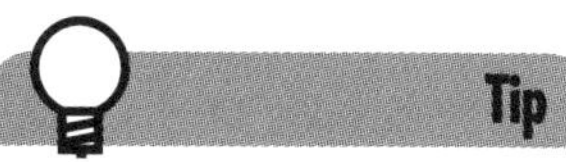

Tip

Save and close a file before you attach it to an e-mail message. Some software, like Word, can keep a file in its clutches until the file is closed.

Right-click anywhere in a message to see all your styling choices (type size, style, color, and so on).

Changing Message Font

The simplest way to embellish a message is to change the font used in e-mail, chat, and instant messages.

To change the default font (the one used in every message), choose Settings⇨Preferences. In the Preferences window, click Font, Text & Graphics to bring up a window with that name, shown in Figure 11-6. There, you can select a different font type, size, style, and color. There is no substitute for playing around with the fonts installed on your system until you find something you like. You can view different combinations of font effects in the viewing window, clicking Save when you are happy with one choice or another.

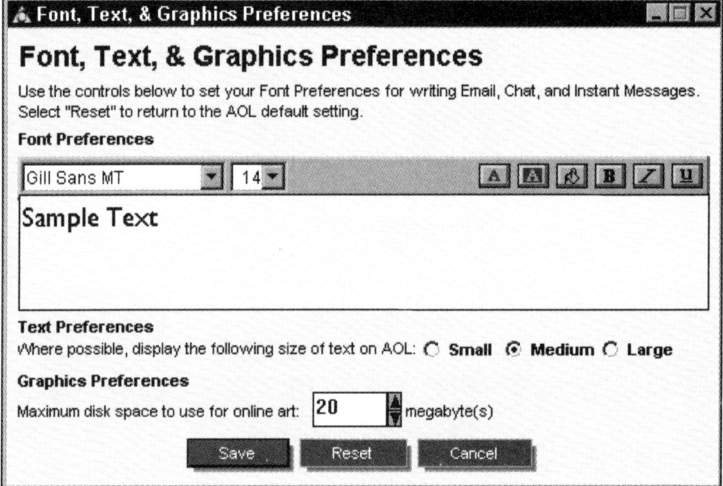

Figure 11-6. Changing the default font that appears when you type e-mail, chat, and instant messages.

Emphasizing Letters and Words

While writing a message, you can override your default text by using the button bar just above the large message window. Here are some of the variables you can play with using these convenient buttons. Figure 11-7 illustrates all of these effects, though you won't be able to see the colors in this illustration.

- Type style (bold, italic, underline).
- Type size, color, and face. You may find more than 100 typefaces in the list. AOL can use any of the fonts installed on your system.

- Background color. A background color can emphasize letters or enhance the legibility of your words. First select the letters, then click the background color button (a white A set in a blue box). If nothing is selected, the entire message background is highlighted.
- Text justification (left, right, center).

To apply a text effect, open a Write Mail window (Ctrl+M or click Write on the toolbar). Type a message in the big box. Select the words you want to enhance and click the appropriate buttons, as shown in Figure 11-7. Or you can set up your text settings and then begin composing the e-mail message.

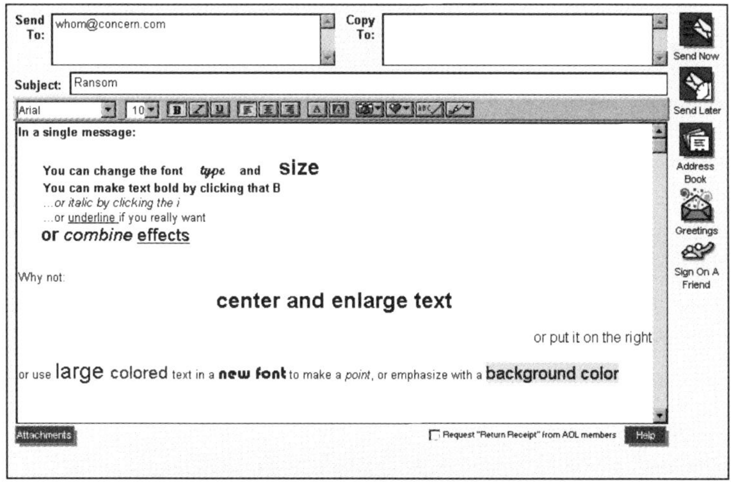

Figure 11-7. No more boring text: The Write Mail's toolbar lets you add effects. This message overdoes it without exhausting the possibilities.

Applying a Background Color or Picture

Web pages have gotten people used to background colors and pictures as a decorative touch or design element. You can add backgrounds to your AOL messages; they'll be visible to AOL members and most Internet recipients having an image-capable mail reader. To use a digital picture as a background, click the Camera button, choose Background Picture, and select the background image. It's best to use a simple pattern and light color so that your text can be read against the image. To add a color background, make sure nothing is selected in the message. Use the button bar's Background Color button, an A set against a blue background.

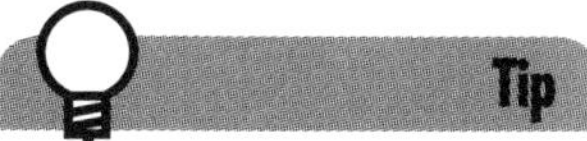

Usability pros suggest the use of complementary (contrasting) colors for text and background, to make the text easy to read.

Using Caffeinated Stationery

In your mail to AOL members, you can choose from a wide variety of pre-made sounds, photos, mail art, banners, and smileys. To do so, click Greetings from any Write Mail window. A single banner or piece of mail art can brighten up a message.

When you forget a birthday, use a greeting card to send someone a card right away. You can personalize your cards with messages and your own digital pictures. Try AOL Keyword: **Beat Greets** to find and send musical greetings to your friends and family.

Click Greetings again to use American Greetings card designs and services. You can send a variety of free online cards to anyone on AOL or the Internet. Some of these cards include multimedia effects, such as animations and Java programs.

Adding Links, Images, and Text

E-mail messages once consisted strictly of words. Now they can carry all sorts of additional information such as links and images. The following brief sections highlight these important additions to your e-mail repertoire.

Adding a Link

Adding a link to your messages lets your recipients click to visit the link to a Web page or AOL area. To link to an AOL area, recipients must be AOL members. You can create a link in a message you are writing in one of these ways:

- Link to a Favorite Place. With nothing selected in the body of your message, click the Heart button on the Write Mail toolbar. A list of your Favorite Places comes up. Select a favorite to add the link to your message. The Favorite Place's name (what you see in your Favorite Places folder) appears as clickable text; the Favorite Place's AOL or Web address specifies where the link will take the recipient. You can view the Web address by moving your mouse over the link.
- Link to a displayed page. Click the Heart button in the page's upper right corner. From the little window that pops up, click Insert in Mail.

  To create your own text for the link to a displayed page (the clickable part that the reader sees), display the page, as in Figure 11-8. Type the text you want in the body of your message. Drag the heart in the upper-right hand corner of the Web site or AOL window onto the selected text. Doing so automatically creates a link from your text to the Web site or AOL area.

- Create a link from scratch — if you know the URL (Web address). With a message open and without anything selected, right-click inside the message and select Insert Hyperlink. The Edit Hyperlink window, with two text boxes (Description and Internet Address), pops up. Provide both a description of the link (this is the text that recipients can click) and a URL (the destination where your recipients go if they click); click OK. Click Launch to make sure you've chosen the correct URL. Click OK if the link works.

  Or select words in the message, right-click, and select Insert a Hyperlink. The Edit Hyperlink window appears, but this time with a single box, in which you enter the link's Internet address.

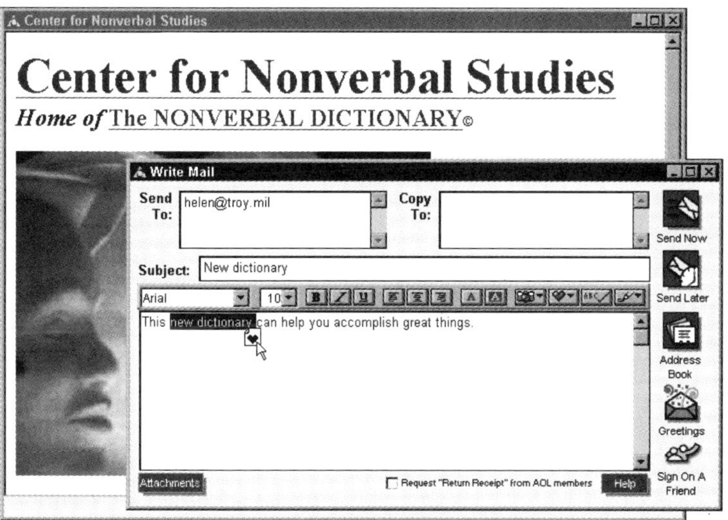

Figure 11-8. Insert a link by dragging the heart from the Web page (shown in the background) to the message (shown in the foreground).

Inserting an Image

Attaching images *to* messages is a convenient way of sharing them with someone on the Internet. For your AOL recipients (or for most Internet recipients who have an image-capable mail reader), you can include any number of messages directly *in* messages. Use this technique to share any clip art or digital picture that you have stored on your computer.

To insert an image in a message:

1. Open the Write Mail window (Ctrl+M).
2. From the mail toolbar, click the Camera button and select Insert a Picture.
3. Find the picture and double-click. You can insert small images directly into text (even in a sentence). To align an inserted image, use the Write Mail button bar's right, center, and left align buttons, which apply to the whole paragraph in which a picture is inserted (or the picture itself, if it's not part of a sentence).

If you insert a large image, you'll probably get a message asking you if you want to resize the picture to fit the message window. Choose Yes to automatically resize the picture and No to insert it full-size. Once inserted into a message, a picture can be resized by right-clicking it, selecting Resize Picture, and choosing a size from the pop-up menu.

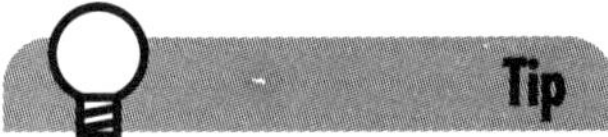

For details about "You've Got Pictures," as well as digital cameras and scanners, see another book I wrote, *Your Official America Online Guide to Digital Imaging Activities* (Hungry Minds Inc.).

Some AOL members may have set their personal preferences to block messages that have pictures inserted. If any of your intended recipients has chosen to block e-mail with inserted images, you'll receive a message from AOL notifying you. To set up or change this preference, go to AOL Keyword: **Parental Controls** and choose Mail Controls.

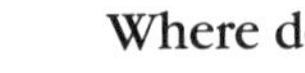

Where do you get pictures?

- AOL Keyword: **Web Art** has many public domain images you can use. Look under Miscellaneous Imagery.
- You can use a scanner to turn your photo prints into digital pictures. The scanner creates digital picture files that you can store on your hard drive. From there, they will be available when you go to insert a picture from the Write Mail window.
- You can use a digital camera to create digital pictures instead of paper ones, which you can then transfer directly to your computer using your camera's cable or removable memory card.
- You can use AOL's "You've Got Pictures"SM service to get digital pictures without owning a scanner or a digital camera. With this service, you take your traditional film to the photo store. Your prints are scanned and then posted directly to AOL as digital pictures. To use a picture in AOL Mail, select and download it to your hard drive.

When you send an inserted image to AOL members, they see a picture icon: an Envelope icon with a small rectangle in the lower right-hand corner. When they double-click the message, a message pops up with a warning about opening unsolicited messages from unknown parties. As soon as they click OK, the image appears a little at a time until it's fully displayed.

Double-clicking an inserted picture received on AOL opens the AOL Picture Finder. From there it can be cropped, edited, and saved.

Inserting a Text File into a Message

Inserting a text file into the Write Mail window can save you from typing the same text again and again if you'll be sending similar messages to many people. It also gives you the chance to draft and edit important messages without using Write Mail until you are ready to send the message. In either case, after you finish, a copy of the original text file remains on your hard drive to use later. Use a word processor, or AOL's text editor (File⇨New), and save your message as a .TXT file.

To insert the message: From the body of the Write Mail toolbar, click the Camera button and select Insert a Text File. Find your file and double-click to insert it. Once your message is in Write Mail, you can style text, add colors, and insert pictures and links.

Closing with a Signature

Signatures, or *sigs,* are bits of text automatically added to the end of all your e-mail messages. With AOL you can create five signatures and use the appropriate signature, or no signature, depending on the occasion.

To create a signature

1. Click the last button on the far right of the mail toolbar:

    - To create a new signature, select Setup Signatures from the menu.
    - To use an existing signature in a message, select the signature's name from the same menu.

In creating a new signature, you'll see a window like the one shown in Figure 11-9, which already lists several signatures. You're allowed a maximum of five signatures.

2. Click the Create button to bring up the Create Signature box.

   The box has two fields for a signature's two elements: *the signature's name,* which you use to identify a particular signature (when you have several signatures), and *the signature,* consisting of text and optional formatting.

Tip

make a signature your efault so that it is added to every message you send, go to the Set up Signatures window (Figure 11-9), select a signature, and click default On/Off button. You can also use the Webdings and Wingdings fonts to dress up signatures or add your e-mail address as a clickable URL.

Note

The formatting for signatures used in e-mail bound for the Internet may not be visible to all recipients. For your messages to AOL members, you can format your signatures all you want. Consider making a special sig just for AOL messages.

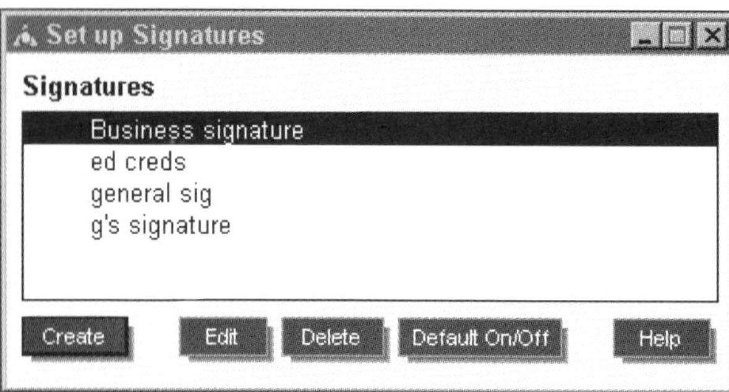

Figure 11-9. Create a signature to share contact information or a favorite quote.

3. Give the signature a name and type in the actual text, with any effects you want. The name is merely used to identify it in the list of signatures available from the Write Mail toolbar.

   To add styling, use the toolbar. It has different fonts, type sizes, styles, and colors — even backgrounds and links. Have fun with them, and click OK when you're done.

   To edit an existing signature, select Set up Signatures from the mail toolbar. In the Set Up Signatures box, select the signature and click Edit. Make your changes and click OK.

To add a signature to a message, open the Write Mail window. Type your message as usual. When done, click the Signature button and select a particular signature to use, which is automatically added to the end of your message. Send your message.

Where to Go from Here

In this chapter, I wanted to show you how you can create e-mail to communicate with anyone in the world who has an Internet account, including the 30 million or so AOL members. Among other things, you learned to write an effective message, embellish a message, send a message, use your Address Book to keep track of more than addresses, and insert personality into your messages with smileys, links, pictures, signatures, and even Web pages. Two other chapters in this book focus on aspects of electronic mail:

- Chapter 10 has everything you need to know about receiving and managing mail as well as downloading and storing mail.
- Chapter 13 is devoted to my favorite topic: mailing lists, dynamic and enduring communities based on nothing more than e-mail and shared interests.

Chapter 12

Taking Part in Live Messaging and Chat

With instant messages on AOL and the Internet, you get quick, easy, live communication that bypasses all the teeth-grinding time delays caused by phone tag, unanswered e-mail, and uncommunicative coworkers.

In this chapter, I provide what you need to know about instant messages on AOL. You use instant messages, or *IM*s, to have live electronic conversations with AOL members and people on the Internet. Later in the chapter, I discuss AOL Instant Messenger. You can use AIM whenever you are using a computer where AOL is not installed. You can also use AIM to take advantage of certain features, such as file sharing.

One of the important innovations in AOL 7.0 is the increasingly similar look and feel of instant messaging on AOL and instant messaging with the AIM software. The most important shared feature is the Buddy List, which you learn all about in this chapter.

I end with a discussion of Groups@AOL, a tool for building online communities with the people you know on AOL and the Net.

Using Instant Messages on AOL

As an AOL member, you can use instant messages to carry on electronic discussions with buddies who are online while you are.

Using AOL's Parental Controls, young teens are allowed access to IM by default. You can block the instant messaging feature for children who have their own screen names. See Chapter 4 for more information.

How do you find out whether a buddy or colleague of yours is online?

- The older and still useful method is to press Ctrl+I. In the Send Instant Message window, shown in Figure 12-1, type a screen name and click the Available button. A message informs you whether your friend is online and able to receive instant messages.

Figure 12-1. To find out if someone is online, you can type a screen name in this window (Ctrl+I) and click the Available button.

- The newer, more automatic method involves your Buddy List (see Figure 12-2). The Buddy List is the customizable list of your online buddies. It is available whenever you are online and shows you which of your buddies are online at any moment. If you don't see your Buddy List, use AOL Keyword: **Buddyview**.

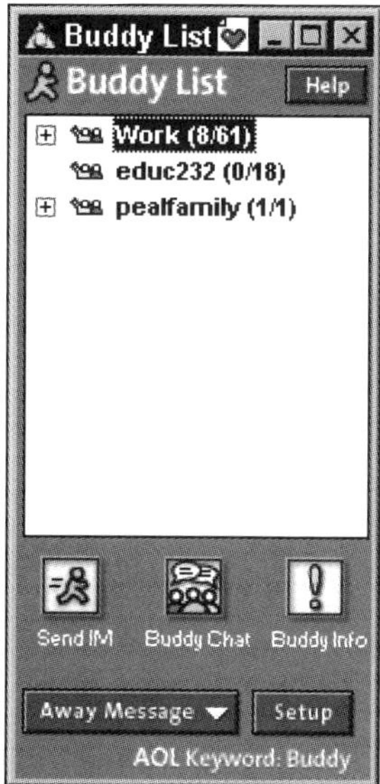

Figure 12-2. The AOL Buddy List window appears when you sign on to AOL. If you should ever close the window, use AOL Keyword: **Buddyview**.

You can find out who's online no matter how you access AOL — by using a handheld computer, wireless phone, Mobile Communicator, AOLTV, or other AOL Anywhere device. Your Buddy List is also available when you use Netscape and when you access AOL Mail on the Web (`www.aol.com`).

Sending and Receiving Instant Messages

To send an AOL instant message to any buddy currently online, simply double-click that person's name in your Buddy List. The Send Instant Message window (refer to Figure 12-1) appears, with your buddy's screen name filled in.

Note that the look of the Send Instant Message window varies when you use an AOL Anywhere device, such as a wireless phone, handheld computer, AOLTV, Mobile Communicator, or Instant AOL (a new service that uses an "Internet appliance" called the Connected Touch Pad, made by Gateway).

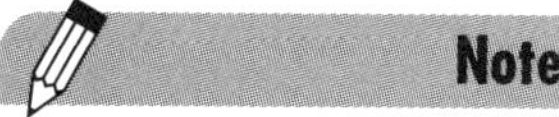

Your AOL Buddy List can include the screen names of Internet buddies who use the AOL Instant Messenger service and thus have an AIM screen name. You cannot add an Internet e-mail address to the Buddy List.

Type your message in the box and click Send. People usually aren't fussy about spelling and grammar in instant messages, so don't worry. When your buddy replies, the appearance of the window changes to support a two-way conversation, like the IM window shown in Figure 12-3.

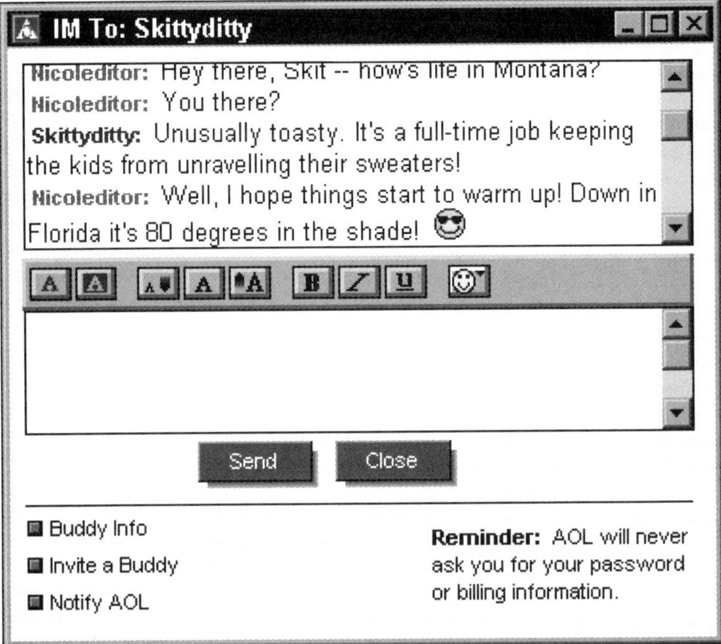

Figure 12-3. Use the top box to see your words and your buddy's responses. Use the box at the bottom to type your messages.

If an Internet buddy (someone using AOL Instant Messenger) sends you a message, you use the same window shown in Figure 12-3. In other words, it doesn't really matter how your buddies get online; AOL lets you interact with them in the same way. Type your message in the box shown in the bottom half of the figure, and click Send to take part in a conversation.

At the bottom of the IM window, you'll notice a Get Info On button. If the person has created a profile (AOL Keyword: **People Directory**), you can read it by clicking the button.

In AOL 7.0, you now see a new button, the Add Another Buddy to This Conversation button. Click it to invite another person to join your conversation, which turns the two-way chat into a larger conversation.

Adding Style and Links

Like the Write Mail window, described in Chapter 11, the IM window has its own toolbar between the two message boxes. Use these buttons to apply color to the text; create a colored background for messages; vary the type size; and apply bold, underline, and italics to text.

Note that any formatting changes you make at one point in a conversation remain in effect until you change them or sign off AOL.

Within your instant message, you can include a link to a Web page in several ways:

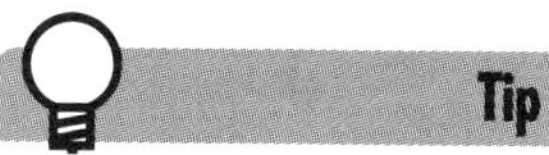

Right-click the message area to see your formatting and linking choices.

- Open the site to be linked to. Drag the site's Favorite Places heart from the upper-right corner into an open IM window. The name of the online destination appears as a hyperlink (it's underlined and the font is a different color).
- Type some text describing the link, select your description, and drag the heart to the selected text to make the words appear as a link to the page. Instead of dragging the heart, you can right-click the selected text and choose Insert a Hyperlink from the menu. Type in a Web address.

Creating Buddies and Groups of Buddies

Your buddies are grouped into convenient categories, such as Co-Workers or Family. To add someone to one of the categories in your Buddy List:

1. With your Buddy List displayed, click Setup.
2. From the Buddy List Setup window (Figure 12-4), click Add Buddy.
3. In the little Add Buddy window, type a screen name and click Save.
4. You can add more buddies at this point if you want. Close the Setup window when you're done.

Creating a group is just like creating a buddy, except that in Step 2 you click Add Group. Then in the little window, type a group name and click Save.

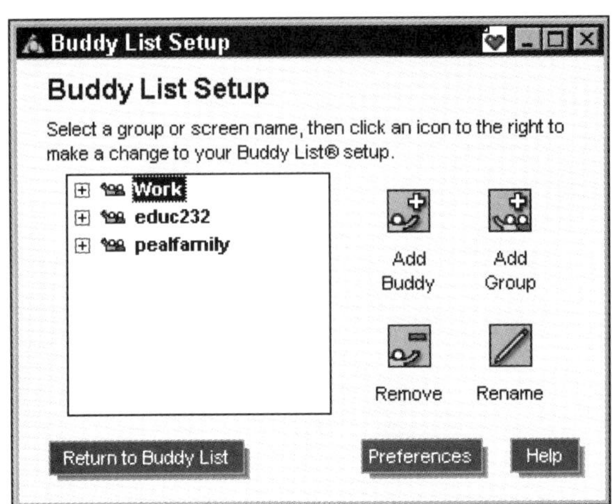

Figure 12-4. The Buddy List Setup window.

You can add your AOL Instant Messenger (AIM) friends to your Buddy List.

A *Buddy Group* is a folder to hold several buddies. You can use your Buddy List to arrange buddies into groups of work colleagues, bridge partners, neighbors, classmates, or any groups you wish. Each of the groups in your Buddy List consists of individual buddies (refer to Figure 12-2). The final group, pealfamily, consists of a group that I created by using the Address Book's Share feature. I go into more detail about Groups@AOL later in this chapter, and introduce the Share feature in the section on creating mailing lists in Chapter 13.

For each group you create, the main Buddy List window subsequently shows the number of buddies and the number of those buddies who are online. For example the 8/61 in Figure 12-2 means that 8 buddies of the 61 in this group are currently online. Click a folder to open it and see who is online in the group; click the folder again to close it.

How do you add a buddy to a group? Whenever you are adding a buddy in the Buddy List Setup window, you can first open the group folder (click the Plus sign by its name in the Buddy List Setup window). Alternatively, simply click a buddy's screen name, and drag it from one group to another. At any time, you can add and remove buddies and groups, or move buddies between groups.

You can use your Buddy List to find out more info about an online buddy. Select any buddy on the list and click the Buddy Info button (which looks like an exclamation point) to do the following:

- Get your buddy's Web address and Member Directory profile (if your buddy is on AOL and has created a Web page or directory entry).
- Find a buddy's e-mail address so that you can add it to your Address Book.
- And if your buddy is online, you can use the AOL Buddy List to send him or her an e-mail message if you're not in the mood to send an instant message.

Setting Instant Message Preferences

Your instant message preferences have grown into a large set of choices in AOL 7.0, and all these options can enhance your messaging. To get to the Preferences window, click Setup in the main Buddy List window and then click Preferences in the Buddy List Setup window.

The Buddy List Preferences window, shown in Figure 12-5, has three tabs:

- **Buddy List:** These preferences also control how your screen name appears on other people's Buddy Lists. Options let others know whether you have been idle for a while and whether you are using an AOL Anywhere device. Finally, you can attach sounds to events, such as a buddy's coming online or signing off. Return to these options from time to time as your needs change.
- **Instant Messages:** Here, you can choose a graphical Buddy icon that represents you online in the messages you send. You can also have icons appear automatically as pictures or as text. Another option enables your software to automatically complete screen names from your address book as you are typing them into the instant message box. With each letter you type, the Address Book narrows the choices of possible screen names, making name entry quicker and more accurate.

Children should never provide a last name or any contact information, and children should be at least 13 years old to create a profile of any kind.

Creating a Member Profile

When you add people to your Buddy List, you usually know their screen names because you've received instant messages or e-mail messages from them.

Sometimes, you might want to use the AOL Member Directory (People➪Member Directory). You can search the directory by name, location, hobby, birthday, language, country, and other identifying information. People on the Internet do not have access to your personal information, but with AOL Instant Messenger, you can create a personal profile viewable by anyone who uses AIM.

To make your personal information available to anyone in the AOL community, choose Settings➪My Directory Listing. Fill in any or all of the boxes with quotes, the type of computer you have, your city, and so on, and then click Update.

- **Privacy:** Use this tab to control who can and can't see whether you're online and send you a message. You can allow everyone online to send you an instant message, narrow your preference down to everyone on your Buddy List, or designate specific people and ignore the rest.

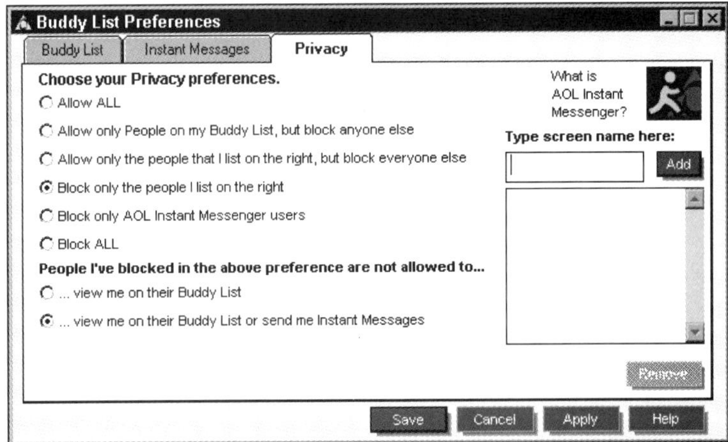

Figure 12-5. Adjust your privacy preferences to control other people's access to you. Use the other preferences to control how your Buddy List works and how messages look.

Getting Started with AOL Instant Messenger

The AOL Instant Messenger (AIM) software extends instant messaging in many ways. With AIM you can

- Get news feeds and stock tickers.
- Exchange files and photos with buddies.
- Have a virtual phone conversation with AIM Talk and AIM Phone, which I discuss in Chapter 18.
- Play online games.

AIM is a great tool to use if you're away from your home PC and using a computer that doesn't have AOL installed, or if you want to take advantage of certain features like the ones just listed. If you don't have the AIM software or can't install it on the computer you're using for some reason, you can use AIM Express on the Web, which I discuss later in the chapter.

People who use AIM can be students in a distance-education class who live in different states, or business people using different Internet service providers. With AIM, distance and type of Internet access simply do not matter anymore. And think of the savings in long-distance phone bills.

AIM's benefits include the following:

- Costs nothing, for either AOL members or anyone on the Internet.
- Comes in versions for Windows, Macintosh, and UNIX.
- Uses the same Buddy List as the one you use on AOL.

Note

The following few sections are based on AIM 4.7. You can find out about new versions at `www.aol.com/aim`. Upgrading is free and requires only a few clicks.

Find It Online

If you ever do need help using AIM, choose Help⇨Help Topics from the main AIM window.

Downloading and Installing AOL Instant Messenger

Here's how you can get AOL Instant Messenger so that you can use it on AOL or on any Internet connection. Read the online directions for the most up-to-date steps.

1. Go to the AOL Instant Messenger page (`www.aol.com/aim`). Click the Get It Now (or similarly named) button.
2. You'll first be taken to the AOL Instant Messenger page. Here you indicate:

Cross-Reference

Netscape Instant Messenger, a version of AIM, is available from Netscape's Tasks menu and as a panel in My Sidebar. See Chapter 7 for more information.

Make sure your screen name has fewer that 16 characters and doesn't contain punctuation.

- **Whether you want to use your AOL screen name and password with AIM:** If you do, click the link at the top of the page, which takes you to a new page where you can type your AOL screen name. Do so, and click Continue.
- **Whether you want a different screen name:** If you do, type the desired screen name and password, and click Continue. If your desired screen name is accepted, you proceed to the next step. If it's not, try a new screen name; it may take several tries before you find an unused name.

You're now taken to a page from which you can download AIM.

If you have ever registered at Netscape's Netcenter, My AOL, CompuServe 2000, or AOL Hometown, or if you already have an AOL screen name, you can use it with AIM. For more about AOL's Screen Name Service, see Chapter 3.

3. To make sure that you get the correct software, click the button that matches your computer and operating system (for example, Windows).
4. A standard Windows box now appears, asking you whether you want to save the file. Do so, using default download directory. Press Enter to start the download process.
5. When the download is finished, find the file and double-click to install it. Or, if you see a Download Complete window, click Open Folder to quickly find the file and double-click it.

   You may be asked some standard installation questions: where to install AIM (choose the default) and whether you accept the licensing terms (click Yes).

To avoid entering your password every time you use AIM, check the Save Password box in the AIM window. Also check the Auto-Login box if you want AOL Instant Messenger to automatically sign on whenever you launch the AIM software.

6. The page from which you downloaded AIM in Step 3 is still displayed after AIM is installed. Click the prominent link that lets you add your new screen name and password to the copy of AIM just installed on your system.
7. You'll be taken to the AIM main (Sign On) window, where you can sign on.

After installation, the AIM icon will be placed on your Windows desktop. In the future, double-click the icon to start the program.

Using Multiple AIM Screen Names

With AIM you can use more than one screen name. You can use a screen name for work purposes, another for play purposes, one for the kids, and so on.

If you ever want to add a new screen name to your new copy of AIM, choose New User from the Screen Name drop-down list in AIM's Sign On window. Click Sign On.

In the New User registration window, indicate whether you want to use your AOL screen name as your AIM screen name or whether you want to register a brand-new screen name. If you've already registered on AIM with your AOL screen name, then you need to click the Register New Screen Name button. You'll be taken to a Web page where you can register your new screen name and password, and other information as required.

When your name is accepted, you'll be sent an automatically generated e-mail message, which you have to respond to before you can use AIM.

To switch between screen names:

- When you are not signed on to AIM, select the screen name from the main Sign On window's drop-down list of screen names, and click Sign On.
- When you are signed on to AIM, choose My AIM⇨Switch Screen Name. You are signed off the AIM session for one screen name and taken back to the Sign On window. Choose another screen name from the drop-down list, and click Sign On.

Starting the AIM Software

When you install AIM, an AIM icon is automatically placed on your Windows desktop and your Windows Start menu.

To start AIM, double-click its icon on the desktop. Or, choose Start⇨AIM.

When you first go online with AIM, you see three windows:

- **AIM Buddy List window:** Exactly like the AOL Buddy List, this Buddy List shows you which of your AIM buddies are online and lets you add and remove buddies

Note

To start AIM, you must be signed on to AOL or the Internet.

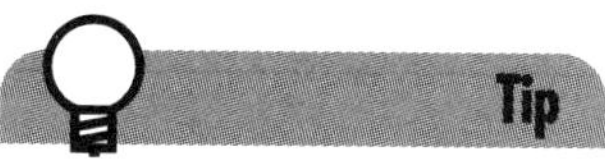

Tip

To get up to speed quickly, start up AIM and choose Help⇨New User Wizard.

and buddy groups. If you use an AOL screen name on your AIM account, your AOL buddies are already listed. Changes made to your AOL Buddy List take effect on the AIM service, and vice versa.

- **The AIM Today Web page:** This entertaining, up-to-date Web page lets you find a buddy, join AIM chats on specific topics, take polls, link to cool Web sites, get tips on using the AIM service, and more. To close the window, click the X in the upper-right corner, and to reopen the window, click the Today button, just below the AIM Buddy List window shown in Figure 12-6.
- **The AIM Headline service:** This window shows you the latest headlines in two formats: scrolling (right to left) and listed. Each headline is linked to the news story on the Web. You can read more about news and stock tickers toward the end of this chapter.

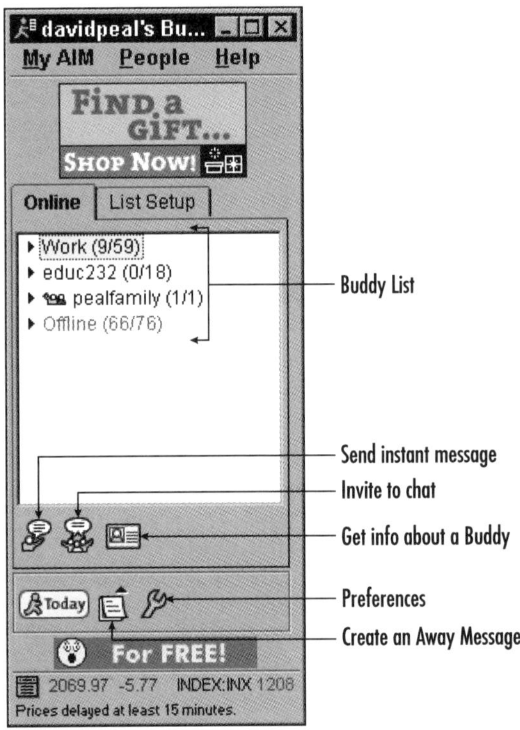

Figure 12-6. AOL Instant Messenger's Buddy List window.

Finding Buddies

AIM doesn't do you much good if you don't have anyone to talk to. With over 31 million people on AOL and more than twice that number using AOL Instant Messenger, there's a good chance you already have friends on AIM. There's an even better chance that you'll find people who aren't friends but who do share a hobby or career interest. AIM makes it simple to make new buddies and to find people whose location or e-mail you know.

To identify people who might share one of your interests, you can use AIM's built-in tools:

1. From the AIM Buddy List, choose People⇨Find a Buddy Wizard.
2. In the Wizard, select one of the three options for finding a buddy:
   - **By e-mail address:** To find someone by e-mail address, you obviously need that person's e-mail address to proceed. Use this method when, for instance, you have a friend at work whose e-mail address you know, but you're not sure whether the person uses AIM.
   - **By name and address:** To find someone by address, you need to know the first or last name, or both. These are people who might be neighbors or PTA friends. You know them by name and community, but don't know whether they have AIM.
   - **By common interest:** To find someone by interest, choose from a comprehensive list of hobbies and interests, such as photography or bird watching. You'll probably find some people you don't know this way.
3. In the next screen, type the required information to help you find a buddy. Depending on your previous choice, the information you need to provide varies.
4. The final screen lists matches. If you're looking for people with common interests, the list of matches can be quite long. You can now send an instant message to any of these people, making sure to introduce yourself, avoid intrusions, and so on.

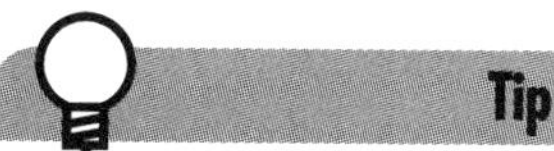

A *wizard* is software that steps you through a series of screens to help you make a decision or, in this case, retrieve useful information.

Setting Up Your AIM Profile

If you want to be included in other people's AIM searches, you need to create your own profile. Your profile says who you are, whether you're available for chatting about topics of interest, and anything else you want to share. If you make your profile available for searching, others can then use the Find a Buddy Wizard to look for you by interest, name, or e-mail address, as described in the previous section. Anyone who adds you to his or her Buddy List can click Buddy Info to see pertinent highlights from your profile.

Creating an AIM profile is entirely voluntary, just as it is in the AOL Member Directory.

1. Choose My AIM➪Edit Profile from the AIM main window.
2. In the Create a Profile window, enter as much or as little information as you wish.
3. When you've entered information you feel comfortable with, click Next.
4. You are then asked if you are available for chat and, if so, what your interests are. Make the appropriate selections, and click Next.
5. You can then, if you'd like, enter a brief text description, formatted as you want. Click Finish.

You can edit your profile at any time by choosing My AIM➪Edit Profile from the Buddy List menu.

Adding Buddies to Your Buddy List

After you obtain the screen names of some friends and acquaintances, you'll want to add them to your AIM Buddy List. Here's what you need to do:

1. First, you need to create a Buddy Group, because on AIM every buddy must be in a group, even if it's a group of one. To create a group, click the Add a Group button.
2. Give the new group a name by typing over the default name, `*New Group*`.
3. To add a buddy to a group, click the List Setup tab (see Figure 12-7).
4. Click the Add a Buddy button and replace `*New Buddy*` with your buddy's screen name.

To move a buddy from one group into another, simply open the buddy's current group and drag the buddy's screen name to the other group's folder.

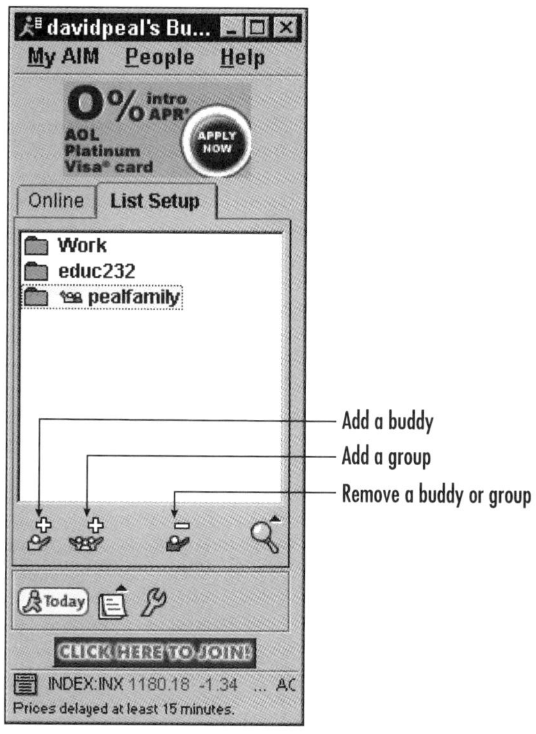

Figure 12-7. Add buddies and groups of buddies by using the List Setup tab.

Using Buddy Alert

Buddy Alert lets you know audibly when someone on your AIM Buddy List starts AIM or signs on to AOL and is available to exchange instant messages. You have a variety of sound options available, such as the sound of a door opening or even a cow mooing.

Here's how to set an alert for a buddy:

1. On the List Setup tab, find the screen name to which you want to attach an alert.
2. Right-click the name and choose Alert Me When Screen Name Is Available.

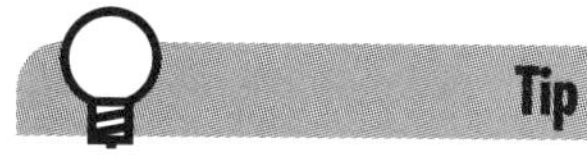

Tip

You can use your Buddy List as a mini-Address Book. Choose icons that represent your buddies, jot down comments about buddies, and store buddies' phone numbers.

In the Edit Buddy Alert window, you can provide more details about when you want to be alerted (when your buddy comes online or comes back from an idle state), and how you want to be alerted (with a pop-up window or sound).

3. Save the alert by clicking in the Save This Alert check box (a check mark appears in the box). Click OK.

Signing Off

Closing the AIM window differs from signing off the AIM service. To end an AIM session for a screen name, merely close the Buddy List window by clicking the X in the upper-right corner. The Buddy List window closes, but the AIM application continues running in the background. You can reactivate AIM by double-clicking the AIM icon in the Windows system tray, which is in the bottom-right corner of your computer screen.

With AIM maximized and showing on-screen, you can choose My AIM⇨Sign Off. Or right-click the AIM icon in the system tray and choose Exit.

Exchanging Messages with AIM

Using your AIM Buddy List, you can see when your buddies are online. To send a message to someone online, double-click the person's screen name. If you initiate an AIM session while you're signed on to AOL using the same screen name, you receive messages in the IM window. If you are on AOL but sign on to AIM with a different screen name, you'll receive messages in the AIM window.

As with AOL e-mail, your messages can contain more than text. Figure 12-8 shows a few ways to enhance a message: smileys, links, a background color (called *window color* in AIM), and styled text (big, bold, blue letters, and so on).

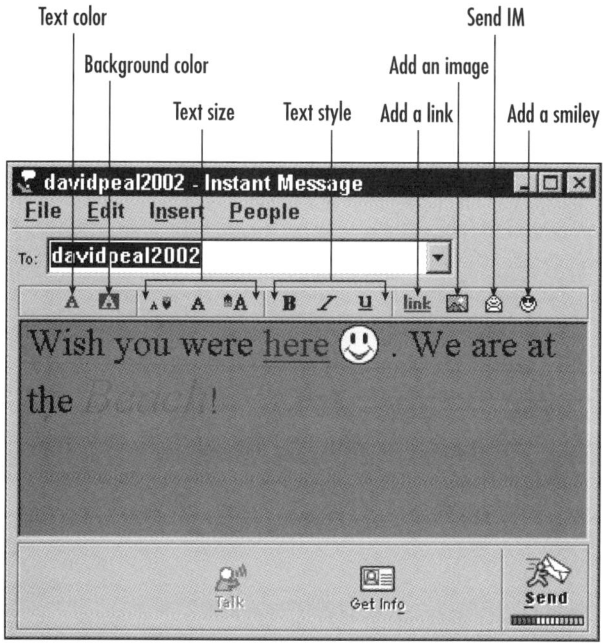

Figure 12-8. Some of the graphical and formatting effects possible with AIM.

When you type a smiley, for example

:-)

AIM brings cheer to your buddy with a right-side up, yellow happy face. Many other smileys are available from the smile button on the AIM message window. You can turn off graphical smileys on the IM/Chat tab in the AIM Preferences window, discussed later.

To add a link to a Web site, think of appropriate text for your reader to click. Then type text, select it, and click the Link button. In the window that appears, type the Web address of the linked-to site.

Receiving AIM Messages While on AOL

When you're on AOL, you can receive instant messages from Internet friends who use AIM, but first you receive a notification that someone on the Internet has sent you an instant message (the screen name is provided). The message gives you the option of receiving the message or ignoring it.

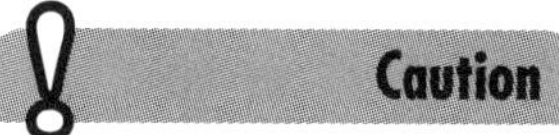

Before you click a link in an instant message or an e-mail, it's a good idea to verify that the link came from someone you know. Strangers may send you links that you find inappropriate.

Have you changed your e-mail address or AOL screen name? Choose My AIM⇨Edit Options⇨Update E-mail Address. Fill in the box and click OK. A current e-mail address gives online buddies another way of staying in touch.

When you're on AOL and talking with an Internet buddy who is *not* an AOL member, you are not protected by AOL's Terms of Service guidelines and protections. Here's the AOL policy:

```
Instant Message conversations with people using
AOL Instant Messenger are not subject to AOL's
Terms of Service. When you receive an Instant
Message note from an Instant Messenger user,
you will be asked if you want to accept or
ignore the message. To further control who can
send you Instant Message notes, use the Buddy
List feature's Privacy Preferences.
```

Privacy preferences can be found by clicking the Buddy List window's Setup button, and the Setup window's Preferences window. See "Setting Instant Message Preferences" earlier in this chapter. To find out more of AOL's policy, go to AOL Keyword: **Notify AOL**.

Creating and Joining AIM Chats

AOL made chat famous; AIM is making it ubiquitous. With AIM, AOL brings a powerful chat tool to users everywhere, no matter what Internet service they use.

To join chats on predefined topics, start with AOL's Chat Room Directory (`www.aol.com/community/chat/allchats.html`). Find a topic of interest and click it. The conversation takes place in the chat window shown in Figure 12-9.

To start up a chat with your own buddies, simply go to your Buddy List and make sure the Online tab is showing. Click the Send a Buddy Chat Invitation button at the bottom of your Buddy List window; it's the button in the middle, just below the AIM Buddy List (refer to Figure 12-6). In the Chat Invitation box, type buddies' screen names and separate the names with commas. When you click Send, the chat window appears. Your invitees need only click a link in the message they receive to join you in the chat room.

When you are in the chat room, you type your comments in the blank message field in the center. Click Send to transmit your message to the rest of the chat room participants. You see your messages, along with everyone else's, in the order they were sent.

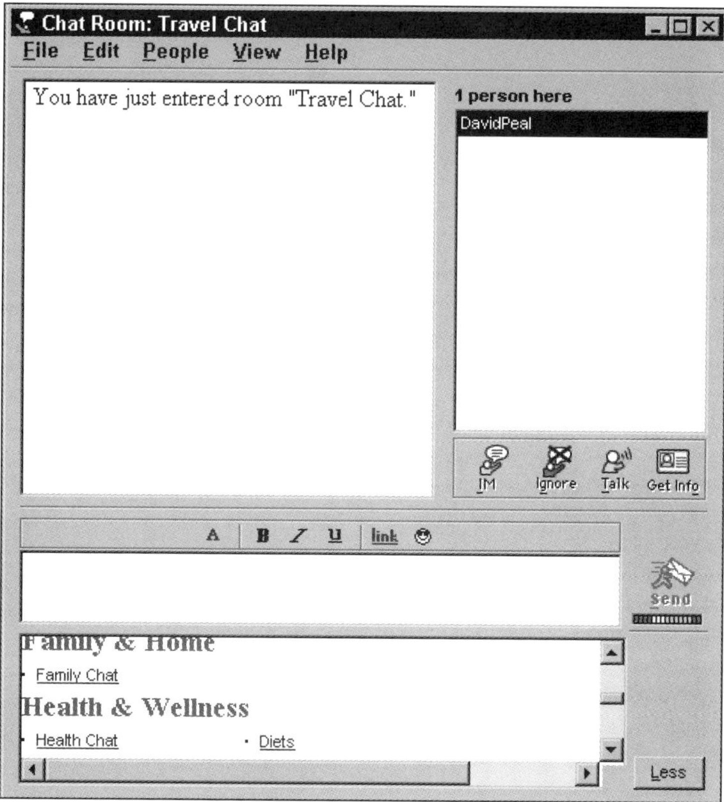

Figure 12-9. The AIM chat environment.

Sending Files with AIM

Want to send your friend a new MP3 file, the latest digital picture of the new baby, or Web pages that you are developing in a group? Exchanging files with AIM offers the kind of immediacy that e-mail sometimes lacks.

Before you exchange files with AIM, both you and your buddy must make sure that the AIM preferences settings allow file exchanges. To check your preferences, follow these steps:

1. From the Buddy List window, click the Preferences button, represented by a wrench.
2. Click File Sharing for options related to sending files. (Click File Transfers to set your file-receiving options.)
3. Click the Browse button to define a default folder where AIM should first look for files to send.

You can also exchange images with AIM by inserting them directly in messages. Highlight an online buddy and choose People⇨Send IM Image. You need to have the image file on your hard drive.

When you receive files, have them checked by your antivirus software. In the File Sharing preferences category, click the Virus Checker button and indicate which antivirus program you want to do the checking.

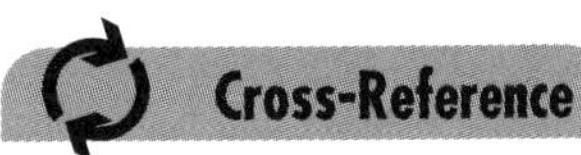

See AOL Keyword: **Virus** for general information, and Chapter 16 for more information.

Use the File Transfer preferences tab to specify where others can put files they send you.

AIM Express: When You Don't Have AIM

What if you're on the road and can only manage a brief visit to the Internet by using someone else's computer? Or you don't have AOL on your work computer, that summer laptop, or a rental computer?

AIM Express, special software designed for use on the Web, provides AIM's essence — a Buddy List together with messaging and chat — even if you don't happen to have AOL or AIM at the moment. The interface looks similar to AIM, but simpler. (AIM doesn't yet support Parental Controls or Notify AOL features.) With AIM Express, you use the same screen name and password that you use with AIM. When you have your screen name and password, start at `www.aol.com/aim` and look for the AIM Express link. You must be using a recent browser, such as Netscape or Internet Explorer.

4. Use the File Access section to indicate people who can receive files (for example, only people in a specific buddy group or your entire Buddy List).
5. Click OK.

Then send a file:

1. Double-click a buddy's name in the Buddy List.
2. Choose People⇨Send File.
3. In the Set File to [*buddy's name*] window, click the File button to find the file to send. You can browse to any directory on your system if the file's not in the default folder. In the special message window, type a few words if you want.
4. Click the Send button.

AIM takes file sharing a step further by letting people help themselves to your files. In the Preference window's File Sharing tab, you can specify a folder of files that you want to make available to specific people or to anyone. Think of this as a type of personal FTP (file-transfer) service. In a work project, others can help themselves to any of the files you make available. They cannot, however, access any other folder on your computer. You can have AIM display an Approve dialog box on your screen each time someone requests a file from the designated folder, or you can permit access to files in a directory to anyone or to people on your Buddy List.

Using AIM's News and Stock Tickers

When you sign on to AIM, you may notice an additional News Ticker window with headlines that scroll across the screen. This window, shown at the top of Figure 12-10, looks like an old-fashioned stock ticker. The News Ticker brings you the latest news, entertainment, business, and sports headlines. You can click any headline to read the story. To see an easier-to-read list of headlines in addition to the ticker, click the button on the far left of the ticker. A News Headlines window like the one on the left in Figure 12-10 appears, and this window displays best if you make it as wide as possible by dragging one side of it.

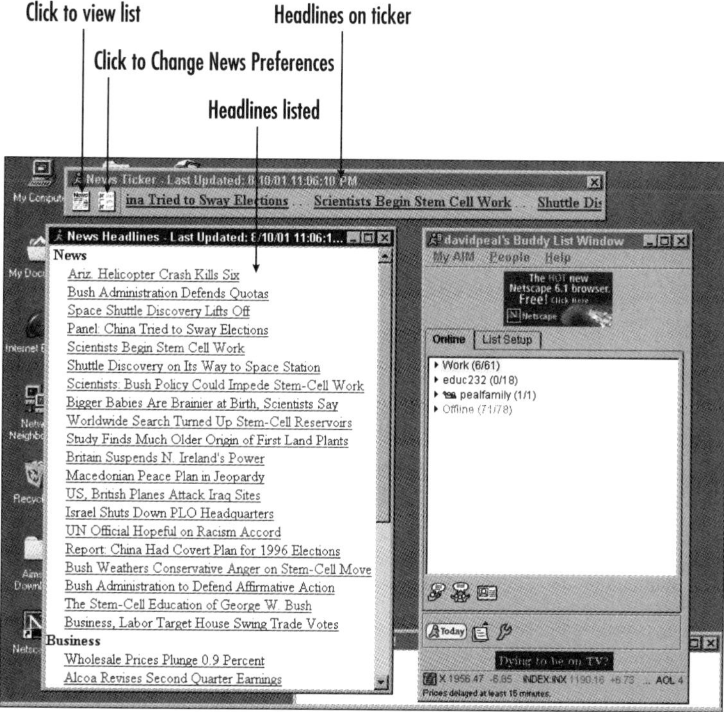

Figure 12-10. Use AIM Express when you don't have AOL or AIM, but do have an Internet connection and an up-to-date browser.

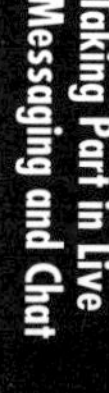

The News Ticker options can all be set in the AIM preferences window, a click away from the ticker itself. Preferences are also available by clicking the wrench icon in the main AIM window. The News Ticker options let you choose the type of headline (business and sports, for example), the update frequency (from every 30 minutes to daily), and the ticker's speed. Right-click the scrolling ticker for similar options.

The second flow of information you can receive on AIM provides customizable stock information. This information appears as a scrolling ticker, too, but within the main AIM window. In AIM's Stock Ticker preferences, click Edit Stocks to add companies' symbols as well as the major indexes to your stock tickers. The Stock Ticker options on the main Ticker preferences page, again, are pretty straightforward, giving you control of how often the data is refreshed and how fast the scroll moves.

Setting Your AIM Preferences

As in any program, in AIM, your preferences tell the software exactly how you want it to work. You have already encountered some of AIM's preferences in this chapter, including file-exchange preferences. In the new version of AIM, preferences are simpler to use than in earlier versions. Figure 12-11 shows the Preferences box, available from the Buddy List window (My AIM⇨Edit Options⇨Edit Preferences).

To use the box, just select a type of preference from the category list on the left (for example, Buddy List, IM/Chat, or File Sharing). Each category has a different set of preferences, which appears on the right. AIM preferences let you alter the look of your messages, the sounds that announce them, who can contact you, and all kinds of other things.

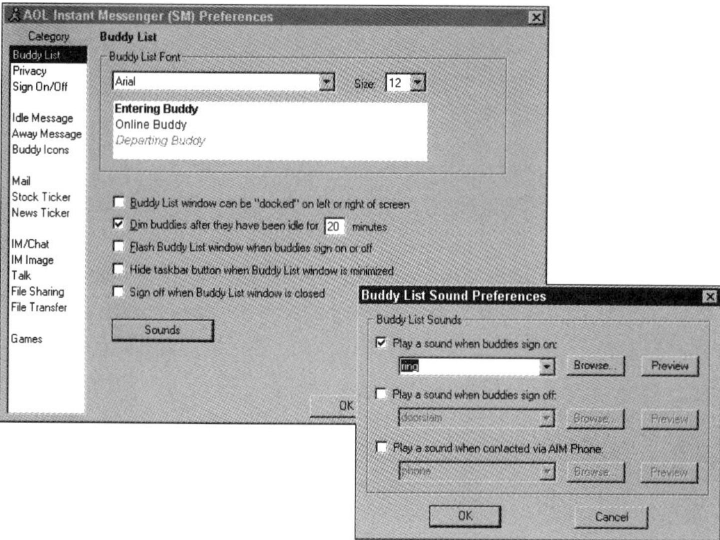

Figure 12-11. Edit your preferences to make AIM work your way. Clicking the Sounds button brings up the window on the right.

Here are a few other useful preferences.

- **IM/Chat:** These preferences let you adjust the default fonts, font sizes, font colors, and background colors used when you type messages, so you don't have to keep setting up the effects you like. In the Text Magnification box, you can adjust the text magnification (up to 200%) in the messages you receive so you can read them more easily. Of course, when you type messages, you can override the defaults and apply the styles and colors in any way you want.
- **Stock Ticker:** You can choose which stocks to include in the scrolling ticker shown in your Buddy List window.
- **Privacy:** AOL's privacy preferences, mentioned earlier in this chapter, apply to AIM messages arriving while you're on AOL, but do not apply to messages exchanged with the AIM software. AIM's privacy preferences allow you to prevent some, all, or no users from contacting you when you are using the AIM software. You can determine how much information other users can find out about you.

If you want a sound to accompany an incoming message, click the Sounds button in the IM/Chat category.

- **Away Message:** Another way of ensuring privacy is to use an Away Message, which you can activate when you step away from the computer or go to lunch. An Away Message is a specific message that is automatically sent to people who message you; it's similar to a "be right back" note tacked to your door.

  You can use a default message or create one of your own. To design a message, click the Away Message button (shown in Figure 12-6) and choose New Message. Give the message a name and type in the message to be sent when buddies message you.

  To activate the Away Message, click the same Away Message button and choose the name of the message you want to activate. When you come back, click the window's I'm Back button.
- **Idle Message:** An Idle Message works like an Away Message but turns on automatically after you've been inactive for a specific amount of time (about ten minutes). Your Idle Message preferences let you define a message that is automatically sent to anyone who sends a message while you're idle. A single keystroke (any key will do) makes you an active AIM user once again, able to receive messages.
- **New versions of AIM:** Using the AIM preferences box (Sign On/Off category), you can choose to be notified when new versions of AIM can be downloaded.

Taking AIM the Next Step: Groups@AOL

This section discusses Private Groups. AOL has just launched a new service called Public Groups, described in the "Public Groups" sidebar.

Think of a Group as a circle of family, friends, coworkers, people in your profession, hobbyists, or students in a class. Now think of a central online meeting place where the Group, and only the Group, can meet (AOL Keyword: **Groups**).

A Group gives its members control of its purpose and content. Every Group you create automatically includes a Group mailing list, flexible chat tools based on AOL Instant

Messenger, and a Group bulletin board where members can post messages for other members to see and respond to. Group members can also create lists of favorite restaurants, movies, books, Web sites, and more, providing, if they choose, ratings and Web addresses of their favorite destinations. Creating and maintaining such lists can provide a tangible focal point and a good way of generating new things to share (see Figure 12-12), such as books, movies, jokes, and so on.

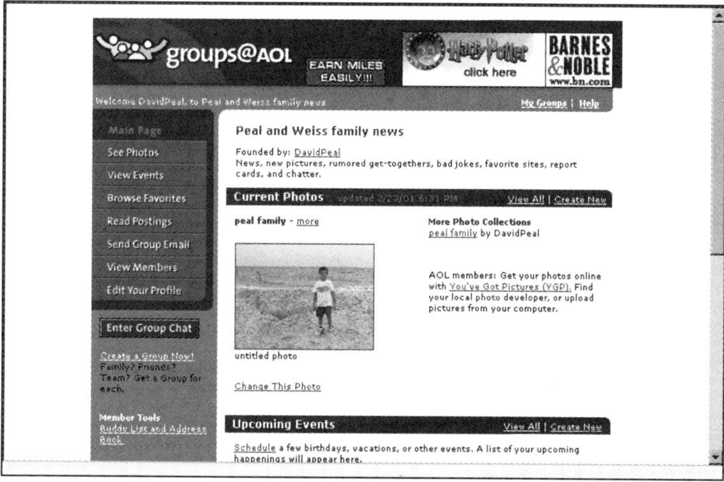

Figure 12-12. Groups@AOL: A Group's main page (the opening page when someone visits the Group).

Any member of your Group can upload pictures to the Group's photo collections, where the pictures become instantly available to other Group members.

Groups@AOL is open to anyone, AOL member or Internet user. Although only AOL members can *start* a Group, anyone can be invited to join. The Group's founder — the person who starts the Group — has control over membership. In fact, Groups don't really exist until the founder sends invitations to people and those people join it. The other side of the coin is more sensitive. Founders can remove participants for any reason, but can also have any participant (a co-owner) share the responsibility of inviting people and kicking them out.

Cross-Reference

A Group mailing list is similar to the Address Book groups discussed in Chapter 11.

Note

Each Group has 12MB (megabytes) of storage space. Images may take up most of that space.

Find It Online

At AOL Keyword: **Groups@AOL**, you can find a directory of public Groups and complete instructions for creating and managing private and public Groups.

Find It Online

At AOL Keyword: **Founders Forum**, Group owners can find message boards, tips, and answers to frequently asked questions.

Public Groups

Until now, Groups have been invitation-only. In a Group for family members or a local investment club, restricting membership keeps the Group focused and familiar. However, in a Group for Britney Spears fans or *X-Files* enthusiasts, such restrictions make less sense. Many people would want to open such Groups to all Britney or *X-Files* fans.

AOL recently announced its public Groups service to complement its existing private Groups service.

The community features of a public Group are similar to the features in a private Group: chat, message boards, a Group mailing list, photo collections, and so on. Also like private Groups, any AOL member can create a public Group.

Public Groups differ from private Groups in two ways. The topic of a public Group is much broader, and although people must be invited to join a private group, founders can allow anyone to join a Public Group or approve requests from anyone who wants to join. In both types of Group, anyone on the Internet can join.

Where to Go from Here

Instant messages enable true conversation. Although this conversation requires typing and networks, with a little practice, sending instant messages becomes as simple and natural as talking. On AOL, instant messaging has been a mainstay of community life for a long time. With AOL Instant Messenger, this tool goes to Internet users everywhere. As an AOL member, this means that you can now communicate with any Internet user, thanks to a Buddy List that can include anyone with AIM or AOL.

Groups take the idea of AIM a step further. Messaging, e-mail, and message boards form a group's core, and the members can include AOL members and Internet folk alike.

- The best way to learn about instant messaging is to use it.
- The best way to learn about Groups@AOL is to experience a public Group. A directory is available at AOL Keyword: **Groups@AOL**.

Chapter 13

Joining Focused Communities: Mailing Lists

IN THIS CHAPTER **PAGE**

Internet mailing lists begin with a great idea — e-mail — and improve upon it. A mailing list gives you a way to stay in close touch with a group of people who infrequently, if ever, have face-to-face meetings. Suppose, for example, that you work offsite for a company that has employees in different states, or that you belong to a PTA committee that meets only monthly. The work list could keep subscribers informed about projects, events, and company news, while the PTA list could plug subscribers in to the day-to-day school issues that arise between those monthly meetings.

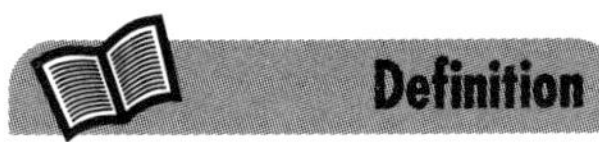

Definition

A *mailing list* is a list of e-mail addresses used by people on the list to send everyone the same message at the same time. *Subscribing* to a list means joining it.

Lists serve different purposes, focus on a wide range of topics, and vary enormously in size (the number of people on the list) and volume (the number of messages sent per day). Some lists are *interactive,* meaning anyone can send a message that will reach everyone on the list. Some lists are passive, meaning that people on the list receive a more-or-less regular message, or *newsletter,* from the person, organization, or business running the list. You'll find out about the world of mailing lists on AOL in this chapter.

Despite the tens of thousands of lists out there, you'll sometimes *not* find one with a specific focus. What to do? Start a list. This chapter shows how.

Mailing Lists and the Web

Not only has the Web simplified sending mailing lists across the Web in all sorts of ways, but it has also encouraged their popularity. It has also become easier for individuals to start and manage lists, and to take part in them. Here are some of the many ways in which mailing lists have become intertwined with the Web:

- Lists have always been a good way to share news about Internet resources with a group of people who share an interest. Because hyperlinks can be used in e-mail sent from and received by AOL, sharing discoveries is now a more immediate experience. An example is To Your Health, the Health Channel's weekly newsletter, which has several links to health-related resources on AOL and the Web.
- Many lists now have searchable Web archives of list messages so that even if you don't subscribe you can find messages to read on particular subjects. Just keep in mind that if you don't subscribe to a list you can't send messages to the list. Searching such archives can help you decide whether list members are interested in the same things as you. If you don't want to subscribe to a list or you want to limit the amount of e-mail you receive, you can check its archives and just read messages for the day or week of your choice.

- Increasingly, you can join mailing lists on Web sites or start you own. On sites such as the one shown in Figure 13-1, all you have to do is fill in your e-mail address and click to join. Likewise, Web fill-in-the-blank forms let you set your preferences and unsubscribe from (leave) a list. Many such sites use lists to keep in touch with their communities — the people who frequent them and share the same interests.

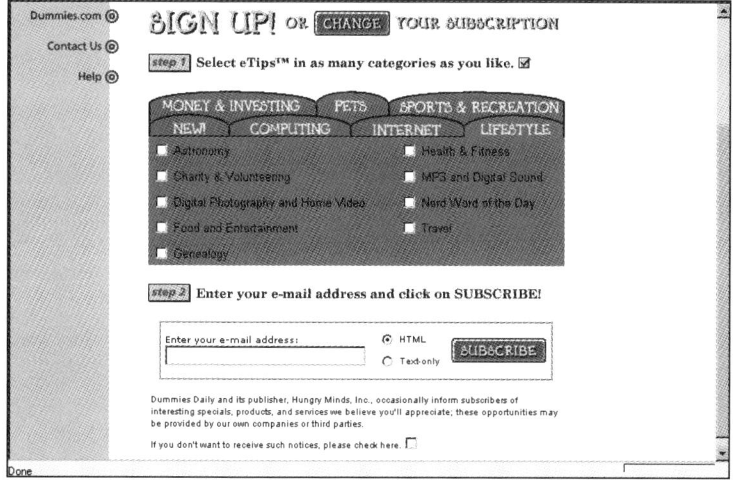

Figure 13-1. Join a Dummies Daily newsletter on any of several dozen topics.

- Companies such as Topica make it possible for anyone to set up and manage a list on the Web. With such services, subscription requests can be managed and the actual messages read on the Web. See "Creating Your Own Mailing List" later in this chapter.

Taking Part in Discussion Lists

E-mail has many advantages as a communication tool, and so, by extension, does the mailing list. One advantage is that you're under less pressure to respond than if you were having a face-to-face conversation or a live electronic conversation. With mailing lists, you don't have to respond at all, but can instead *lurk* (listen in on the conversation).

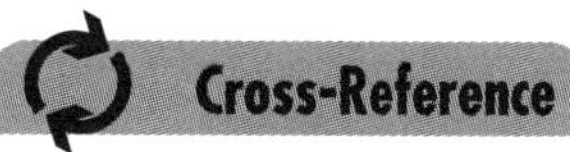

Groups@AOL, discussed in Chapter 12, supports small communities on the Web. Formed around a shared Web site, Groups include their own mailing lists, among other communications tools.

All you need to take part in any mailing list is an e-mail address. Using an AOL Anywhere device or service (outlined in Chapter 10), you can receive e-mail and mailing lists when you're away from your PC.

The first lists covered technical subjects. Created in 1975, Telecomm Digest, which is still active, claims to be the first list. You can find the list's archives, together with informative Web sites dealing the history of telecommunications technology, at `hyperarchive.lcs.mit.edu/telecom-archives`.

To save any message to a file, open it and choose File⇨Save As. Give the file a name and put it in a convenient folder on your hard drive.

Listiquette (Mailing List Etiquette)

Lurking on lists is okay. That is, feel free to listen to what others have to say without saying anything yourself. As in any community, such observation is often the best way to figure out how things are done and to learn about a list's subject. No rule says you *ever* have to take part — in fact, most lists expect you to participate only if you have something to say.

On the other hand, on smaller lists or support groups, not speaking can make you conspicuous. Introducing yourself to a smaller group through e-mail is fine. People in a very large group are likely to be less interested in knowing about every new member. And they definitely don't appreciate responses, such as, "Right on" or "Me too!" because these responses don't add substantively to the discussion.

Avoid asking basic questions that can be answered through other resources.

When you reply to messages, make sure to copy bits of the message to which you are responding in order to provide some context. Select this material before clicking Reply. Selective quoting is critical because the quoted material goes into the mailboxes of dozens or perhaps thousands of other people. Rereading entire messages is annoying because a few quoted words often provide enough context for a person's response.

Another bit of listiquette carries over from simple e-mail: Humor and sarcasm can backfire in an environment of strangers, sometimes from different cultures, regardless of their shared interest in the list's theme. Write clear subject lines and respect the diversity of your audience in your messages. Use *smileys* to show when you're not meaning exactly what you say, as in the following wink (tilt your head to see the wink effect):

```
;-)
```

Many people like to know who is behind a mailing list message. On AOL you can create a *signature,* which is text that identifies you to the others. For Internet mailing lists, make sure to use plain (not formatted) text and, depending on the list, provide enough background information to give an idea of where you are coming from. Chapter 11 provides steps for creating a signature.

Discussion lists differ among themselves in two major ways:

- **How they're managed, or what software keeps them going:** This isn't your problem, but the business of the list's owner. However, the software does affect mechanical details, such as how you join a list and how you leave it. These details are discussed later in this chapter for *Listserv,* the original and still leading type of mailing list software.
- **Whether they're moderated:** A list's moderator screens messages to keep out the offensive or off-topic ones. A moderated list is more likely to be useful and focused than a list that isn't. Good lists also thrive on trust and sociability, however, and subscribers usually don't like one person silencing members without a good reason.

You can find discussion lists that cover every subject. For example, I receive a handful of education-related discussion lists. In these lists, teachers discuss how they use the Internet in the classroom (WWWEDU) and distance educators relate how they adapt their teaching for students who are not in the classroom (DEOS-L). Because of the sheer volume of daily messages, I receive these lists as daily *digests* (a digest is a single message containing all the day's individual messages). Later in this chapter, you can read about digests and find tips for identifying lists that best address your interests.

Staying Informed with Newsletters

A growing number of lists do not allow subscribers to carry on discussions with each other. These more passive lists work like paper newsletters, with the same message and same information going out from one person or organization to many people. Here are a few informative newsletters to serve as examples:

- AOL publishes many weekly channel and forum newsletters to highlight events and new areas of interest in the channel. Some include members' letters, poems, and pictures. You can join any AOL newsletter at AOL Keyword: **Newsletter** (Figure 13-2). Later in this section, you'll see how to get AOL newsletters.

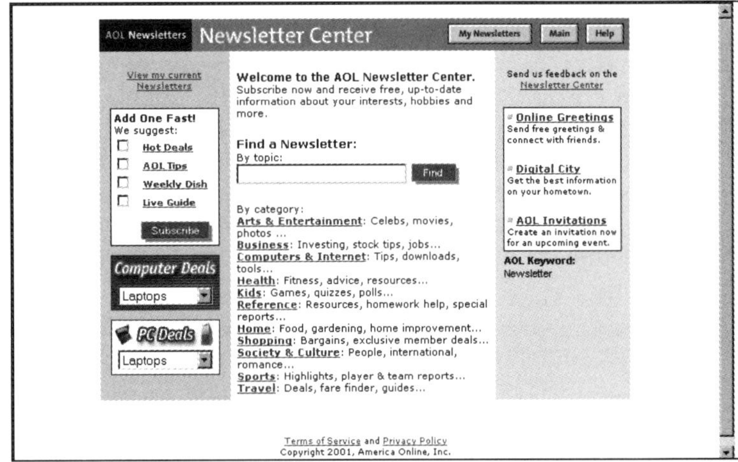

Figure 13-2. Join any of AOL's mailing lists at AOL Keyword: **Newsletter.**

- Some newsletters are a part of a much bigger show. The Net Music Countdown lists, created by radio broadcaster and Internet geek David Lawrence, give you an inside look at the world of popular music on the Internet. At Lawrence's fun and informative Online Tonight site, you can subscribe to the lists (`www.online-tonight.com`). While there, take some time to immerse yourself in the world of Net music, online radio, edgy humor, and headlines.
- Organizations that have a Web presence often offer mailing lists to keep members, donors, and other interested parties up-to-date. Such informational mailing lists can provide a key professional service while also promoting the organization's work. For example, I receive a mailing list on learning disabilities called Schwab

Learning Online. At the very informative Web site (www.schwablearning.org), you can join the list by merely typing in your e-mail address. Look for the newsletter under the Connecting with Others heading.

- Sometimes a newsletter's information is strictly commercial. For example, if you buy books, CDs, and software on the Web, most big online stores make it easy for you to join a mailing list that brings special sales and offers to your attention. Joining such lists is always optional, but whenever you register at a site make sure you are not also registering for a list that you might not want. Read the fine print whenever you sign up for a newsletter or other service.
- Some electronic newsletters have a strong personal point of view and share editorials, essays, links, and perspectives. Created by individuals, they serve specialized audiences. One such list is David Strom's Web Informant, which you can join at www.strom.com/awards. A networking guru who writes clearly on a wide range of computing topics, Strom uses Web Informant to share his insights on subjects like preparing video for the Web and creating a mailing list.
- Many newsletters want to offer you something new every day. For example, A Word A Day (AWAD) brings a new word into your mailbox every day, based on themes that change every week or so. Each day's word includes a definition, a quote, and a link to an audio file in which the word is pronounced. At AWAD's Web site, you can search archives of words. You can subscribe by merely typing your name and e-mail address into a form on the list's Web site (www.wordsmith.org/awad).
- Several big news services bring the day's news to your mailbox — before you see it on TV. Wired Daily is one such service, which (along with a dozen other Wired newsletters) you can join at hotwired.lycos.com/email/signup/.
- At Backwire (www.backwire.com) you can subscribe to newsletters with a business, technology, or family focus. Editors go through key magazines and essential Web sites for stories and links of interest, which are delivered by daily e-mail newsletter. Infobeat (www.infobeat.com) offers more newsletters of this kind.

Subscribing to AOL Newsletters

If you want to subscribe to any of AOL's newsletters, visit the Newsletter Center (AOL Keyword: **Newsletters**). Newsletters are grouped in big categories like Arts & Entertainment, Health, Kids, Sports, and Travel.

To join any AOL newsletter:

1. Go to AOL Keyword: **Newsletters**. A window appears displaying several categories. Each category includes several newsletters.
2. Click different categories to see the available newsletters. Click individual newsletters to read a description. The current issue of each newsletter can be previewed here.
3. When you find a newsletter of interest, simply click to put a check in the box next to the newsletter's name and click the Save button at the bottom of the window. A new window next to it appears, confirming that your e-mail address has been added to the list. Click AOL's Back arrow (or press Alt+Left Arrow) to continue choosing lists.
4. Close the Newsletter Center when you're done (click the Close button — the X in the far upper-left corner).

Whenever you want to unsubscribe from a newsletter, return to the Newsletter Center, find the newsletter under the appropriate category, uncheck that newsletter (click in the check box), and then click Save.

Sampling AOL's Newsletters

AOL channels and forums use newsletters to let you know about new features, events, and other goings-on. Many have a strong point of view and give you a good sense of an AOL area's content and style. Taking advantage of AOL's e-mail features, many channel newsletters come formatted like Web pages, with splashy color, photos, and links. You may need to maximize the Mail window to view these creative newsletters (see Figure 13-3 for an example). To maximize, just click the box showing the outline of a box in the upper-right corner of the message window.

Here's a sampling of the newsletters you can find on AOL in the Newsletter area (AOL Keyword: **Newsletter**).

- **Kids Only:** Uses large colorful text, with background colors and an easy-to-read typeface. Kids' poems and messages are often featured.
- **Picture This!:** Gives a weekly overview of the world of digital pictures on AOL. This attractively laid out newsletter can help you learn all about AOL's "You've Got Pictures"[SM] service. Regularly featured are photos by AOL members.

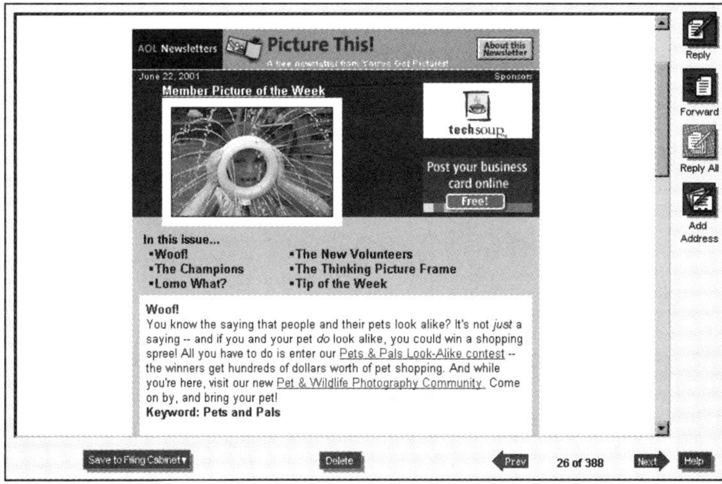

Figure 13-3. Picture This! This newsletter plugs you into digital imaging on AOL.

- **Weekly Byte:** The growing and informative Computing Channel, which caters to everyone from the greenest newbie to the most seasoned Internaut, puts out the Weekly Byte, a newsletter that conveys the breadth of the channel's offerings. A typical issue tells you about forums, classes, new downloads, bargains, and contests. Live links take you directly to the forums and areas described.
- **Deals and Steals:** Find the best bargains on Shop@AOL with the Deals and Steals newsletter.

Finding Lists to Join

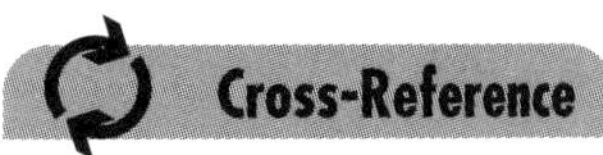

Consider starting your searches for lists with AOL Search, which I discuss in Chapter 8. For example, search for *mailing list Labrador* to find Web pages with mentions of, or subscription information about, Lab-related lists.

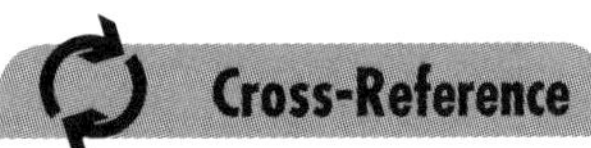

Topica makes creating even sophisticated lists simple. This service is discussed later in this chapter.

Whether it's a discussion list or newsletter you're after, searching for mailing lists is easy, thanks to general tools, such as AOL Search, and list directories, such as the following:

Topica

Liszt (like the name of the composer) once was the name of the largest searchable database of mailing lists of all kinds. Formerly, you could reach Liszt's Web site by going to AOL Keyword: **Liszt**. Today, the keyword takes you to Topica, which recently acquired Liszt. Topica is the largest provider of comprehensive mailing-list services. You can reach Topica directly at `www.topica.com`.

More than 12 million people belong to one or more of Topica's lists. At the Topica Web site, you can quickly search the approximately 100,000 Topica mailing lists. Figure 13-4 shows Topica's search page, where you can browse for a list on a certain subject, search across categories, or search messages.

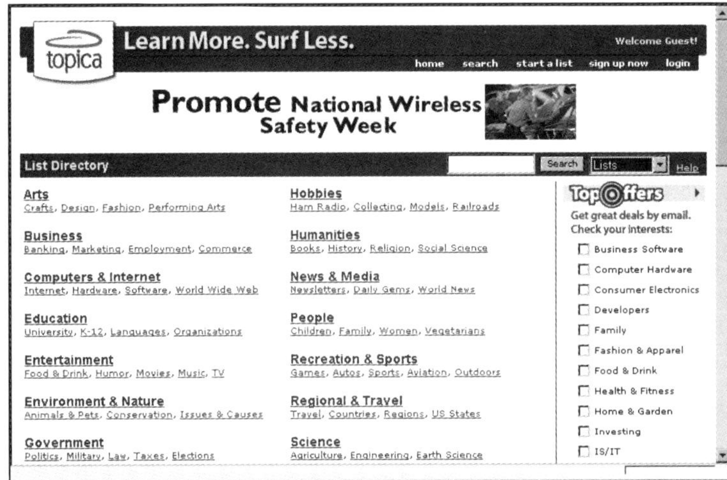

Figure 13-4. Topica: Find a list or start one.

Publicly Accessible Mailing Lists (PAML)

PAML is an annotated directory of mailing lists, usefully organized into subjects, going back to the 1980s. Since 1992,

Stephanie da Silva has kept this Internet classic current. Today, it is available at `www.paml.net`. Browsing PAML's subjects and mailing-list names can turn up many valuable lists.

Listserv's Catalist

Catalist is the search tool for Listserv mailing lists (`www.lsoft.com/lists/listref.html`). Listserv is one of the first programs used to manage a mailing list. Because Listserv has been around for so long and can *scale* (support very large mailing lists), some of the Net's most popular mailing lists run on Listserv software. Using Catalist you can find the size and purpose of any public Listserv. When possible, you can also link to a list's home page on the Web. You can find subscription information here as well, and links to a list's searchable archive if one exists.

Using Listserv Lists

Listserv software is an Internet institution, and the word has even entered day-to-day language as a generic word for any type of mailing list. That's not quite accurate, because *Listserv* merely refers to the software used to manage a particular type of mailing list, not the lists themselves — or all mailing lists. The next few pages show how to take part in a Listserv list.

On L-Soft International, which currently owns the Listserv software, you can search for the world's approximately 50,000 public Listserv lists, but not the much larger number of corporate and other nonpublic lists.

The Listserv software automates most of the work of joining, customizing, and leaving lists. You communicate with the software by e-mail. Because you are sending and receiving mailing list postings using automated processes (run on *software*), you need to follow a few specific but simple rules.

Listserv Primer (1): Joining a List

To subscribe to a Listserv list, you send an e-mail message to the software's e-mail address, often called the *administrative address*. An administrative address looks like `listserv@maelstrom.stjohns.edu`.

You also use the administrative address to set preferences or to leave a Listserv list.

You can type Listserv commands and list names in capital letters or lowercase letters. When you are writing to the administrative address to join or leave a list, you can leave the Subject line blank. The message itself consists of one or more commands, such as `subscribe` and `help`. For a comprehensive list of Listserv commands, send a message to any Listserv administrative address, such as `listserv@listserv.aol.com`, with the command `info refcard` in the body of the message.

Remember, because your message is processed by software, it's important to get the address and command just right.

After you've subscribed to a list, you use the *list address* to send messages to the people on the list. A list address looks like `our-kids@maelstrom.stjohns.edu`. The name of the list, Our Kids in this case, precedes the @ symbol.

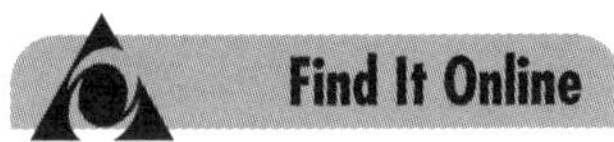

A comprehensive Listserv user's guide is available on AOL at `listserv.aol.com`.

AOL newsletters are all managed by Listserv, so I'm using AOL's Home Page Journal, the newsletter that serves AOL members who use AOL Hometown, to show you how to join a mailing list. (AOL Hometown provides tools and storage space for making and publishing your own Web pages.)

Of course, it's much easier to use AOL Keyword: **Newsletter** to join a mailing list, but to join one of the tens of thousands of Listserv lists available on the Internet you need to know how to subscribe the old-fashioned way. Figure 13-5 shows the message you write to the Listserv software.

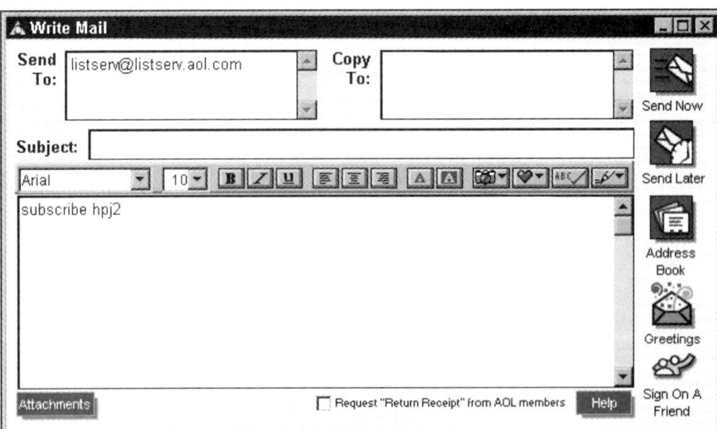

Figure 13-5. Subscribing to a Listserv list requires a simple e-mail message like this request to subscribe to AOL's Home Page Journal.

To join a mailing list:

1. Click the Write icon on the toolbar. A new Write Mail window appears.
2. In the Send To box, type the administrative address, **listserv@listserv.aol.com**. These administrative lists often begin with *listserv@*.
3. Leave the Subject box blank.
4. In the body of the e-mail, type the subscribe command and then the name of the list. For Home Page Journal, you would type **subscribe hpj2**. This is a *command*.
5. Click Send Now.
6. Soon after subscribing, you receive an e-mail acknowledging your request, similar to the e-mail shown in Figure 13-6. Reply as the message requests, and you'll be ready to go.

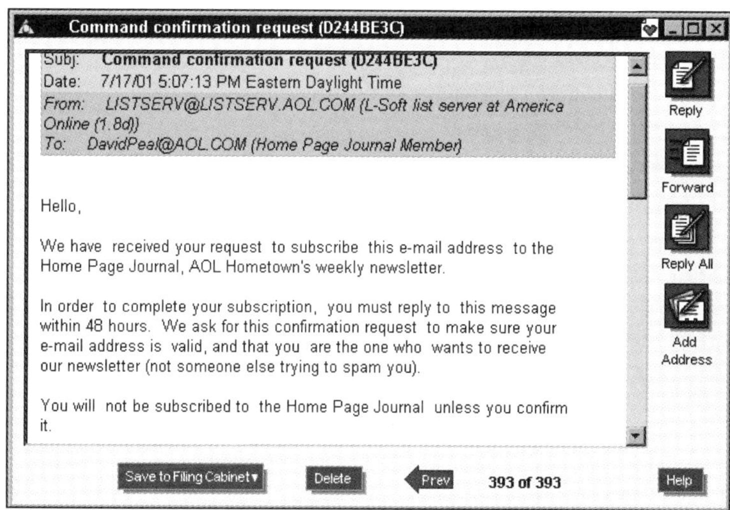

Figure 13-6. After subscribing, you receive a confirmation letter to which you must respond before you start getting the newsletter.

Sometimes you'll receive a welcome message almost immediately. The welcome message tells you how to take part in the list, how to get a list of commands for the list, and how to unsubscribe. Save this message. In fact, it's a good idea to save all your welcome messages in a safe place. Or, print them and keep them in a folder.

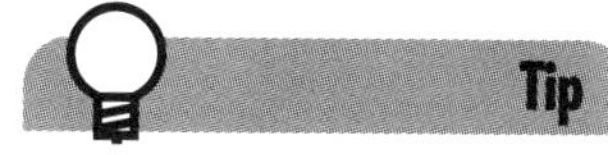

Save the welcome message you receive so that you can refer to it later if you have questions about using the mailing list.

Listserv Primer (2): Sending a Message to the List

Try to use a brief, precise subject line to clarify your new topic. Your message will reach many people, and you want them to know what's in the message before they open it.

After you join a Listserv-type discussion list, messages from the list start coming into your AOL Online Mailbox. The number of messages per day depends entirely on the list.

If you want to participate by replying to another message, then you're taking part in a *thread,* as in the *thread* of an argument. Each response or reply to a posting continues the thread until another topic is posted. You can start a topic of your own by sending an e-mail message to the list address. Several new topics and current threads can be going on at the same time.

Most lists reject commercial postings and unsolicited mail. For example, a list for English teachers is not the place for textbook salespeople to make an unsolicited pitch for their new titles. *Spamming* a list, which involves sending unsolicited commercial messages without any relation to the list's purpose, is not smart and is likely to have some negative consequences, like getting you kicked off the list.

Listserv Primer (3): Customizing a List

Listserv lists offer a wide range of commands that enable users to choose how and when they receive messages. People rarely use many of these commands, probably because the commands' usefulness isn't obvious or because many subscribers don't know the commands exist. These commands can be helpful, however. For example, the `digest` command tells the Listserv software to send you the list in a special format (see the sidebar, "Digests: A Message a Day"), and the `vacation` command lets you temporarily stop receiving messages without leaving the list altogether.

You use a command by sending a message to the list's administrative address, with the command in the message body. For example, to get a summary of available Listserv commands, send a message to `listserv@listserv.aol.com` with the word `help` in the message's body.

Responding to the List or to an Individual

It's not always clear whether you should reply to the individual who sent a message or to the group. Generally, you should respond to the entire list only if your response is of likely interest to most list subscribers.

- Sometimes a message to a list requests specific information of clearly personal interest. In this case, you should probably respond directly to the sender. A subscriber looking for homework help should get the answers directly — and probably shouldn't be posting the question to the list in the first place.
- Sometimes, people request specific information, such as list members' personal experience with a certain piece of software or topic. Often, they'll ask that responses be sent directly to them, not to the list. If the responses are of group interest, some people summarize such responses in a message to the group.
- If you know the sender and have a personal response, write that person directly.

To respond to the group, use the Reply button, first selecting any text to be quoted in your reply. To respond to the individual, you'll find the person's e-mail address in the message header.

Listserv Primer (4): Leaving a List

You can leave a mailing list for many reasons. You don't like it, it takes too much of your time, it's not what you thought it would be, you never look at it, and so on. When you're ready to leave the list (or *unsubscribe*), send a message to the list's administrative address. In the message body, include the `signoff` command followed by a space and the name of the list. For example, if you want to leave Home Page Journal, send a message to the same address that you used to join the list and, in the message body, type **signoff hpj2**.

Caution

If you ever cancel your AOL account, first make sure to unsubscribe from all your lists. If you don't unsubscribe, list messages that are sent to your account bounce back to AOL, creating unwanted mail and extra work for list administrators.

Other types of list software, such as *listproc*, use similar procedures but different commands. For every list you join, make sure to save the welcome message, which includes information about leaving. Many newsletters include information about unsubscribing toward the end of every message.

Creating Your Own Mailing List

Taking part in a few good lists can inspire you to create your own list for a Girl Scout troop, your extended family, a neighborhood association, or another group. Creating a mailing list requires no more than the AOL Address Book. If you want to create, manage, and host a larger or more complex list, Topica probably offers the services you need.

Before creating a list with the Address Book, be sure to tell people what you are trying to do and find out whether they want to join.

To create your own AOL mailing list:

1. Open the Address Book, which is available offline as well as online by choosing Mail⇨Address Book.
2. Click Add Group.
3. In the Manage Group window, shown in Figure 13-7, give your list a name. Then select e-mail addresses to include in the list. For addresses not in the Address Book, type them into Additional Contacts in Group box and separate addresses with a comma.

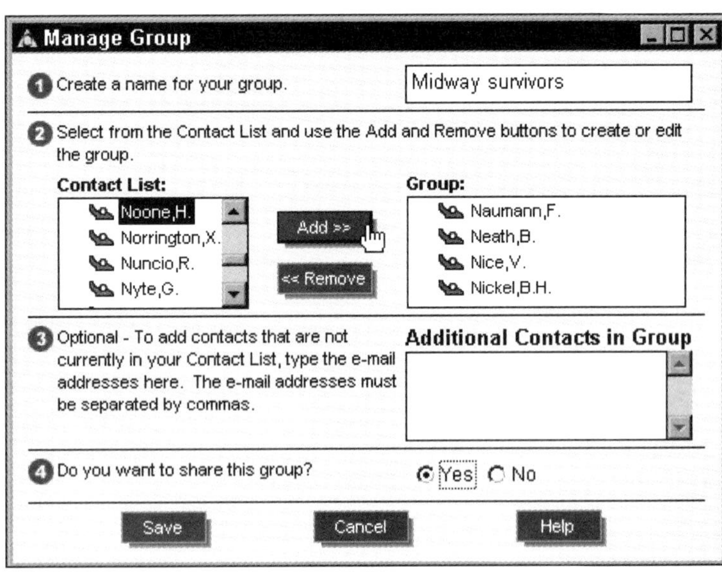

Figure 13-7. The Manage Group window. E-mail addresses from the Address Book and other sources still need to be added.

Digests: A Message a Day

Of all the Listserv commands, `digest` is, for many people, the most useful. A *digest* combines all of a list's messages for the day into *a* single message. Getting all your messages at once is easier than reading a dozen messages throughout the day, unless you take active part in the list. For a lurker, a digest provides a perfect overview of what's happening on a list.

On AOL, you receive digests as e-mail attachments from the list. These attached files have specific filenames. To use an attached file, you must download it to your computer and read it in a word processor or a text editor, such as AOL's, available by choosing File⇨Open. Chapter 10 has more to say about working with attachments.

To find information in a message containing a digest, you can

- **Use the list of headers.** The subject headers for the day's messages are listed at the top of the digest, as in the following figure, so you can find interesting threads easily. The following figure shows an example of a digest.

```
There are 16 messages totalling 1610 lines in this issue.

Topics of the day:

  1. student publishing
  2. Jobs vision (fwd) (4)
  3. Teacher publishing (6)
  4. Why education doesn't change (4)
  5. English Teachers: Literary Criticism Resources
```

- **Use the Find dialog box.** On AOL you can search for specific words in a long digest by pressing Ctrl+F and doing a search.

One drawback of digests is that you can't click the Reply button and respond to the people on the list or even to the individual whose message you are reading. Instead, you must look for the list address or an individual poster's e-mail address, depending on whether your reply will go to the individual or the group, and then copy and paste it into a new message.

4. To share the new list, click the Yes radio button. By sharing an Address Book group you have the opportunity to set up a Group consisting of the people in your list. A Group includes your mailing list as well as a message board, a list of favorites, a photo collection, and other shared tools.

   If you click the No radio button, the group of names will be for your use, and the group's, too, if you wish, but all communication will take place by e-mail only.

5. Click Save when you are done. If you chose to share your Group, the Groups@AOL Web page comes up, with your list name filled into the Unique Name field. On this page, confirm the e-mail addresses of the group members, provide other e-mail addresses if you wish, and click Create Group. You will be the list's Founder. You and group members you invite can now use the group's message board, chat tool, and photo collections.

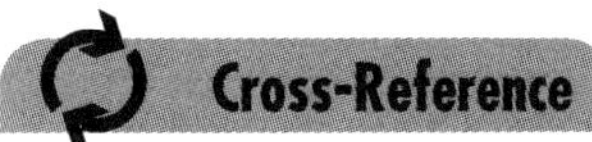

Groups@AOL, introduced in Chapter 12, provides tools for communities of people with a strong shared interest.

The Address Book doesn't care whether the people you include in your list, or in a Group, are AOL members, as long as you provide the full Internet addresses for non-AOL addresses (for example, `ccggaatt-ccggaatt@double-helix.nih.gov`). When you're done, the list's name appears in the alphabetical list of contacts in your Address Book. Use the list name to send one message to everyone on the list.

When choosing a company to host your list, look beyond the price (especially if a company's services are free!) to see whether the list provider can guarantee security, offer technical support, allow your list to grow and provide the degree of moderation you want.

For larger lists and additional features, such as availability on the Web and access to file libraries, you may want to use the services of a company that creates and hosts lists. Topica (`www.topica.com`) lets anyone set up a mailing list at no cost. You can transfer existing lists to Topica and create new lists by filling in a Web form with your name and e-mail address, the list's name and purpose, and the associated Web site, if any. Potential subscribers can find the list in the Topica directory, subscribe to it by filling in a simple form, and take part by using the Web or AOL Mail. It's a good, popular service, but as always, read the fine print.

Using Lists to Keep Up with the Net

Not surprisingly, the Net provides the best resources for keeping up with the Internet itself. Mailing lists in particular, because they are up-to-the-minute and all the information comes from people, can let you know about Internet resources relating to the subjects that interest you, as well as larger trends in the Internet world. From the lists I read, I learn about online content in my areas of interest almost every day.

A perfect place to start is the Scout Report, created by a team at the University of Wisconsin led by Susan Calcari, an Internet pioneer who died in the summer of 2001. The Scout Report is a weekly e-mail newsletter containing information about and links to the best new informational resources. Subscribing ensures that you don't miss an issue, but you can always see the current issue (and every previous, archived issue) on the Web at `scout.cs.wisc.edu/report/sr`. Figure 13-8 shows part of the Web version of the Scout Report.

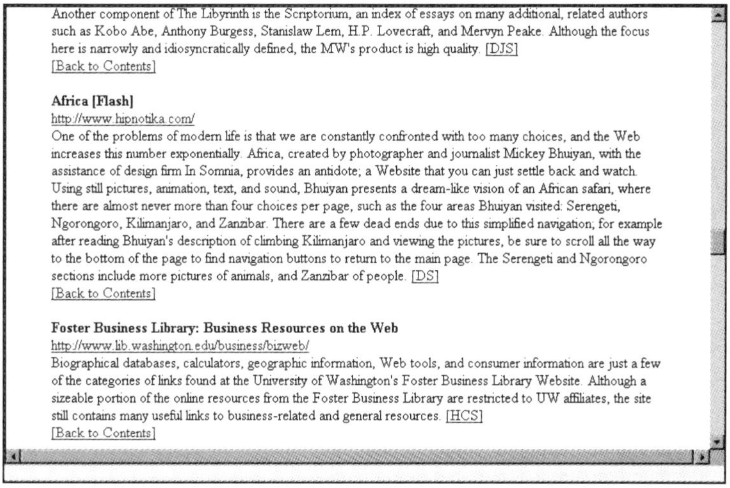

Another component of The Libyrinth is the Scriptorium, an index of essays on many additional, related authors such as Kobo Abe, Anthony Burgess, Stanislaw Lem, H.P. Lovecraft, and Mervyn Peake. Although the focus here is narrowly and idiosyncratically defined, the MW's product is high quality. [DJS]
[Back to Contents]

Africa [Flash]
http://www.hipnotika.com/
One of the problems of modern life is that we are constantly confronted with too many choices, and the Web increases this number exponentially. Africa, created by photographer and journalist Mickey Bhuiyan, with the assistance of design firm In Somnia, provides an antidote; a Website that you can just settle back and watch. Using still pictures, animation, text, and sound, Bhuiyan presents a dream-like vision of an African safari, where there are almost never more than four choices per page, such as the four areas Bhuiyan visited: Serengeti, Ngorongoro, Kilimanjaro, and Zanzibar. There are a few dead ends due to this simplified navigation; for example after reading Bhuiyan's description of climbing Kilimanjaro and viewing the pictures, be sure to scroll all the way to the bottom of the page to find navigation buttons to return to the main page. The Serengeti and Ngorongoro sections include more pictures of animals, and Zanzibar of people. [DS]
[Back to Contents]

Foster Business Library: Business Resources on the Web
http://www.lib.washington.edu/business/bizweb/
Biographical databases, calculators, geographic information, Web tools, and consumer information are just a few of the categories of links found at the University of Washington's Foster Business Library Website. Although a sizeable portion of the online resources from the Foster Business Library are restricted to UW affiliates, the site still contains many useful links to business-related and general resources. [HCS]
[Back to Contents]

Figure 13-8. The Scout Report reviews new informational resources every week. This figure shows the report's Web edition.

The monthly Search Engine Watch analyzes new features of individual engines and new trends in the search industry. Searching is fun and essential, and this newsletter is a good way to stay informed about the many types of search open to you. To subscribe, just go to `searchenginewatch.com/sereport/` and fill out the form.

Bob Rankin and Patrick Crispen's Internet Tourbus, hosted on AOL's Listserv computers, brings you an inside look into a special Internet topic every few days. Topics range from useful ("sending a fax over the Internet") to fun (a recent newsletter on "LEGOS and crayons"). The popular list has its own Web site, where you can both read back issues and subscribe (`www.tourbus.com`).

Where to Go from Here

The word *community* is a hot topic when pundits write about the Net, but mailing lists have been quietly and successfully supporting communities for more than two decades now. This chapter looked at the concept of the mailing list, explained the mechanics of joining and taking part in lists, provided examples of valuable lists, and suggested ways to find lists and newsletters of interest to you. You even found out how to create a list of your own.

- To enjoy lists, all you need is e-mail. Chapters 10 and 11 provide thorough overviews of reading and sending mail on AOL.
- The wilder world of public newsgroups is the subject of Chapter 14.
- For more on Groups@AOL, which combines mail, mailing lists, and messaging, see Chapter 12.
- Join a mailing list today!

Chapter 14

Global Bulletin Boards: Newsgroups

Newsgroups provide a central, public place for sharing opinions, gathering information, and requesting advice. They are open to anyone in the world with an Internet connection and newsgroup software. This software is included with AOL, along with access to thousands of newsgroups. Each newsgroup is devoted to a focused topic, such as rugby or digital photography.

Newsgroups (also called *bulletin boards*) have been archived into massive collections, and their collective wisdom has been condensed into informative overviews, or *FAQs*, which serve as knowledge bases. You can turn to newsgroups, newsgroup archives, and FAQs for answers to difficult questions on just about any subject. Read on to find out what newsgroups are about and how you can take advantage of them.

A *FAQ* is a document maintained by people in a newsgroup in which frequently asked questions are answered and related resources are provided.

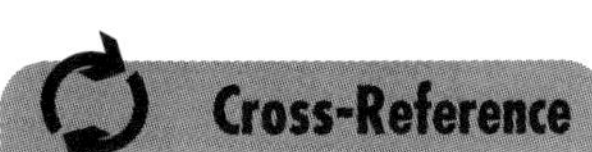

Chapter 4 shows how to use Parental Controls (AOL Keyword: **Parental Controls**) to prevent children from accessing newsgroups and from viewing newsgroup postings that have files attached.

A *posting* is another word for a message. A *newsgroup* contains postings about a specific subject. An *off-topic posting* is one that has nothing to do with a newsgroup's subject.

Newsgroups are more public than mailing lists (which you can read all about in Chapter 12). Because newsgroups are meant for public access, you can move in and out of them as your information needs change.

Using Newsgroups on AOL

AOL helps you find real treasures buried in newsgroups — from diverse opinion to advice — by setting up tools that help you avoid off-topic newsgroup postings. AOL's Parental Controls ward off the folks who send unsolicited commercial messages and advertisements that are inappropriate for children. In addition to Parental Controls, AOL's junk filters weed out these nuisance posts.

Traditionally, newsgroup users are responsible for respecting both the overall system and each other. Unlike mailing lists, many of which have administrators to moderate and guide posts, most newsgroups have no effective mechanism for focusing discussions and preventing flaming (conflicts) or spamming (unsolicited messages). That's why a little self control matters more in newsgroups than in other, less anonymous environments. See "Playing Nice" for a few guidelines.

You have two easy ways to get to newsgroups on AOL; both take you to the Newsgroups window, shown in Figure 14-1.

- AOL Keyword: **Newsgroups**
- Choose Services⇨Internet⇨Newsgroups

How Newsgroups Are Organized

Newsgroups are organized in what seem like nested boxes, one inside another, inside yet another. The largest box is the *category,* which is broken into smaller categories called *topics.* Some bigger topics are broken into *subtopics.*

For example, the rec category is broken into individual recreational topics and subtopics ranging from autos to photography. Figure 14-2 shows part of the list of rec topics, with a specific topic highlighted.

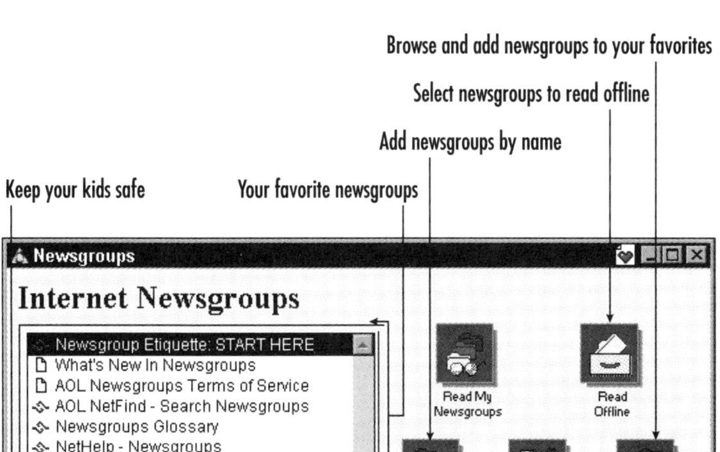

Figure 14-1. Start at AOL's Newsgroups window to find newsgroups, set your newsgroup preferences, and set Parental Controls.

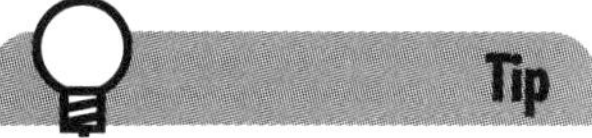

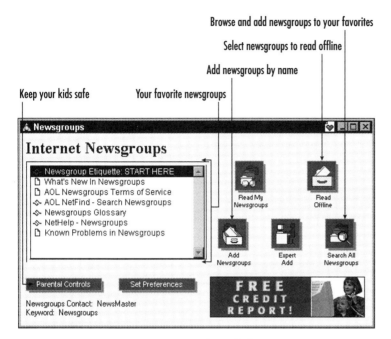

If you have a question about newsgroups, click NetHelp in the Newsgroup window's list box.

At AOL Keyword: **Newsgroups**, click Add Newsgroups to see which topics, subtopics, and individual newsgroups are available for every category.

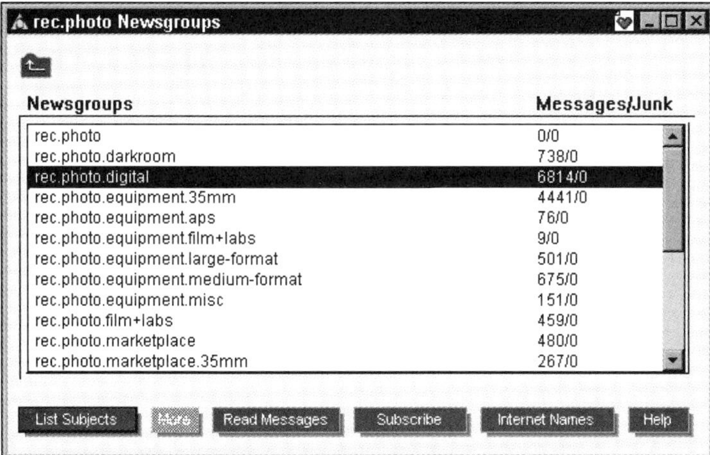

Figure 14-2. Newsgroups, like this one devoted to photography (rec.photo) are divided into categories and topics.

Replies to messages form *threads*. An asterisk (*), as in `comp.dcom.*`, refers to all the newsgroups in a topic.

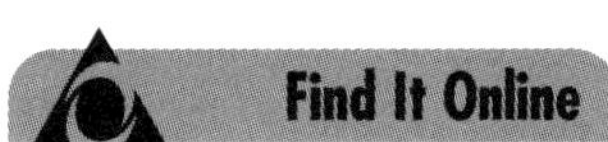

If you are having trouble with Windows, check out `comp.windows.misc`.

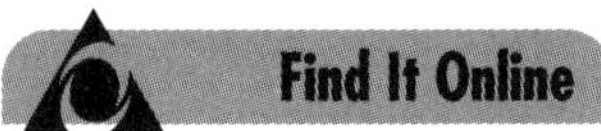

For current national, business, sports, and other areas of the news, visit AOL's News Channel (AOL Keyword: **News**).

Newsgroup names look like e-mail addresses (which I explain in Chapter 10), but don't get the two confused. The first bit of text in a newsgroup name always represents a general category, and the text in the middle represents a topic and perhaps a subtopic. The element at the end of the name defines the focus of a specific newsgroup. A newsgroup like `rec.photo.digital` is part of the photo category, which is part of the larger rec category. The focus of the newsgroup is, of course, digital photography.

You can find some of the largest and most established newsgroups in the so-called Big Seven categories:

- **comp:** As you might expect, this category is devoted to computers, software, programming, and related topics. Computer novices can find much value in this category. If you want to learn more about using HTML, for example, the newsgroup `comp.infosystems.www.authoring.html` remains useful after many years of activity and includes discussion of more advanced topics.
- **misc:** This category includes newsgroups that don't readily fit easily elsewhere, or that fit into more than one category. You can read about parenting in `misc.kids` and about immigration in `misc.immigration.usa`. Or, you can talk about schooling in the `misc.education` newsgroups. The best way to see what's available in this category is to browse (from AOL Keyword: **Newsgroups**, click Add Newsgroup, and double-click the misc category).
- **news:** Look here for information about newsgroups, not political news. For example, you can find answers to a lot of your questions about newsgroups in the `news.answers` group, which is very popular. Read about proposed new groups in `news.groups`.
- **rec:** This category covers recreational subjects. For example, look in `rec.travel.*` for newsgroups devoted to traveling; check `rec.travel.air` for a place to grouse, Find cheap tickets, and get tips. The `rec.sports.*` newsgroups focus on numerous sports. Or, browse `rec.pets.*` for advice about buying or caring for pets.

- **sci:** This category is devoted to newsgroups with an academic scientific orientation. The participants tend to be well informed, and many are pursuing advanced degrees. Interested amateurs have a strong place, also. Some newsgroups in the sci category include `sci.astro.amateur`, `sci.physics`, `sci.environment`, and `sci.lang`, which focuses on linguistics.
- **soc:** This category embraces newsgroups that focus on big social issues or big personal issues, like relationships; `soc.support.pregnancy.loss` is a moderated group for parents who have suffered early bereavement. If you're studying another country or traveling abroad, ask a question in `soc.culture.*` to get inside info and perhaps learn the point-of-view of someone who lives in the place where you will be traveling. Watch out, though, because postings in soc may lead to heated debates about culture and ethnicity.
- **talk:** This category provides a forum for the discussion of a variety of issues, usually relating to public policy. Be careful — this category can be divisive. You can spot the potential for controversy in newsgroup names, such as `talk.politics.guns`.

Note

Every category is diverse. Be prepared for differences of perspective throughout the newsgroup world.

The following alternative newsgroups have surpassed the Big Seven in popularity. *Alternative* refers to non-Big Seven categories in general and to the alt category in particular:

- **alt:** This is a messy category, containing newsgroups that are far from the mainstream as well as newsgroups that aren't very alternative at all; newsgroups on theology and numerology can both be found in this category.
- **aol (only on AOL):** AOL's own newsgroup category, for AOL-related newsgroups. The newsgroups in this category tend to meet the needs of AOL members in specific parts of the U.S.
- **bit:** Based on the old BITNET network, which housed the Net's early mailing lists, bit consists of the newsgroup versions of serious mailing lists. For example, `bit.listserv.blues-l` contains postings from the BLUES-L mailing list and `bit.listserv.autism` carries messages from the AUTISM-L mailing list.

Regional categories for state newsgroups use the two letter postal abbreviation, such as `ca.*` (for California) or `co.*` (for Colorado). The prefix for cities or other regions may be three characters or longer, such as `atl.*` (for Atlanta) and `triangle.*` (for the Research Triangle area in North Carolina).

- **biz:** For the most part, blatant profit-making attempts are discouraged everywhere — except this category. In fact, in the appropriate biz newsgroup, these efforts can be welcome and won't shock anyone. Whether people notice them is another question. The `biz.marketplace.*` category is particularly busy.
- **Regional categories:** Newsgroups within regional categories may be divided into subtopics that focus on issues relevant to particular regions if the traffic is heavy enough. Often, the individual newsgroups are practically empty. Local Web sites and destinations, such as AOL's Local Guide Channel, are replacing these newsgroups.

Adding Newsgroups to Your Favorites

As with mailing lists, which I discuss in Chapter 13, a subscription to a newsgroup merely simplifies the process of taking part; in neither case do you have to take part if you subscribe. On AOL, *subscribing* means adding a newsgroup to a list called Read My Newsgroups. Adding newsgroups to this list gives you quick access to them.

In the main Newsgroups window (refer to Figure 14-1), clicking the Read My Newsgroups button takes you to a window, shown in Figure 14-3. The Read My Newsgroups window displays your favorite newsgroups — the ones you want to read regularly. You can easily add lists and remove them as your needs change.

Including a newsgroup in Read My Newsgroups is required if you want to keep track of which messages you've read in any newsgroup. Further, if you want to use Automatic AOL (AOL Keyword: **Auto AOL**) to download postings from a particular newsgroup, you must add the newsgroup to the Read My Newsgroups list.

To add groups to Read My Newsgroups, you can proceed in two ways:

- If you know the full name of the newsgroup you want to add (for example, `rec.pets.cats`), click the Expert

Add button in the Newsgroups window. Clicking Expert Add saves a few steps but makes sense only if you know a newsgroup's full name and don't want to know what else is available in the same topic.

- If you want to browse categories and topics or view a newsgroup before subscribing to it, click the Add Newsgroups button.

Suppose, for example, you want to subscribe to a newsgroup about cooking but aren't aware of what's out there. After clicking Add Newsgroups at AOL Keyword: **Newsgroups**, double-click rec (the category where hobby topics are kept) and then rec.food (topics about food). Select a newsgroup and click the Subscribe button in the newsgroup window. In Figure 14-3, `rec.food.chocolate` has been added to Read My Newsgroups. Repeat the process for any other groups you want to read regularly. When you click Subscribe, a message confirms that you are subscribed; the Group Preferences window comes up, which allows you to set preferences that apply only to this newsgroup. (I discuss preferences in more detail later in this chapter.)

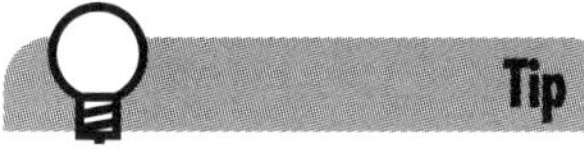

To remove a newsgroup from your list, select it and click the Remove button.

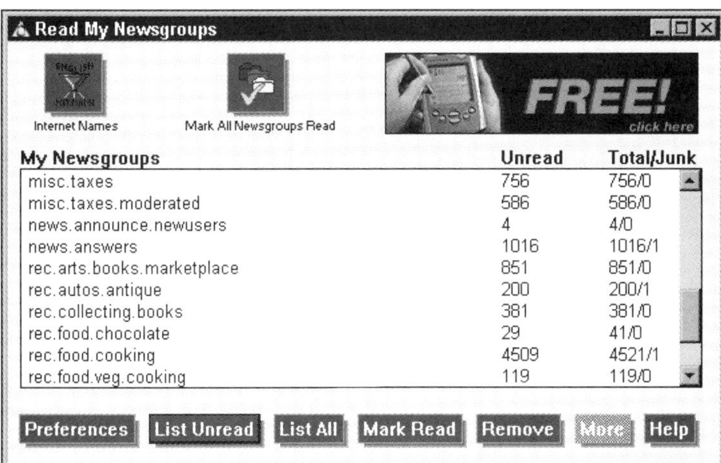

Figure 14-3. The Read My Newsgroups window contains the newsgroups to which you subscribe.

Searching for Newsgroups on AOL

Burrowing through levels and levels of topics and subtopics can leave you empty-handed. To search for newsgroups containing certain words or parts of words in their names, click the Search All Newsgroups button in the Newsgroups window to display the Search All Newsgroups window. Use this window to search for newsgroups (by name), not postings (by content). For content searching, see the next section.

You can create a Favorite Places folder devoted to a very specific topic and put all sorts of content — e-mail messages, newsgroups, Web sites, FTP sites, and more — into the folder.

Suppose you want to find newsgroups about cars. If you are confident that car will be in newsgroups' names, type **car** in the box at the top of the Search All Newsgroups window, and click the List Articles button. You see a list of 20 newsgroups containing articles on the subject. Change **car** to **auto**, and your search retrieves more than 100 newsgroups (see Figure 14-4).

Double-click the newsgroup you want to read. In a new window, you have a choice. You can either list a newsgroup's articles or subscribe to the newsgroup (add it to Read My Newsgroups). Actually, clicking either List or Subscribe has the same immediate effect: Both allow you to read the newsgroup. The difference is that when you subscribe, the newsgroup goes into Read My Newsgroups, which means you can quickly retrieve the newsgroup for future reading. Think of it as a Favorite Places folder for newsgroups.

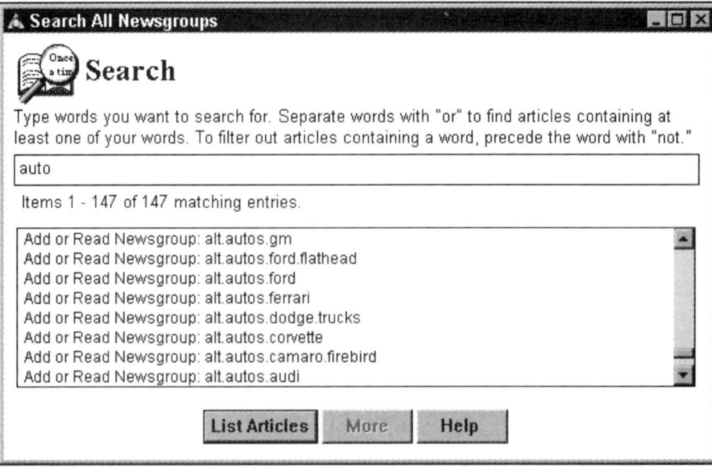

Figure 14-4. The search results for newsgroups with *auto* in their names. Double-click a newsgroup to read it and have the option of adding it to Read My Newsgroups.

Reading, Searching, and Posting on Google Groups

Google.com, one of the biggest and most popular Web search sites, recently acquired Deja, the Internet's biggest newsgroup archives. Updated several times a day and consisting of "upwards of 650 million messages," according to Google Groups' Help page, Google now applies its innovative search and directory technologies to a mountain of newsgroup postings dating back to 1995.

Caution

Google searches are not subject to AOL's Parental Controls. See Chapter 4 to find ways your whole family can surf the Net safely.

To access Google, go to `groups.google.com`, where you can use Google Groups to search for individual postings on any subject, in any newsgroup. Starting here, you can also post messages to newsgroups, taking advantage of Google's Web-based tools for participating in newsgroups.

At the Google Group home page, you can also browse for newsgroups on the Web. Simply click one category or another, browse topics within categories, and read messages in newsgroups that interest you.

To read a message thread, just click it to see all the messages for the thread. Scroll up and down to read the thread. You see several messages in the browser window at a time, so you can quickly scan a thread.

Finding a Message about a Specific Subject on Google

Google Groups has picked up Deja's capability of searching for newsgroup messages going back to 1995. To find a newsgroup (regardless of its category) from the main GoogleGroups page, click Advanced Groups Search. Enter your search terms and click the Google Search button.

Note

In the messages that Google finds for you, your search word or words are highlighted so you can readily assess whether messages are relevant to the topic that interests you.

Messages containing your search term(s) are listed. A search for **basset hounds**, for example, retrieved more than 3,000 messages (see Figure 14-5). Messages can be sorted by date (most recent at the top and the oldest at the bottom of the list) or by relevance (the messages that appear to best match your query are at the top of the list). Just click your preference in the upper-right corner of the search results page.

To access a specific newsgroup from any Google Groups window, simply type the name of the newsgroup into the Google search box.

Use Advanced Search at `groups.google.com` to search for phrases, search within an individual newsgroup, search subject lines, search for messages from specific people, restrict the date ranges of the messages to be searched, and search for messages within the last week or month.

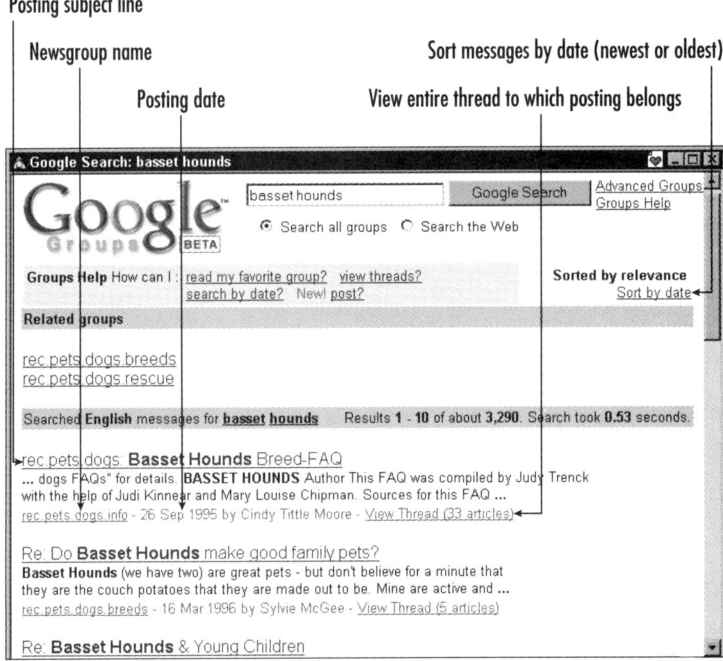

Figure 14-5. A few of more than 3,000 newsgroup postings about basset hounds. Notice the Related Groups category in the upper left, which recommends related newsgroups.

Reading Newsgroup Postings

From AOL Keyword: **Newsgroups**, click Read My Newsgroups to see the newsgroups to which you have subscribed. Double-click the newsgroup you want to read. The newsgroup comes up in its own window (like the one in Figure 14-6), with all the subjects displayed.

Here are some tips to help you read newsgroup messages.

- Double-click to select the subject you want to read about. Subjects consist of several messages about the same thing. (They have the same subject line.)
- To read the messages with this subject, click Read. The first message with that subject appears in the window.
- To jump to a specific message in a subject, simply click List instead of Read. The authors of posts with that subject appear in the window. Double-click the message you want to read.
- To proceed to the next message within a subject (same thread), click the Message -> button. To proceed to the next subject, click the Subject -> button. You can read previous messages and previous subjects by clicking the left-pointing arrows, as shown in Figure 14-6.

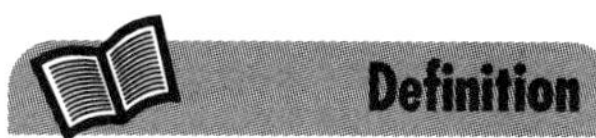

On AOL, a newsgroup *subject* is the same as a discussion *thread*. A *thread* consists of two or more messages with the same subject. A one-message subject is, well, just a message.

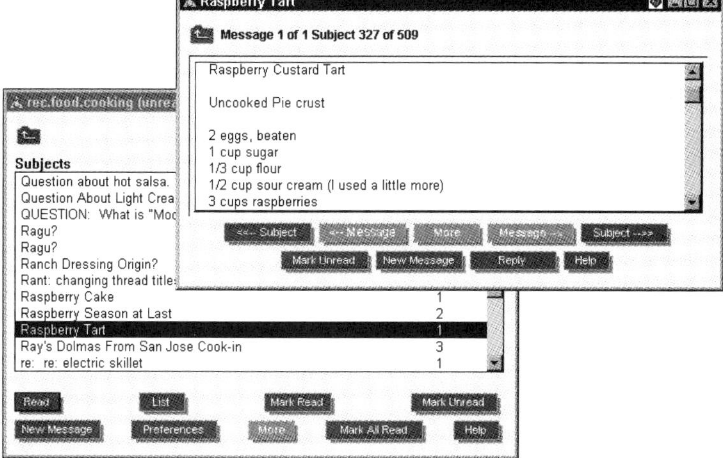

Figure 14-6. You can see a list of subjects (threads) in the newsgroup window in the back. In the front is a single message (not a thread) where someone is sharing a recipe.

Viewing and Hiding Messages

When you open a message in a newsgroup on AOL, the message is automatically marked as read even if you don't read it. Click the Mark Unread button if you think that, the next time you look at your newsgroups, you'll want to see the message again. You can also hide a thread from view by selecting it and clicking the Mark Read button. Unlike your electronic mailbox, a newsgroup is a public bulletin board to which anyone has access. You cannot delete messages, only hide them from your view.

Saving Newsgroup Messages

You can save a newsgroup message for future reference by displaying it and choosing File⇨Save. Give the message a name and put it into a folder on your hard drive. Messages are saved as text documents, so you can later view them in AOL's text editor (File⇨Open) or any word processor.

Discovering Message Boards on the Web

Newsgroups and AOL message boards have been migrating to the Web. These Web-based message boards, or simply *boards,* can add a valuable, social dimension to a Web site, in that they give people a chance to linger at a site, read and reflect upon postings, respond to them, and get to know other people who also have an interest in the site's topic. Web boards tend to be on-topic, and spam and cross-posting are rare.

Here are ten good boards that I happen to know about; you can find countless others:

- Café Utne (`www.utne.com/cafe`)
- GardenWeb (`forums.gardenweb.com/forums`)
- iVillage (`www.ivillage.com/boards`); on AOL use AOL Keyword: **PS Messages** for the Parent Soup boards
- IndependentTraveler.com (`www.independenttraveler.com`)
- LDOnline (`www.ldonline.org`)
- Photo.net (`www.photo.net`)
- Salon (`tabletalk.salon.com`)
- Time (`www.time.com/time/community`)
- WashingtonPost.com (`www.washingtonpost.com`; click Live Online)
- YouthTech (`www.youthtech.com/boards.htm`)

If you're reading a message on the Web with Google, you can choose File⇨Save to save the message on your hard drive as a Web page (an HTML file). I cover saving HTML files in Chapter 6.

As always on the Net, be mindful of copyright laws and common courtesy. You can't redistribute a great message or borrow large parts of it just because you like it. Ask the poster's permission. If you haven't done so already, familiarize yourself with the information at AOL Keyword: **Copyright**.

If you want to print a message that you're reading, choose Print⇨Print from the AOL menu bar.

Posting Messages

You can post a newsgroup message of your own in one of two ways:

- The easy way is to reply to someone else's message, which is just like replying to a mail message. Doing so contributes to a thread.
- Or, you can start your own subject by asking a question, making a comment, or sharing a recipe or opinion — whatever is appropriate in the newsgroup.

However you decide to take part, bear in mind the netiquette guidelines outlined in "Playing Nice."

Replying to a Newsgroup Message

To reply to a message you are reading, click Reply. The Post Response window appears, with the original message in the Original Message Text box at the left. See Figure 14-7. If you are taking part in a thread, you will want to keep the Subject line as is.

You can send your reply to the sender of the original message as an e-mail message (click in the Send Via E-mail box). Or you can send the message to the entire newsgroup as a newsgroup message (click in the Post to Newsgroup box). Or check both boxes.

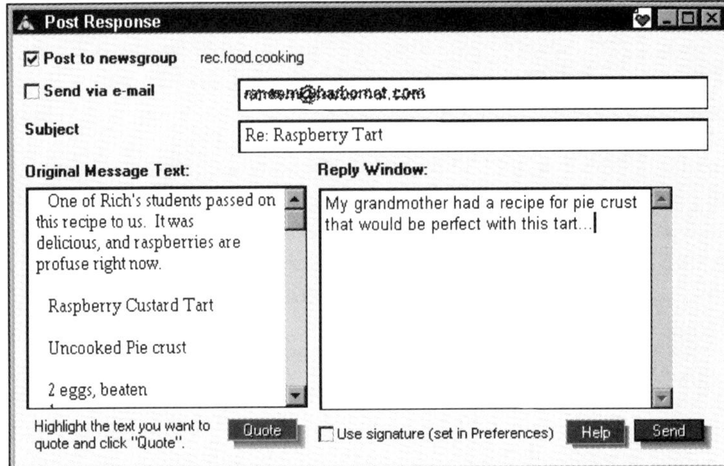

Figure 14-7. Replying to someone else's message is easy in a newsgroup.

Proceed by highlighting, in the Original Message Text box on the left, the portion of the post to which you are responding. When you have selected the text that you want to include, click Quote. The quoted text appears in the Reply Window box on the right, serving as context for your reply. Now, type your response.

If you want to include your signature in your post, click in the Use Signature check box. You can find instructions for creating a signature later in "Setting Newsgroup Preferences." All done? Click Send.

Composing a New Message

If you want to post a message with a new subject, click the New Message button in a newsgroup's window, which displays the group's messages. Your message can revive themes of common interest or be entirely new (if it's on-topic, of course). Figure 14-8 shows the Post New Message window. Clearly characterize your subject in the Subject box, and type your message in the Message box. If you want to include your signature in the post, click in the Use Signature check box. Click Send when you're done.

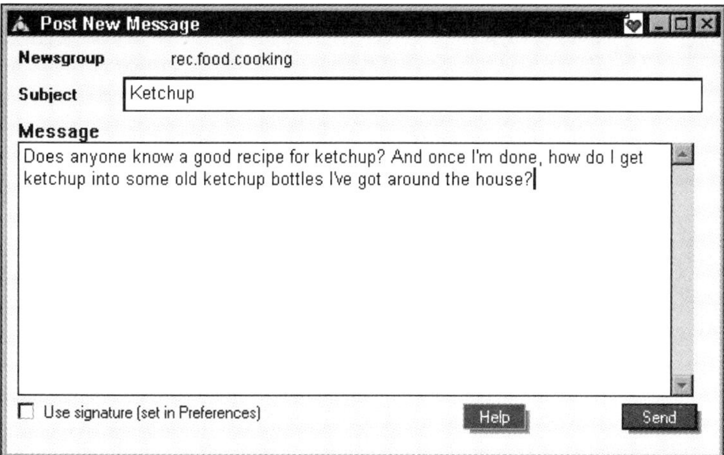

Figure 14-8. Start a new message in the Post New Message window. If others reply, then you've started a thread.

Deleting Your Messages

Oops. If you post something you wish you hadn't, you can sometimes delete the message before anyone catches your blunder. You have no guarantees, however. Your message may have made its way from AOL to the Internet's countless newsgroup computers. Here's how to delete a message: Click Read My Newsgroups and select the newsgroup to which you posted your message. Open your message, and click Delete.

You see the Delete button only in messages that you've posted. You'll be asked if you're sure you want to delete the posting. If you're sure, click Yes.

Playing Nice

Getting along in newsgroups is not much different from getting along with your neighbors — in a very big city. Unfortunately, newsgroups are even more anonymous than cities. In the absence of other people's sighs, smiles, smirks, grins, and countless other subtle, visual cues, the full meaning of any newsgroup message can be unclear.

Online, common sense serves as the best guide. If you were attending your first meeting about a topic, you probably wouldn't shout out a question to the expert at the microphone or ask a simple question of an expert when you know you could get the answer on your own. Where newsgroups are concerned, you may want to listen and read for a while in order to figure out what behavior is appropriate.

Taking Part in a Newsgroup on Google

Taking part in a newsgroup on Google Groups (`groups.google.com`) means posting messages of your own. From the main Google Groups page, either enter a specific newsgroup name in the Google Search box or click topics until you see a list of threads for a specific newsgroup.

To start a new subject/thread, click the Post a New Message link on the page that lists the newsgroup's threads.

Click threads to open and read them. To post a response to a specific message or thread, click the Post a Follow-Up link that appears after the message.

In either case, you'll be taken to a window where you will have to register with Google Groups before proceeding with your posting. There is no cost, but you must provide your name and e-mail address, and create a Google Groups password. Follow the on-screen procedures. In the future you can sign on with your e-mail address and Google Groups password.

Older threads may not have a Post link. After all, when a thread is dead, there is little point in responding to it. In this case, just start a new thread.

Always read a newsgroup's FAQ to get up to speed. Many newsgroups create an FAQ to distill the group's point of view and collected wisdom. See "FAQs: Essential Reading."

Flaming Hurts

To *flame* someone is to lash out in a post or message; it's a fairly obnoxious newsgroup tradition. Such verbal abuse makes people look aggressive and insensitive, and is generally discouraged in newsgroups.

AOL's message boards have explicit rules regarding flaming. If you aren't sure whether the message you are going to send is a flame, save it as a text file and look at it tomorrow, or ask someone else to look at it.

You don't have to curtail your style completely on newsgroups, just use the same degree of discretion you would if you were speaking to an audience of thousands. That is, after all, what you are potentially doing in newsgroups.

 **Note**

You can't save a newsgroup message to be sent later as you can with AOL Mail. If you want to wait before you send a message, create your message as a text file in Word and read it over once or twice before sending it.

Lurk Before Posting

Before you post anything to a particular newsgroup, read the group's messages. You will probably be accepted by the group much easier if you just watch and come to understand the group dynamics before sending a message for the first time. This practice is called *lurking*.

Many newsgroups and mailing lists have distinctive cultures, and some are more hospitable to newcomers than others.

Setting Newsgroup Preferences

AOL gives you three sets of controls to improve the newsgroup experience for you and your family:

- **Parental Controls:** You can prevent kids from seeing all newsgroups, certain newsgroups, or newsgroup postings with files attached. These controls are discussed in Chapter 4.
- **Global newsgroup preferences:** These preferences affect how you read your newsgroups on AOL. They govern how newsgroups appear, whether a signature is added to all of your messages, the level to which newsgroups are combed to remove irrelevant postings, and more.
- **Newsgroup-specific preferences:** You can control just the newsgroups in the Read My Newsgroups list. For example, if certain subjects in `rec.creative-cooking` simply don't interest you, you can use the newsgroup's Preference button to specify filters for words you don't want to see in Subject lines.

The following sections review global and newsgroup-specific preferences.

Setting Global Newsgroup Preferences

Global controls apply to every newsgroup you use on AOL (excluding non-AOL services, such as Google Groups, described earlier). At AOL Keyword: **Newsgroups**, click the Set Preferences button to display the Global Newsgroup Preferences window, shown in Figure 14-9. The window has three tabs: Viewing, Posting, and Filtering. Click a tab to see a different set of preferences. All the global preferences deal with the most general aspects of using the newsgroup window, not with the content of individual newsgroups.

Newsgroup-Viewing Preferences (Viewing Tab)

Click the Viewing tab to control how the messages appear.

- **Headers:** In actual messages, a *header* provides data about a posting's path to your PC. If you aren't deeply interested in network routing, you can place headers to the bottom of the message or hide them altogether.

Spamming means sending an unsolicited commercial posting to a newsgroup whose scope is clearly unrelated to the product or service being peddled.

Post Appropriately

Here are some don'ts to live by in a newsgroup:

- Don't post chain letters, get-rich schemes, multilevel marketing plans (even if you are convinced of their worth), or anything clearly unrelated to the newsgroup.
- Don't *cross-post,* which means to send the same posting to many newsgroups.
- Don't *spam!* AOL is very clear about the consequences of sending unsolicited commercial messages. You can read AOL's unsolicited mail policy in the Community Guidelines available at AOL Keyword: **TOS**.
- Don't post questions for which the answer is readily available elsewhere, such as in an encyclopedia or the newsgroup's FAQ. Later in this chapter I provide a section on FAQs, with places where you can find FAQs for many newsgroups.
- Don't quote an entire message if you're responding to a single sentence or phrase. Quoting excessively wastes people's time and gets on their nerves.

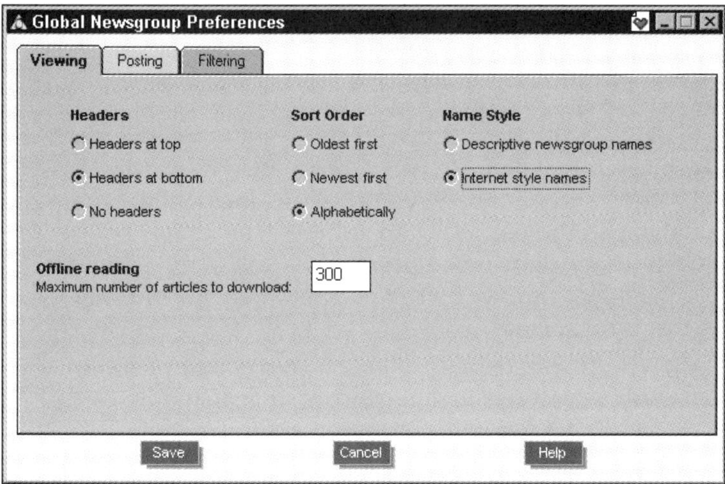

Figure 14-9. Control how you view, post, and filter *all* newsgroup messages in the Global Newsgroup Preferences window.

- **Sort Order:** You can view postings with the oldest message first, or the newest. Starting with the newest posting first can help you get up-to-date quickly, while starting with the oldest lets you follow discussions as they develop. If you choose to view messages alphabetically, you can scan through the subjects and quickly identify threads that interest you. Alphabetical order gives you a good, quick overview of a newsgroup.
- **Name Style:** If you have used other Internet providers besides AOL, you are probably accustomed to "Internet-style" newsgroup names. This is the naming scheme introduced earlier in this chapter, with its categories, topics, and newsgroup names (for example `rec.food.cooking`). AOL applies its own descriptive names to many newsgroups, such as those relating to food, cooking, cookbooks, and recipes.
- **Offline reading:** Use this box to limit the number of messages downloaded when you use Automatic AOL. See "Using Automatic AOL for Your Newsgroups."

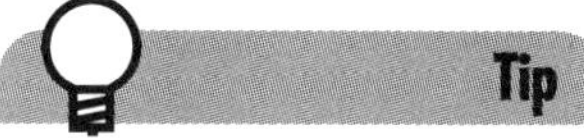

Because descriptive names aren't available on AOL for all newsgroups (and they're not available on the Net), it's a good idea to get comfortable with the Internet style.

Posting Preferences (Posting Tab)

Click the Posting tab to fine-tune the messages you post on AOL. These preferences relate to whether and how you want your identity to be perceived by others when you post. Do you want to use your real name? Do you want people to know your e-mail address? Do you want to provide some personal information about yourself, using a signature?

- **Using Your Real Name:** If you want to be identified by your real name in parentheses after your e-mail address when others read your postings, enter your name in the box. You can also use a nickname or choose to provide no personal information. Use your judgment, and weigh the risks and benefits of using your real name.
- **Junk Block:** Senders of unsolicited e-mail, or *spammers,* are always looking for new e-mail addresses. One way to help deter unsolicited e-mail from finding its way to you is to add a Junk Block to your e-mail address. For example, if someone with the screen name `PineFirForest15` puts applepie in his Junk Block, his posting address appears as `PineFirForest@aol.comapplepie`. Any attempts to send e-mail to this nonexistent e-mail address will obviously be unsuccessful. Enter whatever word you like. The drawback is that legit readers who want to e-mail you may have a more difficult time because they won't be able to use the Reply-To feature without editing the Junk Block address.
- **Using a Signature:** You can use a signature to express your personality, tell a joke, display your insight, provide business contact information, or all of the above. You type a signature in the lower box. A signature block is shown in the box. Note that people who don't use AOL may not see any color, size, or type effects — stick with simple text.

AOL cannot control the content of specific postings. Instead, AOL gives you the tools to avoid what you dislike.

Filtering Out Unwanted Messages (Filtering Tab)

Unwanted online content consists of any e-mail messages or newsgroup postings that you didn't ask for; you may find a message simply obnoxious or completely out of line. Newsgroup filters are a good way to supplement the newsgroup Parental Controls (described in Chapter 4) so that you don't have to see anything that you don't want to see.

Your filtering preferences let you block messages that contain a particular word or words in the subject line. You can also block messages from particular people and messages from

particular domains. (In message boards, all the messages are within the AOL domain.) Here are the different ways to filter postings:

- If you want to filter out all messages containing a particular word in the subject, select Subject Contains from the Select Filter Type drop-down list. Enter the word in the Enter New Filter box and click the Add Filter button. Add as many filtering words as you want.
- If you want to avoid all posts from the person who is sending unsolicited messages, select Author Is from the Select Filter Type drop-down list and enter the appropriate e-mail information.
- If you notice that a particular domain seems to produce many unwanted postings, select Domain Is and type in the name of the offending domain.

Here's a more benign use of filters: If you're an avid cook but you don't like certain vegetarian foods, you could just block messages containing *tofu* or whatever you would not like to see in your `rec.food` newsgroup.

Setting Preferences for an Individual Newsgroup

You can refine your newsgroup-reading experience by setting preferences for individual newsgroups. Preferences for individual newsgroups are applied in addition to Parental Controls and global preferences. The Preferences window is available in two places:

- At AOL Keyword: **Newsgroups**, click Read My Newsgroups. Select a newsgroup, and then click the Preferences button.
- Open any newsgroup in Read My Newsgroups and click Preferences.

Figure 14-10 shows you how you can loosen or tighten the application of global controls to specific newsgroups. The check boxes allow you to determine which messages are downloaded during an Automatic AOL session, described in this chapter. You can choose to see messages up to 30 days old and enable offline reading of messages fetched with Automatic AOL.

Tip

Off-topic messages usually appear at the very top of a newsgroup's list of messages, because they begin with nonletter, nonnumeric characters (" - ^ # < > etc.). These messages can be tricky to filter out. Just scroll past them to read the real messages.

Cross-Reference

A domain is the part of an e-mail address after the at symbol (@). See Chapter 10 for more information.

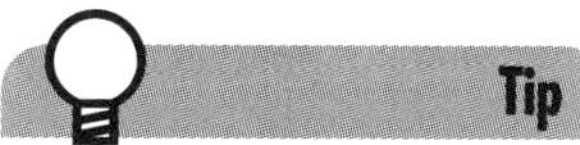
Tip

Try filtering messages that contain the following words and symbols: adult, ADULT, 18, 18+, FREE, free, teen, porn,!!, !!!.

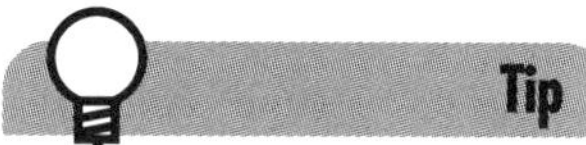
Tip

You can always change your global preferences. The Remove Filter and Clear Filter List buttons at the bottom of the Filtering tab let you remove or clear your filters.

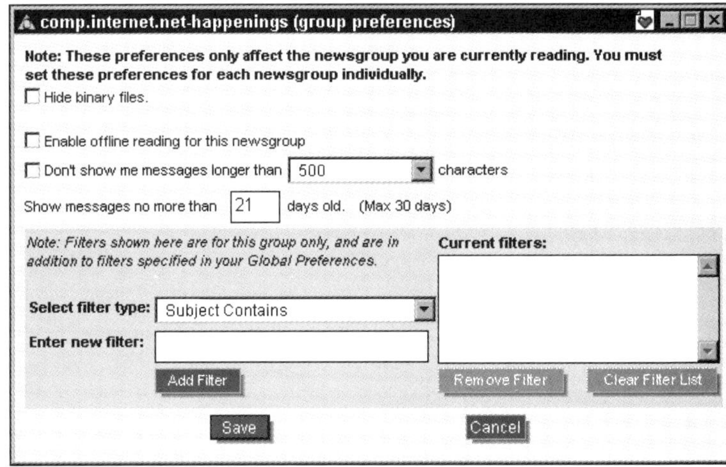

Figure 14-10. Setting preferences for an individual newsgroup.

FAQs: Essential Reading

FAQ is short for Frequently Asked Questions. Some people pronounce it F-A-Q, and others pronounce it to rhyme with *black*. FAQs include answers to common questions and offer background knowledge of interest to newcomers to a field or newsgroup. The Internet FAQ Consortium (`www.faqs.org`) currently archives 3,300 FAQs covering 1,700 newsgroups. Most of these repositories of knowledge are voluntarily created and maintained.

FAQs were invented in the context of newsgroups, but people have created countless FAQs on Web sites to answer recurring questions about the sites or their subject matter. Many big Web-based stores have their own FAQs about products, transactions, and customer service. You need to use AOL Search to find Web FAQs about specific subjects — just add the word FAQ to your query when you do a Web search on a topic of interest (for example, **Basset hound FAQ**).

Tip

AOL has its own newsgroup category — called *aol*, of course. The `aol.newsgroups.help` newsgroup is home to FAQs on subjects like participating in newsgroups, handling files, and using your Filing Cabinet.

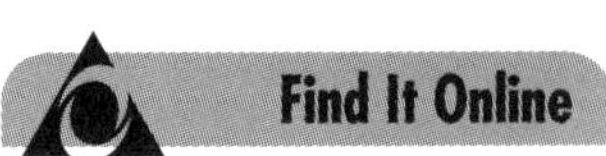

At AOL Keyword: **Newsgroups**, use Expert Add to read `news.answers` for a crop of current FAQs.

Handling Postings with Files

Sometimes newsgroup postings contain multimedia files — music in MP3 format, pictures, or short movies, for example.

Before people insert these files into postings, the multimedia files are scrambled into a text document that's unreadable to people but that can (because it's text) move easily around the Internet. Such files must be unscrambled before you can view or play them. AOL automatically unscrambles these files for you.

When a file is attached to a newsgroup posting and you attempt to open the posting, you see a message giving you a choice: Download File or Download Message? Click Download File. You are then prompted to save the file on your computer. Accept the default folder and then click Save. As the file downloads, a progress indicator tells you how much has been downloaded. Most MIDI (sound) and JPG (image) files download quickly because of their small file size. Video and MP3 files take more time unless you have a high-speed connection (see Chapter 17).

When you retrieve a file from a newsgroup, make sure you scan it with an up-to-date antivirus software program from a reliable vendor such as McAfee or Norton.

Parents concerned about kids' access to objectionable files on newsgroups should refer to the discussion of Parental Controls in Chapter 4.

Using Automatic AOL for Your Newsgroups

Downloading newsgroup messages one at a time, particularly if you subscribe to even a few high-volume newsgroups, can eat up much of your time online. Why not read those postings offline or at least when you have more time? Using Automatic AOL, you can automatically download messages while you're doing something else. Later, at your leisure, you can browse the postings in your Filing Cabinet without having to sign on. The messages will be in the Newsgroups folder under Incoming/Saved Postings.

All you need to do is tell AOL what you want to download, for what screen name, and when. At Mail⇨Automatic AOL, you can walk through the entire process with the help of clear on-screen instructions. To download postings into your Filing Cabinet:

1. Add any newsgroups you want to read offline to Read My Newsgroups. See "Adding Newsgroups to Your Favorites."
2. Go to AOL Keyword: **Newsgroups** and click Read Offline. The Choose Newsgroups window appears, with

the names of the newsgroups to which you subscribe. Click Add All if you want to read all of these newsgroups offline. Alternatively, you can select specific newsgroups and click Add to include them one by one. Clicking Remove All removes all of your offline choices, and clicking Remove applies to a single, selected newsgroup.

3. Choose Mail⇨Automatic AOL.
4. Put a check by one or both of the following options:
   - **Send Postings from the Postings Waiting to Be Sent Folder:** These postings are the newsgroup messages you wrote offline either as new messages or in response to other messages.
   - **Get Unread Postings and Put in Incoming Postings Folder:** This choice retrieves messages from the newsgroup for offline reading. This is the one you're probably interested in.
5. Click Select Names. Select one or more screen names whose postings are to be uploaded or downloaded, and type in the password for the screen names, so that the sign-on process can be automated. Click OK.
6. Click Schedule Automatic AOL and indicate when you want postings sent or retrieved. Probably, you want postings retrieved regularly but sent only when you have something to send. In the latter case, just click the Run Automatic AOL button to send the messages you have written.
7. Make sure to put a check in the Enable Scheduler check box. Click OK when you've decided on a schedule.
8. Close the Automatic AOL window when you're done. Make sure your computer is turned on and the AOL software is open during the time when you have scheduled automatic uploading and downloading.

Where to Go from Here

Chapters 10 through 14 covered the many ways of communicating on AOL and the Internet. AOL gives you access to the tools you need, including e-mail, mailing lists, chat, instant messages, newsgroups, and message boards. Don't worry about figuring out all of them. Instead, pick tools one at a time as you see the need and remember that you can always find help at AOL Keyword: **Help**.

- Find a newsgroup to join.
- To create your own community with a Web-based bulletin board, you can read all about Groups@AOL in Chapter 12.

Chapter 15

Downloading Files and Software from the Internet

IN THIS CHAPTER **PAGE**

Everything you see or hear on your computer, and everything your computer does, requires files. If you ever typed and saved something by using a word processor, you created a file.

What is a file? A *file* has a name, such as `letter.doc` or `butterfly.jpg`, and it takes up space on your hard drive or a disk. A file has information that you need, in a format that you (or your software application, such as AOL) can use. The file `butterfly.jpg`, for example, is a picture that you can see by using the AOL software.

Software is a special kind of file. Usually, software is made up of a single file containing many small files. Together, these files give you the ability to do something on a computer — play a song, connect to the Internet, make a Web page, and so on. In practice, downloading software is exactly the same as downloading a file; you are transferring a single file to your PC. The difference lies in what you do next.

- To use a file, you need a player, viewer, or other kind of software (see the sections about image, sound, video, and text files later in this chapter).
- To use software, you must install it, as described in "Downloading from the Web."

Downloading a file means copying it from an Internet computer (server) to your computer; *uploading* means copying a file from your computer to a server, where others can use it.

Just as files can be stored on a computer, they can be transferred from one computer to another. This chapter shows you how to copy (or *download*) files to use on your computer. Downloading software and files with the Web and FTP (the Internet's File Transfer Protocol) can add tremendous value to your Internet experience on AOL.

Chapters 15 and 16 work as a pair:

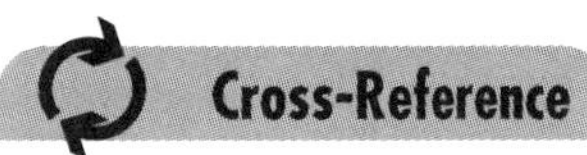

Chapter 7 shows how to download the free Netscape software, and Chapter 12 shows how to download AOL Instant Messenger.

- Chapter 15 provides all you need to know about files and the tools for downloading both files and software. I also mention some of the techniques for uploading files, which is especially useful for people who make Web pages.
- In Chapter 16 you can find examples of some of the great software you can find online to manage, play, and create files, enhancing your overall experience online.

Viruses are small programs that may be attached to files, and they can mess up your computer. You can trust files downloaded from AOL's software libraries, but there's no guarantee regarding FTP files. Stay informed at AOL Keyword: **Virus**. Chapter 16 profiles antivirus software.

Downloading from the Web

Downloading software from the Web has become pretty much point-and-click. Follow these steps to download software or files:

1. Go to the Web page from which you want to download the software.

   How do you know where to start when you want to download software? You can search a download site like Tucows (profiled in Chapter 16), which has well-organized links to thousands of programs around the world. Or, if you know the company that makes the software, go to its site. Or, simply do a search for the program's name by using AOL Search.

A high-speed connection like AOL High Speed Broadband can greatly speed up downloading.

2. Look for a Download link. Make sure the software you download is for your operating system (for example, Windows 98). Click the Download link.

Sometimes the link is on the opening page, and sometimes you have to dig a bit. You can also do a site search if one is available.

3. After a moment or two, the File Download dialog box appears, as shown in Figure 15-1. This dialog box asks whether you want to save the file (the default choice) or open the file after it has downloaded. As a rule, you want to save what you're downloading. Click OK.

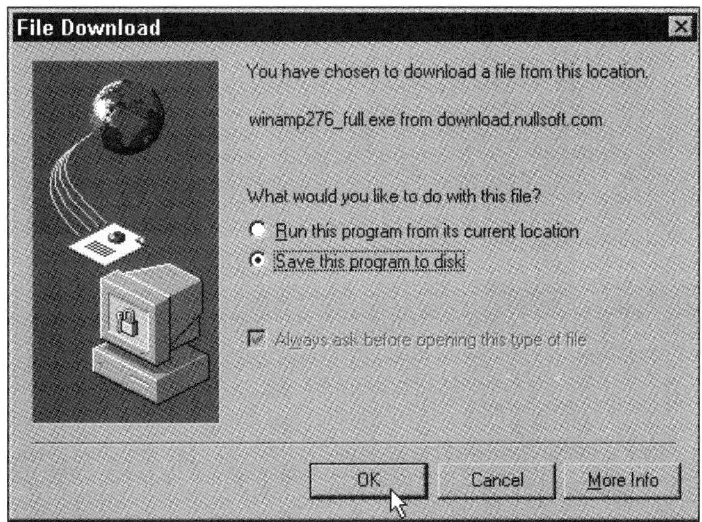

Figure 15-1. This standard Windows box asks you whether you want to save or open software after you download it.

4. In the standard Save As box, shown in Figure 15-2, navigate to the folder on your hard drive where you want to save the software. You want to use the file's name as is, so don't change it. Click OK to download the file and save it in the place you indicated.

   Depending on your connection type and speed, the download can take seconds or minutes. While it takes place, you can do something else online. (Or, keep a book handy just for these moments.)

5. When the download completes, a box like the one in Figure 15-3 appears.

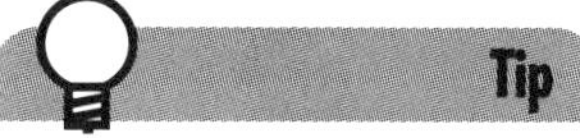

If you don't see the Download Complete box, go to your Windows desktop. Right-click Internet Explorer and choose Properties. Click Advanced. In the Browsing section, make sure there's a check for Notify When Downloads Complete option. Click OK.

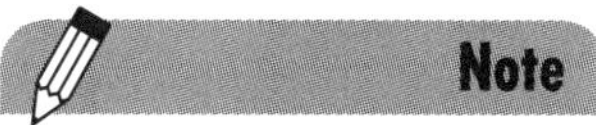

Sometimes downloaded software arrives in the ZIP format, meaning the file must first be decompressed. AOL can decompress a zipped file: Choose Settings⇨ Preferences. Click Download. Under Automatically Decompress, make sure the When I Sign Off option is checked. Click Save.

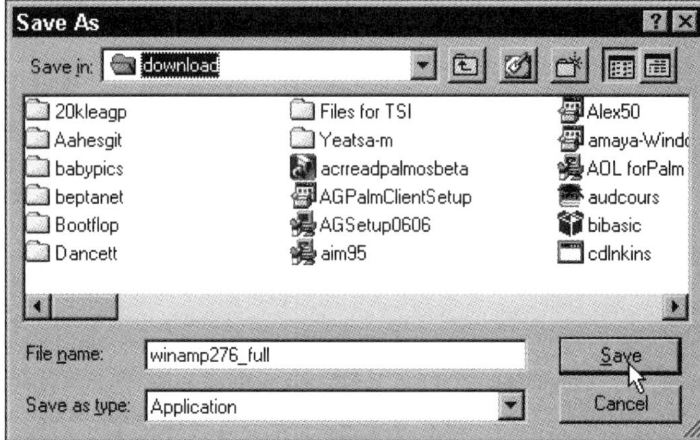

Figure 15-2. Indicate where you want to save the downloaded software on your computer.

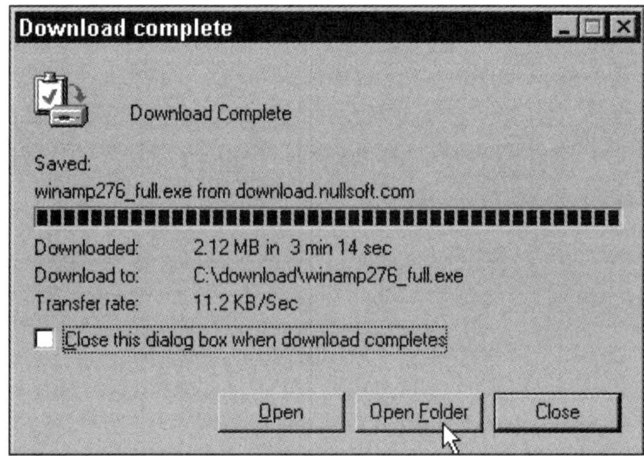

Figure 15-3. To retrieve the file just downloaded, click Open Folder.

To find the file you just downloaded, click Open Folder. The folder you selected in Step 4 comes up, with the downloaded file selected. If you are downloading files (songs, for example), you're finished downloading. If you're downloading software, go to Step 6.

6. To install your new software, double-click the selected file and follow the online instructions.

Installation differs from program to program. More and more programs use a standard program called InstallShield that makes the process practically identical no matter which program you install. With or without InstallShield, the process is automatic (the software installs itself, asking you for information whenever necessary). Your role is mostly passive; the software does most of the work. You'll be asked the following questions:

- **Do you accept the software's licensing agreement?** Click Yes.
- **Where do you want to install the program?** Make sure to choose both a folder where similar programs are installed and a drive with enough room. In most cases, you can accept the default.
- **Do you want to do a typical or custom installation?** Choose typical.
- **Into which program folder do you want to install the various files?** Accept the default.

With the program downloaded, you are ready to use it. The software will be available from the Windows desktop or by choosing Start⇨Programs and then choosing the program from the Programs submenu.

Using AOL's Download Manager

You use the AOL's Download Manager (AOL Keyword: **Download Manager**) to keep track of files downloaded from AOL or downloaded with AOL tools. It is *not* used when you download from the Web.

More precisely, Download Manager can be used to:

- **Keep track of where you download files.** Download Manager keeps track of files downloaded from an e-mail message or newsgroup posting, as well as from an FTP site.

  If you ever forget where you downloaded a file, go to Download Manager, highlight a file, and click Locate to see where it was downloaded.
- **Specify where files and software are stored.** After you specify a default folder, the files and software that you download from AOL or with an AOL tool (except the browser) are saved in this folder.

To change the default, click Download Preferences and change the folder indicated at the bottom of the Download Preferences box.

- **Decompress files.** A file is compressed (or *zipped*), if several files are reduced in size and combined into a single file for speedier uploading and downloading. Zipped files have a filename ending in ZIP or SIT.

Use Download Manager to decompress a ZIP file that you've downloaded:

1. Go to the Download Manager (File⇨Download Manager). Click the Show Files Downloaded button to bring up the Files You've Downloaded window, shown in Figure 15-4.
2. Select the file you want to decompress, and click the Decompress button. The file is unzipped; if there are several files, they are kept in a folder whose name matches the filename of zipped file. You can find this folder nested inside the folder where the zipped file was downloaded.

After your files are decompressed and installed, programs take up much more hard-drive space than you may expect from the size of the downloaded file.

To decompress files automatically upon sign off when you download or delete the compressed files, click Download Preferences and uncheck those preferences.

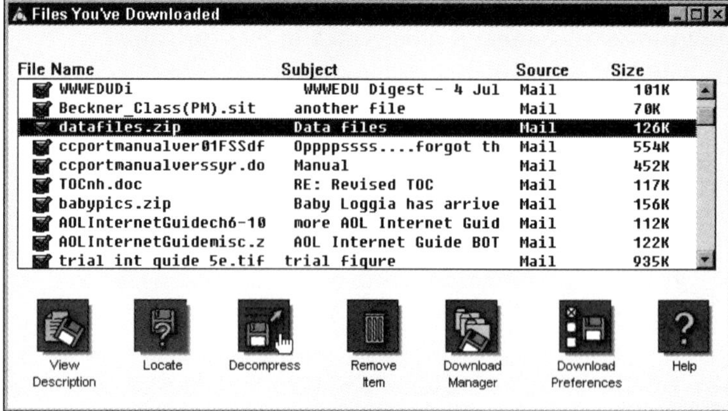

Figure 15-4. Decompressing a zipped file with Download Manager.

Getting Files and Software by Using FTP

In addition to the downloads that you can do on the Web, you can upload and download files by using FTP. *FTP* stands for the Internet's file transfer protocol. The FTP software based on that protocol is used for copying files from one computer to another over the Internet. When you copy a file from a computer, you *download* the file; when you copy a file to a computer, you *upload* the file.

Before the Web, FTP was the workhorse for moving files from one place to another on the Internet. You may encounter FTP when you download files from software vendors and big shareware archives like Tucows.

See Chapter 16 for more about archives, such as Tucows.

You can download more than 100 million files for using FTP software. How do you find what you're seeking among the 100 million?

FTP space refers to a person's space on an Internet server, where files can be uploaded, stored, shared, and downloaded.

Using an FTP site on the Internet is like using your own hard drive. Both your hard drive and an FTP site consist of folders containing either files or more folders. Figure 15-5 shows MIT's FTP site, home to the Frequently Asked Questions documents generated by newsgroups.

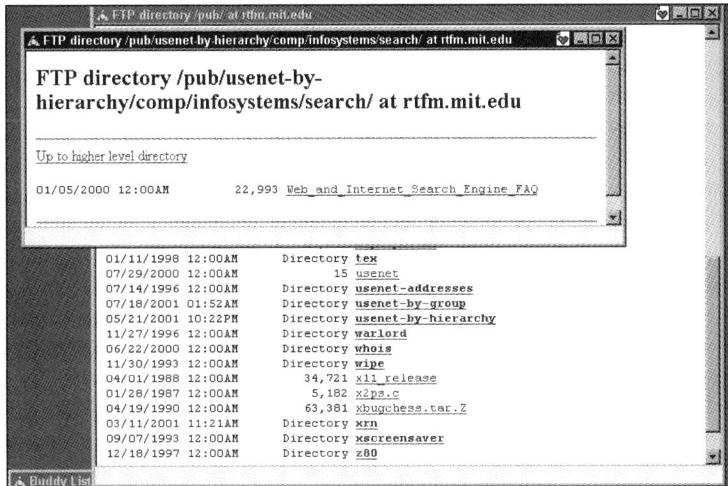

Figure 15-5. MIT's RTFM FTP site, one of the oldest and most useful collections of newsgroup FAQs.

Chapter 14 has more to say about FAQs.

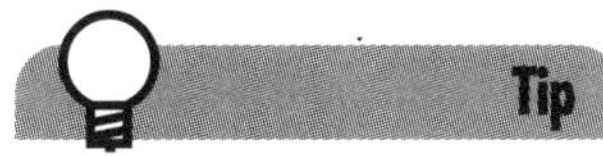

In exploring FTP sites, you often start with the pub directory, to which the public usually has access. Some FTP sites, such as those available at AOL Keyword: **FTP**, are entirely public, so you can use any directory.

To download a file from an FTP site using the AOL browser, simply type the site's address into the AOL address box and press Enter. An FTP address looks something like the following addresses:

```
ftp://rtfm.mit.edu/pub/usenet-by-hierarchy/
ftp://ftp.aol.com
```

Simply click a file to download it. If you're downloading a simple text file (like a FAQ), the file displays in the browser. If you're downloading a file (such as a song in MP3 format), the process works exactly as described in "Downloading from the Web."

Using an FTP site opens a connection that is usually limited in duration. Many sites, too, place a limit on the number of visitors who can use the site at the same time. That's why you may not be able to access an FTP site right away and might be disconnected after a few minutes.

Using My FTP Space (AOL Keyword: My FTP Space)

Nothing on FTP is quite as instantaneous as clicking links on the Web. Sometimes you will need to wait. Another minor drawback: Although your browser is perfectly adequate for downloading files from public FTP sites, you can't use the browser to upload files.

Each AOL account can have *seven* screen names.

Enter My FTP Space. Every screen name on AOL automatically has 2MB of FTP space at AOL Keyword: **My FTP Space**. Use this online storage space to hold three kinds of files.

You can use My FTP Space for at least three purposes:

- If you use non-AOL software, such as FrontPage, to create Web pages, you can upload the HTML files to My FTP Space. That way, you can make the pages available to everyone through AOL Hometown.
- My FTP Space is also the place where the Web pages that you create on AOL Hometown are *automatically* stored.
- You can also use this space to share documents, spreadsheets, PDF files, and so on, with coworkers or classmates.

Anyone who adds a Web page to AOL Hometown receives an additional 2MB of space. More precisely, this space is allotted to the screen name used to add the page. Anyone who adds all Web pages (that is, all pages stored at My FTP Space) on AOL Hometown receives a total of 12MB.

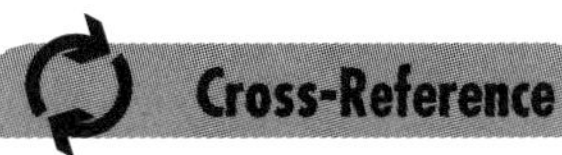

For more about AOL Hometown's Web publishing tools, see *Your Official America Online Guide to Creating Cool Web Pages*, 2nd Edition, by Ed Willett (Hungry Minds, Inc.).

Uploading a File to My FTP Space

If you create Web pages with an HTML editor, such as FrontPage or Dreamweaver, you can upload the HTML files and associated style, image, and other files to My FTP Space. Then, from AOL Hometown, you can add the pages to a Hometown community (member pages on a certain theme) and receive your free, additional FTP space (2MB extra for adding one page; an additional 8MB for adding them all).

To upload a file to My FTP Space, follow these steps. If you have many files to upload, you have to upload them one at a time by using these steps:

1. Go to AOL Keyword: **My FTP Space**. At the My FTP Space information window, click See My FTP Space. After a slight delay, a list of files and folders appears. My current FTP space is shown in Figure 15-6; yours will differ, depending on the files and folders in it. This is your area, accessible only to your screen name.

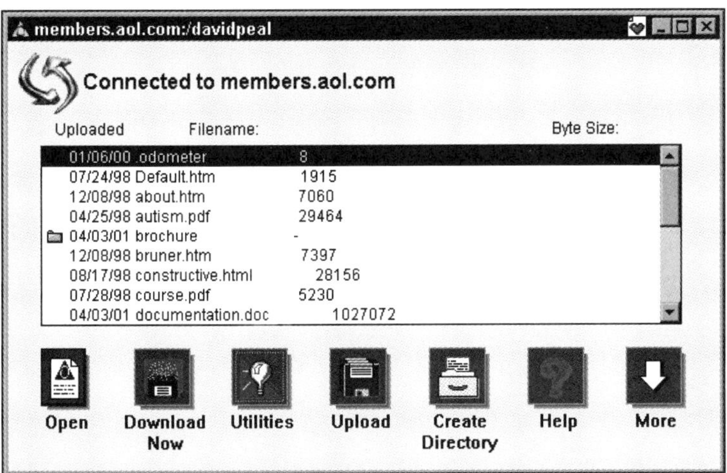

Figure 15-6. My FTP Space: for storing and sharing pages online.

2. Click Upload. The Remote Filename box appears, as shown in Figure 15-7.
3. In the Remote Filename text box, type the name by which you want that file to be known when it's online. Yes, you provide this name before uploading the file. Often, you want to use the same name as the file on your hard drive. Sometimes, however, your own naming scheme may require some tweaking: You cannot use spaces in your online filenames, and you'll probably want to give your online files simple names that make the files easy to identify.

   Notice that Binary is selected under the Remote Filename text box. This setting helps FTP recognize all file types, including simple text. Keep this setting as it is, regardless of the kind of file you are downloading.
4. Click Continue. The Upload File dialog box appears.
5. Click Select File and use the dialog box that appears to browse to the file on your hard drive. Double-click the file when you find it. The filename appears in the File box at the bottom of the Upload File dialog box.
6. Click Send. A little box that looks like a thermometer tracks the progress of your file transfer. Next time you visit My FTP Space, your file will be there.

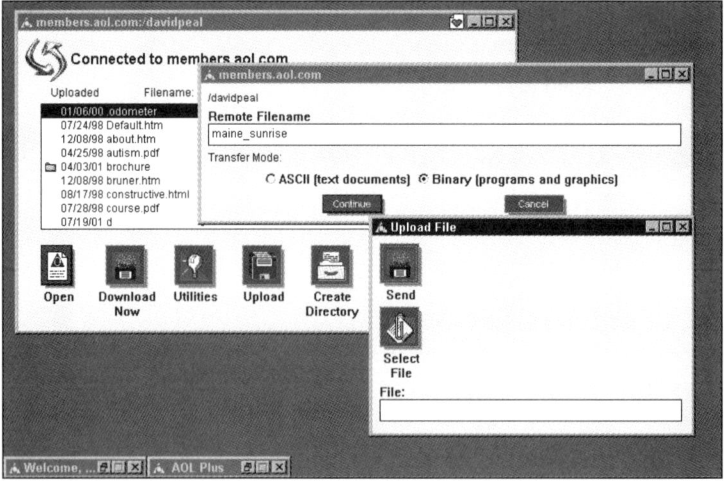

Figure 15-7. You use a series of dialog boxes to upload a file to My FTP Space.

Adding an Uploaded Web Page to AOL Hometown

You may want to register your page with AOL Hometown, as described in this section. Registering a page allows others to find the page by searching AOL Hometown. If you want all your published pages to be searchable in Hometown AOL, return to the Add & Manage Pages screen and click Add All. You can increase visits to your Web site by making all the pages searchable.

To transfer a Web page (HTML file) from My FTP Space to AOL Hometown, follow these steps. This activity takes place at AOL Hometown (AOL Keyword: **Hometown**).

1. After you have created a page and uploaded it to My FTP Space (either automatically by using 1-2-3 Publish or Easy Designer, or manually, when you use another HTML editor), click the Create link at the top of any AOL Hometown page to open the Add & Manage Your Pages screen.
2. Click Add. A list of all your HTML files appears. This is just a file listing of the pages in My FTP Space (the pages automatically stored there as well as the ones you stored there manually). Choose the page (filename) you want to add by clicking in the circle next to its name. Click Next.
3. You can now type a short description of the page, which gives folks in Hometown some idea of what your page is about and why they should visit it. This information is searchable and is one of the ways by which other people can find your page. Click Next.
4. Answer the subsequent questions, clicking Next after each one. After this brief process, you're informed that your page has been added to AOL Hometown. You now have an additional 2MB of space in your FTP space.

   Click Add All to make all your pages in My FTP Space available for searching and viewing at AOL Hometown — a low price for an extra 8MB of storage space.

To see what a page looks like, click View Page next to the page's filename.

From the Add & Manage Pages screen (available from the window that appears in Step 1), you can edit the descriptions of your pages. The descriptions can help searchers find your page.

Managing My FTP Space

Any computer storage space, such as your hard drive or My FTP Space, can quickly get overgrown with many files. Over time, you won't remember the names of the files you've uploaded and downloaded, let alone their purpose.

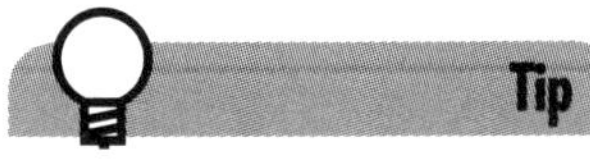

If you do change filenames, delete files, and move things around My FTP Space, make sure to change the links in your Web pages that refer to those files.

On My FTP Space, housekeeping requires a good organizational scheme. "Good" means that it works for you, that you can find files when you need them, and that filenames correspond to how you think of the content.

On My FTP Space, every item is either a folder or a file. You can create and name folders and files intuitively so that you remember what they contain, and others will grasp the content from the filename. You can also add subfolders within a folder to organize similar files. For a work-related Web site, you could, for example, create a folder called WorkPage and subfolders called Projects and Partners.

Here are the primary functions that can help you keep My FTP Space files in order:

- **To delete a file or folder:** Highlight the file, click the Utilities button, and click Delete.

  You can delete only one file at a time. Note that you cannot delete a folder until all its files have been removed; when the files are removed, highlight the folder and delete it as you would delete a file.
- **To create a new directory (folder):** Click the Create Directory button. In the Remote Directory Name box, type the name of your new directory. Click Continue to create another folder or subfolder. Using forward slashes (/), you can create a subfolder, such as `/pub/work`. Close the box (click the X) when you're done.
- **To change the name of a file or folder:** Select the file or folder to be renamed, click the Utilities button, and click Rename. In the New Name box, type the full new name, including all the folders and subfolders, separated by forward slashes.

  If you want to make files available to others, you must create a `/pub` directory in the top level of My FTP Space. If you want people to share files with you, you must create an `/incoming` directory. Make sure to let people know about these directories!

- **To move a file or folder:** To move a file or folder within your FTP space, you merely change its name from one reflecting its old location to one reflecting its new location. First select the file or folder, and click the Utilities button. Then click Rename. You then provide a different path to the file. For example, `/README` could be moved down a level by changing it to `/pub/README` (you can create a pub directory if you don't have one). You can also change the filename in the process by moving the file to a different directory *and* changing its name.

Downloading Files (AOL Keyword: FTP)

My FTP Space gives you access only to your FTP space on AOL. AOL Keyword: **FTP** gives you access to public FTP sites as well as to FTP sites to which you have access. You can also upload files if you have access to sites with incoming directories or other sites where you have your own space. For example, your college or office may provide such sites. Figure 15-8 shows the window you see at AOL Keyword: **FTP**.

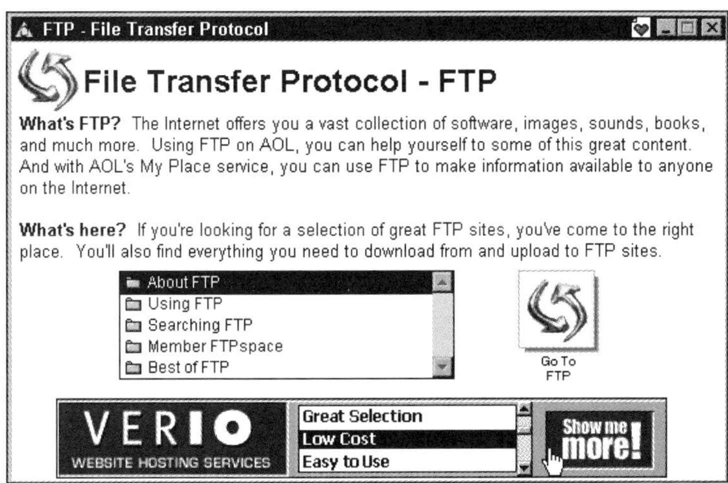

Figure 15-8. Go to AOL Keyword: **FTP** to use an FTP site outside AOL.

Anonymous FTP (available at AOL Keyword: **FTP**) lets you access public FTP sites. From these sites, you can download files. Public FTP sites often restrict public access to certain folders, such as folders named *pub*. Why are the sites called anonymous? Because your login name, literally, is the word *anonymous*. AOL supplies it automatically for you.

AOL's Anonymous FTP tool also gives you access to private FTP sites that require individual logins and passwords (which you can get by asking the person who told you about the site). After you get access to a private site, AOL's FTP tool takes care of the rest. The interface looks just like the one in My FTP Space, so you can upload and download files, as well as move, rename, and delete them.

Here's how to download a file by using AOL's general-purpose FTP tool:

1. At AOL Keyword: **FTP**, click Go To FTP (refer to Figure 15-8).
2. In the Anonymous FTP window, click Other Site.
3. In the Other Site box, type the address of the FTP site. To download a file by using the Anonymous FTP tool, you must first identify the exact address of the site where the file is located. Knowing the whole directory path, with full filename and extension, is best.
   - For anonymous FTP (public) sites, leave the Ask for Login Name and Password box unchecked, and click Connect.
   - For private FTP sites, put a check in the Ask for Login Name and Password check box. Click Connect. You are prompted for your login and password, and if you enter them correctly, you are admitted to the site.

   If the site is busy, try again!
4. In the folder to which you have access, double-click other folders to see the files in them. With a file selected, you can either:
   - **Download it:** Click Download Now and use the Download Manager box to save it on your hard drive. Note that no Download Later option exists for FTP downloads.
   - **View it:** The View File Now box is active (clickable) when a selected file is simple text.

Using Third-Party FTP Software

Commercial and shareware FTP programs give you additional features not available in either AOL's browser or its built-in FTP program. For example, programs like WS_FTP provide a visual display that shows your hard drive's folders on one side and the Internet (FTP) computer's folders on the other, so that uploading and downloading involves no more than dragging files from one panel of the window to the other. (See Figure 15-9.) Your hard drive is shown on the left (Local System), and the FTP site is shown on the right (Remote Site).

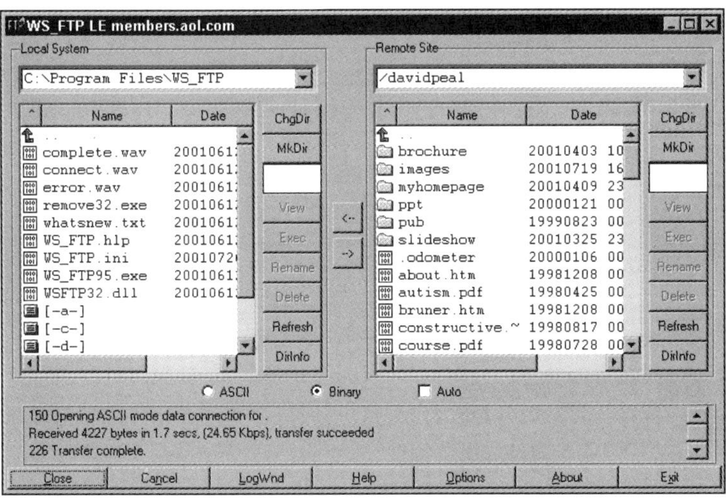

Figure 15-9. I'm sending the files on the left from my hard drive to AOL Hometown on the right. The files that appear in the right window are files I've already uploaded to Hometown.

You can use third-party FTP software like WS_FTP to transfer many Web pages at a time from My FTP Space to your storage space on AOL Hometown. Before accessing My FTP Space by using third-party software, you need to give the software some information about your AOL account. When creating an FTP "profile" to access AOL, provide the following tidbits of information:

- Host address: members.aol.com
- User ID or account: anonymous
- Password: *yourscreenname*@aol.com

Just select a file and click a button to upload from your hard drive to the FTP site, or download from the FTP site to your hard drive. You can move many files at once by simply selecting more than one file to upload or download, and clicking the right-pointing upload button. You can use WS_FTP to delete files and folders, and to make online directories (folders) to hold your files.

Understanding Filenames and Extensions

Filenames have two parts, separated by a period. The first part is the filename proper and is provided by a person; it often describes the file's content (`census.pdf`). Then there's the file extension, which is provided by software and indicates the file type (the *pdf* in `census.pdf`). A file's extension provides the information about its format and platform (Windows, Mac, and so on), and about the software applications that can play it. A PDF file, in this case, requires the free Adobe Acrobat Reader (available at AOL's Browser Plug-ins page, `multimedia.aol.com`).

Using Image, Sound, Video, and Text Files

For faster connections, turn off the conversion of JPGs to ART files as follows: Choose Settings⇨Preferences. Click Internet Properties (WWW). Open the Web Graphics tab. Choose Never Compress Graphics, and click OK.

When downloading an image, sound, or video file, you often need to know what software can play, display, or otherwise use the file. AOL plays many file types automatically, but to replay your songs or view your pictures whenever you want, you need to know which software to use.

Microsoft Windows comes with *default* (or preset) programs assigned to perform tasks. As you acquire more software, however, you can change Windows' defaults so you can use your favorite programs to play your songs and other multimedia.

Using Graphics Files

On AOL, when you open a GIF or JPG picture by choosing File⇨Open Picture Finder, the file can be cropped, brightened, reversed, and otherwise edited.

A file with a graphics extension might look like this: `tip.gif`. When opened in a graphics program or in AOL (File⇨Open), you see a digital image. Graphics files can be large, because of the amount of information required to represent the picture's colors and tones (the file sizes are measured in kilobytes). Table 15-1 gives you additional information about common graphics file extensions.

Table 15-1. Common Graphic File Extensions

Extension	*What It Stands for*	*What It's Used for*
GIF	Graphic Interchange Format	Any browser and graphics program on any platform can display GIFs. This format is used for images with simple shapes.
JPG	Joint Photographic Experts Group	Used for detailed, colorful images and digital pictures. They're compressed, hence small. Along with GIFs, JPGs are the most popular format on the Web, and can be viewed with almost any browser or graphics program and browser, on any platform.
ART		ART files are unique to AOL. By default, AOL's built-in browser converts image files in other formats to ART.

Using Sound Files

When you open almost any sound file, AOL Media Player plays a song or other audio clip, such as a speech. To make sure AOL Media Player is available for all supported media types, choose Settings⇨Preferences. Click Multimedia. Check both of the check boxes under Player Preferences, and click Save.

Note

AOL maintains a library of WAV sounds and sound-playing software as part of the Music & Sound community (AOL Keyword: **Music & Sound**).

Sound files tend to be large — 1MB or more for many WAV and MP3 files — but there is no general correlation between file size and song length, because of the different formats used to compress sound files.

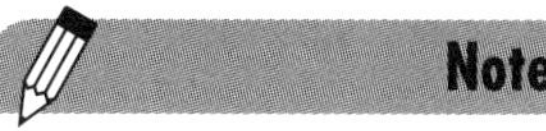

Note

Did you know the "You've Got Mail" message is a WAV file?

Streaming audio formats, such as RealAudio, play right away and usually cannot be saved on your hard drive. Other formats, such as WAV, MIDI, and sometimes MP3, must be downloaded in their entirety and saved before they can be played. The AOL Media Player can play both streaming and downloaded audio. Table 15-2 gives you more info on audio files.

Table 15-2. Common Audio File Extensions

Extension	*What It Stands for*	*What It Does*
WAV	Windows Audio Format	Attempts to faithfully record the original sound. Because of all the information WAV files carry, they can be quite large. WAV is the default sound format used by Windows and AOL.
MP3	MPG/MPEG (Motion Picture Experts Group), layer 3	AOL Media Player plays MP3 files. MP3 is the audio "layer" of MPEG, a standard for compressing digital video.
MID or MIDI	Musical Instrument Digital Interface	Unlike WAV files, which are similar to recordings, MIDI files contain electronically simulated sounds. MIDI files can be opened and played in AOL. MIDI archives can be found on FTP and Web sites around the world.

The Classical Archives (`www.classicalarchives.com`) has a large collection of MIDI music to listen to. For popular music, try `www.musicrobot.com`.

Over a modem connection, even the best-quality streaming video is still jerky, owing to network congestion, modem speed, and compression technology. If you value quality video online, consider a high-speed connection (see Chapter 17).

After you download WAV or MP3 files, you can play them repeatedly. Using the AOL Media Player, you can create playlists of your favorite sound collections, as you'll see in Chapter 16.

Using Video Files

You can watch video files with a video player, such as AOL Media Player or QuickTime. A video player can play a video of any length, from a clip to an entire movie.

AOL's Media Player can play AVIs and MPGs as well as streaming RealMedia, but for MOV you need to use QuickTime to see the movie (if you don't have QuickTime, download from `multimedia.aol.com`).

- **AVI:** The standard Windows video format.
- **MOV:** Short for movie, this is the format used by Apple Computer's popular QuickTime video system; a Windows version is available, too. The latest version of QuickTime supports many types of multimedia files.
- **MPG/MPEG:** Motion Pictures Experts Group. An efficient and popular method of compressing video clips.

Using Text Files

Text files sound dull, but they're actually amazingly versatile. Why? They are small, very fast to download, and can be used on any type of computer system. That's why Web pages are constructed out of pure text — nothing but letters, numbers, and other simple characters. A Web page can be used in a browser or HTML editor on just about any computer out there, and a version of HTML has even been developed for handheld computers.

You are likely to encounter the following types of text files in many places:

- **HTM, HTML:** A file with this extension is a page of HTML code — in other words, a Web page. You can use any browser and can view the file on any platform.

  You might be thinking, "But isn't the Web the visual part of the Internet?" The HTML file itself doesn't contain any graphics or colors. Instead, it either specifies the additional graphics files that are to appear on a Web page or includes instructions for the browser about which colors to display.
- **TXT:** A text file, usable on any platform, with any text editor, word processor, or similar program. Text just refers to simple letters, punctuation marks, and numerals — no formatting or fancy symbols.

Handling File Formats in Windows

In Microsoft Windows 95/98, you can tell Windows which program you want to open when you use a specific type of file. This useful procedure seems difficult because of the cluttered Windows 95/98 dialog boxes and the unhelpfully terse language. In this section, I help you customize Windows to suit your style. Associating a file type with a program is the first step to making files (and programs) useful after you download them.

This example changes the way MPEG video files are configured on my system so that, when opened, such files automatically play in AOL.

1. While using Windows 95/98, choose Start⇨Settings⇨Folder Options and click the File Types tab. The Folder Options window, like the one shown in Figure 15-10, appears.

   In Windows XP (Classic View), choose Start⇨Control Panel⇨Folder Options.

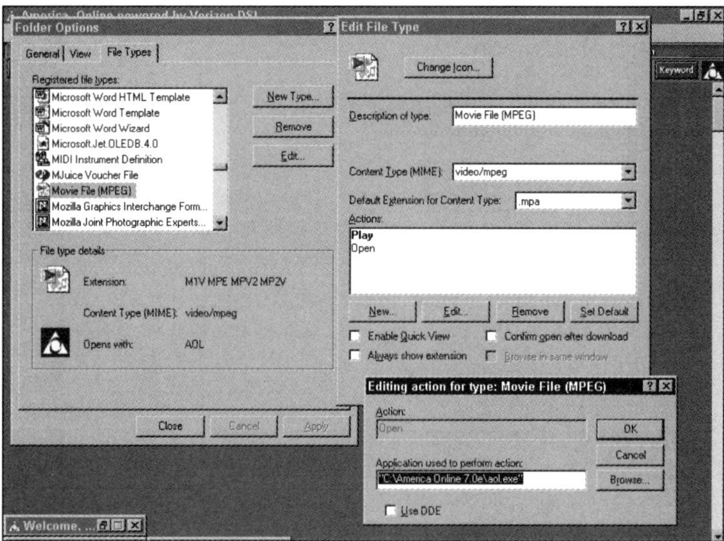

Figure 15-10. Use the Folder Options dialog box to edit file types.

2. In the Registered File Types list box, select a file type. Scroll up and down to see the entire list of file types.

   In the File Type Details area at the bottom of the tab, you can see what player opens the file type that you selected and what file extensions this type may have.

   In Windows XP, you can see a similar area.

3. Click Edit to open the Edit File Type box.

   In XP, click the Change button to use the Open With box.

4. In the Actions box in the lower part of this window, double-click Open to bring up the Editing Action box. In this box, you specify that you want the file to open in AOL. Click Browse to find AOL, which should be in the America Online 7.0 directory on your main drive. Double-click the program when you find it and then Click OK when you're done.

Now, double-click Play and, likewise, specify that you want the file to play in AOL.

In XP, this process is easier. You are given a list of Programs, divided into Recommended and Other. Choose the program to open the file.

5. Click Close OK to close the Edit File Type box. (You don't need to do this in XP.)
6. Test the new association by choosing Start⇨Find⇨ Files or Folders. (In later versions of Windows, the Find menu is called the Search menu instead.) Then search for **.MPG* in your system, and double-click an MPG file.

   The program specified in Step 4 opens automatically. If it doesn't, return to the list of file types in Step 2 and make sure you have chosen the correct file. Sometimes, you will find several versions of the same file type.

Where to Go from Here

Files are everywhere. They make possible all the things that probably drew you online in the first place. AOL's FTP tools help you find and play files of every type: images, videos, songs, and more. The older FTP tool remains the Net's workhorse for storing and sharing files of all kinds, which is why it is available in so many forms on AOL.

- For more about multimedia file types and the way they're displayed or played in the AOL browser, see Chapter 6.
- Chapter 16 suggests some files to download. Many of these downloadable files are programs for making the most of all your multimedia files.
- Everything you need to know about building Web pages and using AOL Hometown (and uploading files) can be found in Ed Willett's book, *Your Official America Online Guide to Creating Cool Web Pages*, 2nd Edition, also published by Hungry Minds, Inc. You can buy the book at AOL Keyword: **AOL Store**.

Chapter 16

Enhancing Your Online Experience with Software

IN THIS CHAPTER — **PAGE**

You can download software from the Internet and run it on your computer to enhance your online experience. To retrieve this software, all the tools you need are included with AOL: the AOL browser, My FTP Space (AOL Keyword: **My FTP Space**), and Anonymous FTP (AOL Keyword: **FTP**).

Chapter 15 showed how to use all these downloading tools. This chapter introduces popular software that you can download for compressing files, playing music files, viewing image files, and creating files for the Web. This list offers just a tiny sample of the software at your fingertips.

Discovering Free Software

You can find and download thousands of programs online. For example, I used a handy and inexpensive program called HyperSnap, from Hyperionics, to capture the screen images in this book. Another example is Netscape, which is available for free. It is the focus of Chapter 7, and is mentioned in this chapter as well.

Software (also called a program) is computer-readable code that lets your computer do something, such as play a sound file or compress a file.

Free software comes in the following two categories, and it's important that you know the difference before you download software from the Web. Both types of free software differ from the commercial software in the computer stores in that they cost little or nothing.

- **Freeware:** This type of software costs you nothing. Freeware products are often every bit as good as expensive commercial alternatives. The Netscape browser and AOL's Winamp player are examples of freeware.
- **Shareware:** This type of software is free — with a couple of restrictions. The most important condition is that you can use the software for free during a trial period (30 days, for example), but after that, you have to pay the software's creator a nominal charge to continuing using it. Sometimes you can't use software after a certain number of days, whether you pay or not.

Sometimes shareware lacks some features that the full version has; sometimes the version of software you pay for is a more up-to-date version of the software. Software makers realize the importance of creating a community of happy users who can spread the word about their creative work. Also, on the Net, there's a strong tradition of "giving back," of creating and freely distributing software for the sake of the community. Unfortunately, there's also a tradition of assuming that others' creations cost nothing, and some developers are harsher than others in restricting use of their shareware. It depends entirely on the specific topic.

So, if you like the shareware you're using, consider paying to register it. In return, you often get documentation and other forms of support, additional features, and notification of new versions. At the least, you avoid having the software become unusable after the evaluation period is over.

Choosing the Right Software

How do you get the best piece of shareware or freeware for your preferences and needs?

The first thing you need to do before you look for software online is figure out what you want the software to do, based on your needs at work, home, or elsewhere. Ask yourself these questions:

- Does AOL already offer what I want?
- Is the required functionality so important to me that I will pay for support and documentation?

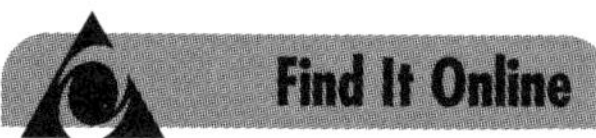

To identify the best products in a specific niche, start your product research at ZDNet (`www.zdnet.com`) or AOL Keyword: **CNET**.

Note that if AOL is your only Internet provider, you won't be able to use third-party e-mail and newsgroup readers (such as Outlook and Eudora) to read your AOL mail.

When you have an idea of what you want, then be sure that the software is compatible with your computer. That means you need to get the appropriate version of the software. Check the following:

- **Operating system:** Buy software for your operating system. If you have Windows 95/98, get software for it, not for Windows 2000 or Windows XP. If you have a Macintosh, you can only use software created for the Mac — unless you have a program that simulates Windows.
- **Software version:** Make sure the version you download is the most recent. How do you tell one software version from another? Look for the version with the highest number (Netscape 6.1 versus Netscape 6.0, for example). Sometimes it is worth waiting several weeks after software is released, to give the developer a chance to fix some of the bugs that seem inevitable in new software.

  If you like older versions of a program (like Netscape 4.7) or must outfit old computers (in a school, for example), you will want older versions of the software. For example, you would want AOL 4.0 if you are using Windows 3.1.

  Beta software is prerelease software, which may be incomplete or unstable, but can also mean that you can be the first to try out cool, new features. Technical support is usually not provided for beta, but that doesn't mean that the products aren't worth downloading. AOL's betas for AOL Instant Messenger and ICQ are usually reliable and stable.

Finding Software on AOL

AOL Keyword: **Shareware** takes you to AOL's Download Center, shown in Figure 16-1, which gives you access to select shareware programs, including Internet tools. The Shareware section of the Download Center is divided into folders, such as Internet Tools and Web Publishing. Open a folder for a list of both programs and the files to use with those programs (for example, WAV players and Star Wars music in WAV format). A search function gives you the ability to search across shareware categories.

You can find the number of times any piece of software has been downloaded by AOL members. A high number of downloads may indicate that users consider the software better or easier to use. However, make sure the high number of downloads is not a mere reflection of the amount of time the software has been available to download.

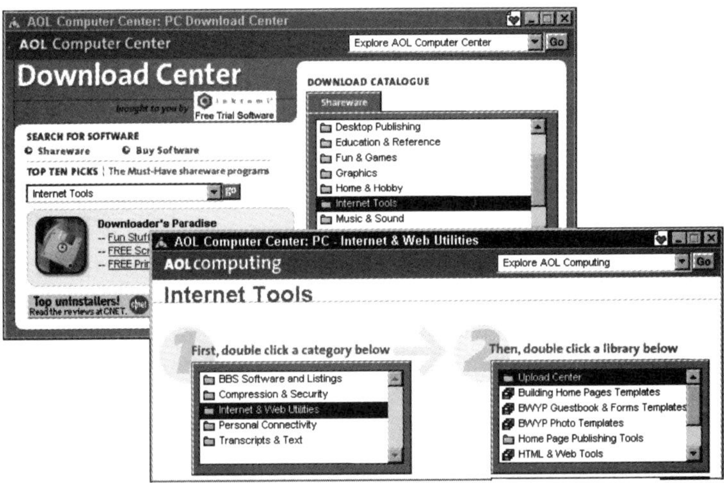

Figure 16-1. AOL's Download Center (AOL Keyword: **Shareware**) is organized into categories for ease of access. The Internet Tools category is one example.

Finding Software on the Web

Online, you can find Web sites that simplify the process of finding and downloading Internet software. The following sites are reliable, and many rate and review software:

- **CNET:** You can access CNET's main page by going to AOL Keyword: **CNET**, where you find links to all of CNET's services. CNET's Shareware.com (`www.shareware.com`) boasts a collection of 250,000 downloadable files distributed across a dozen software libraries on the Internet. CNET's Download.com (`www.download.com`) offers a more select, CNET-only directory of software, which you can browse as well as search. (With Shareware.com, you can only search.)
- **Dave Central (`www.davecentral.com`):** Dave's directory is meticulously detailed. The shareware archive is organized topically. Software types and product names are listed on the left side of the page. Select a product on the left, and a description and download link appear in the center of the page. Downloadable software includes Photoshop plug-ins, Web editors, security software, and many programs for working with multimedia files.
- **Stroud's Consummate Winsock Applications (`cws.internet.com`):** In addition to providing outstanding shareware listings and information, this well-established download site includes updates to major commercial software, such as Microsoft Office, Microsoft Internet Explorer, Netscape, and the Norton and McAfee virus-scanning programs.
- **Tucows (`www.tucows.com`):** In case you're wondering, Tucows stands for The Ultimate Collection of Winsock Software, though it is in no way limited to Windows software. Tucows offers Mac, Linux, and Palm software, as well as software that can be run on all the newest versions of the Windows operating system. Figure 16-2 shows Tucows.

  One thing that sets Tucows apart is its inclusion of family-oriented software. Kids in particular will be interested in `www.tukids.com`. Many packages can help kids with homework. Orbit 1.2, for example, displays the motion of objects relative to the Earth.

Note

Tucows and other big companies like Netscape and Microsoft give you a choice of the site from which to download. Downloading from a computer in your region can reduce your wait time.

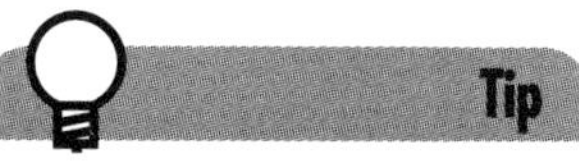
Tip

Tukids (`www.tukids.com`) is the place to find kid-friendly software.

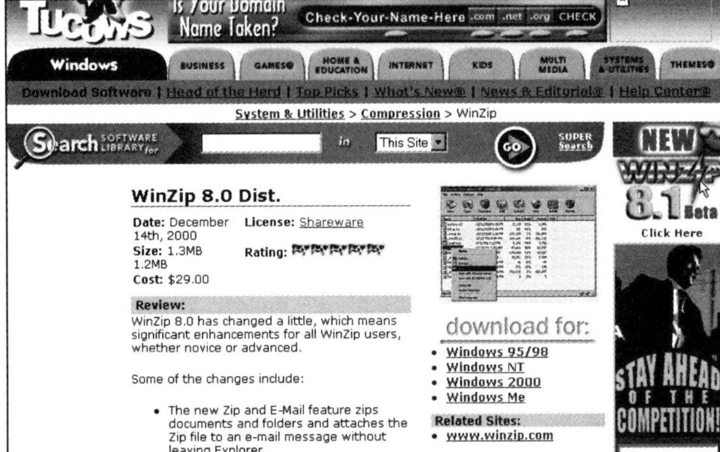

Figure 16-2. Tucows has a clear organization and offers ratings and reviews. Note the five-cow rating for this software (WinZip), which is profiled in this chapter.

- **ZDNet (`www.zdnet.com/download`):** This site features reviewed software, with recommendations and related content from Ziff-Davis's large family of online and print magazines. ZDNet's reviews, user's ratings, and helpful downloading information all make ZDNet worth a visit.

At the sites profiled in this section, you can find the software discussed in this chapter and countless other programs.

Finding Software on FTP

Used to be, downloading FTP files required that you knew the following:

- The FTP site where the file could be found
- The file's location (folder) on the FTP site

You still need this information in many work and college situations. But if you're a home user and looking for music, games, or software, it has become much easier these days to do a simple search of files available by FTP.

FTP Search, available through the Web, was developed by a Norwegian company called Fast Search and Transfer. This company is creating tools for finding and transferring images, videos, MP3s, and other types of files. You can use the company's FTP search engine at `www.alltheweb.com`. Figure 16-3 shows a search for Beatles at this Web site.

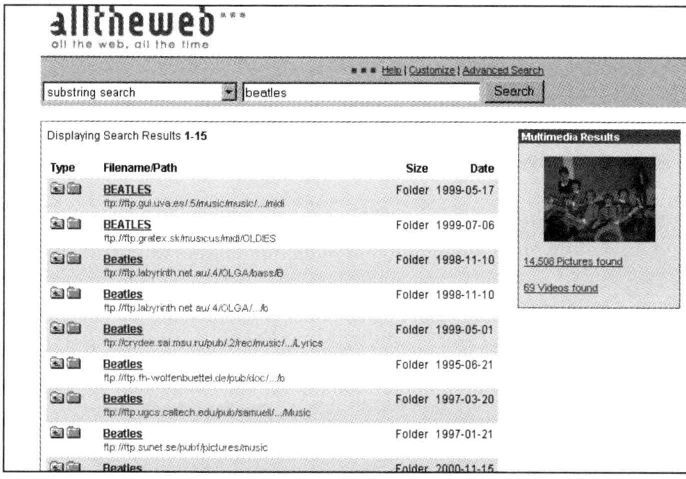

Figure 16-3. FTP Search simplifies your search for FTP files, and combines it with other multimedia searches. This search for *Beatles* returned lyrics and some songs (left), plus pictures and videos (right).

Your results consist of both files and folders. You can open files directly by simply clicking. As described in Chapter 15, you will need to identify a place to save the file and then retrieve it when it has completely downloaded. You may encounter many older file types such as *z* and *tar,* which are intended for use on older, academic computers. Good online Help is available at this all-around search site.

The Norwegian developers of FTP Search have created a large, fast, and reliable Web search engine called All The Web (`www.alltheweb.com`).

Simplifying Life Online with Software

There are several shareware and freeware software packages that directly or indirectly improve your online experience:

- By giving you control of downloaded files
- By helping you create files and build your online content, such as Web pages

The following sections list a short, selective group all readily available from one of the big archives outlined in the previous section.

Compressing Files: Aladdin and WinZip

Cross-Reference

Chapter 15 explains how to tell Windows to open a file type with a certain program. You can use the steps to set which program opens ZIP files. Chapter 15 also covers the Download Manager.

When sending a file attachment to an e-mail message, selecting more than one file automatically creates a ZIP file. This feature works only when using e-mail.

Compression software is used to reduce a file's size so that it takes up less space on your hard drive or takes less time when you send it through the Internet. Such software can also be used to combine many files into one file for speedier uploading and downloading. What if you download a compressed file, or someone sends you one as an e-mail attachment? You need a program for *decompressing* them.

In downloading compressed files (often called ZIPs or zipped files), it's usually best to let Download Manager do the work. However, there are two complementary software products that can extend the simplicity and ease-of-use of Download Manager.

- **Aladdin Stuffit Expander:** This freeware program can work with files zipped on Macintosh, Windows, and UNIX computers. Expander works tends to be used with the SIT (StuffIt) files created by Macintosh programs, and can also handle UNIX formats like GZ and Z, which you will see on FTP sites.

  To use the program, just click and drag a compressed file onto the Aladdin Expander icon on your desktop, and the individual files are extracted and placed in their own folder. Figure 16-4 shows the Aladdin software (top window).

- **WinZip:** This shareware program, shown in Figure 16-4, specializes in ZIP files, the popular PC format for compressed files. In addition to unzipping files, you can use WinZip to create compressed files.

  WinZip also supports non-ZIP compressed formats for the UNIX and Windows operating systems. In a word, WinZip handles just about everything but SIT files — the common Macintosh format created by Stuffit (SIT) Expander.

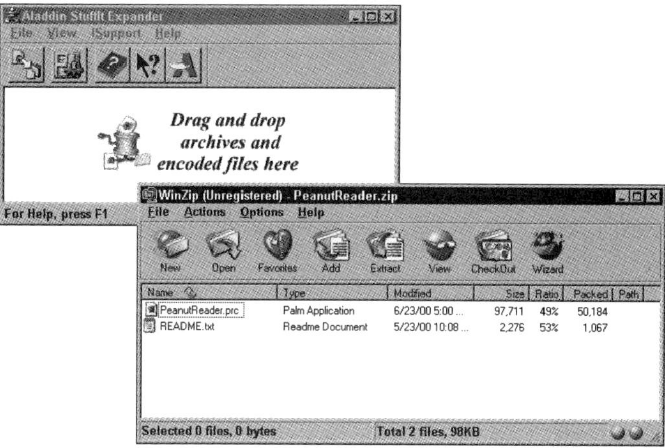

Figure 16-4. WinZip and Aladdin. Together they can handle just about anything.

Viewing and Managing Graphics Files: ThumbsPlus

ThumbsPlus, from Cerious Software, Inc. (`www.cerious.com`), integrates tools for organizing, viewing, and editing graphic images. Unlike many of the products from bigger companies, ThumbsPlus lets you open dozens of file types and convert individual files or batches of files from one format to another. Along the left side of the ThumbsPlus window, ThumbsPlus displays folders and files. On the right, ThumbsPlus displays *thumbnails* (small versions) of individual digital pictures in a selected folder.

A full suite of editing capabilities is included with ThumbsPlus. You can rotate and crop images, alter their brightness and contrast, and improve their color saturation and hue. Finally, you can add keywords and descriptions for your digital pictures so that you can locate files more easily later.

For no-nonsense image viewing and editing, use AOL's Picture Finder (from the File menu).

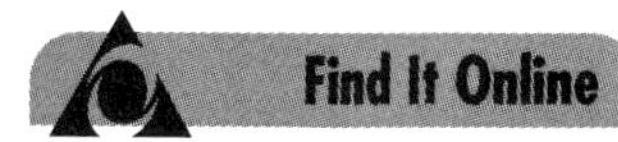

If you want to try ThumbsPlus before you buy it, evaluation copies can be downloaded from Cerious (`www.cerious.com`).

Creating Music Playlists with AOL Media Player

Managing music files means not only playing songs, but also keeping track of them and organizing in ways you like. For all the songs you download, you have what you need built into

AOL. The AOL Media Player can play or display the major formats for both video (AVI, MPG, and RealVideo) and music (WAV, MIDI, MP3, M3U playlists, Shoutcast, streaming MP3, and RealAudio).

To play any sound or video file on your hard drive, launch AOL (you don't have to go online) and choose File⇨Open to find and open the file. The player comes up automatically.

A *playlist* is like your own private radio station. You can group, name, and play a stack of music files on your computer in a certain order, again and again, like a CD you produced yourself. To create a playlist, follow these steps:

1. On AOL, choose File⇨Open.
2. Navigate to a folder that contains your audio files, and double-click the first one you want to add to your playlist. The song plays.
3. In the AOL Media Player window, click My Playlist. The song that's playing becomes the first item in your playlist, displayed in the AOL Playlist Editor.
4. Click Add Item. Navigate to the folder that contains your audio files. Select the file (or files) you want to add to the playlist and click Open.
5. Edit your playlist:
   - To change the order of songs on your playlist, select an audio file and click the appropriate Move Item arrow to change the file's position in the playlist.
   - Click Remove Item to delete it (just from the playlist).
   - Click Add Item to include a new song in the playlist. See Figure 16-5 for a playlist in the making.
6. Click Save.

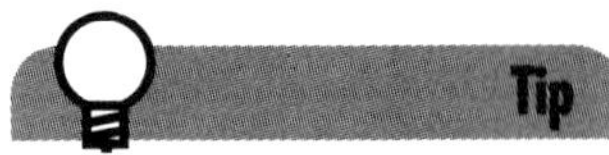

To select more than one file to add to your playlist, hold down the Ctrl key while clicking the files with the mouse.

To listen to the playlist later:

- If AOL Media Player is open, click My Playlist, and then (in the Playlist Editor) click Get One of My Playlists.
- If the player is not open, choose File⇨Open and search for *Files of Type .M3U.* This is a playlist's format, and your playlists should be in the same folder as music files on which they are based. Opening an M3U file opens the AOL Media Player, if it is your default multimedia player.

Figure 16-5. With playlists you can save your favorite downloaded songs in any order, and play the list in its entirety whether you are online or offline.

Finding Music

The AOL Media Player makes it easy to play downloaded music. But where do you *get* all this music, especially the high-quality MP3 music? Here are a few places to start. Using AOL Search, you can quickly find numerous other music destinations.

- Digital Downloads (AOL Keyword: **Digital Downloads**), in AOL's Music Channel.
- MusicNet (`www.musicnet.com`). A new subscription service.
- SonicNet (AOL Keyword: **SonicNet**). Click Downloads.
- RollingStone.com (AOL Keyword: **Rolling Stone**). Includes a subscription service.
- AOL Search (click the Search button on the AOL toolbar). Click Arts⇨Music⇨Sound Files⇨MP3, for dozens of MP3 download sites.

Downloading music is like downloading anything. Chapter 15 has the details.

Playing Music Files: Winamp

Streaming means that you can hear these MP3 files right after they start to download.

Net traffic jams can impair MP3 quality — another reason to investigate a broadband connection. See Chapter 17 for the full story.

Today, there's an amazing variety and quantity of music to download and radio stations to hear on the Net. New formats like streaming audio and MP3 have greatly increased the quality of music. Faster connections have made it possible to listen to all this music without giving it a second thought. Until recently, it took a lot of thought to find music, download it, and play it, and it often wasn't worth the effort. But now, it doesn't take much effort to turn your computer into a music center.

Winamp offers the same functionality as AOL Media Player. You may want to use it on computers where you don't have AOL installed. More advanced users may want to take advantage of features such as the Equalizer, which gives controls of specific frequency ranges.

Winamp, developed by AOL, plays MP3s from your computer or from any online music source; it can also play your audio CDs. The Winamp software, shown in Figure 16-6, has three major parts, as well as a minibrowser (radio) not shown here.

- **Winamp player:** The player has the basic controls: Start, Stop, Pause, Eject, Volume Control, Speaker Balance, and more for the music currently being played. This is the only Winamp component you *must* use to play music.
- **Winamp equalizer:** The equalizer has fancy audio settings, which are very handy if you are audio-savvy and want to vary the sound quality for any range of the frequency. Winamp comes with a list of preconfigured equalizer settings. For rock, as an example, Winamp sets the lower and higher tones above average (louder). Click the Preset button, choose Load⇨Preset, and select the sound configuration you want (Reggae, Classical, Dance, Large Hall).
- **Winamp playlist:** The playlist shows what's playing. To play any song on the list, double-click it. Here's how to create a playlist:
    - To add new songs to the list, click Add⇨Add Dir. In the Open Directory box, navigate to the folder with the music you want to play and select it. Winamp-compatible music, such as MP3 and WAV files, will

now appear in the Winamp playlist. You can add music from several directories and from CDs (by navigating to your CD drive).

- To remove files from your playlist, select an item in the playlist and click Delete.
- To sort displayed music by song title or filename, use the MISC button.
- To save the playlist, click the LIST OPTS button, select Save List, and give the playlist a name; its format will be .M3U, just as in the AOL Media Player.

You can close the equalizer or playlist by clicking the close button (the X in the upper-right corner). To restore the playlist or equalizer, click PL or EQ button on the player. If you align the Equalizer or Playlist under the Player, the windows will latch together so that they can be clicked and dragged at the same time.

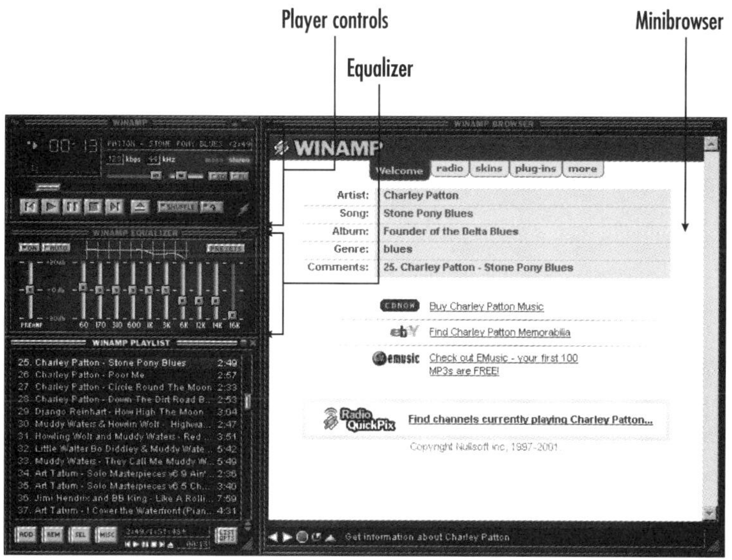

Figure 16-6. The popular (and free) Winamp MP3 player.

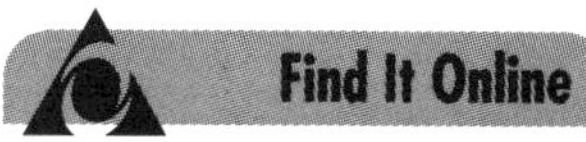

AOL's Virus Center (AOL Keyword: **Virus**) is the place to start when you need general information about viruses, new outbreaks, and software for staying safe.

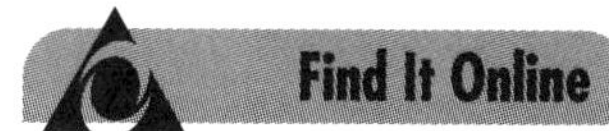

For more information about McAfee visit `www.mcafee.com`. You can reach Norton on the Web at `www.symantec.com`. Both programs are excellent, so if you buy a computer with one or the other already installed, you can't go wrong. Just remember to keep the software updated.

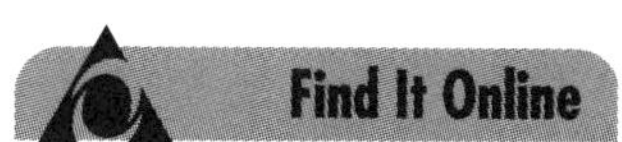

A well-informed and up-to-date review of computer viruses can be found in the Northern Light Special Edition on that subject (`special.northernlight.com/compvirus`).

Tip

If you're new to the Web and want to make a page, start at AOL Hometown and use either 1-2-3 Publish or Easy Designer to get started.

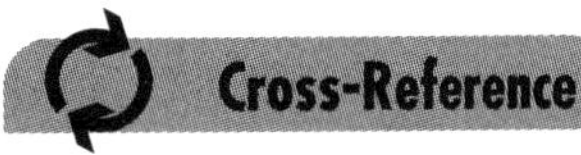

Cross-Reference

Chapter 15 explains how to upload and register Web pages at AOL Hometown.

Software for Creating Web Pages

If you want to make Web pages, you can learn the ropes and download the software you need on the Web itself. Netscape Composer and Paint Shop Pro exemplify the quality of free or inexpensive software that you can download.

Netscape Composer. Composer is a visual tool for building Web pages, and is included in every copy of Netscape 6. To create a new page, click New. As in a word processor, you can type and format your text, and move words around by copying and pasting them. Click the Table button to add a table for structured data, such as a table of prices or a child's growth chart. You can also add pictures by clicking the Image button, and then supplying a filename for the image, and of course you can make pictures and words into links.

Save your page when you're done. You'll be prompted (via one window, then another) to provide a title for your page and then a filename for your page. The title is the part of a Web page that appears in the title bar at the very top of a user's browser window; when a search engine retrieves your page as part of someone's search, it often presents the title. As for filename, this is the name of the HTML file with the script. For others to view your page, you upload it to a Web server. To publish your Composer pages for the world, add your pages to AOL Hometown.

Paint Shop Pro. A proper Web site needs graphics. (It also needs text alternatives of multimedia elements for the benefit of people who have difficulty seeing.) There are many aspects of preparing graphics for the Web, and Paint Shop Pro takes care of all of them. I single out this program because it is well supported on AOL itself. You can download it and learn to use it at AOL Keyword: **PSP**. Paint Shop Pro is free for 30 days, and then costs under $100 to purchase. That's expensive for shareware, but inexpensive for a product that some consider as capable as more expensive programs.

With Paint Shop Pro you can create animated GIFs (simple moving pictures) by using the Animation Shop and create transparent GIFs, which blend nicely into the background of a Web page. You can also optimize images so that they use only colors that browsers can display. You can also create dozens of special effects with filters. Your Paint Shop Pro images can be used with any HTML editor, such as Netscape Composer, and your completed pages can be made available on AOL Hometown.

Protecting against Infected Files: Antivirus Software

A *virus* is a small program that can attach itself to any kind of file except pure text (TXT or HTML). Viruses are usually designed to harm files on a computer system. They can be difficult to detect until they have done their damage. If you do much downloading from the Internet, you might consider protecting your system with antivirus software from a major vendor, such as Symantec (`www.symantec.com`) or McAfee (`www.mcafee.com`). Such programs are not shareware, but they do come free with most PCs these days, and downloading the latest virus definitions and protections usually is free or very inexpensive compared with the benefits of securing your system.

The best way to avoid contracting a virus from a downloaded file is to download software from trustworthy sites like the ones mentioned earlier or the software makers themselves. Infected files can also attach themselves to e-mail messages from friends, owing to security problems with some non-AOL e-mail programs. So, unless you're expecting a file from a friend, don't open an e-mail attachment until you've confirmed its name and contents with the sender.

For general information about viruses, go to AOL's Anti-Virus Center, shown in Figure 16-7. From there, you can connect to the Computer Community's Anti-Virus discussion areas, where you'll find message boards, chat, and additional antivirus resources.

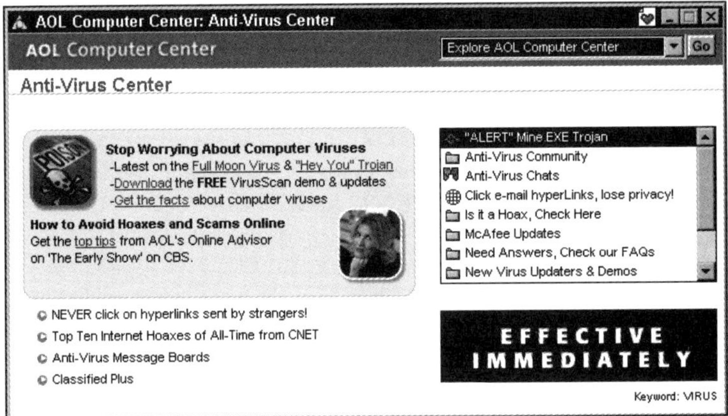

Figure 16-7. AOL's Anti-Virus Center includes general information, breaking news about specific viruses, and links to vendors' sites.

Where to Go from Here

This chapter introduces some of the useful and fun Internet software you can use with AOL to expand and enrich your Internet experience. These programs let you play music, view images, create Web pages, work with compressed files, and find software from many places on AOL and the Net. Two other chapters in this book introduce closely related themes:

- For everything you need to know about the how-to's of downloading from AOL and the Web, see Chapter 15.
- For suggestions about what you can do with the Internet resources at your disposal on and through AOL, see Chapter 18.

Chapter 17

Stepping Up to a High-Speed Connection

IN THIS CHAPTER	PAGE
Overcoming the limitations of traditional modems	381
Getting high-speed access through DSL, satellite, and cable	382
Understanding your choices	390

Your standard 56K modem, which is included with most PCs these days, works fine for everyday online routines, such as reading e-mail and browsing the Web. But for playing music, watching video, using digital pictures, and downloading software, you may want to look into a faster connection if you don't have one already.

Broadband technology now allows several ways to speed up your connection. This chapter gives an overview of high-speed options for accessing AOL and the Internet from your home PC.

Enjoying the Net at Full Throttle

With high-speed access to the Internet, you don't have to deal with dial-up modems, the occasional busy signal, slow file downloads, or conflicts with household members who need to use the phone or fax when you're online. With

AOL High Speed Broadband services, you can just open AOL and sign on in seconds. Plus, your phone line is always available.

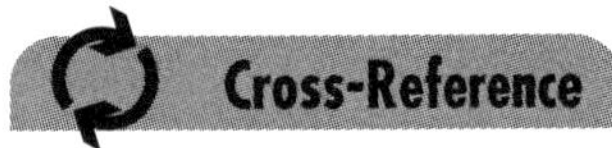

For more on what you can do with high-speed AOL access, see Chapter 18.

Chapter 10 introduced AOL Anywhere, which gives you access to AOL from non-PC devices such as your TV or wireless phone. AOL's *high-speed* services are intended to supercharge your computer's connection to the Internet.

High-speed technologies enable a new crop of services so that you can make the most of your online time.

- **Use your computer as a radio.** AOL Media Player and Spinner make this easy (see Chapter 18).
- **Immerse yourself in online art galleries and other multimedia sites.** Figure 17-1 shows the multimedia art, fun, and learning site created by the Intel and the Whitney Museum of American Art (`whitney.artmuseum.net`). You can also enjoy unique programming, from music videos and movie trailers to the latest headlines and sports highlights.
- **Download large software files from the Internet in seconds instead of minutes.** The software profiled in Chapter 16 can now be yours much more quickly. You are limited only by the hours in the day and the limits of your hard drive.
- **Take part in lifetime education.** With online education, or *distance learning,* you can set your own pace and acquire the knowledge or skills you need, when you need them. For a directory of distance education programs, start at Peterson's directory of programs and courses at `www.lifelonglearning.com`. Distance learning is making use of more and more features requiring a high-speed connection, such as two-way teleconferencing and Flash/Shockwave tutorials.
- **Take part in the MP3 revolution.** Download music files for your favorite bands and performers and find music that you'd never hear on your local radio station. You can use the AOL Media Player to listen to this music when you're on AOL, or Winamp when you are using a different connection (see Chapter 16).

Broadband service helps you take full advantage of real-time gaming. You won't experience as many network traffic jams as you may with a dial-up modem.

Figure 17-1. This presentation by Intel and the Whitney Museum of Art extends the museum experience into the online community.

Understanding Broadband Basics

You don't have to know how your Internet connection works. You may find it useful, however, to understand a few terms before you take advantage of high-speed services, such as AOL High Speed Broadband:

- *Bandwidth* refers to the data-carrying capacity of a communications medium, such as telephone wire or TV cable, as measured in the number of bits of data that can be sent through it per second. A *bit* is the small unit of data; a *kilobyte* is 1,024 bits. An old-fashioned modem, with a speed of 56K, can carry 56,000 bits of data a second (but rarely goes that fast).

  High-speed connections have increased bandwidth, which means that they move more data in less time than ordinary dial-up connections. (A high-speed connection can be about 50 times faster.) In human terms, a bandwidth's speed is relative to what you need to do and how you are used to doing it. For example, some people don't mind waiting ten minutes for a file to download, so the amount of bandwidth they have with a dial-up connection that uses the phone line and a modem is okay. Other people may want to pay a little extra for a high-speed connection so that they can download the same file in less than a minute.

- *Broadband* refers, in technical terms, to the ability of a medium (such as wire or cable) to carry several data streams at the same time. Broadband is commonly referred to as high-speed access, and can be delivered in many ways — over phone lines and cable wires, and even through the air.
- *Downstream* and *upstream* refer to the direction in which data is traveling between an Internet server and your computer. When you download from the Internet, you are moving data to your computer—downstream. You download data each time you view a new Web page. Data is going upstream when you send an e-mail message or upload pages to AOL Hometown.

Note

With a broadband connection, computers can download files faster than they can upload them.

Accelerating the Net with AOL High Speed Broadband

Definition

AOL High Speed Broadband (AOL Keyword: **High Speed**) allows you to access AOL through a high-speed connection and offers multimedia content available only to AOL High Speed Broadband subscribers.

Currently, AOL provides high-speed access to members using a phone line (DSL), cable modem, or satellite dish. Regardless of which type of high-speed connection you use, you have access to AOL's video, multimedia, and other content optimized for a high-speed connection.

I use DSL for my AOL High Speed Broadband connection, and I can speak firsthand of its benefits:

- With AOL High Speed Broadband, connecting to AOL becomes almost as simple as turning on the light. You still have to sign on to AOL, but sign-on is now very fast and you will never be interrupted by busy signals because you're using a dial-up connection.
- AOL features audio and video content from leading broadband programming providers. For example, many of the channels include exclusive content (such as video clips, music, and other multimedia features) that are optimized for high-speed connections. (See Figure 17-2.)

Tip

If you have a high-speed connection, you see bonus links at the bottom of the channel window.

Click to see streaming media

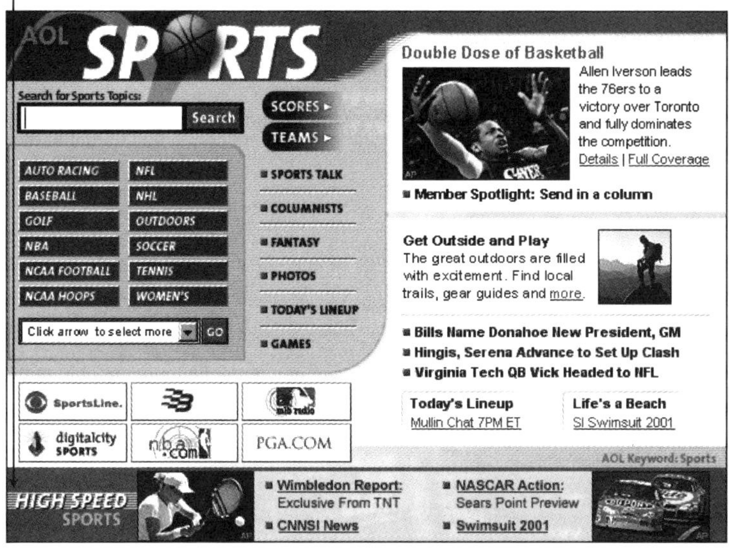

Figure 17-2. With a high-speed connection, you have access to bonus channel content.

Getting Broadband Service

In addition to all of the perks of being a member of AOL's community, the $54.95 monthly fee for AOL High Speed Broadband service gives you the following benefits:

You can instantly access the Internet without worrying about dialing up with a traditional modem.

You can connect at speeds up to 50 times faster than your standard dial-up modem.

You see and hear enhanced multimedia content created by leading news and entertainment providers.

You can download pictures and files quickly and display them without problems.

You can play interactive games online without any lag time.

You also get unlimited access to AOL from any computer (and with any connection) when you're away from the high-speed connection on your home PC.

(continued)

Note

For the monthly fee of $54.95, AOL High Speed Broadband users get everything they need to connect to AOL via a DSL, cable, or satellite connection.

(continued)

For more information on getting broadband service from AOL, go to AOL Keyword: **High Speed** or call the following toll-free number: 800-574-1779.

Accelerating the Net with DSL

Currently, the most popular AOL High Speed Broadband connection is AOL's DSL solution (find out more at AOL Keyword: **DSL**).

DSL technologies pack as much as 99 percent more capacity into existing phone lines by using the part of the wire that is *not* used in voice communication. How is this possible? The frequencies of the human voice don't require much of the bandwidth available in a copper phone line; engineers have figured out a ways to use that remaining bandwidth for data. Here are some benefits to using DSL:

- Someone can use the phone at the same time as you are experiencing the Net at high speed. Using DSL lets you use a single phone line for both data communications (AOL and the Internet) *and* a telephone/fax.
- With DSL, the line by which you connect to the Internet is *your* line, not a shared line. AOL High Speed Broadband is fast and stays fast.

The *central office* is not a place where people work. It is just a piece of equipment that connects local residences and businesses to long-distance lines. To get DSL you must be within a certain distance of your central office.

Ordering DSL service through AOL High-Speed Broadband requires a visit to AOL Keyword: **DSL** or call phone number 800-574-1779. You need to provide information about your phone number. If you can get a DSL connection in your area, the rest is pretty much automatic.

Before your service starts, the following things happen:

- Someone from your phone company arrives at your home to examine the wiring going into your house. This person installs a box on the outside of your house or apartment as a plug for the high-speed copper wire and calculates the distance to and DSL-readiness of your central office. If the technician finds problems in wiring within the house, you may have to pay for materials and labor before starting your service.

- AOL sends you a DSL starter kit with the following equipment:
  - **A DSL modem:** The DSL modem takes data from your computer and encodes it for transmission over the unused parts of the phone line.
  - **A cable:** The cable connects the modem to your PC, and a phone cord runs from your modem to your phone jack.
  - **Filters:** These filters are used to screen out the data traffic from any telephones, analog modems, and fax lines that share the DSL line. If you have more than one phone line, you can identify the DSL line by the phone number for the line used for DSL. Other lines will be unaffected by the DSL line.
- **CDs:** One CD has a special version of the AOL software, and the other CD has software that allows you to use your modem with your operating system.

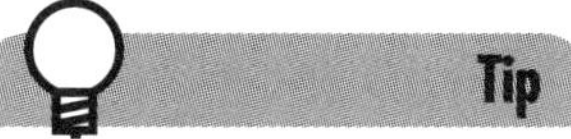

With the new AOL In Home Support service, you can request that an AOL-trained technician come to your house to set up and demonstrate your high-speed connection. Visit AOL Keyword: **IHS** to get information about the service and its availability in your area.

Installing DSL

After you hear from AOL that your service has started, you can go ahead and install the AOL software and modem. Installing the equipment is usually straightforward. Simply follow the instructions in the brochure that comes with your box of equipment. I have installed the service to two external modems and found the procedure simple each time.

The exact procedures you follow depend on the type of modem you ordered. An external USB modem connects to the PC's USB port, while an external Etherlink modem plugs right into a network card, if you have one on your PC.

Setting up DSL for use with an external modem involves several steps. For an internal modem, carefully follow the instructions that came in your package. First, make sure your PC is turned off, and then follow these steps.

1. Put filters on every phone line that shares the same phone number as your DSL line. A filter removes data traffic from your voice line, which otherwise interrupts the signal. *Do not use a filter with the DSL modem itself.*

   To install a filter, remove the existing modem or fax cable from the phone jack in the wall, and put the filter into the phone jack. Then, plug the modem or fax line into the filter.

2. Attach the modem cables:
   - Connect one end of the USB or Ethernet cable to the DSL modem, and the other end to the USB port or Ethernet plug on the back of your computer.
   - Plug the appropriate ends of the electrical cord into the modem and wall socket.
   - Attach the phone cable (the same kind used by your older modems) from the DSL modem to the phone jack on the wall.

3. Turn on your PC. Install two pieces of software on your PC. The software is on the CDs that come with your AOL High Speed DSL package. Both CDs have complete on-screen instructions:
   - First, install the DSL connection software, which makes it possible for AOL and Windows to communicate with the high-speed DSL connection.
   - Second, install a special version of the AOL software, optimized to take advantage of high-speed access but otherwise identical to the software you use now. When you install AOL, you have to go through the process of copying or moving your personal files and telling AOL whether you want to create a new account or use an existing one. You can upgrade your AOL software and DSL drivers online at AOL Keyword: **Upgrade**.

4. When you're done, you are prompted to restart Windows. After you've restarted, sign on to AOL and follow any on-screen instructions to complete the process.

Your new connection is always active, even when you're not signed on to AOL.

Who Supplies Your High-Speed Connection?

Although you order your AOL High Speed for DSL, cable, or satellite service from AOL, it's important to recognize that several companies are involved in the process. With DSL, the phone company ensures the quality of the DSL connection and activates the line. They're responsible for the phone lines, too, at least to the point where they reach your house.

With satellite connections, Hughes Electronics supplies the equipment (the dish and modem), while Hughes-DirecPC supplies the actual satellite service. AOL is also working with Time Warner Cable to deliver high-speed connections via cable modems.

AOL provides the content and coordinates the orders, customer service, and installation of DSL, cable, and satellite services.

Like an amusement park, the Net's biggest attractions often have the longest lines, especially at certain times of the day, and data speed can vary with line quality and the length of copper phone wire over which it must travel from your house to the central office. Even so, you can expect to see an improvement to your online experience when you move to a broadband connection.

Bottom line: Get used to faster downloads, smoother radio, and realistic on-screen movies. Most users never want to go back to an analog modem.

Accelerating the Net with a Satellite Connection

Satellites work by sending data over the high-speed radio waves. The radio waves are transmitted by communications satellites and can carry Internet data, allowing them, in theory, to bring Internet access to every part of the world. The data comes to you via satellite (downstream), but the information you send, like files and e-mail, go upstream via a normal modem. Downstream data speeds are comparable to DSL and cable speeds, but the upstream rates can be a bit slower.

A satellite-based connection to AOL may be right for you if

- You already have (or plan to get) satellite TV service, such as DirecTV.
- You have access to neither cable nor DSL.

AOL High Speed Satellite does not require that you also subscribe to satellite TV.

What do you need to enjoy the benefits of satellite access to AOL and the Net? Most important, you must have a 30-inch diameter DirecPC satellite dish, and the dish must have a clear line of sight to the southern sky.

You will not need an extra phone line to use AOL's satellite service, although you will continue using your dial-up modem with your satellite service.

The satellite dish costs about $150-200 (depending on whether it's TV-ready or just for the PC). Installation is currectly free; AOL arranges for a certified installer in your area to install your dish and activate your AOL High Speed Satellite service.

You also need a satellite modem inside your house, which connects to the satellite line on one side and your PC's USB port on the other.

Accelerating the Net with a Cable Connection

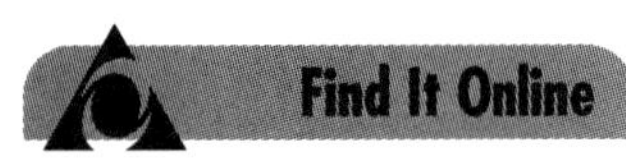

Check out AOL Keyword: **Cable** to find out if AOL's High Speed Cable service is available in your area.

More than 60 million American homes have cable TV, and a growing number of cable companies also offer Internet access services. If your cable company offers high-speed Internet service, you should be able to connect to the Internet over your cable wires. After you're connected to the Net, you can then sign on to AOL and enjoy high-speed access to AOL's programming and the Internet.

If you're using another cable Internet provider, you can still use AOL. How? See AOL Keyword: **BYOA**, short for Bring Your Own Access, for more information.

What You Need for a Cable Connection

To use a cable modem access, you must

- Have access to cable TV service.
- Subscribe to the Internet service offered by your cable-TV provider. (Note that not all cable service providers offer Internet access)
- Have a cable modem, which connects your PC to the high-speed cabling that's ordinarily used for cable TV transmission. Your cable company will tell you what kind of cable modem you need.

Note

High-speed cable access uses your PC, not your TV, to access AOL. Rather than being a high-speed connection option, AOLTV is an AOL Anywhere service actually delivered through your TV via a set-top box. See Chapter 18 for details.

Cable's Benefits

Why would you want to access AOL using cable? Cable-based Internet service is comparable to DSL in many respects, but also differs in important ways.

Note

AOL and Time Warner Cable will be rolling out high-speed cable access in the fall of 2001.

- **Convenience:** If you have cable TV and your provider offers Internet access, you already have most of what you need for cable-based AOL access. And installation is simple.
- **Speed:** As with DSL, the speed you experience on cable is up to 50 times faster than the best dial-up connection using a traditional modem. Unlike DSL, speed is subject to constraints as the number of users on a cable connection increases.
- **Freeing up the phone line:** If you live in a home with a single phone line and find yourself constantly jostling for use of the phone, fax, or Internet connection, you will appreciate an important feature of the cable modem: It runs over a different network from the telephone. And, you can use your PC and TV at the same time.

Cable's downside? Cable is often criticized for putting your connection on a shared line with (potentially) hundreds of other neighbors connecting at the same point of the larger network. If everyone on the block uses a cable connection, performance can slip. Also, your data passes through the local stretch of the network in an unencrypted form. Experts say that a network-savvy snoop can detect and monitor the data being transmitted. If you do any business-related work at home, you may want to seek the opinion of a networking or business consultant if you have concerns here. You may also consider purchasing firewall software.

Signing on to AOL with Your Cable Connection

A cable Internet connection establishes what is known as a TCP/IP connection, over which you run AOL. To use the connection, you need to create a new network *location,* as explained in Chapter 3 and summarized below.

If you have not ordered AOL High-Speed Cable, you can follow these steps to connect to your cable Internet provider:

1. Open AOL but don't sign on.
2. From the Sign On Screen, click Set Up.
3. Click Add Location to create a new location for use with an ISP or LAN. Add a custom (TCP/IP) connection.
4. Sign on to AOL by using this new location.

Find It Online

You will find these procedures at AOL Keyword: **Cable Help**.

Choosing the Right High-Speed Connection

So, you want to take advantage of AOL High Speed Broadband. Which type of connection should you get? The first point to make is that the choice between DSL and cable does not primarily have to do with speed. All three offer comparable speeds and faster download times than the fastest old-fashioned modems.

You should make your decision based on the options available in your area. For example, the availability of cable and DSL varies from region to region. Cable Internet service is still not available in many suburbs — even those that are saturated with cable TV — and is even less prevalent in smaller cities and rural areas. If you don't have cable access to begin with, you have to factor a monthly cable TV subscription into your calculations, plus the cost of cable Internet access.

AOL is working to offer as many solutions as possible, which means AOL doesn't favor one form of high-speed access over another. Here's what the future of AOL High Speed Broadband holds:

- AOL currently provides low-cost DSL connections nationwide.
- Now that AOL is part of AOL Time Warner, check for AOL High-Speed Cable service in your neighborhood soon.

My advice is to start with what you have. If AOL High Speed Broadband for DSL is offered in your area (go to AOL Keyword: **DSL** or **Cable** to find out), it's a solution that offers many advantages. If you have cable and your provider also offers cable Internet access, all you need is to subscribe to the cable Internet service and purchase a cable modem and related equipment. Finally, if you either don't have access to cable Internet service or DSL is not available in your area, consider AOL High Speed Broadband for Satellite.

Securing Your High-Speed Connection

The Internet is made up of networks — and networks of networks. As you might imagine, there can be some risks to taking part in such a big network. If your computer is connected to the Internet all the time, others could try to get access to your computer. In the worst and least likely scenario, they could use your data and computing resources for their benefit.

Fortunately, you can minimize the risks by setting your Windows network preferences to prevent anyone or any computer from accessing any file on your computer. Follow these steps:

Windows XP includes built-in firewall software to protect your computer and its contents.

Firewalls screen out certain types of data or data from certain Internet addresses.

1. Choose Start➪Settings➪Control Panel.
2. Double-click the Network icon.
3. On the Configuration tab, click File and Print Sharing. Make sure that neither of the check boxes is checked. Click OK when you're finished.

For extra protection, you can purchase *firewall* software. Designed originally to keep company Web servers secure from hackers, firewalls are now available to keep home computers from being accessed across the Internet by outsiders. BlackIce Defender (`www.netice.com`), Guard Dog (`www.mcafee.com`), and Norton Internet Security (`www.norton.com`) are a few firewall programs to check out. At AOL Keyword: **Shop@AOL**, you can find the software you need.

Where to Go from Here

The benefits of a high-speed connection could fill a book. After you experience a connection that can be 50 times faster than a modem connection, you won't need any convincing, however. Online movies look like, well, movies, and online radio sounds like the radio, with about a hundred times more stations to choose from. Files download in a jiffy, and JPGs appear in a heartbeat.

- AOL High Speed DSL can be ordered directly at AOL Keyword: **DSL.** Order cable at AOL Keyword: **Cable.**
- The next chapter profiles everyday activities that are greatly enhanced by a high-speed connection—activities such as listening to the radio, talking on the phone, and taking pictures.
- AOL Keyword: **High Speed** gives you solid information on all of AOL's high-speed connection services.
- AOL Keyword: **CNET** has detailed information and product reviews on every aspect of wireless and high-speed computing.

Chapter 18

What's Online?

The most routine daily activities, from using the phone to reading a book, can now be done entirely online. Computer networks won't replace paperbacks, car radios, board games, and the silver screen any time soon. But AOL and the Internet *are* opening possibilities for how and when you take part in these activities and who can join you. For example, AOLTV lets you watch shows with friends across town or in another state, and iPublish lets you try your hand at writing and publishing.

Online activities are great enablers, too. People who can't easily leave home can watch movies online, and people without a fax machine can send an occasional fax online. Here's what's happening online right now.

Watching Movies and Music Videos

As this book was going into print, several major U.S. movie studios announced a plan to develop the technologies and services to distribute full-length movies over the Internet.

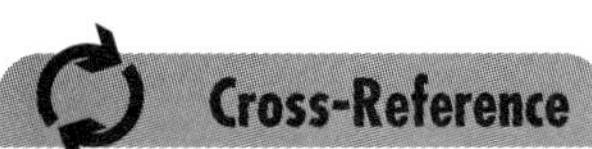

Chapter 17 has the details about your high-speed options.

RealPlayer and QuickTime provide tools for you to make your own streaming video and audio clips. Visit the vendor sites for more information (`www.real.com` and `www.apple.com`, respectively).

Online movies tend to come in common formats, such as RealVideo, which automatically play in the AOL Media Player. Some sites, such as Moviefone, seamlessly embed media players in Web pages for a much smoother viewing experience.

Movies and radio can actively engage the mind and senses in ways that the entertainment world understands very well.

The movies you can watch on the Net are not the same as what you can see in the theater — yet. Instead of studio movies, you can discover an entire world of independent, creative filmmaking. The sky's the limit when it comes to style, subject matter, and point of view. You can also watch any of hundreds of older Hollywood movies.

Even though movies have been on the Internet for several years, the experience has been pretty poor over 56K modems. Unless you have a high-speed connection, watching movies online has about as much appeal as watching spaghetti cook, mostly because of mediocre player software and slow frame-per-second rates over dial-up lines.

Prices for high-speed Internet connections are coming down, and high-speed connection options are increasing. At the same time, media player programs, such as the AOL Media Player, have improved so much that you can now enjoy larger and sharper pictures on your PC, even if you use an older modem. And with a high-speed connection, the quality can be very good. Don't expect TV-quality yet and don't be surprised by the size of the picture, but be prepared for choice and creativity as well as fewer ads.

Check out the following sites for movies you can enjoy on the Internet:

- About.com (`about.com`) includes a guide to Movies On-line (`worldfilm.about.com/cs/onlinemovies/`). This mini-directory has a guide to watching movies online and takes you to many Net movie sites.
- IFILM (`www.ifilm.com`) is the place to start to watch *real* movies on the Web, the kind that are shown in theaters. Along with the handful of gems, there's a collection of awful and highly entertaining B movies. Don't look for recent films; they are heavily protected by the copyright laws.
- Edgy AtomFilms (`www.atomfilms.com`) features independent films and animated shorts. Some of the films are artsy, most of them are irreverent, and a few are not

exactly family-friendly. Through an alliance with Shockwave.com, AtomFilms is home to some very cool Flash and Shockwave animations.

- MTV Online (start at AOL Keyword: **MTV Online**) lets you hear and watch music videos and interviews with band members. You can also chat about the music using AOL chat and message boards.
- RealGuide.com (`www.realguide.com`), from the creators of the RealPlayer (see Chapter 6), provides listings of popular RealVideo movies, including movie trailers, music videos, and cartoons.
- At RollingStone.com (AOL Keyword: **Rollingstone**), click Videos to see music videos of current superstars.
- SonicNet (AOL Keyword: **Sonicnet**) also offers music videos of all genres, including jazz and classical. Look for the All Videos link on the main page to watch movie videos in the embedded SonicNet player.

Exploring Digital Photography

Everyone is familiar with snapshots and photo albums, but you may be less familiar with digital pictures. Put simply, a digital picture is the digital version of a photograph; it consists of *pixels*, instead of paper. Pixels record color and tone information electronically. Because these pictures are *digital*, they can be stored on computers, improved with digital-imaging software, and shared over computer networks like AOL and, of course, the Internet.

A *pixel* is a very small onscreen rectangle, or *picture element*, each one carrying a different color and tone. Together, pixels form an image. The more pixels per image, the higher the quality.

What You Need to Know about Digital Pictures

How do you *get* digital pictures?

- **With a digital camera:** Such cameras take photographs but use light-sensitive hardware instead of film to record an image. Not only do you save money on film, but you can also see the results right away in the camera's integrated viewer. Using a cable or removable memory card, you bring the pictures into your PC, where you can edit, store, and share them with friends and family.

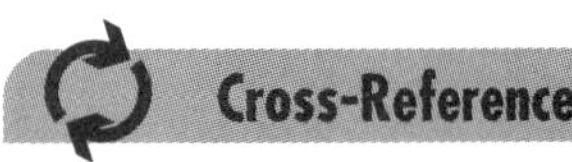

See my other books, *Your Official America Online Guide to Pictures Online* and *Your Official America Online Guide to Digital Imaging Activities*, both published by Hungry Minds, Inc.

AOL frequently has good deals on scanners and digital cameras. Start at AOL Keyword: **Shop Direct**.

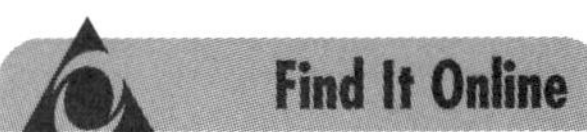

Quality color inkjets can be found for under $200 at AOL Keyword: **Shop@AOL**.

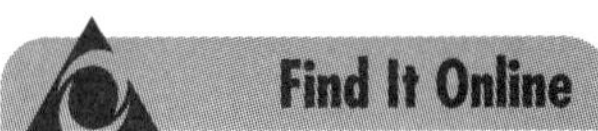

AOL's Printer Supplies service (Print⇨Printer Supplies) simplifies the regular purchase of printer supplies, such as inkjet cartridges and specialty papers.

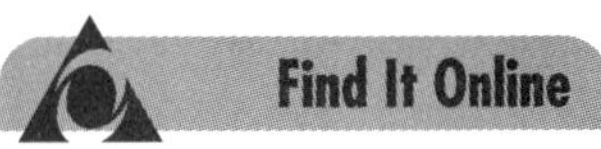

At AOL Keyword: **Pictures**, click Help for a short tutorial that reviews how the service works.

- **With a scanner:** A scanner is a piece of hardware that works like a photocopier machine but creates digital files instead of paper copies. You start with a photographic print, and the scanner converts it into a file — a digital picture, which you can then use on your PC. With a scanner, you don't need a digital camera to create a digital picture.
- **"You've Got Pictures":** The "You've Got Pictures" service (AOL Keyword: **Pictures**) is the easiest way to get digital pictures. This new service is described in the next section. When you have your film developed at a participating "You've Got Pictures" photo retailer, you get prints *and* digital pictures. You pick up the prints, as usual; the digital pictures are delivered to your AOL account, where they can be viewed, edited, and shared.

What can you do with digital pictures?

- Make a T-shirt or mousepad by using iron-on transfer paper.
- Assemble an inventory of household valuables for insurance purposes.
- Make your own greeting cards and invitations by using the special papers available today at any office supply store and at AOL Print Central (Print⇨Print Central).
- Use graphics software to remove red-eye, boost contrast, crop out unwanted parts of the picture, and improve color balance.
- Make your own business cards, tweak them for special purposes, and print only as many as you need.
- Make baseball cards for a Little League team.
- Make your own photographic prints by using the glossy, matte, and other inkjet papers available online and at office supply stores.

Using AOL's "You've Got Pictures"

If you want to get the most out of your digital pictures, the place to start is AOL's "You've Got Pictures" service, available at AOL Keyword: **Pictures**.

Here's how "You've Got Pictures" works. You don't need any new hardware or software; you don't even need a digital camera. Instead, with your film camera (whether it's a $50 point-and-shoot or $2,500 Leica), you shoot a roll of film as you've always done. When the roll is done, take it to a participating photo retailer for processing. AOL works with the PhotoNet network of some 40,000 retailers to get your roll of pictures from the photo bag in the drugstore to your account on AOL. The fee for getting digital images is currently $5 or $6.

When your digital pictures are ready, you hear a voice saying, "You've Got Pictures!" when you sign on to AOL. Click the "You've Got Pictures" icon on the Welcome Screen to go directly to the "You've Got Pictures" main window. From there you can view rolls of film, share pictures, and create collections of pictures called *albums,* like the one shown in Figure 18-1.

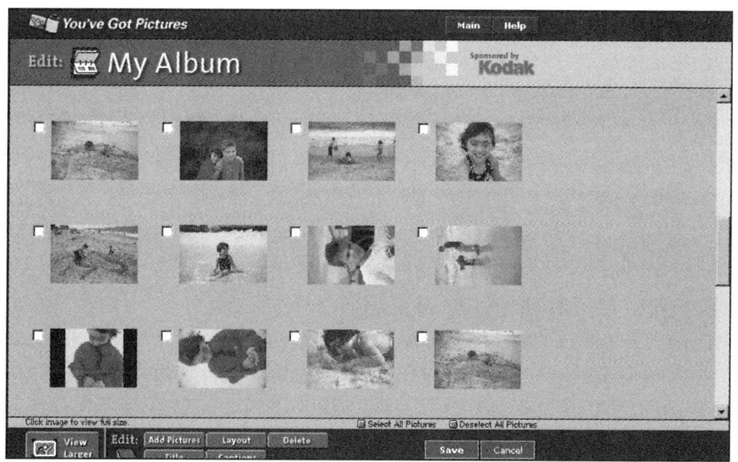

Figure 18-1. From "You've Got Pictures," pictures can be e-mailed one at a time, or grouped as albums, to friends and family.

At AOL Keyword: **Photo Developer**, you can quickly and easily find the name and address of the closest PhotoNet developer. You also get names and addresses of mail-order photo participating developers.

To view your pictures, start at AOL Keyword: **Pictures** and click Go to My Pictures. The My Pictures window has three tabs. Click a tab to switch to a different section.

- **New Pictures:** This tab contains digital pictures from rolls of film you've had developed (the retailer scans the film and posts the images here). Pictures stay on the New Pictures tab until they've been viewed.

Unlike previous versions of "You've Got Pictures," in the new version you now have no limit to the number of pictures you store online or to the length of time they're stored.

On AOL, an *album* is a collection of pictures, from any roll and from any source, that you want to keep together (for example, a family reunion or birthday party).

- **My Rolls & Albums:** This tab contains viewed rolls and collections of pictures *(albums)* that others have shared with you. Note that when using "You've Got Pictures" you are always working with rolls and albums, not individual pictures, as in the earlier version of this service.
- **Buddy Albums:** The Buddy Albums tab includes albums that people have shared with you.

With your digital pictures, you can

- Order prints and photo gifts such as mugs, T-shirts, and mousepads.
- Download your digital pictures to your own computer, where you can edit them in any graphics program, such as Adobe PhotoDeluxe, Paint Shop Pro, or MGI PhotoSuite IV. On your computer, you can also use pictures in your own Web pages.
- Share pictures with others online, one at a time, using the "You've Got Pictures" e-mail feature. Or, you can share several pictures at the same time by creating *albums*.

After you download pictures, you can upload them to AOL Hometown.

Listening to the Radio

Did you know you can listen to the radio while using your desktop computer? You can, but the experience differs from listening to the radio in your car or on your alarm clock.

In the first place, you can choose from thousands of online stations. You probably don't want to listen to that many stations, but the chances of finding a station that plays just the music you like (and none of the music you don't like) are much greater when you tune into the radio from you computer. You can also explore new genres in depth — and without advertising. As for sound quality, MP3-based music can be pretty close to CD-quality, especially if you have a high-speed connection.

- Radio@AOL, new in AOL 7.0, carries more than 75 radio stations, and the number is growing all the time.
- The latest version of AOL's Spinner software has been greatly improved and is the ideal radio when you are using a computer without the AOL software.

Using Radio@AOL

Radio@AOL, shown in Figure 18-2, can be accessed from the AOL toolbar or at AOL Keyword: **Radio**. You can listen to the radio whenever you're online.

Radio@AOL differs from the AOL Media Player, profiled in Chapter 16, in what it plays:

- The AOL Media Player appears automatically to play sounds and show videos that you find on the Web. The radio stations you can hear on the AOL Media Player are, for the most part, the networked versions of real stations, such as the BBC.
- The radio stations you hear on Radio@AOL are Net-only stations organized by genre. As Figure 18-2 shows, the genres run the gamut from alternative rock to world music, such as reggae and salsa.

Using Radio@AOL is a snap. Start by clicking the Radio button on the toolbar. When the player appears, select a genre and a specific station (also called *channel*) from the list on the left. If you see a plus sign (+) before a genre, click the name to see more stations for that genre. The controls in the lower left let you play, stop, adjust the volume, and even mute the music entirely.

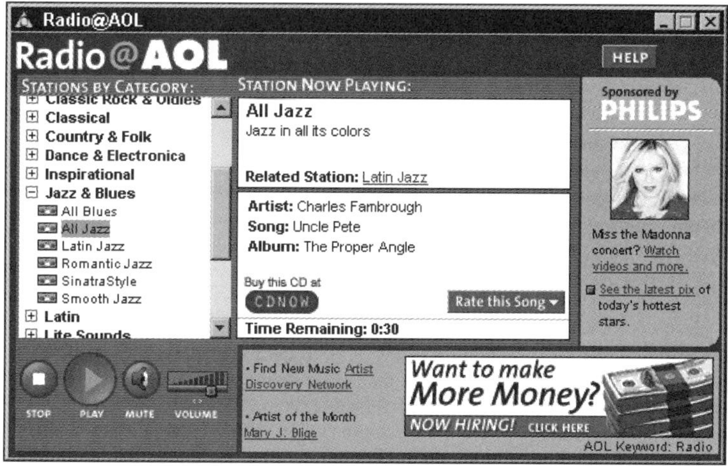

18-2. Rock around the clock with AOL Radio.

To use the AOL Media Player as a radio, choose from the stations listed in Real Network's Guide (`realguide.real.com/tuner/`). The Radio Tuner link takes you to a list of several thousand online radio stations.

Using Spinner

When you use a computer without AOL, you can listen to your favorite music with Spinner. The Spinner software can be downloaded from `www.spinner.com`.

Spinner gives you a selection of more than 100 channels, and the latest version makes it simple to select the channels you like. You can also create a list of favorite channels, which Spinner remembers every time you use the software. Each of Spinner's stations is carefully programmed, and there are no commercials except for occasional spots for Spinner itself.

Spinner has features that enhance your listening. For example, Spinner lists channels related to the one you're currently listening to. You can also easily get information about the artist who's currently playing. And Spinner simplifies the process of finding and ordering CDs from Amazon or CDNow. That means that if you like a song, you're only clicks away from getting more good tunes.

Here are some tips for using Spinner:

- Create a list of your favorite channels by clicking Edit Favorites on the right side of the screen (see Figure 18-3). Select stations from the list of Spinner channels on the left, and click Add to move them to your list of favorites.
- Click Now Playing to see what's playing now on all your favorite channels.
- Click File to find and play individual MP3 songs and M3U playlists on your hard drive.

Spinner is the software used for both Radio@AOL and Netscape Radio, and as a result all three radios work in a similar fashion.

Here are three additional sources of online radio programming:

- Real Network's Guide (`realguide.real.com/tuner/`), like Spinner, works like a radio tuner that covers the globe or at least many of the world's current musical genres. Follow the Radio Tuner link for a searchable list of (currently) about 2,500 online radio stations, consisting of "real" radio stations with an Internet presence and online-only stations.

- Shoutcast (`www.shoutcast.com`) takes you to many online-only MP3 stations from around the world, serving alternative, jazz, international, and other types of music.
- The Global Music Network (`www.gmn.com`) features recorded and live jazz and classical music.

Figure 18-3. Spinner (available at `www.spinner.com`) is better than having the radio on.

Reading Books

Why in the world would you want to read a book on a computer or a handheld computer? Digital versions of printed books, or *eBooks,* aren't about to replace books, but they do have many benefits:

- **eBooks don't weigh anything.** They can be carried anywhere. They make sense on long trips when you want to travel light. Palm and PocketPC handheld computers also weigh less than a book, but they can store many eBooks at a time.
- **You can search them.** Most eBook readers provide a button allowing you to search eBooks for a word or phrase.
- **You can take notes.** In most eBooks, you can attach the electronic equivalent of a post-it at any point if you want to jot down a note.

- **You can look up words.** Some eBooks can be linked to digital dictionaries, for very quick look-up of unfamiliar words.
- **eBooks offer usability features.** Fonts can be increased in size, and some eBook readers speak the words of a text, making eBooks useful while driving and indispensable for the visually impaired.

What do you need to read an eBook? To read an eBook on a PC, you need software. The two major software formats, Adobe eBook and Microsoft Reader, can be downloaded free and run on any Windows or Mac PC or laptop.

Hardware eBook readers, such as the Gemstar eBook from RCA and the Franklin eBookMan, have failed to catch on to date but may become popular when the supply of eBooks becomes much greater. For owners of handheld computers, Palm-compatibles can be outfitted with the free PeanutPress reader to become eBook readers, and PocketPCs can run a handheld version of the Microsoft Readers software.

Adobe's eBook Reader is based on the familiar Acrobat PDF format, which was introduced in Chapter 6. (PDF allows highly formatted documents, complete with page numbers, links, and illustrations, to be published online.) Versions of the eBook Reader are available for both the Mac and the PC, as well as handheld computers such as Palm. The eBook Reader has accessibility features, so that on a sound-enabled PC or handheld computer, words can be spoken aloud by a voice synthesizer. Like other readers, eBook in the Adobe Reader can be searched, annotated (with your notes), and bookmarked.

Where do you get eBooks?

- **eBooks.com** (`www.ebooks.com`) specializes in books formatted for Adobe's eBook reader, but the company is currently expanding to provide books for the Microsoft Reader and other platforms. Most of the books are not free; they are the digital version of recently published books. You'll find, in general, that digital books cost less than their commercial counterpart, and can often be downloaded on the spot.
- **Adobe's eBook Mall** (`www.adobe.com/epaper/ebooks/ebookmall/`) offers free classics, just-released trade books that are available as eBooks, and links to

other online stores where you can get eBooks. The mall is a collection of links to non-Adobe vendors and can be reached from the Adobe eBook Reader itself.

- **iPublish** (`www.ipublish.com`) is a new venture from AOL Time Warner Trade Publishing. iPublish will eventually bring you electronic versions of traditional books, plus books written especially for the new medium. You can sample a chapter from a new book before buying it. iPublish also has an entire channel devoted to new works (iWrite). The opportunity could benefit writers who have had a difficult time getting distributed or finding a niche. In addition to new publishing opportunities, look for new publishing formats, such as the publication of books and articles too specialized for general publishers or too short for the tastes of traditional booksellers, who like books to be readily visible on the bookshelf.
- **Barnes & Noble** (AOL Keyword: **BN**) and **Amazon.com** (`www.amazon.com`) both have special sections devoted to eBooks.
- **PeanutPress** (`www.peanutpress.com`) sells eBooks for Palm-compatible handheld computers as well as for PocketPCs. A few free books are available. This large and well-organized collection consists primarily of newer trade books (digital versions of the same books you see in the bookstores), which you have to pay for. eBooks usually cost less than the print version, and because you download directly, there is no shipping cost.
- **NetLibrary** (`www.netlibrary.com`) provides digital content to libraries, along with the tools required to manage this content. NetLibrary has also pioneered multimedia textbooks. To use NetLibrary's free online e-texts requires the free NetLibrary eBook Reader. You can read a small stack of eBooks, selected from the 3,500-plus classics here.
- **MemoWare** (`www.memoware.com`) is perhaps the most interesting collection of eBooks, because of its diversity and the selection of books and documents in other languages. MemoWare offers eBooks in many different formats, and you need to familiarize yourself with the FAQ to use the files effectively.

Note

PeanutPress books are available for PocketPCs, Palms, and Palm-compatible devices. At the PeanutPress site, you can find instructions for making your own eBooks.

Tip

After you register at NetLibrary (it's free), you can read books online as well as download them. Double-click a word when you're using the NetLibrary reader, and you get a definition from the *American Heritage Dictionary of the English Language!*

Watching TV

Sometimes you hear silly reports that the Internet and television are locked in some sort of mortal combat for the hearts and minds of viewers. In fact, new technologies usually complement old ones instead of replacing them. Such is the case with AOLTV, shown in Figure 18-4.

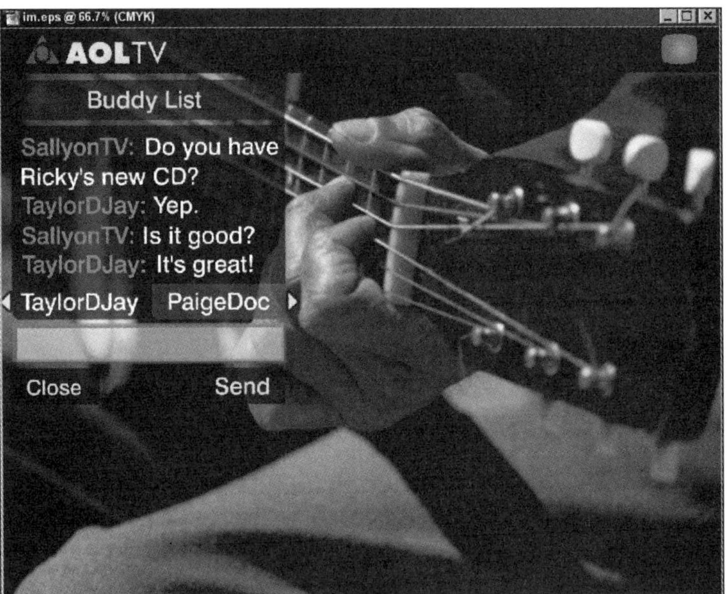

Figure 18-4. AOLTV: Why choose a favorite medium when you can have both?

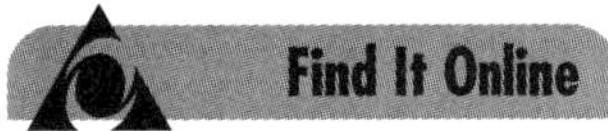

At the Entertainment Web Center (`www.aol.com/webcenters/entertainment`), click Television to see news about your favorite TV shows. Also check family-oriented networks. Try AOL Keywords: **PBS** and **NickJr**.

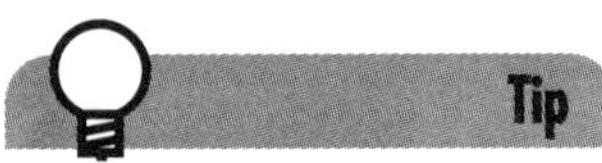

You can be online with the AOL service while you're using AOLTV, or any other AOL Anywhere devices for that matter.

AOLTV is delivered over the television set. It offers a set of essential AOL features on the same screen where you watch TV. The features include e-mail, instant messaging, and Web browsing. The available features and their format complement TV in many ways:

- The Program Guide provides television listings and show summaries, making it easier than ever to find something of interest. Never miss another show again, thanks to the one-touch Remind/Record feature.
- With AOLTV you can talk with friends and share your thoughts and TV experiences through e-mail and instant messaging. With an AOLTV account, you get seven screen names, each with its own mailbox and Buddy List. The same screen name can be signed on to both AOL and AOLTV.

- Use any of AOL's 16,000 chat rooms, many of which are devoted to soaps, stars, and shows.
- Share your pictures with friends and family with the "You've Got Pictures" service, described earlier in this chapter.
- Imagine watching television and being able to access complementary Web sites without leaving your seat, or vote in online polls and see how your opinion compares to others watching the same show.
- As on the PC-based AOL service, on AOLTV, Parental Controls are in effect to make sure younger people in your household don't visit inappropriate places or receive unwanted e-mail.
- Through AOLTV you have access to Shop@AOL and Quick Checkout, both described in Chapter 5.

Note

At press time, AOL Time Warner was developing a version of AOLTV designed for cable lines instead of phone lines.

What does it take to use AOLTV? AOL provides everything you need:

- A Philips set-up box with a 56K modem (AOLTV is not high-speed). The set-top box can work if you already have cable service, or if you use a DirecTV or other satellite TV service and the Philips set-top box.
- A wireless keyboard.
- Cable (coaxial) wiring.
- A phone splitter, so that the telephone and the TV's modem can share the same line. However, you can't use the phone and AOLTV at same time.

Note

A second variety of AOLTV is currently under development for people who subscribe to DirecTV, the digital TV service delivered by satellite (`www.directv.com`).

Currently, AOLTV costs about $200 (for the set-top box, wireless board, remote control, wiring, phone cord, splitter, and documentation). The service itself costs about $15 a month for AOL members, somewhat more for nonmembers. You can find all the information you need at AOL Keyword: **AOLTV**.

AOL In Home Service

With the new AOL In Home Support service, you can request that an AOL-trained technician come to your house to set up, register, and demonstrate how to use AOL products or devices. Visit AOL Keyword: **IHS** to get information about the service, find out if it's available in your area, and request the service.

AOL Meets the Telephone

AOL and the telephone are changing each other in pretty basic ways, too, and the influence goes both directions.

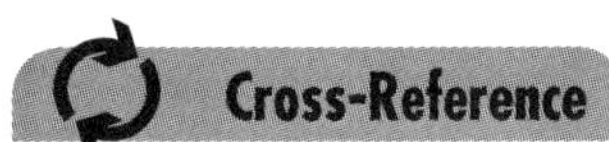

I discuss how to access AOL over a wireless phone and through AOLbyPhone in Chapter 10.

- You can get the AOL service over a telephone (a wireless cell phone, to be precise).
- You can use AOLbyPhone to access select AOL features over any telephone.
- You can do the opposite, too: use software and an AOL Internet connection to make or receive phone calls, and send or receive faxes.

It's all possible on AOL, as you'll see in this section.

Using Buddy Talk

Using the AOL Instant Messenger (AIM) service, Buddy Talk lets you speak directly to your buddies who are signed on to AIM. Your Buddy List will inform you of online buddies. You and your buddy need to use AIM, and you both need to use a computer microphone and a computer with sound.

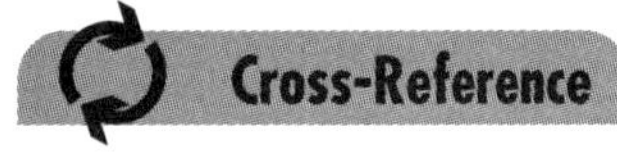

Chapter 12 is devoted to AOL Instant Messenger (AIM).

To use Buddy Talk:

1. While signed on to AOL, open the AIM software.
2. Select the name of a buddy who is online from your Buddy List, and choose People⇨Connect to Talk or press Alt+T. Your buddy receives a message saying that you would like to talk.
3. If your buddy accepts your invitation, you can begin your conversation. When you are finished talking, either of you can click Disconnect.

With AIM Talk, you can talk in full- or half-duplex mode. *Full-duplex* mode allows you and the other person to speak at the same time. *Half-duplex* allows only one of you to talk at a time; you and your buddy must wait until the other one finishes before talking.

Your sound card supports either full- or half-duplex mode. If you and your buddy are using different modes, the Talk feature uses the lowest mode. For example, if your buddy is using a half-duplex sound card, and you are using a full-duplex sound card, Buddy Talk places both of you in the half-duplex mode.

Using half-duplex can make for a smoother conversation. Use your preferences to switch to half-duplex:

1. Choose My AIM⇨Edit Options⇨Edit Preferences.
2. Click the Talk category.
3. Click the option: "Always Talk in Half Duplex mode, even if sound card reports Full Duplex." Click OK.

Using AIM Phone

AOL Instant Messenger's Phone service allows you to initiate a call by using your computer. While you start the call on your PC, the other person receives it on a regular phone. The service is provided through Net2Phone, and it supports full-duplex (two-way) conversations, because the calls are placed through a switched phone network.

To place calls from your computer, you need the additional AIM Phone software, which is shown in Figure 18-5. While the AIM Phone software is free, the service, offered by Net2Phone, is not free. Charges apply only to toll PC-to-phone calls and toll PC-to-Fax calls. Calls can be made anywhere in the U.S. and around the world at competitive rates.

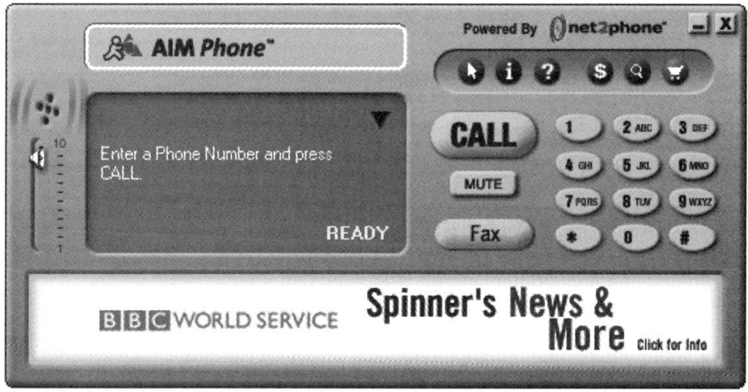

Figure 18-5. AIM Phone enables you to call people on the phone while you're at your PC.

AOL Phone is yet another way of staying in touch with people on your AIM Buddy List. You'll need your buddy's phone number handy, of course. To call a buddy on the telephone (with you on the PC and your buddy on the phone):

1. Open AIM. Right-click on your buddy's screen name in your Buddy List window, and choose Contact Using AIM Phone.

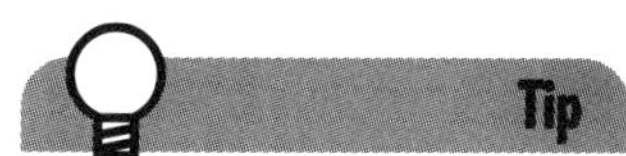

Complete online help for AIM Phone is available at `aimphone.aol.com/help.html`.

To keep track of phone numbers, right-click a buddy and choose Store/Edit Buddy Numbers. Enter a work, home, and cell phone number. These numbers are used automatically when you want to place an AIM Phone call to someone on your Buddy List.

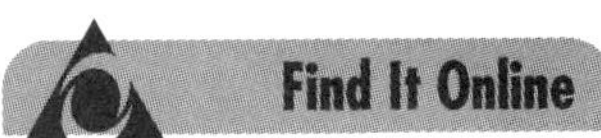

For more information, go to `www.net2phone.com/net2phone/` and click the Net2Phone Pro link.

- If you have not registered for AIM Phone, the AIM Phone registration page (`aimphone.aol.com`) appears in your browser. Register and download the software. Then you can continue with these steps.
- If you have stored a phone number for your buddy, AIM dials that number automatically. If you have stored several telephone numbers, you are asked to select the number you want to use.
- If you have not stored your buddy's telephone number, you see a box where you can enter the number.

The AIM Phone window appears on your screen.

2. Begin speaking into your PC's microphone after your buddy answers the phone.

Sending a Fax over the Internet

Phone lines can be used to send faxes as well as phone calls. Just as you can use the Internet to place calls, you can use it to send and receive faxes. Why would you want to send a fax over the Internet? A fax machine is not cheap, especially if you rarely send faxes, and takes up space. Many Web services now make receiving and sending faxes over the Internet possible without cumbersome and costly equipment.

The Net2Phone Pro service expands on the basic AIM Phone service described in the previous section. With this service, you can send a fax from your PC to any fax machine or e-mail address in the world. Like using a fax machine, you start with a document (it can be a file on your computer), dial in the recipient's fax number, and click OK.

Where to Go from Here

Where to go from here? Anywhere! With AOL as your online home and AOL Anywhere wherever you go, you can take control of your own online adventures:

- Use AOL's channels and AOL Search, learn something new and maybe even find a new hobby.
- Use the Favorite Places feature to keep track of your favorite communities, destinations, and activities.

- Use e-mail, mailing lists, newsgroups, and instant messages to stay in touch. Then, use your Address Book and Buddy List to keep track of your friends and acquaintances.
- Whenever you have a question about using a tool, AOL Help is always available, online or offline, from the AOL Help menu.

Index

A

Continued

B

Continued

D

E

F

Continued

Continued

L

M

Continued

T

U

V

W

Continued

Y

Z